CORRECTIONS CRIMINOLOGY

The power to punish is not essentially different
from that of curing or educating

Michel Foucault

CORRECTIONS CRIMINOLOGY

Editors

Sean O'Toole and Simon Eyland

HAWKINS PRESS
2005

Published in Sydney by:
  Hawkins Press
  An imprint of The Federation Press
  PO Box 45, Annandale, NSW, 2038
  71 John St, Leichhardt, NSW, 2040
  Ph (02) 9552 2200 Fax (02) 9552 1681
  E-mail: info@federationpress.com.au
  Website: http://www.federationpress.com.au

National Library of Australia
Cataloguing-in-Publication entry

  Corrections criminology.
  Bibliography.
  Includes index.
  ISBN 1 87606 717 9

  1. Corrections – Australia. I. O'Toole, Sean II. Eyland Simon.

365.994

Typeset by The Federation Press, Leichhardt, NSW.
  Printed by Southwood Press Pty Ltd, Marrickville, NSW.

Contents

To Norval Morris (1923-2004)
the pre-eminent criminologist of his generation

Contributors

Bill Anscomb is Senior Lecturer in Human Services at Charles Sturt University.

Dr Eileen Baldry is a senior lecturer in social policy in the School of Social Work at the University of NSW.

Mike Bartlett is the Manager, International Programs for the NSW Department of Corrective Services.

David Biles is Professorial Associate in Corrections at Charles Sturt University. For the past ten years he has been the Coordinator of the annual Asia and Pacific Conference of Correctional Administrators.

Professor David Brown teaches criminal law and criminal justice at the University of NSW.

Dr Tony Butler is the research manager for Justice Health Service in NSW.

Pat Carlen is Honorary Professor of Criminology at Keele University, Staffordshire, and Visiting Professor of Criminology at Westminster University, London.

David Daley is the Director, Community Correctional Services, Victoria. He has also been General Manager of Community Based Services in Western Australia.

Dr John Dawes was the Director of Correctional Services in Victoria and head of the South Australian Department of Correctional Services (1982-93). From 1993 to 1998 he was South Australia's first Public Advocate. He currently holds adjunct appointments at Charles Sturt University and Flinders University.

Al Dawood is currently the Manager of Workplace Development for the NSW Department of Corrective Services.

Dr Greg Dear has worked in the School of Psychology at Edith Cowan University since 1996.

Simon Eyland is the Director, Corporate Research, Evaluation and Statistics for the NSW Department of Corrective Services.

Dr Tony Falconer is a consultant, Health and Medical, for the Department of Corrections, Queensland.

Anna Grant is a Crime Prevention Officer at the Queensland Crime and Misconduct Commission.

Professor Richard Harding is the inaugural Inspector of Custodial Services for Western Australia, having taken up this position in August 2000. Previously he was Director of the Crime Research Centre at the University of Western Australia (1989-2000) and Director of the Australian Institute of Criminology (1984-87).

Kyleigh Heggie is currently the Research and Information Manager for the NSW Department of Corrective Services.

Professor Ross Homel is Foundation Professor and Head of Criminology and Criminal Justice at Griffith University in Brisbane, Australia. He is also Deputy Director of the Key Centre for Ethics, Law, Justice and Governance at Griffith University.

Dr Ole Ingstrup is the current President of the International Corrections and Prisons Association. He was appointed Chairman of the Canadian National Parole Board in 1986 and in 1988 he was made Commissioner of the Correctional Service of Canada, retiring in 2000.

Dr Don Josi is an Associate Professor of Criminal Justice/Criminology in the Department of Government, Armstrong Atlantic State University, Savannah, Georgia.

Maria Kevin is currently a Senior Research Officer with the Corporate, Research, Evaluation and Statistics Unit, NSW Department of Corrective Services.

Associate Professor Michael Levy is the Director of Population Health with the Justice Health Service in New South Wales and has an appointment with the Department of Public Health at the University of Sydney.

Dr Alison Liebling is Director of the Prisons Research Centre at Cambridge University's Institute of Criminology.

Professor Lucien Lombardo coordinates the Individualised Interdisciplinary Studies Program at Old Dominion University in Virginia.

Judy McHutchison is a Senior Researcher with Corporate Research and Statistics NSW Department of Corrective Services.

Sean O'Toole is the Assistant Director of Learning and Staff Development for the NSW Department of Corrective Services.

Dr Stuart Ross is the Project Manager for the Centre for Criminological Research and Evaluation, a joint venture between Melbourne University Private and the Department of Criminology at the University of Melbourne.

Rick Sarre is Associate Professor of Law and Criminology with the School of International Business, Division of Business and Enterprise, University of South Australia.

Professor Dale Sechrest, University of California Berkley, has practised, taught, and published in the field of corrections for over 30 years.

Eileen Skinnider is a Canadian lawyer who has been conducting international legal research for the International Centre for Criminal Law Reform and Criminal Justice Policy (ICCLR) since 1997.

Carleen Thompson is a PhD student at Griffith University.

Brian Tkachuk is currently the Director of the Corrections Program at the International Centre for Criminal Law Reform and Criminal Justice Policy (ICCLR), a United Nations affiliate institute located in Vancouver, Canada.

Professor Paul Wilson is the Chair of Criminology at Bond University.

Ron Woodham is the Commissioner of the NSW Department of Corrective Services, Australasia's largest corrections agency.

Acknowledgements

This book would not be possible without the support of Commissioner Ron Woodham, Lindsay Cotton and the Board of Management for Learning and Staff Development of the NSW Department of Corrective Services. Thanks must also go to Robyn O'Toole, Margaret Buttenshaw and Lisa Elias for their proof reading and to the many generous contributors whose efforts make this book an important contemporary contribution to the corrections literature. The editors would like to express their thanks to Margaret Farmer, Chris Holt, Clare Moss, Diane Young and all the staff at Federation Press.

Detailed profiles covering all of the Australasian correctional jurisdictions and important international agencies can be found on the NSW Corrective Services Academy Website <www.csa.nsw.gov.au>.

Corrections criminology

Sean O'Toole, Assistant Director, Learning and Staff Development,
NSW Department of Corrective Services
Simon Eyland, Director, Corporate Research, Evaluation and
Statistics, NSW Department of Corrective Services

Introduction

The genesis of this publication was twofold: the Australian and New Zealand Society of Criminology conference *Controlling Crime: Risks and Responsibilities* held in Sydney in 2003 and the need to produce a book which would serve as a reader for those interested in corrections or undertaking training to work in this field.

At the ANZSOC conference, it became clear that even within the criminology community, debate on what we have come to term *corrections criminology* was not as widespread or published as some other areas of criminological study. Studies into police, sentencing or various other specialist sub-genres like restorative justice and the process by which juries come to their decisions attract a populMarist appeal in criminological circles. This is quite surprising given the importance and high calibre of work done by those involved in matters correctional, some of whom are included as authors in this book. The reluctance to publish on corrections research is one which remains even in the literature specifically aimed at this task. Tewksbury and Mustaine's (2001) analysis of all the corrections specialty journals published between 1990-1999 revealed that nearly one in six articles contained in these journals focused on non-corrections topics.

Why should such a situation have arisen? At many levels this is perplexing, as prisons, correctional officers and the building of new prisons certainly attract the attention of the general public and media. We are all regularly subjected to an extensive coverage of the crimes committed by those currently in prison as well as those high profile prisoners and parolees – which is often overwhelming to the administrators concerned.

In some ways this situation is a mirror image of a current debate in sociology on "making social science useful", that is, by using it to inform governmental policy. As Wiles (2004) argues, "the more directly populist nature of contemporary politics ... have speeded up political debate and made it more difficult for specialist and nuanced voices to be heard".

Notwithstanding the central role of politicians in such a debate, that there is a muted voice on matters correctional by professionals and the general public alike is even more surprising given the increasing use of imprisonment both in Australia and worldwide. This is detailed in the first two chapters of this book by Mike Bartlett and Kyleigh Heggie.

Although the underlying reasons why both the actual numbers of those imprisoned and the rate of imprisonment per head of population has dramatically risen worldwide (a point sometimes confused by the unwary student) are not totally apparent, the clear delineation of this phenomenon provided by Garland (2001) is an excellent starting point to examine this issue.

As Garland's (2001) latest work stresses, the force for imprisonment is all pervasive. Australia provides a clear example of this, demonstrated by the significant increase in imprisonment rates in the past two decades. What is also of interest is that this increase has also directly affected the traditional balance within and between Australian jurisdictions, with the clearest example of this contained in any comparison of the imprisonment rates for NSW and Victoria in recent years. Victoria has traditionally recorded an imprisonment rate of almost half that for NSW, yet Victoria's rate of imprisonment has approached that of NSW in recent years despite Victoria maintaining a similar crime rate and rate of police employment to that of NSW.

This is an area rich for research – as any careful examination of the nexus between crime and imprisonment rates reveals far more about a society's promotion of and attitudes to social control than merely its apparent preference for imprisoning its people.

Although criminal justice rhetoric would posit that imprisonment must always be a last resort, the worldwide experience of increasing imprisonment rates belies this and is only matched by an increasing pressure on community corrections. David Daley points out that although rooted in an historical objective of rehabilitating offenders, modern community corrections now faces the double yoke of having to maintain its position as a cheaper alternative to imprisonment while also achieving a level of public protection equivalent to imprisonment. Accountability and extensive performance measures provide a spotlight on offender interventions in the community that has not been present before. Currently based on the "What works" literature, Australian community corrections interventions can often be seen to be at odds with populist wisdom backed by media commentators who remain confused as to what the purpose of community corrections should be.

Lucien Lombardo's chapter on prisonography is an apt counterpoint to the confusions surrounding the purpose of community corrections through his development of the concept of multiple realities. He addresses how such realities reflect the many different players involved in any examination of the prison – the public, the prisoner, the policy maker, the correctional officer, the politician, the lawyer, and the reporter, to name but a few. The narratives of each of these players will often be very different, resulting in a complex mix of understandings that are recreated throughout the world.

The difficulty of understanding such narratives becomes even more important when Commissions of Inquiry are undertaken after the apparent break down of existing systems of correctional administration. In Chapter 5, David Brown pursues three themes to examine such inquiries – namely their ability to establish the truth, to settle accountability for any wrongdoings proven, and to provide for any long-term reform. Although acknowledging the political context within which they operate, Inquiries are charged with providing enough evidence, or to establish their own "authority" to provide for the future. Truth requires hearing the voices of all those concerned – and clearly delineating between what has happened in the past and what should happen in the future. It is an important to remember that any Inquiry will also be subject to discourses over which it can have no direct control.

Control is a central concern for any correctional administrator according to Ron Woodham, Commissioner, NSW Corrective Services. What is of interest is not only the use of ever increasingly sophisticated technology to ensure the secure custody and control of prisoners, but the recognition that real control or influence can only come through the effective use of individual case management and the gathering and dissemination of intelligence.

Brian Tkachuk and Eileen Skinnider posit that control must protect the rights of prisoners and prison staff alike. This challenge cannot be met by merely applying international and domestic law. The observance of ethical and human rights standards in prisons must be viewed as an effective aid in the reintegration of prisoners into their communities.

Another challenge for correctional administrators has been the push by some governments to increasingly involve private enterprise in punishment. As Sean O'Toole demonstrates, such pressures are hardly new. Examples of privatisation of our system of punishment date back to the 16th century. With no evidence of any increase in effectiveness being provided by private enterprise management in corrections, it would appear that advantages may be only realised in opportunities for innovation or re-examination of traditional management practice.

In Chapter 9, Ole Ingstrup discusses what constitutes "Good Corrections" and how correctional administrators should lead in the changing environment of political policy-making and public sentiment. Good correctional systems address where they are going (aims), have a defined character (its people and levels of communications and trust) and, finally, get things done. Good management is characterised as that which places a high priority on teamwork and the ability to manage change.

Good management also requires an intimate understanding of both staff and clients. Bill Anscombe provides a salutary reminder that Indigenous over-representation in prisons has increased in Australia in recent years, despite major inquiries aimed at combating just such an increase. The level of Indigenous disadvantage in Australia is profound and has obvious connections reaching far beyond the criminal justice system.

Pat Carlen provides an important chapter which brings into focus an essential debate on imprisonment. Raising basic questions on the moral and social dimensions of life in prison, she identifies a risk of imprisonment that may not be as obvious to those outside corrections – a "growth in women's prison business". With sentencers increasingly sending women to prison in the belief that in-prison programs will directly rehabilitate and prevent future criminal acts, it is argued that a shifting of emphasis from the community to prison "treatment" has occurred. This is seen to be paralleled by "a translation of welfare need into psychological need" with the state seen to distance itself from initiating general crime control measures in favour of making prisoners solely responsible for their own rehabilitation.

While women still make up a small proportion of the overall Australian prison population (7%) their rate of incarceration has steadily increased in recent years. Female inmates can be characterised as "high need-low risk", meaning they generally have greater needs and issues relating to mental illness and alcohol and other drug abuse than male inmates – and do not pose the same overall level of security threat. The approach to the security, care and management of females is also different to that of males. However, the Australian correctional system is still coming to terms with the best programs and infrastructure to properly care for women in custody. It is a fact that there are often not enough appropriate employment and education programs. In some Australian jurisdictions, many of the programs that are available haven't yet moved away from the traditionally genderised stereotypes regarding rehabilitation programs. Women of varying security categories are often housed together because there is not a range of facilities for them to be placed in. However, their increasing numbers mean construction of new correctional centres for women are underway in many States, offering choices and the latest programming models. New specialised training programs for staff who work with female inmates are also available and will ensure both the infrastructure and support is in place to offer them the best opportunities for rehabilitiation.

With increases in the prison population not being restricted to women alone, John Dawes provides a timely reminder that all Australian correctional systems must face the prospect of caring for increasing numbers of elderly prisoners. Such a population requires specific management considerations including all its concomitant impacts on finances, health services and physical infrastructures.

Adding to the consideration of the health needs of prisoners, Michael Levy, Tony Butler and Tony Falconer detail the implications of caring for the health of an Australian prison population. Caring for the complex health problems of the prison population – characterised as disproportionately Aboriginal or Torres Strait Islander, young, male, infected with hepatitis C and survivors of childhood sexual abuse – can present profound difficulties that have led to large health differentials between prisoners and those in the community.

Of particular concern to NSW and several other Australian jurisdictions has been the push for the deinstitutionalisation of the mentally ill. In NSW there has been a very significant growth in the number of imprisoned people who suffer from some form of mental illness. Long Bay Prison Hospital, which was specifically designed and built to house the medically and surgically ill, has been virtually devoted to the secure custody of those with a mental illness. NSW Prison censuses reveal that there were 21 Governor's Pleasure Inmates (now termed Forensic Patients) in prison in 1982, representing 0.7 per cent of the total prison population compared to 100 in 2003, some 1.1 per cent of the total prison population. While there has been some governmental interest in investigating this situation (see NSW

Parliament, Legislative Council, Select Committee on Mental Health, 2002) there is very little Australian literature published in this important area.

We are grateful to Dale Sechrest and Don Josi for their chapter outlining the situation in the US for inmates and mental health issues. Prisons serving as "revolving doors" for the mentally ill, the inability of prisons to provide treatment essential for the proper management of a mental illness and the difficulty of handling such prisoners by officers with little specific training in mental health nursing have direct resonance with the Australian situation.

Similarly, Maria Kevin's chapter provides a far-ranging examination of NSW prisoners with drug and alcohol dependencies reflecting the situation in all Australian jurisdictions. Although over three-quarters of those who enter prison do so because of drug-related crimes is largely matched in prison populations around the world, the relationship between drug type abused, and criminal activity committed, requires further study. Those studies already completed raise as many questions as they answer. The concept of "recovery from inside" – knowing the prison population and responding to its particular needs is of particular interest. Investigations into drug misuse in prison can only lead to better treatment engagement by prisoners, with the emphasis on harm-reduction responses being a principle which seems both practical and humane.

Discussions concerning illicit drug use and the relatively high concentration of the mentally ill housed within prison inevitably leads to considerations for minimising the incidence of self-harm in prison. Greg Dear has provided a framework for just such an examination. Prison represents a mixing pot of those who have many personal vulnerability factors for self-harm which can only be amplified by the deprivations present in any prison setting. The development of "healthy prisons as inoculations against self-harm" truly is an ideal which prison administrators must strive towards in order to overcome the many ambivalences (to live, to succeed, to overcome difficulties) that face all involved in the process of incarceration.

That many concerned with corrections were in fact ambivalent about what they were to do with those they imprisoned was clearly encapsulated in the "Nothing Works" literature. Rick Sarre refreshes our memories on the often erroneously reported beginning of this era in correctional thought. He presents compelling arguments that simply using recidivism as a measure of success and not promoting psychologically-based treatment programs targeting offence behaviour will naturally lead to the failure of the rehabilitative ideal. The use of meta-analysis, although still subject to debate has, at its heart an implied emphasis on the need to provide quantifiable and scientifically rigorous research and evaluations. Sarre's reminder to correctional researchers of their responsibilities in the area of rehabilitation is even more valid given the three decades of pessimism that has been allowed to continue with little intervention.

Stuart Ross stresses that the work of rehabilitation cannot simply be restricted within the prison walls. The successful transition back to the community by a prisoner is a complex story which has only been carefully examined in recent times. Problems with material security, personal relationships and personal identity are all matters which extend beyond the prison wall. The role of post-release supervision in its attempts to re-connect the prisoner with a community and government agencies which can effectively exclude access to social services and support is critical. This is an essential component for the 'Throughcare' of any prisoner and forms the basis for a return to a productive social and working life.

In any society an individual is expected to work to the best of their ability, with the association between crime and unemployment being indelibly made in some commentators' minds. As in all matters to do with human beings interacting in a fluid society, the situation is not always so clear cut. Judy McHutchison presents a rare foray into research on the effect of prison-based industries on re-offending. Problems with defining "industries" as a specific and separate program in corrections makes it difficult to design any evaluation which seeks to isolate employment experience as a single variable. Further work in developing appropriate evaluation methods is needed in this area as although prison industries may provide scope to inculcate pro-social values and address some criminogenic needs of the prisoner, both very important areas for rehabilitation, the differing nature of its prison industry operations will always present the corrections researcher with difficulties.

The recent work by Eileen Baldry in constructing a research framework for examining post-release support for prisoners has provided many important elements of a complex picture. The specific focus on ex-prisoners and homelessness provided by Baldry reminds us of a vitally important and basic human need that can become a critical factor for ex-prisoners – the provision of adequate housing.

The requirement for adequate housing for all those in society should not stop at the prison wall. Anna Grant provides a clear exposition on the responsibilities for those who house our prisoners, the ethical difficulties they often face and the need for them to protect those basic human rights even for those who may have rejected such considerations themselves. The clash between the legislated duty of care requirements incumbent upon each individual correctional officer and the force of cohesiveness which motivate correctional officers to comply with group norms through group loyalty, compliance and conformity set the stage for a continued debate that found such vivid expression by Erving Goffman in 1961.

The multitude of accountabilities incumbent upon those who imprison its citizens are often seen to be merely an extension of those operating outside prison even though the physical circumstances are vastly different. Alison Liebling presents a seminal work which questions the how and what should be measured in a prison setting. Using an appreciative inquiry technique to reveal how a prison would operate when at its best, the results found stress a basic need for all prisons to encompass fairness, justice and respect. This reflects those values usually found in any civil society which may come as a surprise to those unfamiliar with prisons. Similarly, correctional officers are seen to have more in common with prisoners than is often first assumed.

Liebling's *Measuring the Quality of Prison Life* survey for the UK Home Office is an exciting development which re-orients prisoner management from a purely "What Works" perspective to one which also asks "What is just?"

Sean O'Toole provides an analysis of just who staffs the corrections industry in Australia, the roles they must successfully undertake and the career paths available to them. With the industry changing from an out-moded security oriented model to embrace a human services approach, correctional staff training and career development are the key factors in providing a fully trained and professional staff capable of meeting the challenges that must now be faced in correctional settings.

David Biles summons the complexities that underlie the functioning of any criminal justice system with the many inter connections between the different agencies providing for sometimes unexpected results. He raises the issue of whether some criminal sanctions should be termed "alternatives to custody" at all. The call to view correctional workers as specialists in crime prevention is a salutary one which reminds us that corrections must remain a vital and equal partner in all criminological examinations of society.

Confusion remains about the specific role that the prison plays in society. Paul Wilson re-examines the issues of increasing numbers of women prisoners, Indigenous prisoners and the involvement of private enterprise in prisons from recognition that "a prison sentence can never be a neutral experience". The question of why a large and rising prison population should be a source of pride to many in society is a valid question for any corrections criminologist to examine and lies at the heart of the development of a corrections criminology.

CHAPTER 1

World correctional population trends and issues

Mike Bartlett
Manager, International Programs,
NSW Department of Corrective Services

Comparing the use of imprisonment

In attempting to "take the pulse" of international corrections, some general limitations need to be acknowledged from the outset. Comparative criminology is fraught with definitional and methodological difficulties, which restrict our ability to make conclusions about similarities and differences across international jurisdictions.

When comparing imprisonment rates and prison populations, definitional problems arise from differences about what constitutes a prison and who counts as a prisoner. Most countries typically use the "total prisoners divided by total population" method to work out their imprisonment rates. As this depends on an estimate of the national population, the calculation isn't precise, particularly when age distribution is not factored in. Other problems arise from using the number behind bars at a particular time (stock statistics), rather than the number of admissions to prison over a specified period (flow statistics). Although serious offenders with longer sentences tend to be over-represented in stock statistics, (Reichel 2002), these figures are much more widely available and are therefore currently more useful for the purpose of international comparison.

A nation's rate of incarceration describes only so much of its criminal justice or social policies. At best, imprisonment rates indicate the extent to which prison is used as a sentencing option by the judiciary in a particular jurisdiction. We cannot make reliable assumptions about crime rates, punitiveness or prison conditions from imprisonment rates alone. As Mauer (1995) suggests, many Third World nations may maintain a low imprisonment rate simply because the cost of large-scale incarceration is so prohibitive.

World prison population growth

Throughout the 1990s, imprisonment was a growth industry. The decade saw a relative boom in prison populations across the world. According to Walmsley (1998; 2001), growth in Europe during this period was generally over

20 per cent and at least 40 per cent in half of its countries. In the six most populous countries of the Americas, prison populations rose by 60 per cent and 85 per cent. Australia saw growth of 50 per cent, New Zealand's prison population grew by 38 per cent, Canada's by 12 per cent, South Africa's grew 33 per cent and Japan by 10 per cent.

The prison population in the US effectively quadrupled between 1980 and 2002 (US Department of Justice 2004). It currently has the highest incarceration rate in the world with 701 prisoners per 100,000 of the national population. This is five to eight times that of similar industrialised countries such as Canada and parts of western Europe. With about 5 per cent of the world's population, the US holds a quarter of the world's prisoners. Notably, one in five new prisoners (18%) is in Texas, which reportedly has a rate of 1,035 people behind bars for every 100,000 in the population (Centre on Juvenile and Criminal Justice 2002).

Population rates can differ significantly between different parts of the same continent. Australia has a prison population of approximately 22,500 and is among 60 per cent of countries which have an imprisonment rate below 150 per 100,000 (Walmsley 2003). While the Australian national rate (115) has generally been increasing, patterns vary considerably between States. Similarly, China has a rate of 117 inmates per 100,000 population, however, increases have been much higher in some provinces than in others (Biles 2001). There is also considerable variance between different regions of the world, as shown in Table 1.1.

Table 1.1

World regions	Median rate of imprisonment per 100, 000 of the general population
Western & central African countries	48
Southern African countries	327
South American countries	126
Caribbean countries	297
South central Asian countries (mainly the Indian sub-continent)	59
Central Asian countries (ex-Soviet)	390
Southern European countries	76.5
Central and eastern European countries	200
Oceania (including Australia and New Zealand)	111.5

Source: Walmsley 2004

In Asia – home to more than half of the world's total population – approximately 90 per cent of countries have seen recent rises in their prison population. Thailand, for example, increased from some 73,000 prisoners in 1992 to over 250,000 in 2002. Cambodia and Sri Lanka also had rapid increases over 1996 to 2000 (Kidata 2001). Comparatively low rates of imprisonment are found in the Philippines, Indonesia and India. In western

Europe there have been considerable rises in the United Kingdom and the Netherlands. Though the Netherlands has long been renowned for its low prison population rate, in the 1990s it had the largest rise of any west European country, and its prison population almost doubled (Walmsley 2001).

There are now at least 9 million people held in penal institutions throughout the world, half of which are incarcerated in the US (2.03m), China (1.51m) or Russia (0.86m). With a global population of 6.2 billion people, this means that the world prison population rate is approximately 145 per 100,000 citizens. The international trend of increasing prison populations has continued well through the turn of the century and shows no promise of abating. Countries with the highest prison populations are incarcerating as many as 1 in 80 of their male citizens (Walmsley 2001).

Features of the world prison population

The offender make-up of correctional populations differs due to a complex variety of factors. Two common features of the international use of imprisonment are high proportions of pre-trial detainees (remand prisoners), and the over-representation of Indigenous offenders in custody.

Pre-trial detainees

Most developing countries and particularly parts of South America and Asia have extremely high percentages of unconvicted prisoners. Approximately 20 per cent of Australia's prisoners are on remand. Proportions of between 15-25 per cent are found in Israel, the UK and US, Canada, Russia and Poland. Within the range of 30-50 per cent remandees are jurisdictions such as Brazil, Thailand, Papua New Guinea, France, Kenya and Mexico. Countries with well over half their prison population on remand include, Saudi Arabia 65.8 per cent, Pakistan 66.1 per cent, Peru 67.2 per cent, India 70 per cent, Timor Leste 70.9 per cent, and Haiti 83.5 per cent (APCCA 2002; World Prison Brief 2003).

Socio-economic factors at individual, State and national levels help to explain the reason why large numbers of people are held awaiting trial. In South Africa for example, 34 per cent of the remand population in 2001 was in prison because they could not afford to pay bail (Ntuli & Dlula 2003). High remand populations are also supported by hard-line criminal justice policies. In certain countries "preventive" imprisonment has become the rule and rather than the exception. Often, unsentenced prisoners can spend months or years awaiting trial. The status, proportions and imprisonment conditions of remand inmates have become a global human rights issue and high on the United Nations agenda for criminal justice reform. Gross breaches of international treatment standards tend to be commonplace wherever high proportions of remandees exist.

Indigenous over-representation

The systemic disadvantages that Indigenous peoples face around the world are strikingly highlighted by their over-representation in prisons. Punishment and imprisonment have been the most commonly used political responses to deal with a range of Indigenous problems stemming from colonisation and conquest by other cultures. Wherever Indigenous peoples exist, they tend to be disproportionately represented in criminal justice systems and therefore in the offender groups that correctional systems manage.

The proportionately significant numbers of Indigenous prisoners in many correctional systems and their cultural difference to the general population, present particular challenges for correctional administrators. According to Ingstrup (1999), although corrections cannot directly influence the rate at which the courts sentence Indigenous offenders, a positive impact may be made in reducing their rate of recidivism. In the Australian context, this requires closer collaboration with Indigenous communities themselves and intervention strategies which include Aboriginal people, Aboriginal beliefs and traditional mechanisms of Aboriginal "lore" (law).

Reasons for increasing prison populations

The latest figures available from the World Prison Population List, (Walmsley 2003), show that prison populations have risen in 71 per cent of the 205 countries listed. A deceptively simple reason is that imprisonment is being used more often as a sentencing option. As rates are generally calculated using the amount of inmates on a given day, increased sentence lengths are another straightforward explanation. At a deeper level, causation can include combinations of socio-economic conditions, crime rates, criminal justice policy, correctional efficiency and public attitudes.

Prison population fluctuations in some countries can be attributed to particular occurrences. Korea's economic crisis of 1998 is linked to an increase in their inmate population by 10,000 in less than a year (Lee 2003). In Eastern Europe, the collapse of communist and socialist regimes were followed by a marked rise in both criminality and prison populations at least until 1992-93 (Walmsley 2001). The abolition of the death penalty in South Africa in 1995 resulted in magistrates opting for longer sentences (Ntuli & Dlula 2003).

From a global perspective, some common themes surrounding the increased use of imprisonment emerge. Criminologists seem to agree that there is no predictable relationship between the size of a country's prison population and its crime rate (Rutherford 1991; Ingstrup 1998; Aebi et al 2000; Mauer 2003). This is contrary to the popular myth that a nation with a high rate of incarceration must have a high crime rate or vice versa. In many jurisdictions, such as Singapore, crime rates have been stable or declining while inmate populations have continued to rise. In Canada, crime rates had declined for most of the 1990s, while incarceration rates remained relatively stable (Biles et al 2000).

Increasing imprisonment rates are generally rooted in policy choices. Regardless of whether crime rates are rising or falling, punitive attitudes across much of the world, particularly in Europe and North America, have moved towards favouring severity. Public fear of crime, real or perceived, has been compounded by a lack of confidence in the criminal justice system. These sentiments, fuelled by the mass media, have promoted ill-informed legislative responses. As criminal policy has increasingly become a favourite item in the toolkit of general politics, legislative emphasis has returned to retribution and deterrence as the hopeful goals of punishment.

In such a climate, slogans like "three strikes", "zero tolerance", "tough on crime" and "truth in sentencing" abound. These catch-cries impact sentencing culture, if not law. The use of bail and conditional release measures, where they exist, is increasingly restricted. As the authorities in numerous countries fight "wars on drugs" and similar campaigns, prisons are over-relied upon as combat support. In many jurisdictions, lengthy sentences are still pursued as the primary deterrent against crime. Incapacitation is employed in the hope of decreasing crime rates and improving public safety. This is despite at least a decade of research proving the limitations and even counter-productivity of such strategies (Matthews & Francis 1996; Ingstrup 1998; UNAFEI 2003). In short, societies are sending an increasing flow of people into prisons, even though the prison system is not working.

Prison overcrowding

Inevitably, and almost invariably, the increased use of imprisonment has led to prison overcrowding throughout the world. Although prison systems have no control over the number of those imprisoned, they nevertheless have to deal with the consequences (Coyle 2002). Along with Indigenous over-representation, the global epidemic of overcrowding represents an acute crisis for correctional administrators.

Overcrowding is no new phenomenon. It was the burgeoning prisons of 18th century England that resulted in the voyage of the First Fleet to Australia (Morris 1988). Today, prison overcrowding is manifested in a system's occupancy rate (actual prison population compared to the official capacity), as well as less tangible factors such as institutional conditions. In the majority of jurisdictions, increases in prison capacity have not kept pace with increases in prisoner numbers, with some countries incarcerating over double their official capacity.

When the weight of offender numbers overwhelms physical and human resources, correctional service delivery is handicapped in many respects. Prison administrations can struggle to guarantee basic human rights and honour their duty of care. Overcrowding is often related to reductions in living and exercise space, lowered sanitation and hygiene standards, inadequacy of basic supplies, poor nutrition and health care, and limited access to legal assistance. Deterioration of the prison environment contributes to instances of violence, self-harm and suicide.

Increased prisoner numbers means more enrolments in our proverbial "universities of crime". During incarceration, inmates can become saturated with criminal ideology and often take it with them upon release. As Posmakov (2002), suggests, by allowing a significant part of a country's population to pass through prisons, ultimately contributes to the deterioration of society.

Another effect of overcrowding is seen in the ratio of prison staff to prisoners. As influxes of inmates widen this gap, the level of prisoner supervision declines. Treatment and activity programs suffer, disciplinary problems are common, breaches of security increase and officer/offender relationships fray. The increased stress of the working environment negatively affects staff morale, heath and attitudes. While the United Nations requires a minimum standard of one officer for every four prisoners, a number of countries are operating with ratios beyond one to every ten.

The high costs associated with the use of imprisonment pose tremendous difficulties in some countries. Although custodial corrections often compete directly with funding for education, health and other vital services, the public is rarely aware of how huge correctional budgets actually are. In many developing countries, billions of dollars are diverted away from needy communities in order to incarcerate offenders, a high proportion of whom have lengthy sentences for minor offences. In industrialised nations, the massive fiscal burden of imprisonment has been accepted as a "necessary evil" until very recently. Los Angeles County has given early release to nearly 50,000 inmates in 2003 due to budget cuts in the order of US$166 million over the previous two years (*Sydney Morning Herald* 2004). Some of these offenders had served only 10 per cent of their sentence. As public accountability for correctional spending increases and budgets are squeezed tighter, these sort of radical responses to overcrowding are set to continue.

For many countries, the immediate "answer" to the pressures of overcrowding has been to simply build more prisons. In 2002, the United Nations Economic and Social Council invited Member States to report their efforts in solving the problem of prison overcrowding. Of the 15 national responses, prison-building programs were the most common measure of reform (Commission on Crime Prevention and Criminal Justice 2003).

Expanding prison capacity, apart from being enormously expensive, generally offers only interim respite. Many correctional administrators will have seen this borne out in practice. New prisons are quickly filled, outdated facilities constantly renovated, de-commissioned facilities perpetually reopened, yet problems of overcrowding continue. There is also a danger that new prison space can in fact prompt further additions to the prison population (Rutherford 1991).

In parts of Europe and Asia, amnesties and mass pardons have been used to reduce inmate populations by tens of thousands at a time with only temporary effect. The most promising counters to overcrowding are alternatives to imprisonment which (broadly defined) include bail, non-custodial sentencing options and conditional release. In many countries these options are often unavailable or under-utilised and tend to be frustrated by a lack of public/political support.

Alternatives to imprisonment

The continuous increase in prison populations and the damaging effects of incarceration demand new strategies for managing offenders. Recognition of this need has caused many countries to at least consider various non-custodial sanctions, diversionary programs and conditional release mechanisms

Cost savings are certainly an incentive. In Australia, for instance, managing an offender in custody costs 20 times more than if they were supervised in the community. It is also widely agreed that non-custodial measures offer the best hope for offenders' reintegration, rehabilitation, and to help them avoid stigma and further criminal association. In some forms, alternatives to custody provide opportunity for offenders' reparation to the community.

In many countries where alternatives to custody exist, they are often limited to "classical" pre-sentence sanctions such as fines, suspension of imprisonment and probation. Extremely common across western Europe, North America and Oceania, these sentencing options have the potential to provide graduated levels of punishment across offences of varying severity (Hillsman 1998). Monetary penalties are the most common non-custodial sentencing option found around the world, followed by unsupervised probation.

Notable innovations in the area of community corrections are restorative justice programs, court-monitored treatment programs and home detention (with electronic monitoring). Restorative justice, in the form of victim-offender reconciliation and group conferencing has been pioneered in Australia and New Zealand. In Canada, the concept has been culturally tailored and applied in a number of Indigenous communities as an alternative to the mainstream system (Zubrycki 2003). The "Drug Court" is a diversionary scheme which has also been piloted in Australia. The Drug Court can send an offender to community-based treatment after pleading guilty to possession or use of drugs before sentence is passed (UNAFEI 2003). Home detention (house arrest) can function effectively as a direct and constructive alternative to imprisonment, particularly when electronic surveillance is supplemented by an appropriate level of case management. Programs of this nature are operating in the UK, Sweden and Australia.

Community Service Orders (sentences to periods of unpaid work) are growing in popularity as an alternative to imprisonment which allows offenders to give something back to the community. There are legislative provisions for this measure in numerous jurisdictions, however, it is an option which is often underused by the judiciary and under-resourced in terms of supervision. This is particularly the case throughout Asia, Africa and South America. Post-sentence options, such as parole and remission, while generally available, are also substantially under-used in these regions and much of eastern Europe. This is often due to extremely rigid release criteria. The limited use of parole plays a large part in maintaining the high daily average of prison populations around the world. Compared to pre-sentence options, conditional release mechanisms have more potential to lessen imprisonment rates because they directly affect sentence length.

Of the alternatives implemented in western European countries, community service has been the most successful (Lappi-Seppala 2003). It is functioning well in Finland, England, France and the Netherlands. In a number of central and eastern European countries, community service and probation are conspicuously absent and legislation often precludes the application of non-custodial sanctions to all but first-time offenders and petty offences (Joutsen 1998).

The developing nations of Asia have had a particularly slow uptake of contemporary community-based sanctions. Nevertheless, some national imprisonment rates remain relatively low due to informal mechanisms such as the "village court". In the Philippines and Indonesia, for example, traditional interventions operating in local communities help to reduce the total number of criminals who would otherwise be processed by the official criminal justice process. In the Maldives, banishment remains an available sentence which is frequently used. The court may order the offender to be re-located to another inhabited island for a specified period (UNAFEI 2003).

A major impediment in South Africa and southeast Asian countries is the lack of community corrections professionals. The operational dilemma of massive community caseloads has necessitated citizen involvement to prop up various systems. In Korea there are about 125 trained probation officers to 140,000 probationers. Thailand has community caseloads of 500 to 600. Volunteer officers in these countries are responsible for supervising up to 80 per cent of all community-based orders. While the nature of these societies has facilitated community engagement, varying levels of volunteer expertise and training and have posed additional challenges.

In the US, the number of people serving community-based orders is more than double the prison population. Over 80 per cent of these offenders are on some form of probation, with the remainder on parole (Sourcebook of Criminal Justice Statistics 2003). This equates to approximately 6,730,000 people being under some sort of correctional supervision in the US alone. Australia has over 50,000 offenders serving sentences in the community, which again is more than double the number in prison. Australian Indigenous offenders continue to be over-represented, with a community corrections rate ten times higher than the rate for non-Indigenous offenders (Australian Institute of Criminology 2003).

Australia's probation and parole rates (per 100,000 population) are among the highest in the world. Other jurisdictions making frequent use of pre-sentence alternatives and conditional release mechanisms include the UK, Hong Kong and New Zealand. Canada is arguably the world leader in the development and use of alternatives to imprisonment. About 80 per cent of its offenders under sentence (or on remand) are being dealt with in the community. Zubrycki (2003), describes a number of characteristics of the Canadian correctional system which provide a conducive framework for community-based corrections including a principles-based sentencing system, a research and risk-based correctional system, an active and committed voluntary sector, and community corrections professionals who can secure community acceptance while they implement and operate community programs.

The mere number of non-custodial alternatives that a nation has, or even their rate of use, do not automatically translate into a reduced use of imprisonment. It deserves reiterating that in community corrections, "one size does not fit all". Effective diversion in one country may be net widening in another. Reports to international symposiums and conferences are littered with examples of borrowed community-based management strategies that have been force-fitted onto offender populations simply because they have worked elsewhere. Given differences in expertise, implementation, cultural heritage and socio-political climates, "world's best practice" is not always as universal as it sounds. What is clear across the international literature is that community understanding and engagement is crucial. The financial, administrative and rehabilitative advantages of alternatives to custody remain out of reach wherever the public feels endangered by the prospect of offenders in the community or rejects the notion as too lenient.

– CHAPTER 2 –

Prison populations in Australia

Kyleigh Heggie
Research and Information Manager,
NSW Department of Corrective Services

Introduction

Despite the immense cost of incarceration and the general lack of evidence to its efficacy as a rehabilitative stratagem, it is well recognised that the number of people imprisoned throughout the world is continuing to increase. This increase has had a profound impact on general societal perceptions of crime, justice and social order. Some of the most influential factors related to the growth of prison populations can be found in the shift of both cultural and political imperatives towards the reliance on the use of imprisonment to segregate "unwanted" citizens.

Along with most other developed countries over the past ten years, Australia has experienced a steady increase in its total prison population and significant changes to its general characteristics. As in Australia, the most pronounced increases in the world's prison population have involved female prisoners, Indigenous prisoners and unsentenced or remanded prisoners. This chapter details these specific prison population increases within Australia and more specifically within NSW.

Prison population trends in Australia

According to recent published statistics, the Australian prison population has increased by nearly 50 per cent over the past ten years (ABS 2003). This reported increase has exceeded the 15 per cent growth in the Australian adult population for the same period. On 30 June 2003, there were 23,555 prisoners in Australia.

With the exception of South Australia, all Australian States and Territories have experienced increased prisoner populations. The following table illustrates the steady increase in overall Australian prisoner numbers between 1993 and 2003.

Table 2.1 Prisoner Characteristics – Australia (1993–2003)

Year	All prisoners No	Female proportion (%) of total prison population	Indigenous proportion (%) of total prison population	Remandees proportion (%) of total prison population
1993	15,866	4.8	15.2	12.0
1994	16,944	4.9	16.5	11.5
1995	17,428	4.8	17.1	11.5
1996	18,193	5.3	18.0	12.7
1997	19,128	5.7	18.7	13.4
1998	19,906	5.7	18.8	14.0
1999	21,538	6.3	20.0	14.9
2000	21,714	6.4	18.9	17.4
2001	22,458	6.7	19.8	19.3
2002	22,492	6.6	20.0	19.6
2003	23,555	6.8	20.5	20.5

Source: Australian Bureau of Statistics Prisoners in Australia 2003

More alarming than the 50 per cent increase in the overall prison population in Australia over the past ten years is the reported 110 per cent increase in the female prisoner population over the same period. Other changes in the Australian prisoner profile include an 8 per cent increase in the unsentenced prisoner population and a 5 per cent increase in the Indigenous prisoner population.

Cost of imprisonment

The cost of imprisonment is of concern to all Australian State governments. The overall cost of imprisonment has escalated as a direct result of increased prison populations. In 1994-95, the total Australian national expenditure on corrective services was $883 million. In 2002-03 this figure had risen to $1.7 billion, according to the Productivity Commission (2004). In 1994-95 the Australian national average cost per prisoner per day was approximately $135. In 2002-03 this figure had risen to $159 (Productivity Commission 2004). It is likely that the cost of imprisonment will continue to rise notwithstanding the huge burden on government expenditure. Despite evidence to suggest that most Australian jurisdictions are tentatively embracing less expensive alternatives to full-time custody – such as home detention schemes and other types of intensive supervision programs – there appears to be no firm commitment to the promotion of such alternatives in the published literature.

Australian women in custody

Before discussing any changes to the population of Australian women in custody, it is important to stipulate that, on the whole, women prisoners represent less than 7 per cent of the total Australian prison population. For example, in 2003 there were 1,594 women imprisoned in Australia compared with 21,961 men (ABS 2003).

In 1993, there were 648 women imprisoned in Australia. In 2003 this number had risen to 1,594 an increase of over 110 per cent (ABS 2003). This percentage increase is mirrored in countries such as the UK. For example, in 1992 the number of women prisoners in the UK was 1,180. By 2002, the female sentenced prisoner population had increased by 184 per cent to 3,340 (Home Office 2003).

There is little discourse as to why there has been an increase in the number of imprisoned women. The community pressure placed on governments in response to heightened sensitivity to media has fuelled legislative promises of "getting tough on crime". The inevitable conclusion is drawn between prisoners and violence. This conclusion, perpetuated by media attention, detracts from the realities of female criminal activity and women prisoners. The most recent statistics indicate that over 68.5 per cent of the female prisoner population were serving sentences for non-violent offences. These offences largely involved offences against justice procedures and social security fraud (NSW Corrective Services Inmate Census 2003).

Despite the fact that a large percentage of crimes committed by women are regarded as non-violent, there is some evidence in Australia to suggest offending patterns of women are changing. In recent years the number of women in NSW convicted of violent offences has escalated. The number of women prisoners in NSW serving sentences for major assault offences has increased by over 100 per cent, although the actual number of female inmates remains low.

Australian Indigenous people in custody

As with women prisoners, the number of Indigenous prisoners in Australia is continuing to increase. On 30 June 2003 there were 4,818 Indigenous prisoners in Australia, representing 20 per cent of the total Australian prison population (ABS 2003). The imprisonment rate of Indigenous people in 2003 was 1,888 prisoners per 100,000 adult Indigenous population. This is a 5 per cent increase on the reported 2002 rate. Indigenous people are 16 times more likely than non-Indigenous persons to be in prison. The highest Indigenous rate of imprisonment in 2003 was recorded in Western Australia. The Indigenous imprisonment rate in Western Australia was 2,744 prisoners per 100,000 adult Indigenous population (ABS 2003).

It is difficult to say whether these statistics are galvanising the Australian community into positive action. Despite the high profile needs of Indigenous Australians, there is little evidence that Australian society is willing to acknowledge and proactively seek measures to reduce these disturbing imprisonment rates. Rather, the persistent community demands for tougher penalties for offenders and the increased resources and power for law enforcement have meant that policies directed at addressing Indigenous imprisonment rates are subsumed into the larger rhetoric surrounding crime and justice. Chapter 12 on the over-representation of Indigenous people in the criminal justice system by Bill Anscombe will explore many of these issues in greater detail.

Increase in the remand population

Over the past ten years, Australia has undergone a high-profile public debate over crime, justice and social order. Politicians on all sides of the political spectrum have called for tougher sentencing, a proactive prison-building strategy and a general tightening up of legal procedures for granting bail. For the most part, the community response to the political rhetoric has been taken up with enthusiasm. Opponents of this so-called "law and order auction" are concerned with the seemingly intolerant attitude of the general public to criminal justice issues of fairness and social understanding. According to Garland (2001), the public acceptance of tougher social control is in direct response to societal rejection of crime as a social justice issue. Rather crime is now viewed as an unwanted entity that needs to be expelled at all costs from the "world of consumerist freedom":

> Crime control and criminal justice have come to be disconnected from the broader themes of social justice and social reconstruction. Their social function is now the more reactionary, less ambitious one of re-imposing control on those who fall outside the world of consumerist freedom. If penal-welfare conveyed the hubris and idealism of twentieth-century modernism, today's crime policies express a darker and less tolerant message. (Garland 2001: 199)

The consequences of this so-called "darker and less tolerant message" are reflected in the prisoner population trends. In NSW, the recent *Bail Amendment Act* 2003 has made it harder for repeat offenders arrested for crimes of serious personal violence to secure bail. This, coupled with the acknowledged delays in court procedures due to over-demand and with no apparent change in social attitudes, it is likely that the escalation in the remand population will continue.

Conclusion

There is no doubt that there has been a move in Australia towards the use of imprisonment as the preferred means of dealing with crime. The increasing reliance on imprisonment to segregate criminals has been profoundly influenced by shifts in cultural and political imperatives which propel the public's perceptions and responses to crime. The general lack of evidence to the efficacy of imprisonment has failed to halt its seemingly unstoppable momentum.

Australia has been inextricably drawn into an increased reliance on imprisonment, as have most other developed countries. The most pronounced increases in the Australian prison population can be found in the increased number of women prisoners, Indigenous prisoners and the number of remand prisoners which continue to spiral upwards. With little change in sight, Australia will continue to experience upward-spiralling prison populations. The cost of imprisonment is felt by the Australian society both in financial and social terms. The high cost of maintaining the current rate of imprisonment without convincing evidence to its efficacy as a means of rehabilitating offenders comes at the cost of developing social policies and initiatives aimed at addressing problems such as crime and social exclusion.

– CHAPTER 3 –

Australian Community Corrections population trends and issues

David Daley
Director, Community Corrections Victoria

Introduction

Unlike prisons, which offer bricks-and-mortar evidence of their presence in society, Community Corrections is less visible and less well understood. Prisons regularly attract public attention and reaction, whereas Community Corrections goes about its business in a way that seldom enters public consciousness. Despite its lack of profile, Community Corrections manages more than 70 per cent of all offenders in Australia under correctional services' jurisdiction. Australian Institute of Criminology statistics reveal that on 30 June 2001 there were 22,458 persons in custody, compared to an average daily community correctional population of 59,733 during the same year. Figures for adjacent years show similar ratios. On such numerical comparisons, Community Corrections should merit greater public awareness and critical scrutiny than it has received. In recent years, Community Corrections in Australia has absorbed a diversity of influences in step with contemporary correctional thinking and practice worldwide. This chapter examines the influences which have shaped its present contours, considers present-day trends, and points to potential future directions.

Historical antecedents

In Australia, there were rudiments of probation in the late 19th century, and the colonial ticket-of-leave system is a well-known forerunner of parole. Queensland introduced an early form of probation in 1887, marginally ahead of South Australia, although both had very limited scope and intent. The *South Australian Offenders Probation Act* 1887, which also followed the British *Probation of First Offenders Act* 1887, was restricted to first offences of a minor nature. An offender released on probation would have no conviction recorded. Although probation in South Australia was acknowledged by Graycar (1997) as a means to save the government money:

> the thrust of the debate was on rehabilitation, avoidance of "contamination", and offering a second chance.

The sentiments of 1887 still resonate, although prevailing social values and ideologies have shifted immensely in the intervening period.

Modern statutory probation and parole systems are mostly the product of the 1950s and 1960s. The adult probation service in NSW was established in July 1951, with South Australia following suit in 1954. Queensland created a statutory probation and parole service in 1959, and Western Australia borrowed heavily from Queensland in setting up its legislation in 1963. In the same era, the growth of parole systems around the country was profoundly influenced by Sir John Barry, a judge of the Supreme Court of Victoria from 1947, and the first chairman of the Victorian Adult Parole Board.

The common historical thread in each State and Territory was the shared belief until the 1970s that the objective of probation and parole (then the core components of Community Corrections) was the rehabilitation of offenders. Sentencing was the catalyst for a "treatment" process to enhance offenders' social functioning and overcome problems assumed to underlie their offending behaviour. Supervision failures were usually explained by the offender's unwillingness or inability to respond. The suitability or adequacy of the supervision was less frequently called into question.

Disillusionment with rehabilitation grew in the late 1960s and reached a crescendo in the 1970s. There was no universally agreed definition of rehabilitation, and measurable criteria of success were difficult to find. Conservatives were uneasy about rehabilitation as the primary goal of corrections, and liberals were alarmed at the discretionary power exercised by correctional personnel and their inconsistent decision-making. Amongst the most persuasive influences on the correctional policy climate was Robert Martinson (1974), whose so-called "nothing works" doctrine is typified in the following quote:

> With few and isolated exceptions, the rehabilitation efforts that have been reported so far have had no appreciable effect on recidivism.

By the 1980s, rehabilitation had largely given way to a "just deserts" or "enforcement" approach to Community Corrections. The shift away from a rehabilitative to a retributive focus was accompanied by the political rhetoric of "law and order", and "getting tough on crime" (Clear 1994; Cullen and Gendreau 1988). The shift supported the position of public commentators who blamed the assumed prevalence of crime on undue sentencing leniency. Tougher sentences and rising prison rates have been a hallmark of the past two decades, and this climate has indelibly changed the character of Community Corrections.

Contemporary Community Corrections

Bhui (2002) records that in England and Wales:

> The probation service is now seen as a "public protection"' agency in which "enforcement" has become all important as the service seeks to live up to the government's ambition to portray community penalties as genuinely "tough" alternatives to prison sentences.

The same paper attributes to the UK Probation Service:

> An essentially managerialist ethos, stressing efficiency, performance and effectiveness over all other organizational virtues.

These themes have echoed in Australian Community Corrections. Corporate accountability and performance measurement initiatives introduced to the public sector in the 1980s also suited the enforcement model. Many of the performance measures adopted (the proportion of orders successfully completed, breach rates, community work hours performed, treatment program attendances) were essentially compliance-based. These are still common measures but their impact on recidivism or social reintegration is increasingly questioned. More recent offender programs are likely to specify recidivism reduction measures or other positive indices of personal change, although many have not yet been operational for sufficient time to provide reliable data on their results.

The "just deserts" approach to Community Corrections has itself been criticised in the past decade. Tough regimes of order enforcement have produced mixed consequences. Daley (2003) argues that instead of acting as an effective alternative to imprisonment, a narrow focus on enforcement can feed higher levels of incarceration through rising breach rates.

In the past few years, Community Corrections has embraced a more eclectic range of objectives. Elements of enforcement and rehabilitation are found side by side, along with reparation, community protection, restorative justice, and victims' rights. In those States that have introduced home detention, incapacitation has also become a component of service delivery through curfew enforcement.

Despite the diversity of current approaches, there is a unifying thread. The dominant position of the past decade is encapsulated in the so-called "What Works" literature, mostly emanating from the UK and Canada. Its focus is empirical rather than ideological, concerning itself principally with research evidence about what is most effective in reducing rates of re-offending.

In the late 1980s, new statistical analysis methodology allowed earlier research to be re-assessed, and it showed that some things did have a positive impact. This had a seminal influence in restoring the credibility of rehabilitation. In retrospect, the pessimism of Martinson in 1974 may have said more about the limitations of the analytical tools available at that time than the intrinsic merits of rehabilitation

According to "What Works" principles, the primary target group for supervision should be those offenders who represent the highest risk of re-offending (McLaren 1996). Low-risk offenders are less confronting but intensive supervision will at best result in them remaining at low risk. There is suggestive evidence that intensive work with this group might even make things worse. The reasons are debatable but it is not in dispute that working with high-risk offenders offers the best chance of reducing recidivism, with corollary benefits for community protection.

Effective high-risk offender intervention is founded on:

1. *Risk Classification* – using a reliable risk assessment-screening instrument to determine who is at the greatest risk.

2. *Assessment of criminogenic need* – the identification of problems or needs that contribute to, or are supportive of offending. Programs should target these needs, which include:

   - Changing antisocial attitudes and cognitions;
   - Reducing antisocial peer associations;
   - Promoting identification with anti-criminal role models;
   - Reducing chemical dependencies;
   - Increasing problem-solving skills;
   - Helping the offender to recognise risky situations and to have a plan for dealing with them;
   - Decreasing problems related to re-offending – eg, lack of work skills and employment, lack of leisure and recreational skills, drug/alcohol abuse, poor impulse control.

   Offenders have many other legitimate needs, but programs not related to their offending behaviour will not impact significantly on re-offending rates.

3. *Responsivity* – matching programs and intervention strategies to the offender's learning styles. Active and participatory programs are generally more effective for pro-social skills acquisition. Effective staff develop good rapport with offenders but also enforce rules fairly and consistently. They should use and teach problem solving skills, and help offenders apply these skills to real life problems.

4. *Program integrity* – Standardised delivery of programs in accordance with a validated program design, avoiding ad hoc localised variations.

An emphasis on cognitive-behavioural techniques predominates. The primary aim is to improve the thinking, reasoning and decision-making skills of offenders through:

- teaching the offender to identify thinking patterns which led to a particular problem;
- considering the consequences of one's actions, both personally and for others;
- controlling anti-social impulses;
- correcting perceptual distortions; and
- developing a repertoire of pro-social behaviours.

As a simple example, an offender misses a reporting appointment and fearing the consequences, avoids arranging another appointment. This turns a small problem into one with potentially severe consequences, but cognitive training techniques would offer an easy solution.

Cognitive skills programs do not negate the need for other programs to address psychological or psychiatric difficulties, substance dependency, sexual or violent offending, or other issues requiring clinical services. However, for many offenders cognitive-behavioural programs will reduce re-offending risk. They may also serve as useful "gateway" programs to treatment interventions for those with specific needs.

The accumulated evidence does not necessarily match populist wisdom about what works. Interventions which consistently show up as ineffective include:

- Harsh deterrent interventions – short, sharp shock regimes such as boot camps, heavy discipline, physically demanding routines, submission and compliance do not reduce offending.

- Programs which emphasise control more than rehabilitation. McGuire (1995) found that both in the UK and the US, the emphasis on punitive measures alone was counterproductive. Any positive outcomes on recidivism were attributable to program components providing positive service delivery to offenders.

- Client-centred and psychodynamic therapies which focus on development of insight. If the problems and habits related to the offending behaviour are not directly addressed then re-offending rates are not reduced.

- Focus on problems such as low self-esteem, anxiety, depression, etc. These problems are worthy of attention because of their disabling effects, but this will not suffice to reduce recidivism rates.

- Working with low-risk offenders. As previously indicated, intensive intervention achieves little added value, but diverts scarce resources into unproductive work.

Some recent commentators have pointed out if offenders lack readiness or motivation to change, the best of programs may still be frustrated. Victoria now offers training for all staff in motivational interviewing as a precursor to other interventions.

Not everyone is convinced that "What Works" represents the peak of achievement in Community Corrections to date. Its critics argue that its focus on effective offender interventions has obscured the equally crucial role of social exclusion factors (poverty, unemployment, inadequate housing, poor educational attainment, discrimination, etc) as causes of offending behaviour. The debate is beyond the scope of this chapter, but there is no doubt that "What Works" has re-shaped the Community Corrections landscape. It is no longer possible to rely on beliefs about good practice based on intuition, experience or ideology.

Sentences administered by Community Corrections

Community Corrections administers a diverse range of sentences. They vary from State to State, as does their terminology, but the "What Works" principles are applicable to most of them. Community work is an arguable exception; its primary goal is completion of the work rather than casework to reduce recidivism. At the same time, it is desirable that community work offers exposure to a positive social learning environment and an opportunity for acquisition of skills.

Sentences administered by Community Corrections include:

- *Probation:* The English criminologist Nigel Walker (1985) has referred to the concept that probation may be imposed "instead of sentencing", which suggests an intent to avoid retribution or punishment for offenders who are not a significant threat to the community. Others have argued that the imposition of mandatory supervision obligations with sanctions for non-compliance cannot logically be considered an alternative to sentencing. Leaving aside this debate, the ideal of providing a second chance permeates probation thinking. The aim of avoiding the burden of a conviction for an offender on probation is also a feature of many probation systems. The now superseded Western Australian *Offenders Probation and Parole Act* 1963 is an example. It provided that offenders who completed probation and did not re-offend would be deemed not to have incurred a criminal conviction.

  The benefits claimed for probation include the offender's maintenance of community contacts, avoidance of the negative effects of imprisonment (association with a criminal sub-culture and absorption of its values), financial cost-effectiveness in comparison to imprisonment, and reduced stigma on family members.

- *Community-Based Orders* and *Intensive Supervision/Correction Orders*: Some States still use probation orders, but others have replaced them with a hierarchy of community-based sentences, reflecting the application of risk assessment principles to differential levels of supervision intervention. These sentences may include components of supervision, programs to address the causes of offending behaviour, and community work. In Queensland and Victoria, an *Intensive Correction Order* is a prison sentence served in the community, and breach of the order renders the offender liable to serve the sentence in prison. *Intensive Probation Supervision* in South Australia provides curfew monitoring with intensive supervision for offenders who would otherwise have been sentenced to imprisonment, but where their disability or ill health would make such a sentence unduly harsh.

- *Community Service/Work Orders*: Tasmania introduced Australia's first community service order scheme in 1972. It now operates in all States, either as a sentence in its own right or as a condition of another order. Community service as an alternative form of recovery of unpaid fines is also widespread. Common to all is unpaid community work, usually for a stipulated minimum number of hours per week. The scheme has elements of reparation, punishment and rehabilitation. It requires offenders to put something of value back into the community, subjects them to a disciplined regime, and offers opportunities to acquire social or employment skills.

- *Parole* involves conditional release from prison under supervision after serving part of a prison sentence. In some States the sentencing court specifies the minimum period of the sentence to be served before eligibility for parole. In others, the proportion of sentence to be served before eligibility for parole is fixed by legislation. Post-release supervision is similar to other forms of order. Failure to comply can result in the cancellation of parole and return to prison for the balance of the sentence. Parole primarily aims to assist and support offender rehabilitation and re-integration into the community.

- *Home detention* was introduced in South Australia in 1986, and is now in all mainland States, although recent legislative changes in WA have absorbed it into other supervision orders. Home detention can be a form of bail supervision, a sentence imposed by the courts, or an early prison release option for selected low-risk prisoners. It can also exist as an intermediate sanction for offenders who risk imprisonment for breach of a community-based supervision order. In each case an offender is placed under curfew at an approved residence except for authorised absences for such purposes as community work, paid employment, medical emergency or to report to a Community Corrections officer. Curfew compliance is usually enforced by an electronic monitoring device worn by the offender. This sends an alert signal to a central monitoring station if an offender moves outside the curfew zone or tampers with the equipment.

  Home detention aims to divert suitable offenders from prison, and to reduce pressures on prisoner numbers and costs. It has attracted considerable controversy since its inception. Its detractors point to a highly intrusive management regime for a population of low-risk offenders, contrary to contemporary theory about matching supervision intensity to the risk of re-offending. Home detention has also been criticised for turning households into virtual prisons for other residents. Proponents argue that political realities dictate the necessity for a regime that is accepted by the community as tough, that it is less socially disruptive than imprisonment and is much less expensive.

Other sentences which may be administered by Community Corrections include suspended sentences of imprisonment with reporting conditions, and periodic detention. The latter requires offenders to report to a residential centre during specified times, and to participate in community work, personal development programs or other activities. NSW and the ACT are the only jurisdictions in Australia with periodic detention.

In addition to its sentence administration function, Community Corrections has a pivotal role in providing pre-sentence advice to the courts, and assessment advice to Parole Boards and other bodies. It also administers the rules governing breach action for those offenders who fail to satisfy the conditions of supervision, or who re-offend.

Emerging issues and future directions

Restorative justice

Marshall (1999) defines restorative justice as:

> A problem-solving approach to crime which involves the parties them-
> selves, and the community generally in an active relationship with
> statutory agencies.

The criminal justice system currently operates under a retributive justice paradigm, in which the State is concerned to determine guilt or innocence and allocate punishment. The offender has the right to due process and punishment should be proportional to the severity and circumstances of the offence. The community and the victim have little direct impact on proceedings and critics argue that the offender may also be disengaged. Since the burden of proof of guilt is on the state, there is a disincentive for the offender to accept responsibility or offer reparation, even if the offence is acknowledged.

Restorative justice proposes a different view, which sees the harm done to victims as the defining feature of a crime, rather than the breaking of rules or laws. Its priorities involve making amends to the victim and the community, usually through processes of mediation, reconciliation and reparation. Proponents of this approach view crime as a problem for the whole community and argue that closer relationships between justice agencies and the community are an essential pre-requisite to a more effective justice system.

Elements of restorative justice exist in Community Corrections, but there is still no consensus about its potential scope. Some jurisdictions have established victim-offender mediation processes, and many have victims' registers, which provide for eligible victims to receive information about the sentencing of offenders and their progress through the criminal justice system. There are also limited trials of community participation in the sentencing process, including the Koori (Aboriginal) Court in Victoria and the Nunga Court in Adelaide. It is too early to judge whether restorative justice philosophy will re-shape Community Corrections, but it adds a dimension which will increasingly stimulate thinking over the next few years.

Therapeutic jurisprudence

Wexler (1990) is the best-known proponent of therapeutic jurisprudence, which rests on the premise that the role of judges and lawyers can either contribute to or impede therapeutic outcomes for the offender. Therapeutic jurisprudence erodes the demarcation between the sentencing function of the courts and the sentence administration function of Community Corrections. Drug Courts and other specialist courts (eg, the Domestic Violence Court in WA) are good examples. The judicial officer becomes part of the case management team after sentence is imposed and is actively engaged in monitoring the offender's progress. Community Corrections is but one participant in a multi-disciplinary supervision team.

In some places, therapeutic jurisprudence principles are stepping outside the specialist courts and into the management of mainstream offenders.

As an example, the Ringwood Court in Melbourne has introduced a conjoint case review process by magistrates and Community Corrections for young adult offenders who are on the threshold of breach action for unsatisfactory response to their supervision obligations. For Community Corrections, such pilots could have interesting implications for future directions.

Tracking

Community sensitivities in relation to offenders convicted of certain sexual or violent crimes have seen the emergence overseas of tracking programs, which may prohibit an offender from specified areas. Offenders' movements are tracked, using technologies such as GPS (global positioning systems), or cellular telephone capacity. There is lively debate about related moral and ethical issues and the technology is still being refined, but it is likely that Community Corrections in Australia will be assigned a role in this process.

Crime prevention

In working with offenders and their social milieu, Community Corrections is well placed to identify families and communities at risk. This knowledge could be of major value for crime prevention and early intervention strategies, although historically, the formation of inter-agency partnerships to pool knowledge and develop joint policy has been uncommon. As understanding of community risk factors grows, a challenge for Community Corrections will be to re-assess its role in front-end crime prevention. In light of the offender supervision demands it already faces, the debate may hinge in large measure on the practical limitations to the breadth of Community Corrections' role as much as on policy considerations.

Conclusion

In the past half-century, rehabilitation has fallen from grace in Community Corrections and then been restored, but as part of a much more complex world. A lot of work has been done to develop accurate risk and needs assessment instruments, but there is still a long way to go to develop effective programs to target identified needs. Community Corrections must also put more work into the research and evaluation agenda to measure its contribution.

Community Corrections will continue to wrestle with the balance between its role in managing individual offenders and its part in the wider debate about social exclusion factors as causes of offending behaviour. The future is also expected to see Community Corrections developing closer partnerships with other justice and community agencies, testing traditional notions of confidentiality. Despite these challenges, there are positive signs ahead. Reassessment of the impact of the rapid rise in imprisonment rates over the past decade is causing many jurisdictions in the western world to reconsider the limits to growth and its cost in both financial and social terms. In this environment, Community Corrections has an unparalleled opportunity to prove its worth.

CHAPTER 4

Prisonography: Sources of knowledge and perspectives about prisons

Professor Lucien Lombardo
Old Dominion University, US

By exploring the various sources and perspectives about prisons, one encounters a central problem in knowing about the prison: the problem of multiple realities. These multiple realities of the prison reflect the perspectives, values and experiences of those who gather and present the information. The public, the prisoner, the policy-maker, the correctional officer, the administrator and the politician, the lawyer and the judge all experience and shape the prison environment. In addition, the social scientist (sociologist, psychologist, anthropologist, political scientist all see through different disciplinary lenses), the investigative reporter, the legal scholar, the historian, the novelist and the film maker all interpret data and transmit impressions and images of prisons to the multifaceted audience which consumes the information they produce. Taken together, the matrix created by this information contains the reality of the prison. It is up to us to recognise this diversity of perspective and to select, analyse and interpret this information to improve our understanding.

Sources of knowledge about the prison

During the past 200 years, the sources of our knowledge about prisons have changed and expanded as our culture, its knowledge-producing and disseminating mechanisms, and the prison as an institution have changed. As prisons were developing in the early 19th century, there were no academic social scientists studying such issues as where to place prisons and the impact of prisons on communities where they were built. There were no professional associations like the American Correctional Association to provide recommended standards for the institutional developers to follow. There were no legal experts designing disciplinary procedures. As prisons developed, there were no social scientists monitoring the growth of prison subcultures or the psychological impact of confinement on prisoners and prison staff. What did exist were politicians, legal scholars, penal reformers and reform societies, novelists and the nascent news media.

In 1828, Greshom Powers – the agent and keeper of Auburn Prison – demonstrated the general lack of publicly available information about his prison, which was being touted as the model for the world to follow, when he observed that visitors to the prison regularly requested prison reports or pamphlets, from which they could learn. To his great regret the desired information could not be supplied. Much of it was only to be found scattered in the journals of the legislature, and much, in regard to police and discipline, existed only in practice, and was never reduced to writing.

What follows is a brief discussion of different types of materials from which information about prisons might be obtained and the relative value of utilising these sources.

The reformers and treatise writers

Prison writing for the first 150 years of the institution's existence was generally descriptive, often critical, and prescriptive. That is, it started from a particular set of values that guided a critical appraisal of the penal situation, as it existed at a particular time, and ended by proposing a series of reforms designed to remedy the problems identified.

Volunteer prison reform societies collected and disseminated much of the public knowledge about prisons in the early 1800s. Gathering information from personal visits, legislative documents, prison annual reports, surveys of prison administrators and local facilities the reform societies provided a picture of contemporary penal practice. In addition, they supported lobbying efforts in various state legislatures to improve the quality of prisons in what they believed was a more humane and effective direction.

The reports of the reform societies were supplemented by the work of treatise writers. From John Howard, *The State of Prisons in England and Wales* (1777), Dorothea Dix, *Remarks on Prisons and Prison Discipline in the United States* (1845), Frederick Wines, *Punishment and Reformation* (1895); Thomas Mott Osborne, *Society and Prisons* (1916); to Jessica Mitford, *Kind and Unusual Punishment* (1973; Norval Morris, *The Future of Imprisonment* (1974); David Fogel, *...We are the Living Proof ...* (1975); Gordon Hawkins, *The Prison: Policy and Practice* (1976); Robert Johnson, *Hard Times* (1987); and John Dulilio, *Governing Prisons* (1987) prison reform and the prison treatise have had a long tradition. The treatise writers often blended prison experience (as administrators or as members of reform societies) into their personal critique of and prescription for the prison. These documents are prescriptive and analytical, linking an analysis of the theoretical purposes of the prison with practice and policy. But they are more. They are aimed at the political and professional penal/correctional establishments and are attempts to influence correctional practice. The treatise serves to promote argument and discussion and gives evidence and visibility to the key issues of concern in the penal/correctional imagination and debates of particular times.

Government documents

Government documents concerning penal/correctional practice are as varied as the nature and complexity of the governmental structure of the country where they are produced. In each state there are legislative documents that provide authorisation and funding for penal institutions and their activities. There are records of legislative hearings that provide information about the background for legislative action. Reports of legislative, executive and special investigative committees and commissions explore specific components of correctional practice and make recommendations for reform. In addition, departments of correction at the state level and individual specific institutions often produce statistics, documents and annual reports concerning their activities.

At a more specific level, institutions and departments of corrections publish manuals of policy and procedure. These have become more complex to reflect legislative and judicial mandated changes in correctional practice and the standards developed by professional organisations. Little credence, however, can given to these reports when not checked up by other contemporary comment.

The prison narrative

The autobiography or prison narrative has long been a staple source of information about the character of prison life. It is a direct and personal account of life inside of a prison. Prisoners themselves have most often written these accounts. However, prison administrators such as Thomas Mott Osborne, Lewis Lawes, Joseph Regan, and Thomas Murton have also provided glimpses into their philosophy and the practice of penal administration. In *The Victim as Criminal and Artist* (1978) Bruce Franklin lists over 400 literary works (autobiographies, plays, poetry and novels that comprise a bibliography of the prison narrative from 1800-1977. From the *Confessions of Nat Turner* to Charles Colson's *Born Again*, from Lewis Paine's *Six Years in A Georgia Prison*, Elizabeth Flynn's *The Alderson Story* to the *Autobiography of Malcolm X*, George Jackson's *Soledad Brother*, and Jack Abbott's *In the Belly of the Beast*, the prison narrative has long carried the prisoner's experiences and feelings across the walls that separate them from society.

Franklin describes two types of prison autobiographical narrative – the "confessional" and the "institutional". In the first (historically, the oldest) the author describes the profligate nature of his or her life, admits the error of his ways and describes his reformation. The prison, its characteristics and personal reactions to it are not the focus of "confessional prison autobiographies". However, the criminal and his reformation (often as a result of religious experience) provide support for the institution and practice of the prison.

While institutional prison narrative may describe reformation, it is a reformation achieved in spite of the nature of prison life. It is in the institutional prison biography that we began to see descriptions of the personal and psychological impact of imprisonment on prisoner. Struggles with self-definition and the relationship of the individual and society began to take shape. Unlike the treatise, which presents critique and analysis, the goals of the prison autobiography are to expose the impact of the prison on the self, conveying the personal experience, the changes it brought about and the personal meaning (as opposed to the social meaning) of imprisonment.

Society and its representatives are called to account for their failure in meeting the standards they themselves set. The prisoner's voice thus becomes a voice for social critique, a voice for penal reform, in addition to being a voice struggling to make sense of the prisoner's own life. As critic the prisoner provides a perspective of those who experience the fate and circumstances the prison is designed to control. In the prison narrative, the prisoner describes that experience from a personal, not abstract, perspective.

The institutional prison narrative often reflects the assertion of personhood from within a structure that denies individuality. Feminist, Afro-American and other scholars of the "disenfranchised" have shown that the perspectives of these groups (women, Afro-Americans, slaves) have value and serve a corrective function related to the positions and perspectives of the "dominators", those who exercise power. In this regard, the prison narrative is akin to the slave narratives of the 1800s, the biographies of factory workers during the late 1800s and early 1900s, and those of women who portray a meaningful side of life normally ignored in the male-dominated culture. The prison narrative thus is a form of "resistance literature" (Kaplan 1992) exposing the colonisation of power, law, economy and culture and resisting its imposition.

The literature of correctional professionals

In 1870, the International Prison Congress that met in Cincinnati, Ohio published its declaration of principles that codified from the perspective of "correctional professionals". The foundation of this body in 1870 transferred the dominant place in the debates over penal policy from the essentially religious-oriented volunteer prison reform societies of the early 1800s to associations dominated by a professional penal establishment of prison administrators and experts who had a self-interest in prison issues and reform. From this point, professionals in the field would carry on the debates interested members of the public had carried on before.

Rather than debates over the "separate" and "congregate systems", professionals would deal with issues raised by the reformatory movement (how to integrate components into the existing prisons systems), acceptable forms of convict labour, state-centralised versus decentralised control, and the mechanical questions such as plumbing and heating and making prisons technically more efficient. There was now a professional management interest in corrections. Those in charge struggled with how to make their job of prison administration easier and more "effective". No longer was society to be saved and the perfect society modelled by the prison (Rothman, 1971) as it was thought in the early 1800s; now management details would be the concern (Bacon, 1917).

The application of scientific management principles meant that prison administration would focus on lines of command, communication mechanisms and control of correctional officers by wardens and supervisors and of inmates by correctional officers. There would need to be more detailed descriptions of the duties of the various posts and assignments so that there could be no mistake about what was expected. The emergence of the "professional" perspective in discussions of prison policy lead to what Cohen (1985) calls "the hegemony of professional and expert opinion". That is, those who administered the prisons would now shape our common sense understanding of the prison world, and the government and state whose power the prison reflects.

Legal perspectives

The prison is, above all, a legal institution. When the judge pronounces sentence in a courtroom, for many, it is in the prison where the human meaning of the criminal sentence takes form. Prison administrators do not choose their clients. Neither does the prison administrator decide when prisoners will be released. Indeed, the selection of those who occupy prisons is the result of a highly discretionary criminal justice process based on the definitions of what is and what is not criminal behaviour and law enforcement and prosecutorial decisions concerning which law enforcement problems merit the most attention (eg, prohibition enforcement in the early 1900s and drug law enforcement in the 1980s). Executive pardons (widely used in the early 1800s) and parole and legislative actions determining the length of sentence (eg, sentencing guidelines), completion of one's term, and good-time credits determine when the prisoner is released.

Besides determining the make-up of the prison population at any particular time, the law authorises various prison activities. Executive and legislative budgeting processes structure and provide (or do not provide) support for prison labour activities, educational programming and treatment services. Finally, the law determines the nature of the relationship between the person convicted of a crime and sentenced to prison and the state powers embodied in that incarceration.

Penal codes, codes of criminal procedure, and manuals of correctional legislation provide basic authorisations and limitations on state power in relation to the prisoner. Legal commentary found in law reviews and academic journals provide analysis of the issues and problems of the philosophical and operational difficulties of applying law to specific situations. In addition, decisions of various appeals courts provide valuable material. Not only are the specific holdings in specific cases and jurisdictions important, but also the fact situations which lead to the case provide insight into day-to-day correctional operations and practices. Appellate court decisions supply the reader precedent and interpretation of legislative statutes and penal practice. More importantly for understanding the prison, appellate decisions explore the variety of rationales used by correctional administrations (the state) to justify its activities.

Social science research

With the publication of Donald Clemmer's *The Prison Community* in 1940, the social and behavioural sciences began studying life inside a prison. From the introduction of prisons nearly 150 years earlier, writing about prison and prison life was dominated by prison reformers and administrative and policy concerns. Prison administrators who wrote of their experiences and prison inmates who confessed their crimes and described their individualistic experiences with prison life, and novelists and newspaper accounts provided the bulk of our knowledge about prison life. Until the publication of *The Prison Community*, the issues and topics covered in writings about prisons proceeded pretty much as it had since the Prison Discipline Society of Boston collected and published reports on prison issues and activities from around the country in 1826. There was more information about prisons in the popular culture than there was in the academic literature. In fact, one annotated bibliography of prison movies lists 109 films about prisons made between 1921 and 1940 (Querry, 1973).

In this seminal work, Clemmer moved knowledge about prisons from discussions of administrative and policy concerns to the study, description and analysis of the prison as a unique culture. Clemmer's work built on community studies such as Middletown (Lynd and Lynd 1925; Clemmer 1940: xvi) and the Chicago school of the 1920s and 1930s. In these studies it was assumed that social behaviour and social processes could be studied in the laboratory of specific, ecologies and communities (Bell and Newby 1972: 85-93; Clemmer 1940: vi). In the social laboratory of the prison Clemmer explored communication patterns and language, social group formation, leadership, social structure, prison social control processes and sexual behaviour. A key social process was "prisonisation", the process by which prisoners came to take on, more or less, the characteristics of the culture of which they were a part. Important to Clemmer, where the unique character of the various communities from which the prisoners came. For Clemmer, the prison experience would be shaped by previous experiences and the culture prisoners brought with them to the prison.

Our understanding of the relationship of custodial control over prisoners was addressed by Sykes (1956). Sykes extended Clemmer's contribution by bringing to the fore a more theoretical understanding of behaviour in the prison world. Sykes skilfully blends an analysis of both those who wield formal power and their culture (the custodians) and those who targets of the custodial regime who experience the pains of imprisonment (the prisoners). Sykes' work challenged popular and theoretical assumption that prison custodians had absolute control over prisoners. In doing so, he documented and explained sociologically what correctional personnel and prisoners had in all probability long experienced.

Building on Sykes' work, Giallombardo (1966) demonstrated the importance of perception, expectations and gender in shaping the nature of the prison experience. While argot roles, group formation and relations between staff and women prisoners were described and analysed the women's prison society was different. While conflict, authority and control dominated expectations for the men's prison, Giallombardo discussed women's social organisation in terms of "kinship groups" and the importance of social support such family-like associations provided. Indeed, the terms "power", "control", "conflict" and "violence" do not even appear in the index to Giallombardo's work. It was not until the late 1970s that such ideas as "helping-networks", (Johnson and Price 1981; Toch, 1977); and human service orientations (Lombardo 1981) emerged in relation to the study of men's prisons.

Sykes' description of the "pains of imprisonment" and "the defects of total power" set the stage for two new and related directions in the study of the prison: prisons as complex organisations and the prison experience as a form of psychological survival. In addition, the work of Goffman (1961) on the characteristics of the staff and inmate worlds guided attention to the meaning of both the *informal and formal* prison organisation. The importance of informal work groups and group norms had been long known to students of industrial organisations ever since the 1920s and 1930s when Elton Mayo conducted the Hawthorne studies. With Goffman's work, the ceremonial, meaning-creating rituals of prisons, mental hospitals and other segregated communities deepened our understanding of both community and organisational approaches. Goffman analysed the process of self-identity transformation and modes of adaptation undergone and used by the inmates and staff of total institutions.

Cohen and Taylor (1972) expanded the meaning of prison life approach to describe the psychological, perceptual and behavioural impact of the confinement experience. Rather than looking to other "total institutions" for conceptual links, Cohen and Taylor look to "extreme situations" such as the isolated life of explorers, people who migrate and suffer through natural and man-made disasters (1972: 210-211). Changes in behaviours, lifestyles, perceptions of time, self-identity become crucial dependent variables related to institutionalisation. At this time, the socio-psychological experiments of Zimbardo (1971) Haney et al (1973) and Milgram (1969) began to explore the roots of the abusive dimensions of the authority to be found in transfer of responsibility, role taking and bureaucratic rule following.

In the late 1960s and early 1970s, a series of prison revolts in the US, culminating in the deaths of 43 prisoners and staff at Attica in 1971, high-lighted the extent that prisoner and staff perceptions and rhetoric about the prison community had changed (Ussem and Kimball, 1989). There was a revolution taking place inside the walls as the stability of "The Big House" gave way to a redefinition of the prison as a political instrument of state power and a battle ground for racial and ethnic conflict (Irwin 1980). The "rehabilitative programming" and organisational emphasis of the 1950s and 1960s was supplemented in the late 1970s with political and legal analysis in the social science research focusing on the prison. Accountability concerning the exercise of power would now be required of those who administered the prisons. This led to studies of disciplinary procedures, parole decision-making, program assignment criteria, discrepancies between male and female institutions, medical and mental health services and provisions for prisoner safety and control, and prison crowding.

Institutional and social diversity

In the 1970s the impact of race on the social life of the prison and the experience of imprisonment was explored. In addition, the emergence of race in studies of prisons meant that questions of equality, fairness and the exercise of discretion needed to be addressed. Prison practices were now looked at not only in terms of their efficiency and effectiveness but also in terms of standards external to the prisons main functions. The racial integration of prison officer corps in the late 1970s and 1980s meant that a new dimension of general prison culture and organisation and the correctional officer culture and behaviour could also be explored (Jacobs, 1977; Carroll 1988). In the 1980s, the addition of women to traditionally all-male officer corps in male prisons meant that gender issues could be added to race as variables to be explored in the study of the prison society (Zimmer 1986; Jurik 1985).

In 1977, the publication of Hans Toch's *Living in Prison* added still another dimension to the study of the diversity to be found in the prison experience. Drawing on the study of environmental psychology, Toch left the "criminal" element of the prison and its population aside. Rather than studying the way criminals react to the prison environment, transactions between people and environments became the focus. Whether a prison is intended as custodial or as treatment (as emphasised in earlier organisational studies) has less impact for the individual than how he or she perceives that environment, how that environment fits his or her needs, and how people negotiate with their environment.

In addition, this transactional perspective derived from and led to an understanding that the prison was actually made up of multiplicity of environments, each having specific aggregations of resources with which individual prisoners constructed their responses to the prison environment. The cellblock, the dormitory, the mess hall, the prison school, prison Industries, the yard each had unique characteristics and resources. Death row (Johnson 1980, 1990), and solitary confinement (Jackson 1983) received specific attention. Each environment could provide comfort and each could provide danger depending on the needs and perceptions of the individuals involved. Individual prisoners differed in their needs (environmental concerns) and prison environments differed in their ability to match those needs.

The role of the correctional officer, has from the beginning been deemed central to successful prison administration and management. However, it has only been since the early 1970s that the place of the line-level correctional worker has been studied in some depth. From being described as strictly a custodian and supervisor of inmates, the correctional officer has been studied as a "change agent" (Hall et al 1968) and more recently, as a human service providers (Lombardo 1989; Johnson 1977; Philiber 1987). The impact of the correctional officer as an active and passive participant in shaping the character of the prison community (Crouch 1980; Lombardo 1989; Owen 1988; Jacobs 1977; Carroll 1978; Kauffman 1988) has been studied. In addition, the impact of the prison regime on the prison officer has allowed officer stress and coping strategies to be explored. Finally, the impact of unionisation (Jacobs 1983) and racial and gender integration of correctional officer has also been studied and problems and impacts of these changes on the officers and the institutions in which they operate have received additional attention.

The prison in popular culture

Crime, the criminal and the criminal's punishment have long been a subject of popular fascination within the popular media – such as the newspaper, magazine and film. The print media provide a variety of types of information about policy issues and controversies at particular times, information about specific incidents such as riots and investigations into corruption. In addition, reporting patterns in the popular media provide insights into the relationship between prison and public opinion about the prison. Unlike professional, governmental, legal and social science perspectives that are normally aimed at elite audiences, the popular media translates prison ideas to the mass audience. Those who have studied available research on criminal justice and the popular media agree that studies of the relationship between the prison and the media are woefully lacking (Surette 1992: 67; Lotz 1991: 55; Lombardo 1988).

Prisons in the press

Though research on prison and popular culture is lacking, there is no lack of interest about prisons in popular culture. In-depth stories by investigative reporters concerning correctional issues abound. Such journalism supplements insights gained from other sources with detailed information and explanations from official and expert sources on the state of penal practices. Collectively, newspaper coverage of correctional issues in any particular geographic area provides some indication of the amount and type of information available to the general public about correctional matters. Jacobs' (1983) study of newspaper and television coverage of correctional issues during 1976 showed that there is more information in the public domain than one would expect.

There are a number of concepts that can guide one in thinking about and understanding the relationship of popular media presentations of the prison. One emphasises the "hegemony" producing effects of media images. Hegemony is what might be described as "that which goes without saying", or the "givens" or "the common sense realities of the world, which, it turns out, serve an ultimate purpose – that of maintaining the dominance of the ruling class" (Berger 1982: 63). Here the images of the prison portrayed in popular media can be analysed in terms of the patterns of social relations they emphasise. The production of prison news might also be studied. The development of stories, sources used, editorial gate-keeping decisions to include or delete the writers material can be explored.

The prison in film

Feature films provide visual depictions and symbols of the diversity and confusing nature of reality in the prison. According to Rafter (2000), the nature of justice and attempts to struggle to achieve are reflected in individual and institutional situations. Whether the lead characters are rightly or wrongly convicted, they are all portrayed observing and learning about prison reality (that is, undergoing degradation and prisonisation processes). They interact with guards and with other prisoners. In some films some prisoners demonstrate their humanity, while others are models of economic, sexual and psychological exploitation, demonstrating argot roles described in prison social science literature. Though guards are often portrayed as inflictor of pain (especially in films about Southern American prisons) they are also portrayed doing their jobs – opening, doors and gates, breaking up fights and often treating prisoners with respect when they deserve it and disrespect when they do not. From the experiences of the wrongly convicted prisoners of the 1930s to those of the criminal gangs members of the 1990s, prison films portray the uneasy relationship between the public and the modes of punishment inflicted on their behalf.

I am a Fugitive from a Chain Gang (1932), *Cool Hand Luke* (1967) and *Brubaker* (1980) portray the brutality inflicted on the prisoners by the system in Southern road gangs and prisons. *In Each Dawn I Die* (1939), *The Glass House* (1972), *American Me* (1992) and *Shawshank Redemption* (1994), we see the solidarity of the "prisoners' code" crumble under the pressure of prisoners exploiting other prisoners.

In these films prison officials are either accomplices in the exploitation either through direct participation or by omission. Prison gangs, guard brutality, systemic hypocrisy and the political forces and power that helps perpetuate the status quo become powerful messages. While films from the 1930s and 1940s portray prisoner conflict and status determined by the prisoner's criminal background, more recent films portray racial and ethnic conflict which has come to characterise real prison life.

Conclusion

Over the past 200 years much has been written and said about prison. The multiple perspectives from which the prison world has been described make understanding prison a complex undertaking. However, understanding the nature of the perspectives and the need to recognise bias in all perspectives may help us discuss issues and prison practices with a bit more humility and hopefully more clarity. I recently conducted a workshop on "the prison "for a community housing a prison which was trying to come to grips with complex issues related to social justice, prisons as places of punishment and the heated political debate individuals with different perspectives brought to the discussion.

As part of the workshop, we discussed the problem of "multiple perspectives" and how people with different perspectives often "talked past each other" as if they were speaking different languages. After a couple of hours searching for a common language, agreement on many issues was still elusive. However, much greater understanding replaced the heated political rhetoric. I hope that this chapter can contribute to our understanding of the prison, even if agreement on practical solutions still eludes us.

– CHAPTER 5 –

Commissions of inquiry and penal reform

Professor David Brown
University of NSW

Historical introduction

Royal Commissions of inquiry can be traced back to the Domesday Book of William the Conqueror in England between 1080 and 1086, an early investigation of land holdings for taxation purposes (Clokie and Robinson 1937: 28; Gilligan 2002: 290). Their subsequent history in Britain was closely connected with constitutional struggles between the Crown and Parliament, the centralisation of state power, and bureaucratisation. The high water mark for British Royal Commissions was the 1850s which saw 75 established (Clokie and Robinson 1937: 26). Gilligan (2002: 292) notes that in Britain, departmental committees are now favoured over Royal Commissions; only eight new commissions were set up in Britain in the 1970s and none in the 1980s, compared to 74 in Australia and 89 in Canada since the 1970s.

In Australia, Royal Commissions and Boards of Inquiry with coercive powers to compel attendance, the production of documents and testimony, have been a consistent feature of governance, "an inheritance of Australia's tradition of military influence upon civil administration" stemming from its penal history (Gilligan 2002: 291). Perhaps the most important penal inquiry of the 19th century affecting Australia was the Molesworth Committee on Transportation in 1838, a select Committee of the English House of Commons. Informed by evangelical and anti-slavery sentiments and political jockeying between Liberal, Radical and Tory MPs, a jaundiced picture of the NSW penal colony and the "lottery" of transportation and the assignment system emerged, leading to the cessation of transportation to NSW in 1840 and later in Tasmania in 1853 and Western Australia in 1868 (see generally Hirst, 1983; Ritchie, 1976; Finnane, 1997). The ending of transportation was a spur to the building of prisons, both in England and the penal colonies, as the prison became entrenched as "the archetypal institution of punishment" and as "unequivocally a State institution" (Finnane 1997: 13).

Borchardt's checklists (eg, Borchardt, 1986) of Australian Royal Commissions (including Boards of Inquiry, Select Committees and Royal Commissions) suggest that inquiries into prisons in Australia have been concentrated in two key periods. First, there were inquiries across a number

of States in the (post-convict era) second half of the 19th century. Many of
these were responses to specific events and problems at particular establishments, others were more general. Inquiries were conducted into:

- "Irregularities" (Parramatta, 1861-62, NSW);
- Prison conditions (public prisons in Sydney and Cumberland, NSW, 1861)
- "Penal, reformatory and charitable establishments" (NSW, 1863);
- The death of a prisoner at the Adelaide "Stockade" (1869);
- "General management and discipline", including the use of the gag and "spread-eagling" (Berrima, NSW, 1878-79);
- Payments to discharged prisoners (NSW, 1879);
- The assassination of JG Price, Inspector General of Penal Establishments during an inspection of the Penal Hulks in Hobson's Bay, Williamstown, an inquiry which recommended the abolition of the Hulks as penal establishments (Victoria, 1856/7);
- Management of Geelong Gaol (Victoria) (1866) and attempted escapes from Geelong (1866);
- Penal discipline (Tasmania, 1875 – which recommended the closure of Port Arthur – and Tasmania, 1883 – which recommended that all prisoners should serve part of their sentence in solitary confinement) ;
- "Prison discipline" (Queensland, 1868; Victoria, 1856-57; 1870-72);
- An "outbreak of the inmates at Jika" (Victoria) in 1878;
- "General management" (Queensland, 1887);
- Corporal punishment (Penal Commission, Fremantle, WA, 1899) which recommended the abolition of whipping in prisons.

Some of these inquiries had significant effects. A major prison-building
program in Victoria between 1858 and 1864 followed the 1857 inquiries (Kerr
1988: 101). In NSW the 1861 Select Committee on Public Prisons in Sydney
and Cumberland, chaired by Henry Parkes, was scathing of conditions on
Cockatoo Island and in Darlinghurst and Parramatta gaols and recommended an effective system of classification and segregation of prisoners and
the appointment of an Inspector of Prisons. New South Wales' first comprehensive set of prison regulations was subsequently introduced in 1867,
dividing prisoners into different classifications entailing different treatment
and facilities.

There were few Royal Commissions in the first half of the 20th century
(Victorian Parliamentary Report on Penal Establishments and Gaols in 1910
and Royal Commissions into Fremantle in 1911 and Hobart Gaol, 1943); a few
into escapes in the 1950s (Pentridge, 1955; Langi Kal Kal Training Centre
(1956-58); followed by a rash of inquiries in the 1970s. This pattern was not
the case in relation to Royal Commissions in general (in NSW the high point
for the establishment of Commissions generally was 1912, Borchardt 1986:
viii) nor because there were no prison disturbances between 1900 and the

early 1960s. Finnane (1997) notes press reports of disturbances at Bathurst in 1924, 1928, 1932, 1938, 1939 and 1942; at Parramatta in 1926, 1931, 1934, and 1938; Goulburn in 1939; Hobart Gaol regularly between 1931 and 1334, 1936 and 1939; St Helena in Morton Bay in 1926; Pentridge in 1926, Fremantle in 1930 and Yatala between 1930 and 1931. Finnane comments that "rarely did these incidents seem to provoke concern over institutional conditions, and there was no public inquiry into prisons in these decades. A political consensus on progressive penal reform largely distracted attention from any potential review of conditions within institutions" (1997: 143).

That consensus unravelled in the 1960s and public and media attention over abuses led to the establishment of many inquiries including those into:

• The planning of mass escapes and the bashing of prisoners at Westbrook Training Centre in 1971;

• Assaults against prisoners at Brisbane Gaol (Boggo Road) Qld, in 1972;

• High profile escapes from Boggo Road in 1973 (1974);

• Bashings of prisoners at Pentridge Prison in Victoria in 1970-72 (Jenkinson, 1972/73/74);

• Complaints of brutality against prisoners following an escape attempt at Yatala in SA in 1975 (Johnston, 1975/76);

• Prison conditions and administration in Tasmania in 1977 (Grubb, 1977); and

• Arguably the major Australian prisons Royal Commission of the 20th century, the Nagle Royal Commission in NSW (1978).

These inquiries reflected the upsurge of prison disturbances and increasing prisoner militancy as prisoner action groups drew media and public attention to bashings and brutality. Troubles at Boggo Road continued to generate inquiries, with "escapes, increased disturbances, overcrowding, industrial unrest, widespread media criticism and community dissatisfaction" (McCartney, Lincoln and Wilson 2003: 138) prompting a Commission of Review which made recommendations for wide-ranging changes including the introduction of private prisons (Kennedy 1988). A major riot at Fremantle in 1988 prompted an inquiry (McGiven 1988). Some of the other more recent inquiries include an inquiry into "the incident" at Casuarina prison (WA) on Christmas day 1998 (Smith et al 1999; Carter 2001) and the NSW Legislative Council Select Committee Inquiry into the Increase in the NSW Prison Population (2000-2001) (Brown 2002a).

In this chapter I wish to examine the role of Commissions of Inquiry (excluding inquiries by standing agencies such as the Ombudsman and Inspectors) in bringing about penal reform in the Australian context, with particular reference to the landmark Nagle Royal Commission into NSW Prisons (1978) (see generally, Vinson 1982; Findlay 1982; Zdenkowski and Brown 1982). Of the many and varied criteria upon which the conduct of commissions of inquiry can be analysed, three particular themes will be pursued, all of them interlinked. These are the ability of inquiries to establish the truth, to settle accounts, and to stimulate long-term reform.

Truth-telling

The first theme is the issue of truth telling, or more precisely, the readiness and ability of an inquiry to establish a credible version of "truth" about particular events or a particular state of affairs. This is potentially a highly fraught and philosophically complex exercise, for "truth" is not absolute and, to use Foucault's (1980: 133) definition, is "to be understood as a system of ordered procedures for the production, distribution, circulation and operation of statements" and as "linked in a circular relation with systems of power which produce and sustain it, and to effects of power which it induces and which extend it". Hancock and Leibling (1994) in an assessment of English penal inquiries against the criteria of truth, independence and effectiveness define "truth" as "the extent to which inquiries appear to establish accurately both the *reality of what happened* in a given set of circumstances and *knowledge as understanding about the organisation concerned* more generally" (1994: 100; emphasis in original; drawing on Bottoms 2001). On this definition I would argue that Nagle did produce, against considerable opposition, a credible version of "the truth" about specific events and processes in NSW penal practice. This version was subject to later attempts to rewrite the record and to continual contestation, by sections of the media, the prison officers union and conservative politicians. But the basic credibility of findings of fact in relation to the bashings at Bathurst and the Grafton regime in particular stand firm and provide the moral footings for the whole inquiry. One of the key conditions for this "truth-telling" capacity to be fulfilled, is the recognition that prisoners accounts must be heard and, given their cloistered state, practical mechanisms of access, communication and representation adopted to ensure this.

Without hearing from prisoners we are left with the sanitised prison of official discourse. John Pratt in *Punishment and Civilisation* (2002) examines prisoners' accounts of their conditions, particularly food, clothing, personal hygiene and language, recounted in autobiographies and memoirs. This discussion provides in part a contrast, in part confirmation, of the official accounts provided by way of inquiries and official reports (some 1300 in all).

From examples such as these, Pratt (2002) makes the more general point that:

> There are two very different versions, then, of "the truth" about prison life. On the one hand, we have official penal discourse. Here, prisons came to function as they should in a civilised society ... Prison had become largely conflict-free institutions, the authorities told us; within which they had also maintained that food, clothing and hygiene arrangement had been normalized; the prisoners were being encouraged to improve themselves by making use of educational facilities; now, where there were personality problems, there were treatment and rehabilitation programmes available to remedy them. On the other hand, we have the very different story that the prisoners had to tell. In their accounts, continuous themes of deprivation and degradation characterize prison life; reforms might even introduce new privations and torments ... (2002: 121)

Pratt (2002) suggests that historically it was the authorities' accounts that were typically accepted as true and he suggests that this acceptance was a consequence of the combined effects of bureaucratisation and public indifference. Potential independent voices such as those of doctors, chaplains, official visitors and inspectors were vetted and subject to official departmental control. Prisoner's accounts of deprivations, mistreatment and complaints were routinely denied.

Pratt argues that over the period from the mid-19th century to the 1960s expert knowledges, largely the property of elites such as the penal bureaucracies and penal reformers were increasingly embraced by penal authorities. This language was by and large sympathetic to the circumstances of criminals and prisoners, in contrast to popular discourse which "changed from celebrating and romanticising the criminal in the eighteenth century to fearing and shunning him during the nineteenth and twentieth" (2002: 81). This analysis helps explain perhaps, why there were so few prison inquiries in Australia in the first half of the 20th century. But as noted above, this absence was not for want of complaints leading to disturbances, suggesting that at least in the Australian context, Pratt's argument that the sanitised prison of official discourse "operated in a relatively untroubled way because the prisoners came to internalise their own subjection to it" (2002: 120) overstates the degree of subjection and underplays the degree of continuing resistance to authority.

Finnane (1997) provides an illustration of the ease with which prisoners' accounts can be discounted as untrue, merely by the recitation of their makers' criminal histories, as if the status of convicted criminal carries with it a complete absence of veracity. In 1955 the *Sunday Telegraph* ran a story on the physical abuse of prisoners at Grafton. The editor passed prisoners statements and complaints on to the NSW Comptroller-General who recommended to the Public Service Board that a warder be charged with misconduct for striking a prisoner. At the inquiry the allegations were completely dismissed, being "made by young men with very long criminal records" (attaching the records) while the warder had an "unblemished record" (1997: 158). The "regime of terror" (Nagle 1978: 108) at Grafton continued for another two decades.

Similar tactics were used to deflect demands for a Royal Commission into the bashings at Bathurst in 1970, well captured by Commissioner McGeechan's advice to the Minister that "it comes to whether the word of law enforcement officers is to take precedence over the uncorroborated, probably malefic (sic) allegations of people with long criminal histories and demonstrated inability as responsible members of society" (Nagle 1978: 196). In 1970 the first prisoners to be seen by a doctor were examined "in the presence of Superintendent Pallot [who had led the bashings] and a number of other prison officers, including at least two officers who had been responsible for flogging the three prisoners" (1978: 83). Nagle noted that "the circumstances in which the medical examination had taken place were calculated to prevent legitimate complaints being made". He described Commissioner's McGeechan's report to the minister as "unfair" and "not only misleading but dishonest", adding that "Mr McGeechan thought that it was pertinent for the Minister to have a list of Cornwell's [the first prisoner complainant] previous convictions and disciplinary offences within the prison system".

Nor was such conduct confined to prisoners. Prison officers who spoke out were threatened with disciplinary charges, as happened to Ristau, a union official who had publicly called for a Royal Commission. He was later sacked, then reinstated and demoted (1978: 101, 103) but one example of a wider phenomenon of "promoting the bashers, condemning the critics" (Zdenkowski and Brown 1982: 249-255).

As Finnane (1997) notes, "allegations of abuse could readily find their way into the press, but the path from media attention to satisfactory redress was strewn with numerous hurdles, including the ambivalence of the media itself with regard to prisoners and punishment" (1997: 158-59).

The argument that effective mechanisms for obtaining prisoners accounts are central both to establishing the truth and providing legitimacy and moral authority to an inquiry and its recommendations is not new. Finnane (1997) notes that "a number of the most important inquiries in the self-governing colonies up to 1900 paid particular attention to the grievances of prisoners" (1997: 144). One such was the NSW Select Committee on Public Prisons in Sydney and Cumberland in 1861 which conducted extensive visits to prisons, interviewed and received statements from prisoners and ulti-mately published the evidence of the prisoners, for "the ends of truth in disclosing the actual state of our prison establishments must suffer by its being suppressed or modified" (quoted in Finnane 1997: 145). Another was the Fremantle Commission in 1899 which "was even more impressed with the value of prisoner evidence as a guide to carceral realities". However it appeared to be the "last such official inquiry for many decades to give serious consideration to the prisoner's own experience of the system" (1997: 146). Finnane warns that "it is evident that a penal system in which the prisoner is subject to supervision for the purposes of reform is one in which the capacity to be heard is severely diminished"(1997: 147).

Settling accounts

The second theme is that having established a credible version of the "truth" of particular events, in the Nagle case widespread institutionalised violence and mistreatment of prisoners, the extent to which an inquiry can provide the basis for thoroughgoing reform is tied up with the extent to which individual and institutional accountability for abuses is achieved, or more colloquially, the extent to which accounts are settled as a necessary pre-requisite for a "new broom". The criminal prosecution of individuals is the chief (and far from unproblematic) way in which accountability is measured, especially by the media. While acknowledging the dangers inherent in this measure, such as distraction and scapegoating, the failure to prosecute or otherwise disci-pline certain prison officials, officers and others following the release of the Nagle Report undermined the capacity of the new administration led by

Tony Vinson, to bring about the extent of change envisaged and authorised by Nagle. It still casts a shadow of illegitimacy over the NSW Department of Corrective Services, to this day, leaving a legacy of bitterness among prisoners, particularly those who were charged and convicted of destruction of prison property in the 1974 Bathurst riot and served additional prison terms.

Cohen (1979) uses Mary McCarthy's account of the trial of My Lai massacre defendant Medina (McCarthy 1972) to show how "problematic are the connections between theories ('They were just obeying orders', 'they were part of the system') and assessments of responsibility, culpability, blameworthiness or guilt" (1979: 28). Without some notion of individual responsibility, no credit or blame could be assigned to anybody. Similar questions and similar rhetorical strategies to deny, assuage or attribute guilt are often evident in Royal Commissions and are currently on display in relation to the treatment of prisoners by US forces in Afganistan, Iraq and Guantanamo Bay.

In the Nagle inquiry for example, after initial departmental, government and union denials it was eventually established that there had been at Bathurst Gaol a systematic flogging, cell by cell, of all prisoners in the gaol and that there had been in operation at Grafton prison what Justice Nagle described as "brutal, savage and sometimes sadistic physical violence" and a "regime of terror" (1978: 108) involving reception and repeat brutal bashings of so-called "intractable" prisoners which had operated from 1943 until the establishment of the Commission in 1976 (1978: 134-148). Should the prison officers who conducted these sustained routine assaults, for which at Grafton they were paid an additional "climatic allowance" (1978: 134), and those who had knowledge of the regime and covered it up such as, to quote a *Sydney Morning Herald* editorial, "visiting doctors, Cabinet Ministers and members of parliament, judges, members of the clergy, official visitors, health officers, public service inspectors and departmental administrators, among others" (Zdenkowski and Brown 1982: 185) be the subject of criminal or civil charges?

In relation to the evidence "establishing the admission that prison officers participated in a systematic flogging of a large number, if not all, of the prisoners in Bathurst Gaol in October 1970", the Commission noted:

> The Commission has made findings where it believes that assaults have occurred. It has done so on the evidence and on the inferences which arise from that evidence. Whether prison officers or former prison officers should be charged, either criminally or departmentally, is a matter which the Commission leaves to the appropriate authorities. (1978: 71)

The admission by counsel for the prison officers union that "the systematic flogging" "was carried out under the leadership and control of the Superintendent, Mr Pallot, and was regarded by officers as representing official policy" was treated by the Commission as an attempt to plead superior orders:

> The Commission finds against the Prison Officers Vocational Branch of the Public Service Association in its attempts to have its members escape responsibility on this ground for the floggings they inflicted. The defence did not succeed in the Nuremburg trials; it does not succeed here. (1978: 77)

In relation to the brutality at Grafton prison, the Nagle Royal Commission found:

> That every prison officer who served at Grafton during the time it was used as a gaol for intractables must have known of its brutal regime. The majority of them, if not all, would have taken part in the illegal assaults on prisoners. In the time available, the Commission has not attempted to discover or assess the culpability of individual officers ... The names of these officers would be available to the appropriate authorities, and as previously, the Commission leaves to them to any consideration on their future. (1978: 148)

The Commission did, however, recommend disciplinary proceedings under the *Public Service Act* be taken against one prison officer, Keith Newling, for non-violent homosexual advances towards prisoners, conduct described by the Commission as "disgraceful and improper and likely to prejudice the good order and discipline of the gaol" (1979: 178). Charges were instigated promptly and Newling was dismissed. Non-violent homosexual advances or "touching prisoners in an affectionate and suggestive manner" (1978: 175) was evidently conduct warranting a recommendation of disciplinary charges while acts of extreme, repeated violence and brutality was not (see Zdenkowski and Brown 1982: 255-58).

The issue of prosecutions was central to the political, media and governmental responses to the Nagle Report and as the newly-appointed Commissioner of Corrective Services given the task of implementing the Nagle Report, Professor Tony Vinson has subsequently argued, "the conflict over these issues and uncertainties about disciplinary action based on the Royal Commission findings assumed the proportions of an unending drama that impacted on almost every initiative that was taken" (Vinson 2004: 98; and see more generally, Vinson 1982). Vinson expressed the view that "a clear line had to be drawn between past and future practices and that the prosecution, where warranted, of those who had behaved illegally was one important way to establish that irreversible progression" (2004: 97). He goes on to note that there was little enthusiasm within the government to prosecute staff.

After 18 months, State cabinet agreed that disciplinary rather than criminal action be taken against two officers; but before this could proceed an ill-considered private prosecution was launched by prison activists which took pressure off the state to act. The private prosecution was dismissed and the magistrate involved in the hearings launched an attack on the complainants in terms which were used by the charged officers to undermine the legal and moral authority of the Nagle Commission. Some of the same officers were later charged with disciplinary offences following an inquiry into allegations of abuse of prisoners at Goulburn, although the charges against the most senior officers, ex-Grafton Deputy Superintendent Penning and Goulburn Superintendent Hanslow, were dismissed (Henry 1979; Vinson 1982; Zdenkowski and Brown 1982).

Stimulating penal reform

The final theme is that of stimulating penal reform. There are a number of immediate difficulties with this criteria. As Hancock and Leibling (2004) point out in the English context:

> Inquiries that lead to instant and substantial change are not necessarily the best or the most influential in the medium-long term. (2004: 98-99)

Acknowledging how problematic the change or effectiveness criteria is, how might we evaluate the Nagle Royal Commission on that criteria, some 26 years later? One very obvious change, which might be read as a failure of both prediction and influence, is the significant increase in imprisonment rates since 1978. Nagle predicted that "the prison population will not necessarily continue to increase proportionately to any population increase because of, inter alia, the adoption of alternative modes of punishment and improvements in the organisation of society" (1978: 25). In fact, NSW imprisonment rates, which take account of population increases, have doubled since Nagle.

What are we to make of how spectacularly wrong the prediction that the prison population would not continue to increase proportionately to any population increase, turned out to be? One answer would be that Nagle was in good company, that in the late 1970s what is now often referred to as "the punitive turn" was not widely predicted. There has indeed been an expansion in available alternatives since 1978, but for a whole range of reasons an institution under significant challenge in the 1960s and 1970s, regarded by some as deeply obsolete and likely to be consigned to a marginal status or even abolished, has undergone a revival across a number of jurisdictions internationally, particularly in the US where leading criminologists now talk of "mass imprisonment" (Garland 2001).

In terms of a brief overview of changes in NSW penal practice since Nagle (for a more detailed elaboration see Brown 2004, 2005), support for a "decivilising" trend (Pratt 2000; 2002) associated with the punitive turn might be found in major increases in:

- The prison population as a rate; sentencing changes;
- The muzzling of watchdog agencies;
- Prisoner-on-prisoner violence, some engendered by racial and ethnic streaming; and
- The impact of drug use and responses to it such as delinquent cataloguing, shifts in prison culture and intrusive security measures.

On the other hand, there is less official physical violence, systematic bashings appear to have stopped and animosities between prisoners and prison officers have diminished; riots and major disturbances are down; physical conditions have improved and there are a proliferation of programs oriented around education and rehabilitation. Other facets, such as the legal status of prisoners, have shown continuity rather than change, with lack of action on restricted voting rights (Ridley-Smith and Redman, 2002) and other incidents of a "partial citizenship" (Brown 2002b). In short, penal developments since

Nagle have been complex and contradictory, not the simple unfolding of Nagle's reform agenda nor a uniform movement in the direction of "decivilisation" and the "new punitiveness" (Brown 2005).

The extent to which particular inquiries such as Nagle stimulate penal reform is dependant on a whole host of forces beyond the power of inquiries to guarantee. But particular consequences can be attributed to specific inquiries. In relation to systematic bashings, for example, Nagle's argument was that once the brutality had been revealed for all to see it was unlikely to reappear. Zdenkowski and Brown (1982: 119) were sceptical about this, but it may have turned out to be largely true. Shortly after the release of the Nagle Report, a group of old guard officers, some formerly from Grafton, engaged in a range of violent behaviour at Goulburn. An inquiry (Henry 1979) was quickly called by Commissioner Vinson and some *Public Service Act* charges laid. Since this time little evidence has emerged or complaint been made about systematic bashing, although as noted above, other forms of violence permeate the experience of imprisonment. While the Nagle Commission itself did not result in a legal "settling of accounts", a combination of its moral and political force and Commissioner Vinson's determination to "draw the line", helped ground a significant culture change away from the use and legitimacy of direct physical violence.

Conclusion

There have been varied approaches to analysing the contributions of Royal Commissions and other official inquiries to the history of penal reform. Certain radical accounts of the 1970s tended to locate inquiries as sites for the production of "official discourse", functioning to repair legitimacy crises on behalf of the state (Burton and Carlen 1979). More recent treatments have suggested that royal commissions are not all responses to crisis situations; they can be effective information gatherers; they can generate accountability; some can escape their origins and have profoundly "destabilizing" effects on governments (Gilligan 2002: 294). The conditions of existence, conduct and outcomes of specific inquiries are diverse and contingent on a whole host of factors such as the political imperatives behind their establishment; the broader conjuncture; the type of Commission agency involved; the particular appointments of Commissioner and of key staff; the level of resources supplied by government; the terms of reference; decisions as to rights of standing and legal representation; the level of media interest and coverage and its terms and themes; the timetable involved; types of evidence produced; and chance events, to mention just a few of the more obvious.

Royal Commissions of inquiry cannot control the political context in which their recommendations are implemented, transmuted or ignored. But what they can do is to maximise the authority of their processes, findings and recommendations by ensuring perhaps above all, the integrity of their "truthtelling" role. I have suggested in this chapter that in the penal sphere this entails a commitment to, consultation with, and participation of prisoners themselves: that the expression and hearing of prisoners voices is central to the production of "truth", lest we are to discover only the sanitised prison of official discourse. Secondly, I have suggested that an important precondition of the ability of inquiry reports to stimulate significant institutional change is that the inquiry be used to "settle accounts", or in the words of Tony Vinson, to "draw a clear line between past and future practices". Thirdly, I have argued that evaluating the role of particular inquiries in securing long-term change is difficult precisely because such influence is dependent on the operation of historical and conjunctural forces outside the control of inquiries themselves, such as the role of media constructions and popular sentiment, discursive and political struggle around particular inquiries, and longer-term trends in the structure and conditions of life in late modernity. A sub-theme which has forced its way to the surface and which presents a challenge for accounts which conflate or assume a congruence between inquiries and subsequent reform is the extent to which, historically, it has been precisely when the reform impulse and reform discourse has been strongest, that penal inquiries have been deemed unnecessary and the sanitised prison of official discourse has prevailed.

– CHAPTER 6 –

Security in correctional systems

Ron Woodham,
Commissioner, NSW Department of Corrective Services

Introduction

Prison security means a lot more than razor wire and towers.

As recently as the 1970s, the prevailing philosophy for prison security was management by force. The systematic use of brutal physical force ensured that prison routine was observed. As these management practices were exposed after various commissions of inquiry, prison administrators responded by approaching the questions of control and security in a more sophisticated manner which would stand up to scrutiny from both the public and human rights advocates. Electronic monitoring and surveillance teamed with prisoner classification and placement systems now ensure prisoners are where they should be. Case management and intelligence gathering inform and underpin this structure.

Architecture and design of prisons

In 1791, Jeremy Bentham's panopticon was among the first prison designs to consider more than basic security principles. The panopticon was a multi-storey circular structure where a tower formed the central surveillance point allowing the gaoler to observe all cells both individually and collectively. The Pentonville plan of the 1840s, with its radical corridor wings linked to or converging on a central hall was the most popular of the early Australian prison designs.

The designs upon which both of these early forms of architecture were based have influenced probably the most significant advance in prison architecture in the past 20 years – the butterfly design. The butterfly design is so named because the wings fan out like a butterfly's wings from a central control room. The individual cells are situated around the edges of the butterfly wing, to a maximum of two stories high. This design allows all points of the wing to be placed under visual surveillance and maximises inmate management and supervision.

The other major development in prison building design in recent years that has a flow-on effect for security is the concept of building pre-fabrication off site, allowing the construction of an entire wing or section of a prison without the need to shut down the institution for the duration of the building works.

Electronic monitoring systems

There was a trend in prison design in the early 1990s to abolish towers, a centuries old form of physical surveillance very much a part of the prison landscape. As the towers were brought down, a security concept that was fundamental to prisons for centuries was removed, creating the possibility of a backlash from staff. At the time the question was posed – if you don't have towers how do you counter the incidence of contraband being thrown over the wall? The answer has been the introduction of sophisticated electronic monitoring systems. In Australia today, the best prison design features a mix of towers and electronic surveillance systems. However, in the US, towers are still integral to the construction of all new correctional institutions.

The introduction of a range of electronic monitoring systems over the past two decades has presented corrections administrators with a dilemma. An electronic system that effectively counts prisoners as they escape is hardly desirable, rather a system that provides an alarm and gives a response team enough time to prevent an escape is needed.

Electronic monitoring is best used in tandem with effective sterile zones, video motion detectors and with an inner fence that has size and strength.

In recent years, we have learned that we can't build maximum-security prisons with see-through fences. The escape of Brendan Abbott from the Sir David Longland Correctional Centre in Queensland in November 1997 highlighted this. What is needed is the right mix of the old and new in our institutions – with the old prisons that haven't got dedicated sterile zones; the towers have remained while the latest electronics have been added. In prisons with dedicated inner perimeters and sterile zones in the newer institutions there are less towers and more electronics. Regardless of what the mix is, however, nothing is adequate if the alarm is raised and no one responds. Nothing can substitute for vigilant and well-trained staff.

Securing the entry and exit points

Mobile patrols are an increasingly popular management tool in prison complexes where several facilities are grouped together, often in a semi-rural setting. The mobile patrols operate randomly and detect unauthorised people in the grounds of the complex. At the sharper end of mobile security, armoured vehicles are favoured for these patrols. The armour plating extends from the roof to the sides and undercarriage and the vehicles are not immobilised if their tyres are slashed.

Securing the entry and exit points to a prison and minimising their number is the most effective way to prevent breaches of the perimeter walls.

Getting the technology right at the points of entry strengthens the accountability for incidents that occur within the prison. Among the options available are drug-detection dogs, x-ray machines, and metal detectors.

Visits areas are a feature of all prisons. They also pose a very real threat to security as all manner of contraband can be exchanged, even with the most vigilant staff and sophisticated monitoring systems. Privacy laws prevent the placement and operation of surveillance cameras in the toilets of visits areas. Therefore, visitors in secured institutions should never be allowed to visit the toilet and then return to the visits area to continue their meeting with the prisoner. Another point of entry to each institution is the inner gates where vehicles enter and exit. The best prison design incorporates a vehicle inspection bay where the vehicle is parked upon entry to the prison, so officers can walk down under the vehicle to visually inspect the undercarriage.

Helipads constructed on the sports fields of maximum-security institutions will soon figure prominently in the design of new maximum-security prisons. This will enable the authorities to move terrorist prisoners or other extreme high-risk prisoners without the need to put them in a vehicle for longer journeys and excessive time periods – thus decreasing the chance of incidents occurring on the road and removing the predictability of road transport of prisoners of this kind.

A basic concept in prison security is to restrict the access of pedestrians, such as visitors and staff. The number of breaches of the prison perimeter is critical and must be limited and controlled. In the supermax prison in Goulburn in NSW there is no gate to the outside world. The only access point to the facility is from within the main prison.

Sadly, it is the staff of an institution that is often responsible for bringing in contraband. Comprehensive strategies to minimise corruption generally, and focus on contraband in particular, are essential. A focus for such a strategy in recent years has been the pedestrian entry and exit points in each prison. New metal detection devices, where the technology itself does the challenging, is the greatest breakthrough in this area. In effect, the metal detector won't allow the gate (or door) to open if someone sets off the alarm.

These devices are often combined with an iris (eye) scan to allow a central computer to verify if the person has the authority to enter the prison. Iris scan is more tamper proof and more accurate than other biometric identification systems such as finger scans. In NSW the iris scan is being utilised for methadone distribution to prisoners in some gaols. The iris scan allows staff to correctly align the prisoner with the allowable dose of methadone. The nurse involved in the procedure is also subject to the iris scan in order to give the approval for the dose.

Legislation and regulation also have a role to play in relation to compelling staff to submit to searches on entering a correctional facility. Staff entering a prison should be required to empty their pockets, take off their belts and other items that might contain contraband. Under such legislation, the staff member who sets off the metal detector can then be taken to their car or to their workstation and those areas can also be searched for further contraband.

Security measures within the prison

At night, staff numbers within the prison fall to the bare minimum. We need to be confident that the fabric of the building will contain any prisoner that finds a way out of their cell within their wing.

Prison workshops are a key element in most rehabilitation strategies – they are also an enormous risk if not properly monitored and secured. The key issue is minimising the opportunity for prisoners to convey weapons (tools) back to the accommodation sections of the centre. The most effective deterrent for this is to have shadow boards for all tools and to account for their safe return at the end of each shift.

Control rooms are also an integral part of modern prison design. They are a hub for surveillance and monitoring and orchestrate the level of response to an incident at the local, regional and central levels. The reporting of a suspected breach of security (usually activated by a personal alarm which is carried by each officer on duty) to a control room can bring three levels of response. There is a localised response from whatever staff is nearest the incident. The second level would be a regional response from an emergency unit (these units exist in maximum-security prisons). Finally, there could be a centralised response such as in the case of hostage taking within a prison. This level of threat would be controlled centrally.

In recent years, the concept of prisoner escapes utilising highjacked helicopters became a reality. In 1999 prisoner John Killick was extracted from a Sydney prison when his girlfriend highjacked a helicopter and forced the pilot to land inside the prison so Killick could escape. In France, there were five very violent helicopter extractions within a three-year period. The French put wires across the rooftops to prevent the helicopters landing on open spaces, such as playing fields, within the prison. However, this strategy actually served to escalate the violence associated with these escapes: as weapons were dropped into the prison yards allowing the prisoners to arm themselves while the helicopter dropped a pickup ladder and extracted the prisoners through the wires. An added complication for prison staff attempting to combat the escape is endangering the lives of any civilian on board a helicopter who may be under duress. The real solution to the problem comes back to prison design and limiting the possible landing areas for helicopters within maximum-security facilities.

Escorts and prisoner transport

In most correctional jurisdictions, the escort and transport function is so large that the equivalent of a large prison is managed each day on the road. In NSW alone there are 160,000 prisoner movements over 3.5 million kilometres each year. Minimising escorts and prisoner movements outside the correctional centre is the preferred position. As recently as the 1980s, up to 28 inmates would be moved in what was virtually a modified passenger bus. Up to 22 prisoners can now be moved at a time in specially designed vehicles which contain separate compartments. This means prisoners can't interfere with each other while in transit, and men and women, protection- and general-population prisoners can all be moved together in one vehicle.

It is now standard practice that an armoured vehicle accompanies all extreme high-risk escorts. Increasingly, a network of video links are being installed in all prisons so that evidence can be given by prisoners from within the institution and the signal sent by video link to the court, thus minimising the need for these prisoners to ever leave the confines of the prison.

The correct training for staff in the use and deployment of firearms and restraints is crucial. Regular and systematic refresher training is equally important. The most effective training exercises for the use of these important tools involves real-time responses to scenarios, testing the limits of the decision-making under pressure of both the individual and the organisation.

Special weapons and tactics are called for when someone is taken hostage inside a correctional centre. In NSW, a highly trained Hostage Response Group is available to deal with these scenarios. The Latin translation of their motto *Negotiari Stria Nonvisibles* means, "negotiate and if that fails – then strike unseen".

Intelligence

A well-organised and effective intelligence function can position an organisation to head off riots and major disturbances. The importance of gathering and disseminating intelligence and the role intelligence plays in security cannot be overestimated. Potentially, intelligence can be gathered from any person within or outside the correctional system. Well-established links with external law enforcement agencies are also a crucial ingredient in piecing together the often unrelated or seemingly unimportant data provided from intelligence sources. Intelligence networks are now being established between prison services throughout Australia, an include joint training and national conferences, networking with the police and other relevant agencies.

The use of informants is a key aspect of corrections intelligence-gathering. The creation of reward registers for the provision of information demands that the process be accountable and closely managed. Informant management plans must be designed for both staff and prisoners. Separate registers should be kept, detailing the informants and the rewards they have received. Controlled operations involving informants must be endorsed by law enforcement agencies. Informant-handling is fraught with danger and staff often get too close to informants and cross into territory where they can be accused of being an "agent provocateur", which loosely means they are enticing the informant to act and not merely observe.

It is also possible for prisoners to organise breaches of security over the telephone and through correspondence with the outside world. Authority to record any telephone conversation and to censor mail enable correctional authorities to exercise control in these areas.

As the usage of mobile phones becomes commonplace, and they become smaller in design, they pose a significant threat to prison security. Every Australian correctional jurisdiction currently faces a problem with staff and visitors smuggling phones into prisons. One solution to this problem is mobile phone finder devices. The threat posed by mobile phones can be dealt with if the reception can be jammed. However, at this stage the footprint of the signal to jam the reception will spill over beyond the correctional centre into the surrounding area and interfere with phone receptions in passing traffic and in nearby residences.

Terrorism and security threat groups

Security philosophies in recent years have increasingly had to encompass the threat of terrorism and the containment of terrorists in custody. While the phenomenon of prisoners threatening staff is not new, this situation is particularly acute when members of extremist organisations are taken into custody. The response to this situation is to provide target hardening of staff. This simply means the organisation must be equipped to properly protect staff when a threat is identified. This response can vary, but in extreme cases, 24-hour protection and security for their homes and families may be necessary.

The poor language, literacy skills and work history that are present in the prison population means that prisoners often view crime as their "business". Inmate gangs or groups generally come from cultures where violence is acceptable and is considered normal. These groups of prisoners pose a threat within, and external to, the prison system. In particular, they pose an escape threat as they often have considerable resources at their disposal. This can result in the need for armed intervention and superior levels of planning by prison staff.

There are distinct differences between groups which form for criminal/organised crime purposes and those that form along ethnic/cultural lines. Prisoners who are members of a defined group in prison often try to continue to participate in organised crime activities while in custody. The group helps to facilitate this, and attempt to threaten, to corrupt and intimidate prison staff.

One of the problems that confronts prison administrators in Australia is that there are fewer options available to allow the movement of leaders and members of prisoner groups. In most jurisdictions there are not enough prisons to separate the group leaders from their members.

The first step in combating the emergence of these threat groups is educating staff about specific ethnic and cultural issues associated with the group. The most obvious strategy is to house the different groups in physically separate locations within the prison. This can present logistical and resource issues. Anecdotal evidence suggests that the affiliation and association of the individual within the group tends to weaken towards the end of the individual's sentence.

Prisoner classification

Central to all security-related matters in any correctional system is the prisoner classification process. Prior to the Nagle Royal Commission into NSW Prisons in the late 1970s, the philosophy was to classify all prisoners to the highest possible level. That philosophy still operates in most Australian jurisdictions, however, it can increase the effect of institutionalisation and impede rehabilitation. Post-Nagle, NSW classifies all prisoners to their lowest possible level. The system in NSW has now has a Serious Offenders Review Committee in place to ensure that the most serious offenders aren't moved through the classification system too quickly.

Classifying prisoners to their highest possible level, which in effect minimises the numbers in minimum-security facilities, is justified by most administrations because prisoner escapes are not acceptable to the community. Private prison operators also pursue the philosophy because their contracts have penalty clauses linked to escape rates.

Despite fears that such a philosophy would mean prisoners would have a greater chance to escape, NSW has never had more prisoners and has historically low escape rates. Classifying to the lowest possible level means security can become a more dynamic process and prisoners are more able to access meaningful programs. Having the proper process in place to monitor individual progress as prisoners progress down through the security ratings is also central to this concept.

Conclusion

Secure custody and control of prisoners has always been the cornerstone of effective prison management. It ensures staff have confidence to carry out their duties in a stable working environment. This, in turn, enhances the case management process and allows us to pursue individual rehabilitation programs. Security is never taken for granted by prison administrators despite the application of a range of sophisticated technology. Every officer has a duty to maintain the safety and integrity of their workplace and to see himself or herself as a security technician. Even the most secure institutions are only as technically strong as the weakest link in procedures or the lapses in vigilance of its staff members.

CHAPTER 7

Privatisation in the corrections industry

Sean O'Toole
Assistant Director, Learning and Staff Development,
NSW Department of Corrective Services

Origins of private enterprise involvement in punishment

Private enterprise has been involved in corrections for centuries. In 16th century England and Europe, prisoners were charged fees for their keep. Fees and standards of accommodation varied with one's ability to pay, meaning that prisoner groups were mixed together in quasi-secure facilities regardless of age, gender or offence type. Those occupying more salubrious rooms were often accompanied by their wives and families. After the basic payment to the gaoler, virtually any special services provided to prisoners, such as better meals, attracted a higher fee (Telfer 2003; Morris and Rothman 1995; Austin and Coventry 2001).

During the Middle Ages in England, magistrates controlled the majority of prisons. Each group of magistrates was responsible for those in their district and was also responsible for the community money which funded the prison system. It followed that they were reluctant to invest public money in prison facilities and on a group as unpopular and as powerless as prisoners. According to Thomas and Stewart (1978), prisoners themselves were responsible, for their experience in prison through their payment of fees – payable both upon entering and leaving the prison.

The transportation of convicts to the US was pioneered by entrepreneurs who would ultimately profit from the venture, and recover their outlays for transporting the convicts, when they were sold as indentured servants.

The early Australian experience with privatisation is not dissimilar to that of the US. The lack of gaols and other detention facilities in colonial Australia meant the convict population were assigned to free settlers after the transporter had been paid a fee. This often meant their labour was exploited by individuals or companies for profit.

Prisons in the US also pioneered variations on the privatised model as far back as the mid-1800s, based on the premise that prison labour was expected to turn a profit for the institution. One model involved private companies supplying raw materials to be refined in prison workshops and then returned to the private company for sale. Another involved the lease of prison labour to private farms or businesses. Contractors also paid prisons a fee or percentage of profits to gain the right to employ convict labour (Austin & Coventry 2001).

The introduction of legislation in the early 1900s prohibiting the commercial sale of goods manufactured by prisoners is often cited as one of the major reasons for the decline of the first wave of prison privatisation in the US. The effect of such legislation was to remove the attraction for private companies to utilise cheap prison labour.

The income generated by prison labour was never sufficient to account for the high costs of operating a correctional system. By the early part of the 20th century the convict-lease system gave way to increased government involvement in corrections.

The latest incarnation of privatisation has its origins in the juvenile corrections industry in the US in the 1970s. Austin and Coventry (2001) report that the US Immigration and Naturalisation Service also privatised their detention facilities in the early 1980s and both industries continue to have considerable involvement from the private sector today.

Why do we continue to pursue privatisation of the correctional system?

According to Graycar (2001), one of the reasons privatisation has been such an attractive proposition for Australia's correctional administrators is that by the late 1980s more than half of all prisoners in the country were housed in prison buildings which were constructed 150 years earlier. This ageing infrastructure was inadequate, didn't comply with modern correctional standards and was expensive to maintain.

This untenable situation coincided with a sharp rise in inmate numbers, which paralleled the high rate of imprisonment which prompted the boom in prison building nearly 150 years before. What can now be viewed as the second great prison building boom in Australia's history commenced in the late 1980s and the result was an unprecedented level of private companies becoming involved in the construction and management of private correctional facilities.

In the modern sense, privatisation of the corrections industry has not meant an ownership transfer of the government-run prison system to the private sector. Moyle (2000) argues that the government becomes the purchaser of management and program services and retains the responsibility for the correctional system. It also acts as regulator or monitor of the private provider and applies policies, rules and procedures in the contract, which specify the limits the private sector can apply to existing practices.

There are three basic types of correctional services offered by the private sector (Moore 2002):

- the design and construction of prisons;
- the provision of a range of services for offenders, such as food or medical care, and juvenile or community correctional centres; and
- the contract management of major detention facilities.

In the late 1980s extreme overcrowding issues prompted the French prison service to create a hybrid model of privatisation. In total, 21 semi-private prisons were privately constructed and all non-custodial services contracted out. However, the staff were employees of the State, including the Governor or Director in charge of each institution. This model was later replicated in other European jurisdictions such as Germany and Belgium (Doohan et al 1999; Coyle et al 2003).

A major argument in the literature about the management of private prisons is that it represents major cost savings compared to government-run facilities. However, there is no agreement among academics or professionals in this field on the issue. A nationwide study into private prisons in the US uncovered the fact that the average saving to government from privatisation of corrections was only in the order of about 1 per cent. Most of these savings came from lower labour costs (Austin & Coventry 2001).

Cunningham (1999) provides a very balanced summary of the benefits and pitfalls of privatisation. For example, on the positive side, it is widely accepted that privateers can finance and construct a facility more quickly and cheaply than government, reducing the government's economic and compliance liability. A commonly advanced argument is that government performance in the sector is increased by the introduction of competition. Another central point in favour of privatisation is the escalating labour costs associated with the corrections industry as up to three-quarters of budgets are typically spent on human resources. The correctional workplace is also dominated by a very vocal union presence who strongly influence any attempts to reform work practices.

Moyle (2000) argues that the real catalyst for Australia's first private prison (Borallan in Queensland), was the idea that market forces generated by the profit motive would ensure greater efficiencies and superior performance than the public sector had been able to achieve. This thinking soon spread to other Australian States.

Central to the negative aspects of privatisation of the corrections industry are the precepts that there are certain responsibilities that only government should meet. The right to punish its citizens and deprive them of their liberty is vital to this notion. Contemporary commentators such as Harding (1999) have expressed the view that punishment will always be seen as a "core" state function that can never be delegated. Rather, only the administration of punishment should be delegated to the private sector – and it should be subject to safeguards.

While privatisation can be a generator of competition and stimulate debate and new ideas, the reality is that there are very few private companies involved in the corrections industry. The bottom line profit motive can also compromise correctional operations.

Contracts between the government and private organisations is also a complex area. Lack of enforcement remedies in contracts often mean that termination or lengthy legal actions result when expectations are not met.

Current facts and statistics

The origins of the modern form of privatisation in corrections originated in the US. In 1987, the total number of prisoners managed in privately operated gaols worldwide was 3100. A decade later that number had increased to 132,000. Two American companies, the Corrections Corporation of America and Wackenhut Corrections Corporation (now the GEO Group Inc), account for three-quarters of the entire worldwide market (Thomas 1997; Austin & Coventry 2001).

Private prisons make up less than 5 per cent of the world market and about 7 per cent of the US market. The UK is the most privatised corrections jurisdiction in Europe with 8 per cent of its total prison population under private management. Australia has the greatest amount of privatised correctional services and facilities with 18.8 per cent of its prison population in private hands. There are almost 200 private prisons in the world, holding approximately 140,000 prisoners. The bulk of these facilities, approximately 160, are in the US (Austin & Coventry (2001). Significant levels of privatisation exist within the criminal justice sector in countries such as New Zealand, South Africa, Canada and the Netherlands Antilles. Countries who have engaged in smaller contracts with the private sector or have expressed serious interest include Japan, South Korea, Lebanon, Costa Rica, Mexico, Venezuela and Thailand (Coyle et al 2003).

The US has experienced the largest growth in correctional privatisation in the world, purely in terms of prisoner numbers. In 1995 there were 16,663 inmates in private prisons in the US but by 2000 this figure had increased six-fold to 93,077 according to the US Bureau of Justice (2004). When we include gaols and other facilities, the figure is closer to 120,000, down from a peak of over 130,000 in the late 1990s as reported in the Prison Policy Initiative (2002).

The reason for this dramatic increase in prison privatisation in the US is that most States need to have a referendum or have legislation enacted in order to build a new prison. However, if a private company builds the prison and the government leases it or contracts a private company to operate it, the recurrent expenditure does not need separate authorisation.

In Australia in 2004, there are 81 government-operated and seven privately-operated prisons, four government-operated community custodial facilities (including two transitional centres) and five privately-operated community custodial facilities. A daily average of 4171 prisoners (excluding periodic detainees) were held in privately operated facilities during 2002-03, by proportion the highest level of privatisation for any country in the world. Private correctional facilities operate in five Australian jurisdictions (NSW, Victoria, Queensland, WA and SA). The proportion of prisoners accommodated in private facilities in those States ranged from 39.7 per cent in Victoria to 7.2 per cent in South Australia (Report on Government Services 2004).

There are very few detailed studies on the effects that privatisation has on running costs, recidivism, prisoner safety and conditions of confinement. In those countries where there are private prisons, their presence seems to have encouraged the public facilities to sharpen their programs, procurement, finance and human resource strategies. The one area where the private sector has a discernable edge is in the construction of new facilities, which it does faster and more economically (Austin & Coventry 2001). A good example of the financial rewards available to private prison operators is the revenue available from facilities such as payphones. In the US, a single payphone can return up to $12,000 a year. In 1997 in New York, $21.2 million in commission was declared from inmate phone calls using payphones (Coyle et al 2003).

A range of distinct themes has emerged in the literature on privatisation. The nature of making a business profitable means that operators of private prisons face mounting pressures to cut costs and lower standards. At the beginning of the privatisation debate it was commonly thought that private enterprise could deliver an equivalent or superior service more cheaply than the government-run corrections industry. Over time, and with changing management practices brought about by competition, this argument is no longer sustainable. There is also a danger that in the pursuit of a greater market share, private operators will lobby governments and the media for greater sentences and a harder line on crime and justice (Harding 1999).

While there has been a discernable slow down in traditional markets such as the US, Australia and the UK, the transnational corporations involved in corrections have successfully moved into new markets in Asia and the Pacific, South America and the Middle East where privatisation of government-run correctional facilities has considerable momentum.

Future trends and emerging issues

The privatisation of correctional systems, facilities and services in Australia, the UK and the US probably peaked in the late 1990s. In the years ahead, there is likely to be a gradual increase in the number of private prisons across a broader range of countries but at a slower pace than the past decade. The number of companies involved in the industry is also likely to decrease. The areas of greatest demand for privatisation in the US are now homeland security and immigration detention facilities (Prison Policy Initiative 2002).

The likely areas or inmate populations where privatisation will make advances in the future include the following categories: low-security prisoners; aged or geriatric prisoner populations; mental health facilities; and, corporate services such as food, maintenance and transport (Austin & Coventry 2001).

Privatisation in corrections is not confined to the "for profit" sector. The involvement of voluntary and non-government sectors offers a diverse range of approaches, management styles and service delivery modes to the industry (Harding 1992). This kind of involvement is referred to by Ryan and Ward (1989) as the shallow end of privatisation and predominantly occurs in community corrections. Conversely, the deep end of the system is the transfer of the construction and management of prisons traditionally built and operated by the government to the private sector (Moyle 2002).

In NSW, the government has used the spectre of privatisation to trial a series of operational reforms in its newly constructed prisons at Kempsey and Windsor. Each prison will benefit from a streamlined organisational structure and a renewed emphasis on case management. Staff will receive an annualised salary package, enter into performance agreements and receive a flat rate of overtime. These new prisons will be used to pioneer changes to traditional work practices in the NSW public sector. All of this was made possible because the government indicated that the new prisons would be privatised unless the NSW Department of Corrective Services (with union agreement) could come up with a radical new model.

Conclusion

There is no evidence that privatisation of the corrections industry has had, or will have, a dramatic effect on the way the industry operates or its effectiveness. While its value to the criminal justice system as a whole is only marginal, it is here to stay. Privatisation has offered modest cost savings by making minor modifications to staffing, staff benefits and other labour-related costs. This must be balanced by the potential for operational ineffectiveness linked to inexperienced staff, who may receive inadequate training; and the ongoing difficulties associated with the recruitment of competent staff. The private sector has shown it is also capable of mismanagement. Regardless of these issues, the involvement of private corporations, voluntary and non-government sectors do serve a vital purpose as part of the modern correctional landscape. Their very existence has challenged the industry to innovate and re-examine traditional management practices.

– CHAPTER 8 –

Human rights in corrections practice

Brian Tkachuk and Eileen Skinnider[1]
International Centre for Criminal Law Reform
and Criminal Justice Policy, Canada

Introduction

In recent years, a law and order philosophy has become prevalent in many countries, irrespective of the economic, social or cultural context. This increasing pressure on governments to control crime and enhance public security has been reflected in domestic legislation and policies that have resulted in the increased use of incarceration as punishment; imposition of new restrictions on prisoners; and less emphasis on alternatives to incarceration. In this environment, correctional authorities are increasingly challenged with the difficult task of meeting their obligations to ensure international human rights standards for all prisoners.

All human beings are endowed with basic human rights. People who are detained or imprisoned, including those on remand, pre-trial detention, awaiting sentence or convicted, no matter how serious the crime, remain entitled to their rights. While some of these rights are obviously limited for prisoners, such as the right to liberty and freedom of movement, everyone must be treated with inherent respect and dignity regardless of their circumstances. Human rights in corrections practice recognise the balance between the State's obligation to protect the public from crime and criminals, while ensuring respect for the humanity and dignity of prisoners, the provision of humane conditions in prisons and the legitimate deprivation of liberty.

International human rights

International human rights represent an idea that now has worldwide acceptance. Some regard the formation of the United Nations in 1945 and the promulgation of the *Universal Declaration of Human Rights* in 1948 as the

---

1   This chapter was made possible through the support of the International Centre for Criminal Law Reform and Criminal Justice Policy and the Correctional Service of Canada.

beginning of the protection of human rights. However, others trace the origins of human rights to early theories of "natural law" wherein individuals were entitled to certain immutable rights as human beings (Weissbrodt 1988). While there exist many definitions of "human rights" and debates rage about the importance of different rights and the implementation of those rights in different cultures, what is clear is that human rights are universal legal guarantees protecting individuals against actions which interfere with fundamental freedoms and human dignity (High Commissioner for Human Rights 2000). Human rights provide a moral recognition of the dignity and equality of all human beings and encompass all aspects of the human life, from civil and political rights to economic and social rights. Among the rights guaranteed to all human beings are: the right to life; freedom from torture and cruelty, inhuman or degrading treatment or punishment; freedom from arbitrary arrest or detention; right to a fair trial; freedom from discrimination; the equal protection of the law; freedom from arbitrary interference with privacy, family, home or correspondence; freedom of association, expression, assembly and movement; the right to adequate food, shelter, clothing and social security, the right to health and the right to education.

According to human rights law, States have legal obligations to respect individual and group rights. The General Assembly of the United Nations has repeatedly emphasised the importance of strict compliance with obligations under human rights instruments (Ramcharan 1988). This may mean that the State must do certain things, or refrain from doing certain things, to ensure that human rights are being respected. It is important to distinguish the concept of rights from charity. States do not guarantee "rights" out of benevolence or kindness. Rather individuals hold a claim or legal entitlement and the State has a corresponding duty or legal obligation.

Some of the important characteristics of human rights have been rearticulated in the *Vienna Declaration of Human Rights* following the 1993 World Conference on Human Rights. All human rights are universal, indivisible and interdependent and interrelated (Art 6). Universality means that such rights belong to each and every human being regardless of who they are and where they are, be they free or in prison. Respect for all human rights on a fair and equal basis upholds the dignity and equality of all people. The inalienability of human rights means that they cannot be taken away or renounced. Some human rights can be derogated from or subject to limitations, but only in accordance with the laws of a democratic society and to the extent necessary.

International human rights law standards and instruments

Human rights are enumerated in the *Universal Declaration of Human Rights* (UDHR) and in various treaties, declarations, guidelines and bodies of principles elaborated by the United Nations as well as by different regional organisations. However, states are only legally bound to comply with provisions that they have agreed to. Two sources of international law legally binds states. The first is treaty law or "hard law". A treaty is a written agreement that binds the signatories to its provisions and requires ratification, a formal act of confirmation. The other source of law binding on states is customary international law. Such law has developed through general and consistent practice of states which states have followed because of a sense of legal obligation. For example, while the UDHR is not a binding treaty, it has been held that certain of its provisions are considered to have the character of customary international law which is now binding on all states (Buergenthal 1988).

Some of the human rights treaties cover every aspect of rights, such as the International Covenant on Civil and Political Rights (ICCPR) and the International Covenant on Economic, Social and Cultural Rights (ICESCR). Along with the UDHR, these three instruments are called the International Bill of Rights. Other treaties deal with particular types of violations, such as the International Convention for the Elimination of All Forms of Racial Discrimination (CERD) and the Convention Against Torture and other Cruel, Inhuman or Degrading Treatment or Punishment (CAT). Other treaties deal with protecting particular groups, such as the Convention on the Elimination of All Forms of Discrimination Against Women (CEDAW) and the Convention of the Rights of the Child (Children's Convention). All of these instruments are legally binding on States which have become parties to them.

Human rights norms and standards are further elaborated in other types of instruments such as declarations, recommendations, bodies of principles, codes of conduct and guidelines. These instruments are called "soft law" as they are not legally binding on states. However, they have moral force, being broadly accepted within the international community, usually adopted by consensus at the United Nations. They also provide practical guidance to states in their domestic conduct and policy. Certain provisions or instruments may be regarded as reflecting customary international law when there is a consistent and general international practice among states, and therefore conferring binding obligations upon states. In addition, these instruments may provide indications for determining the development of customary international law (Kindred 1993).

There are a number of "soft law" instruments that are applicable to corrections. The *Standard Minimum Rules for the Treatment of Prisoners* (SMRs) is one of the main instruments that deal with the essential features of daily life in prison. The SMRs embody the principles of humanity, respect for human dignity, social purpose and managerial performance in prisons while recognising the variety of legal, social, economic and geographical conditions that prevail in the world. These minimum rules are seen as generally accepted good practices in the treatment of prisoners and institutional management (Gonsa, 1995). The *Body of Principles for the Protection of All persons under Any Form of Detention or Punishment* (Body of Principles) applies to all persons deprived of their liberty, including those who have been convicted of an offence. The *Basic Principles for the Treatment of Prisoners* (Basic Principles) reinforce the fundamental human rights for prisoners and confirms that the UDHR and other standards apply to prisoners except for those limitations that are demonstrably necessitated by the act of incarceration. Other soft law instruments deal with prison authorities, such as *Code of Conduct for Law Enforcement Officials* and *Basic Principles on the Use of Force and Firearms by Law Enforcement Officials*. Others cover specific groups such as juveniles.

Implementation of international standards in domestic contexts

It is incumbent upon states to take all necessary measures to give force to the standards and norms contained in those treaties to which they are party to and those provisions reflecting customary international law. States do this principally through their domestic legal systems, including incorporation of these standards in their constitutions, bill of rights, domestic law and policies. In addition, states are required to establish internal and external monitoring mechanisms to ensure compliance with their obligations. Training and support mechanisms to ensure that states' agents are aware of these obligations should also be implemented.

Certain resolutions that come out of the various bodies of the United Nations provide guidance to states on how to ensure effective implementation of human rights norms and standards. For instance, the resolution entitled *Procedures for the Effective Implementation of the Standard Minimum Rules for the Treatment of Prisoners* sets out the various implementation measures that can be taken, such as embodiment in national legislation, wide distribution to concerned personnel and prisoners, technical assistance services and training programs.

Standards are also expressed in broad terms, setting out generally accepted principles. They must therefore be implemented in a variety of contexts which have different legal regimes, economic and social standards and cultural characteristics. Countries can use different practices and policies to comply with these standards. As declared in the SMRs, these standards are designed to stimulate a constant endeavor to overcome practical difficulties and encourage experimentation.

Human rights in prisons

The use of imprisonment as a punishment was introduced in Europe in the 18th century and it soon spread to most countries, often as a result of colonisation (Wallenberg et al 2004). In some regions, such as Africa, the concept of prisons had not been found in the local culture, which emphasised reconciliation. In many countries, the debate continues as to the primary purpose of imprisonment. Whether the focus is on punishment, deterrence, reformation, rehabilitation or a combination of those, international law clearly states that the aim and purpose of the penitentiary system is reformation and social rehabilitation (Art 10, ICCPR) and to encourage the prisoner's self-respect and develop their sense of responsibility (r 65, SMRs). International law recognises the necessity of addressing crime and maintaining public order through the use of prisons. The law does not prohibit or seek to abolish prisons; rather it sets out a framework in which states can lawfully and non-arbitrarily detain people in humane conditions and with dignity (Achieng 2004). Respecting human rights enhances the possibility of reintegration of the prisoner back into society upon release as well as being a useful management method to ensure security, safety and good order within the prison (Coyle 2002).

Prisoners are one of the most vulnerable groups in society since they are under exclusive control by the state and its agents. For that reason, international instruments clearly provide that except for those limitations that are demonstrably necessitated by the fact of incarceration, all prisoners retain the human rights that are set out in the UDHR and other treaties, where the state is a party (Principle 5, Basic Principles). Prisoners' rights cannot be taken away without legal justification. Prisons exist to ensure a measure of protection to the public. Therefore restricting movement to individuals and ensuring that they do not escape and threaten the security of the public may be seen as a justifiable limitation to the right of freedom of movement. Limitations may also be justified to ensure there is a safe environment for prisoners and staff by maintaining good order and control, while providing for all basic human needs. Limitations have to be legal, therefore any order for imprisonment must be authorised by a competent judicial authority.

Specific human rights for prisoners and prison staff

As previously mentioned, all human rights apply to prisoners, with, of course, some obvious limitations and restrictions. For the purpose of exploring how these rights apply in the prison context, this part is divided into five categories of rights for ease of discussion:

(i)   broad rights of prisoners;

(ii)   civil and political rights;

(iii)   social and economic rights;

(iv)   rights relating to remedies and disciplinary practices; and

(v)   rights of prison employees. One must remember that these rights are all inter-related and interdependent.

Broad rights of prisoners

International human rights law expressly declares that the treatment of prisoners should aim for their rehabilitation (Art 10(3), ICCPR). The purpose of imprisonment, protecting society against crime, is not met by simply removing offenders from society but trying to ensure, as far as possible, that upon their return to society, the offender is not only willing but able to lead a law-abiding and self-supporting life (r 58, SMRs). States can discharge their duty to protect society against crime by ensuring its fundamental responsibilities for promoting the well being and development of all members of society, including prisoners. Prisons must create favourable conditions for the reintegration of released prisoners into society (Principles 4 and 10, Basic Principles). Therefore all prisoners have the right to participate in rehabilitative programs.

Rehabilitative programs or treatment should encompass education, vocational guidance and training, social casework, employment counselling, physical development and strengthening of moral character (r 65, SMRs). Education should be made available for all prisoners capable of profiting from it and should be based on the state's regular education system to ensure continuity upon release (r 77, SMRs). The education of illiterates and young prisoners is compulsory. All prisons should have a library (r 40, SMRs). The international standards refer to the state's regular education system as the norm to be met. It is important to note that where a state may be unable to meet certain standards due to financial constraints, it must be willing to allow non-governmental organisations access to prisons to provide such programs.

As part of rehabilitation, each prisoner has the right to engage in their own cultural and recreational activities which ensures contact with the community that they will one day return to. Prisons should offer counselling programs, ensuring that informed consent is given by prisoners regarding psychological and psychiatric assessments. In most prisons where prisoners engage in some form of work, the international standards require that the work should maintain or increase the prisoners' ability to earn an honest living after release and should resemble as closely as possible those of similar work outside institutions, so as to prepare prisoners for the conditions of normal occupational life (rr 71 and 72, SMRs). The international instruments also provide for meaningful remuneration for the work done by prisoners (r 76, SMRs).

The principle of equality applies in prisons and to prisoners. Any treatment, program or service should be available to all prisoners equally. That means each prisoner has the equal right to enjoy all human rights applicable to them, including access to services and programs (Art 3 in both ICCPR and ICESCR). Therefore, such programs and services should be tailored to women, ethnic and cultural groups and people with disabilities. The state must also ensure that prisoners have the right to an environment free from practices that undermine the dignity of the person. There shall be no discrimination based on race, colour, sex, language, religion, political or other opinion, national or social origin, property, birth or other status (Art 2, UDHR). This non-discriminatory clause is reproduced in both the ICCPR and ICESCR and is elaborated for specific groups in the CERD and CEDAW conventions. Discrimination can mean imposition of treatment or conditions which are detrimental or disadvantages, or which is substantially favorable to certain individuals or to groups of prisoners.

Civil and political rights

The necessity of confinement in prison does restrict somewhat a person's right to liberty and freedom of movement. International law allows such restrictions but only when they are done on grounds and in accordance with procedures established by law (Arts 9 and 12, ICCPR). The right to freedom of movement is not completely removed since prisoners are rarely held in total isolation. Such isolation would have to be for very good and specific reasons. Generally, it is the prison authorities that are responsible for determining the classification and placement of each prisoner based on security requirements and agreed criteria. In so doing, the authorities must ensure that the extent of the deprivation of liberty and restriction to freedom of movement are justified, necessary and proportional to the security threat of the prisoner. As a general rule, prisoners should only be confined to special maximum-security conditions where their behaviour has shown them to pose a threat to safety and security, and that the prison authorities have no other choice. Any such assignment should be for as short a time as possible and subject to continuous review (Coyle 2002). Any decision regarding segregation, transfer, reclassification or suspension of conditional release needs to be in accordance with the least restrictive measures consistent with public safety and with the principles of fundamental justice.

Deprivation of liberty itself is the punishment and prison staff should not inflict additional punishment on prisoners during their imprisonment. It has been noted that the closed and isolated nature of prisons may allow abusive actions to be committed with impunity, sometimes in an organised manner (Coyle 2002). Prisoners are particularly vulnerable to abuses of use of force. There is a danger that in countries where the punitive function of prisons is given priority, actions which amount to torture or ill-treatment such as routine unlawful use of force and beatings, can come to be regarded by staff as "normal" behaviour (Coyle 2002). The international instruments make it very clear that there is a total prohibition on torture and deliberately inflicting cruel, inhumane or degrading treatment or punishment no matter what the circumstances (Art 7, ICCPR and Art 5, UDHR). Prohibited treatment includes circumstances which deprive the prisoner, temporarily or permanently, of the use of any of his or her natural sense, such as sight, hearing or his or her awareness of place and the passing of time (Principle 6, Body of Principles).

In order to safeguard against torture and ill-treatment, a number of international instruments set out procedures to follow when prisoners first enter prisons. This includes a transparent registry system, the opportunity for prisoners to inform their legal representatives and their family of their whereabouts as soon as possible, and to offer the prisoner a medical examination by a qualified medical officer (rr 7 and 24, SMRs; and Principles 16, 18 and 24, Body of Principles). International instruments also set out the parameters for the use of force by prison staff. Instruments of restraint, such as handcuffs, chains, irons and straitjackets should never be applied as punishment. Chains and irons should never be used as restraints. The other instruments should only be used under limited circumstances (r 33, SMRs). In the use of force and restraints, the procedure must be clear and transparent.

Some countries still allow for corporal punishment, solitary confinement and penal diet. The international standards make clear that solitary confinement is appropriate punishment only in exceptional circumstances. In recognition of studies showing that periods of solitary confinement can destroy the personality and seriously effecting the prisoners' mental health, the standards encourage states to take steps to abolish the use of solitary isolation (Principle 7, Body of Principles; and Coyle 2002). Corporal punishment used for disciplinary offences is completely prohibited by the standards (r 31, SMRs). Although not specifically prescribed in the international instruments, penal diet is now recognised by many as being inhuman and cruel punishment (Coyle 2002).

The human right to privacy must also be interpreted in a prison context. All persons, including prisoners, should be protected from arbitrary interferences with their privacy (Art 17, ICCPR). Any actions that limit prisoners' privacy should not be of an intimidating or humiliating nature or for the purposes of punishment. The right to privacy must be balanced with the legitimate interest of the prison to ensure security of prisoners and staff as well as the public. This balancing should be taking places in decision regarding the designing of the prison, the locations of cameras, monitoring and alarm systems and the establishment of procedures relating to searches of the person and personal possessions. The procedures must balance the objective of preventing escape or limiting contraband with protecting the dignity of the prisoner and their visitors. The Human Rights Committee, in elaborating on right to privacy and personal searches, provides that persons being subject to a body search should only be examined by persons of the same sex (Human Rights Committee 2001). Censoring correspondence and monitoring telephone calls must also be limited only in justifiable circumstances. Authorities have a right to make sure that incoming correspondence does not contain forbidden or contraband material, such as weapons or drugs. Attitudes to privacy vary across cultures and need to be understood in the balancing of what is a legitimate limitation.

The right to maintain contact with the outside world, including family, friends, and various media sources, is meaningful for prisoners in their eventual reintegration into the community. The ICCPR recognises that the family is the natural and fundamental group unit of society and is entitled to protection by society and the state (Art 23, ICCPR). Prisoners have the right not to be subject to arbitrary interferences with his or her family (Art 12, ICCPR). Of course this right is not absolute and the need to hold prisoners in appropriate secure conditions may limit this right. Such right can be subject to reasonable conditions and restrictions as specified by law or lawful regulations (Principle 19, *Body of Principles*). However no matter how strong the emphasis is on security, some contact with the outside world must be allowed.

Other civil and political rights that apply in the context of prisons include the freedom of religion and spirituality, freedom of association, freedom of expression and the right to vote. Freedom of thought, conscience and religion to all persons is guaranteed by Article 18 of the *ICCPR*. Religion also includes belief, which is broadly interpreted to include more than the traditional religions. Freedom of religion within the prison context includes the access to worship, practice and services and encompasses such issues as dietary requirements, religious holidays and wearing of religious symbols. However this special treatment does not mean that prisoners receive additional privileges or be allowed to live in better conditions because of their religious affiliation or practice. Prisoners of the same religion should have opportunity to gather as a group for religious services and on religious holidays. If there are enough numbers, the prison should appoint a qualified representative on a full time basis. Access to any qualified representative of any religion should not be refused. (Rule 41, *SMRs*).

Economic and social rights

There are certain standards that must be met by the State in order to comply with its obligations to respect the prisoner's human dignity. Prisoners have the right to adequate provisions of accommodation, hygienic conditions, clothing and bedding, food, drink and exercise. As previously stated, the punishment for crime is the deprivation of liberty. Further punishment should not be imposed through lack of adequate living conditions. The international instruments provide detailed guidelines on the standards of accommodation, hygiene and nutrition, recognising that such living conditions can determine a prisoner's state of mind, self-esteem and dignity (Coyle 2002). While the international instruments do not explicitly set out the minimum space for each prisoner, they require that they have enough space to live in, with access to enough air and light to ensure good health (Rule 9 *SMRs*). The adequacy of the living space is connected to how much time prisoners will be spending in their cells. Overcrowding has become a major problem in many countries. The international instruments recognised overcrowding by providing a temporary solution of doubling up but the emphasis is on 'temporary' (Rule 9-14 *SMRs*)

The actual implementation of these standards in countries which have varying economic and social realities is a challenge. In countries where the standard of living for the general population is very low, it has been argued that prisoners should not have a higher standard of living than those around them who may be finding it difficult to feed, shelter and clothe their families (Coyle 2002). One commentator responds that if the State takes on itself the right to deprive someone of liberty, for whatever reason, it also takes on the obligation to treat such person in a decent and humane manner (Coyle 2002). Prisons should only be used for the most dangerous criminals and particularly in countries with financial limitations, this is one way to ensure reduction in the prison population if States cannot ensure adequate living conditions.

The right to the best attainable standards of physical and mental health enshrined in article 12 of *ICESCR* is an obligation imposed on prison officials, like any other State agent. As a starting point the health treatment should be of the same quality and standards to those available in the outside community. With the deprivation of liberty resulting in reliance by the prisoners, it is up to the prison authorities to ensure prisoners have access to medical assistance, including physical, dental and mental health services. Prisoners have also the right to an informed consent to the medical treatment to which they are subjected. The international instruments elaborate that every prison should have the services of at least one qualified medical officer who should have knowledge of psychiatry. In women's institutions, female prisoners should have access to pre and post natal care and treatment (Rules 22-26 *SMRs*).

The Principles of Medical Treatment Relevant to the Role of Health Personnel, Particularly Physicians, in the Protection of Prisoners and Detainees Against Torture and Other Cruel, Inhuman and Degrading Treatment or Punishment elaborates further on the duty of health personnel charged with the medical care of prisoners. These principles condemn any acts which constitute participation in, complicity in, incitement to or attempts to commit torture and other ill-treatment. The principles also explicitly provide that the purpose of any relationship with prisoners must be solely to evaluate, protect or improve their physical and mental health. Health personnel are prohibited from applying their knowledge and skills in order to assist in interrogation of prisoners in situations which may adversely affect the health of the prisoner. There are other international instruments, such as the WHO Guidelines on HIV Infection and AIDS in Prison, that deal specifically with such issues as HIV/AIDS in prisons.

Right to remedies and fair disciplinary practices

Fundamental to the protection of prisoners' rights is that they have the right to effective remedies when any of their human rights are violated. States must ensure that there is a fair and expeditious internal prison grievance system without fear of negative consequences with clearly defined internal investigation regulations. Prisoners should also have access to independent external remedies such as courts, tribunals, ombudsmen or human rights commissions to raise issues of alleged violations.

Prisoners also have the right to a fair disciplinary system. Discipline and order is to be maintained with firmness, but with no more restriction than is necessary for safe custody and well-ordered community life (Rule 27 *SMRs*). In all disciplinary hearings, the principles of fairness and natural justice apply. This means that the prisoner has the right to know of the charges under the disciplinary hearing, to be heard without undue delay, time to prepare a proper defence, be heard before a competent authority, and be present at the hearing. There should be clear set of procedures, which describe what conduct constitutes a disciplinary offence, the types and duration of punishment and the competent authority to impose such a punishment, and should be made available to all prisoners (Rule 29 *SMRs*). The international standards clearly stipulate that a prisoner has the right to be heard before disciplinary action is taken and has the right to bring such action to higher authorities for review (Principle 30 *Body of Principles*). Furthermore, international instruments, such as *SMRs* and the *Basic Principles on the Use of Force and Firearms by law Enforcement Officials* elaborate on the use of force in disciplinary scenarios.

Integral to exercising the right to remedies as well as the right to fair disciplinary practices is the right to information and language rights. Prisoners should have access to and protection of personal information. There should be access to legal information and library material as well as access to relevant information to ensure adequate time and facilities to prepare for any response. All programs and services should be in the States' official languages but there is also a right to an interpreter for any hearings affecting the implementation of rights. Everyone, on first admission into a prison, should be provided with written information about the regulations governing the treatment of prisoners, disciplinary requirements, authorised methods of seeking information and making complaints and all such other matters as are necessary top enable him to understand both his or her rights and his or her obligations and to adopt to the life in prison. If a prisoner is illiterate, such information should be conveyed to him orally (r 35, SMRs).

Rights of prison staff

Prison staff, like other workers, have a number of rights that have arisen from various International Labor Organisation instruments that have sought to improve the working conditions of men and women throughout the world. Prison staff should be properly and carefully selected, trained and informed of their legal obligations since it is on their integrity, humanity, professional capacity and personal suitability for the work that the proper administration of the prison depends (r 46(1), SMRs). Staff are to be classified as civil servants with security of tenure and adequate salary to attract suitable men and women (r 46(3), SMRs).

Staff should not only have an adequate standard of education and intelligence but must also have access to a course of specific training (r 47, SMRs). Personnel should include a number of different specialists, such as social workers, teachers, psychiatrists, psychologists and trade instructors (r 49, SMRs). Staff have the right to work in an environment free from practices that undermine their dignity as human beings. For example, female prison officials working in an all male prison would not be required to conduct full body searches of male prisoners or maintain supervision in areas where they would be exposed to nudity, such as in shower areas.

As prison officials may be held accountable for their actions, they must be able to understand, respect and protect the human rights of every person that is in their custody. It is their task to carry out the sentence of the court in a humane and respectful manner. Therefore training for awareness on human rights and obligations under international law is considered essential.

Conclusion

All countries are being faced with the challenges to protect the rights of prisoners, not only developing countries or countries in transition. Guaranteeing the human rights of prisoners continues to be a significant but important objective for countries regardless of their economic or social development or their cultural context. The best argument for observing human rights standards in prisons is not only that they are required by international and domestic law, but also that it is the most effective approach for dealing with offenders and staff for the betterment and protection of society as a whole (Coyle 2002). The effective reintegration of prisoners back into their communities is enhanced, although not guaranteed, with the compliance of human rights obligations. There are also positive economic benefits that can be derived by compliance to human rights. Experiences from several countries show that compliance with human rights standards improve the prison environment which can lead to prisoners being transferred to lower security prisons or being released into the community, which can ultimately lead to financial savings for prisons (Lokdam 2000). This logic can also be used to show that such compliance to individual human rights of prisoners can ultimately lead to more security and protection of society at large as compliance with human rights obligations increases the likelihood of releasing more responsible citizens back into the community.

CHAPTER 9

"Good corrections": Implications for leadership and organisational performance

Ole Ingstrup, Commissioner,
Correctional Service of Canada, (1988-1992/1996-2000)
President of the International Corrections and Prisons Association

In our media intense world – the "sound bite universe" – sensationalising and playing strongman is both easier and apparently more rewarding than it is to show balance and thoughtfulness in the field of corrections. Therefore a dialogue does not have an inviting and fertile environment in which to unfold. One of the characteristics of the political attitudes towards corrections in most developed countries appears to be that politicians have placed themselves and thereby their administrators and advisors, in a next to hopeless position.

On the one hand, the politicians are promising tough and unsentimental measures against criminals, in order to satisfy a mostly perceived, or media-created, need on the part of the public to see "justice" done to those who violate the laws of the land. Super gaols are being built to show that governments are determined and committed to delivering on those promises.

Legislative packages are arriving on parliamentary doorsteps at frequent intervals in order to address (often non-existing) problems by introducing longer sentences, fewer conditional releases, lower age limits for criminal responsibility and even expansions of what is to be considered a criminal act. The money, which could never be found to address the social conditions which have been proven to lead to crime in the first place, seems to be falling from heaven when the need is a punitive one. In the same category falls the ill placed arguments that offenders must serve long sentences and their rights and privileges must be kept to a minimum in order to show respect for the victims of their crimes.

On the other hand, our politicians are also promising the citizens that the system of corrections will – and certainly should – transform offenders into law-abiding citizens and they tend to underscore this view apportioning blame when an offender re-offends seriously while on conditional release or thereafter. I have never heard a politician, or for that matter even a thoughtful journalist, ask questions about accountability for crimes committed by offenders because they were not conditionally released but kept incarcerated to the end of the sentence.

The obvious problem with this line of argument is that the two objectives are incompatible. We know that longer, harsher punishment will lead to more crime – not less. We do not get safer streets and safer homes through that type of intervention. What we do get is slightly less safe streets and less safe homes.

I am not arguing that the criminal justice policy field is the only field which has opened both the goal side and the professional strategy side to public debate, but it certainly is one of the hardest hit areas in that category of politics and policy. Anything similar in the health policy area would be unthinkable.

No matter how complex the situation may be, we still need to strive for high performance in the field of corrections and what follows is my best suggestion to all of those involved in the world of corrections, with respect to a framework and some definitions of what constitutes "good corrections".

The framework which I use in this chapter is based on Ingstrup & Crookall (1998), which was a study of the 40 most effective public sector agencies across 14 countries. Investigating some of the best public service organisations in the world led us to the conclusion that one of the keys to the success of these organisations was that they have an ongoing, open and vigorous dialogue – a Socratic dialogue – in three main areas of their organisations: aim, character and execution.

A good correctional service knows its direction

A good correctional system knows where it is going. It knows its mission and it is also clear about its operating values. It is a system driven by results and based on values. This sounds pretty simple and straightforward – but unfortunately it is not.

The fact that corrections in many countries have become a political football makes it very difficult to decide upon an unambiguous mission. A mission means the ultimate goal: the direction for a never-ending journey of improvements, the organisational North Star or Southern Cross for leadership navigation. The fact that we still do not seem to have a generally agreed-upon understanding of the relationship between criminal justice policy, penal law, the purpose of sentencing and the purpose of corrections do not make matters any easier.

Having said that, what constitutes good corrections still needs to be defined in order to be achieved. Like a good and achievable society needs to be defined in order to provide a chance to improve the existing society, so do the individual parts of a good society need to be defined in order to enable those responsible for the individual areas to make useful changes.

However, no agreement exists as to what corrections is supposed to accomplish. The international community of corrections – as reflected in the membership of the International Corrections and Prisons Association – seems to be divided into at least three groups: the largest group being states and nations who have not even considered the question. The second group seem to prefer or accept a primarily punitive system for which "serving time under tough and severe conditions" is the actual, but most often not explicitly stated, mission. The third group is leaning towards a mission dominated by ideas of rehabilitation, reintegration and assisting offenders to get on with their lives.

Although one should remember that in most countries where the importance of mission is recognised, there seldom appears to be total agreement on what it ought to be. Denmark is a particularly good example where the central correctional administration has decided on a model of reintegration and crime prevention, which is now also enshrined in the newly-passed *Danish Corrections Act* 2000. At the same time one of the respected Danish wardens (head of an institution) continues to argue loudly, repeatedly and publicly that attempts to reduce recidivism is not even part of the business of corrections.

The trend seems to be that more and more correctional systems develop mission statements including a prominent reference to crime prevention, reintegration or rehabilitation. It is difficult to find any system in the world which has a mission statement with no reference to this family of concepts. My suspicion is that it simply is too embarrassing to put out a mission statement which reflects a "punitive only" philosophy and that it is a great deal easier to be punitive in speeches and policy without making an uniquiviquely clear operational statement to that effect.

One of the first mission statements to see the light of day in the area of corrections was developed by the federal Correctional Service of Canada in 1988. The strategic approach to corrections in Canada was inspired by a serious crisis in the Service prior to 1988 and the mission clearly reflects the conviction that corrections best contributes to society by helping and encouraging offenders to become law-abiding citizens. Corrections as crime prevention is key in this directional statement, which in its entirety reads:

> The Correctional Service of Canada as part of the criminal justice system and respecting the rule of law contributes to the protection of society by actively encouraging and assisting offenders to become law-abiding citizens while exercising reasonable safe secure and humane control.

To achieve "good corrections" it is not enough to simply state the ultimate outcome or to identify the desired results as a flow from the mission. It appears that results driven and value-based organisations tend to perform better than other types of organisations. An overall mission statement must be supported by a number of organisational values which have to be defined and communicated as sharply and as vigorously as the mission statement itself.

In the Correctional Service of Canada we identified the following five core values:

> Core value 1: We respect the dignity of individuals, the rights of all members of society and the potential for human growth and development.

Core value 2: We recognise that the offender has the potential to live as a law-abiding citizen.

Core value 3: We believe that our strength and our major resource in achieving our objectives is our staff and that human relationships are the cornerstone of our endeavour.

Core value 4: We believe that the sharing of ideas, knowledge, values and experience, nationally and internationally, is essential to the achievement of our mission.

Core value 5: We believe in managing the service with openness and integrity and we are accountable to the Solicitor General.

Getting the results definition and the values right is critical to success. It also ensures some measure of stability in the evolution of the organisation. In the case of the Correctional Service of Canada, the mission and values and the accompanying long-term (strategic) objectives have remained intact over a period of 15 years. During that time, both a conservative and a liberal government have been in power and nine different individuals have served at the ministerial level of responsibility. This suggests that if the work is thoroughly done, there is no reason to fear that major changes to the mission and values would be requested by incoming ministers. A clearly described, realistic and research based correctional "universe" gives any Minister or government the opportunity to lead both by changing the framework and by setting priorities within the existing framework.

Without "good leadership", "good corrections" is not possible. Good leadership means the kind of leadership which is most likely to move the organisation towards its mission and doing so in a way that clearly and visibly respects the defined values of the organisation.

What constitutes good leadership may vary from place to place. The universally valid and significant elements in leadership include the ability to listen, a desire to involve others and the skill required to delegate without abdicating responsibility. Also, leadership is not "a thing" vested in the CEO but a dispersed phenomenon. Leaders must demonstrate a commitment to their employees and be consistent with the mission and values; there must be consistency among the leaders of an organisation and perhaps most importantly, there must be absolute consistency between the leaders' words and their deeds. They must walk the talk. Furthermore, they must take the long view and they must demonstrate leadership beyond borders.

The third, and in this context the final, element in the area of direction setting which must be solidly in place is accountability. Good corrections cannot be achieved and certainly not be sustained, without the ability on the part of the organisation to clearly explain how and to what extent the organisation is making progress relative to both its mission and its values. One cannot ensure that an organisation is making progress on its mission if the ongoing performance measurements and the performance indicators are not related to that mission. Measuring, for instance, the number of staff training days and costs says little about the success of safely reintegrating offenders into society.

The Canadian Auditors General have repeatedly pointed to the need in the Public Service of Canada to strengthen its accountability frameworks at the departmental level to ensure better coordination between performance measures and the overall purpose – the mission of the department. In my time as head of Canada's correctional system I became convinced that a very close connection exists between the extremely focused accountability system of the Correctional Service of Canada and the fact that the Service has been able to reduce rates of recidivism substantially.

A good correctional service has character

A clear, well communicated and truly driving mission, a good set of operational and ethical values, focused leadership of high calibre and an accountability system adjusted to the directional statement provides corrections with an aim. However, more is needed to deliver "good corrections". The system must pay attention to its character, including people, communications and trust.

A correctional service will most often employ many people, and as the system evolves and becomes more sophisticated, different professions will be represented on staff. Efforts must be made to seek out and retain the very best people for all of the jobs. It is not enough to *say* that "our employees are our most important resource" or "we want to be the employer of choice". The organisation, and especially its leadership, must consistently and visibly make the employees feel that they indeed are being treated as such.

The interplay between the areas of "leadership" and personnel is obvious. It is worth noting that a comprehensive Danish study of personnel issues (not particularly related to the Correctional Service of Denmark) includes among its findings that the most significant reason for employees leaving the public service seems to be bad leadership.

The best organisations in the world understand the importance of good people policies and practices and have such policies and practices in place to guide them in such areas as selection, assessment, training and development, promotion and demotion. This is particularly important for corrections where the environment is often harsh, unfriendly and more often than not littered with frustrating and disappointing experiences. These realities call for an extra effort to be made just to level the playing field.

Communication

It is part of the character of a good correctional organisation that communications occur at a high level and in a systematic manner. Communication must not be an after thought, confined to water-cooler chats and it must not proceed on a need-to know basis.

Communication appears to be an ongoing and universal challenge. Organisations never seem to get it quite right. The best in the world, however, seem to consistently improve and continue to struggle for further improvements in this area. They have recognised the significance of communications and they apply a multitude of strategies in order to get the best out of it.

One key element seems to be in identifying those with whom to communicate by mapping out the hundreds or thousands of lines of ongoing or occasional communications. It is an integral part of this mapping process to determine the nature of the relationship, criteria for success in the relationship and also to assign responsibility and accountability to someone for taking care of the relationship.

Most correctional leaders and senior managers are surprised by the extent and complexity of organisational networks – especially when the network mappings include those relationships which should exist, but do not..

I have personally found it rewarding to think in terms of a number of networks: internal relationships (within the service itself); networks external to the service but internal to government; networks external to government but national in nature; and international networks.

Each of those areas is, or ought to be, huge and constantly expanding. One dimension which regularly seems to be under-emphasised in corrections is the horizontal dimension, that is, the relationship with other departments. It is relatively obvious, for example, that the role and characteristics of corrections is poorly understood and appreciated in the international community, even in the international law enforcement community.

Sadly, the situation is often not much better at the national level. Legislation is routinely passed in one sector of criminal justice with no appreciation for other sectors, most notably corrections. Correctional services are often guilty of the same sins, often acting unilaterally without consulting their counterparts internationally or without the necessary appreciation of the horizontality of most issues such as health, security, minority groups, rehabilitative programming, social control and research, to mention just a few. It appears that correctional organisations themselves must redouble their efforts in order to take their rightful place in the community of government organisations. In some places, governance structures constitute a further impediment to good lateral communications: another hurdle to overcome; another obstacle over which a communications bridge must be built.

Literally thousands of communications strategies are in use, however, the best ones are open, prompt, to the point and brutally honest. It is recognised that often almost anything else would seem to be so much easier and expedient.

In any modern organisation, communications is also a leadership responsibility. It is not something which can be left to a communications officer or, for that matter, to a communications division. Among other things, leadership is about opening new paths and about removing obstacles to organisational development.

Corrections, which want to strive for excellence, must invest considerable effort in its world of communications. If that area fails, the organisation, and its CEO, will inevitably lose standing among peers and in the world external to the public service. That in itself will make the path to excellence even more exhausting to climb.

Trust

Many organisations, including correctional organisations, find it difficult, even embarrassing, to discuss the issue of trust in and around their organisations. They seem to feel that discussing trust becomes too "up close and personal". However, based on my own studies and experience at the organisational level, I have no hesitation in stating that trust is key to good leadership, management and collaboration. Trust is a lynch pin in the effective and efficient operation of well performing organisations.

Employees and partners alike who feel that they have to devote a considerable amount of time covering their backs are not effective employees and partners. The absence of trust creates more than uncertainty. It is the main reason why people will "look after themselves", why good ideas will not be shared, bad news will be held back as long as possible, why staff morale will plummet, absenteeism will soar, why good people will be looking for employment elsewhere and an indefinable negativity will become more and more apparent. An untrusting environment is a poisonous environment.

If trust does not exist, it must be generated. If trust does exist, it must be sustained and nurtured. Ensuring that the organisational character includes trust is first and foremost a leadership responsibility. However, by definition, all members of the organisation must share in that responsibility in order to meet this critical objective. Within the context of a good correctional service, one can look at trust from a variety of perspectives.

One such aspect of trust is personal trust. Personal trust concerns the degree to which people may trust others to say what is true. There is no hidden agenda. Simply put, people are trustworthy or they are not. Ethical behaviour is often included in this area. With respect to leaders, it would appear that trustworthiness must be combined with their ability to trust others. However, leaders may be as truthful as can be but if they do not enjoy the full trust of their employees, they will not benefit from their full energy and ingenuity.

Another aspect of trust is a professional trust. Professional trust involves a trust that the organisation and its individual members know what they are doing and that they are good at it. In corrections, lives literally depend on that trust being justified. One of the important tasks for correctional leaders is to ensure that all the members of the service meet standards sufficiently high to warrant trust in them and in the organisation, and as a consequence to solidify trust external to the organisation. Leaders must also ensure that their employees and subordinates confidently may trust their leaders' ability to lead and to manage–and to engage meaningfully and competently in discussions about correctional subject matters.

A third aspect of trust is political. The politicians responsible for good governance – the government – and especially those who have a direct responsibility for corrections, must be confident that their correctional agency is performing competently and with integrity and is moving performance at a reasonable pace towards a mission which is compatible with the government's overall political agenda. Without that kind of trust, a correctional agency will be less and less able to pursue its mission, more external mechanisms will be imposed, internal self-confidence will be lost, levels of energy and creativity will diminish – and soon there will be good and visible reasons not to trust the organisation. This was the way in which Correctional Service of Canada was perceived by many in 1987-88.

Finally, a good correctional service must enjoy public trust. Public trust is about the degree to which the public at large – often influenced through the media – feel that they can trust their correctional agency to do what corrections is supposed to do.

This area of trust is, at best, very difficult even to sustain. The media often seems to be driven by identifiable incidences for example, an offender on conditional release commits a serious offence and the whole system is questioned. Yet if an offender is not found by the police, the impact on public trust is significantly less. This simple fact allows the police to enjoy a great deal more public confidence than the corrections even if correctional success rates generally are superior to the clearance rates of police.

Whether this is fair or not is immaterial. What it entails is the fact that building and sustaining public trust is a task of great significance in good corrections.

A good correctional service knows how to get things done

Without aim and character as discussed earlier, there will be no "good corrections". Collectively the members of the service must have the skills to translate ideas, attitudes, creativity, energy and intellectual insights into well-directed actions that produce results as defined by the mission.

In order to get things done, leaders need to know how to lead and managers need to know how to manage. Very few are born leaders or managers. Even fewer are born as the best leaders and managers that they can become. As in all types of trades, people need education and exposure to organisational life in order to eventually master the art of leadership and management. Leadership and management in corrections and in public service are no exception to that rule.

Unfortunately, leadership and management training and development are frequently not a high priority in most organisations and certainly not in public service organisations. Developing leadership is often something that happens a long time after the individual has been appointed to his or her position of authority. During the countless hours of my life that I spend travelling by air, I feel very good about the fact that the airlines seem to take a different approach to the training and development of their pilots than most organisations take with respect to their leaders and managers. I particularly like the fact that pilots tend to have been trained before they take up their duties on the flight deck and not at some later point in time. Perhaps the visible and immediate consequence of not training a pilot plays a role here!

Part of being a good manager is being capable of identifying problems and opportunities and seeing solutions or ways of capitalising on opportunities for improvement. Furthermore, leaders and managers must know which tool or strategy to apply and how to handle the tool. They must also know how to maintain a tool, to keep it sharp, and must be able to see the difference between a new solid tool on the market and yet another slick gadget that looks good and promising but which does not match the kind of problems that the organisation is dealing with.

In good corrections, leaders and managers do master the areas just mentioned and those abilities exist at all managerial levels throughout the organisation. Off-the-shelf tools are rarely found in the toolboxes of high performing organisations. Their tools are either tailor-made to fit their problems and opportunities or they are adjusted versions of the "brand names".

The corrections toolbox has two major compartments: management tools are in one and the correctional tools are in the other. Especially with respect to the correctional tools, the International Corrections and Prisons Association has created a "best practices institute" through which members have access to tools that have worked well in other jurisdictions. Other organisations, such as the International Centre for Prison Studies in the UK, also provide valuable insights into this (and many other) areas.

Teamwork

Sophisticated teamwork also seems to be an essential ingredient in good corrections. It appears that well-performing organisations (also outside of corrections) display a very mature attitude towards teams and teamwork. They tend to use teams primarily when the task is one which requires a high level of creativity and/or a relatively high level of skills from different professional areas. Teams should be given broad mandates and, when appropriate, short timeframes. Routine tasks are usually not carried out in teams.

It does not appear that involving team members who have developed the ideas in the implementation process increases the likelihood of success in the implementation. "Implementers" are often individuals with a different personality from those who are natural choices for the idea development phase.

The need to work in teams and to manage teams and team processes will likely grow, rather than diminish. The fact that more and more governments realise that good horizontal working relationships among departments is a key to success entails that teamwork will be in high demand. Teamwork may often be most useful when circumstances are difficult, timeframes are short and multi-disciplinary and/or multi-cultural perspectives are required.

Understanding how to best work in teams and how to get the best from teams, may be one of the most significant keys to success in the "good correctional organisation".

Corrections is not an area which, generally speaking, has been known as a fast moving one. There is movement, of course, but often, lack of significant movement is more obvious than the opposite. A couple of correctional services, on the other hand, have actually placed themselves at the cutting edge of public administration.

It seems obvious that correctional organisations and institutions with any ambition to serve their governments and country well will have to adopt an organisational style of aggressive and decisive, goal-oriented improvement.

An organisation, which is not improving, is decaying. Constant change is part of what makes an organisation good and the only way in which constant change becomes constant improvement is when the mission is clear and present in the minds of people, when the operational values are being adhered to and when the organisation is comfortable with a relatively high pace of change.

In "good corrections", therefore, the mastery of change management and organisational adaptation becomes critical. That is, the kind of change which accommodates a ministerial agenda and a professional, knowledge-based correctional agenda, a mission-driven and values-based agenda; not the kind of change which is driven by mere political opportunism and conflict avoidance.

Leaders in good correctional organisations must understand how to create a change-prone and change-willing organisation. They must also understand the nature of change and not least the art of comforting employees affected by change. They must learn to deal constructively and effectively with the ever-present pressure, or at least inclination, to lower the pace or bring change to an end altogether.

Often processes of renewal and change take longer and move more slowly than leaders had hoped for. In those cases, blaming the "implemen-ting classes" for resistance to change, counterproductive foot dragging and the like, is not uncommon. This tendency to lay blame somewhere is itself a factor which tends to slow down the process of change, and is certainly a factor which is likely to reduce enthusiasm for the continuing process of change.

This chapter is a framework for a constructive dialogue in the area of corrections. Each national system can add and subtract, or they can try to fill the framework with meaningful substance. The only thing they cannot do is stay as a spectator on the sideline of the correctional playing field while claiming that they make an optimal contribution to their society.

– CHAPTER 10 –

Inspecting prisons

Professor Richard Harding
Inspector of Custodial Services for Western Australia

Understanding the context: the limits of standard accountability mechanisms

Closed institutions of all kinds – prisons, juvenile detention centres, police lock-ups, secure psychiatric wards, immigration detention centres and similar custodial services – pose accountability challenges for democratic societies. Sometimes, the accountability processes only cut in when it is already too late – after major prisons riots (eg, the 1978 Nagle Royal Commission Report[1] into the riots at Bathurst and staff misconduct at other New South Wales prisons or the 1991 Woolf Report[2] in England and Wales following the torching of Manchester-Strangeways and six other prisons) or a long trend of avoidable custodial deaths (eg, the 1990 Report of the Royal Commission into Aboriginal Deaths in Custody[3]).

Of course, when situations have been allowed to get to this level of crisis, governments tend to take the subsequent recommendations seriously. The Woolf Report was the catalyst for the most radical improvement of the 20th century to the British prison system, and all Australian governments likewise tried to respond positively to RCIADIC. However, these responses lose momentum, as David Brown has shown with regard to the Nagle Report.[4] There are complex reasons for this, but a crucial one is that usually no machinery is put in place to check and maintain implementation of the policies to which governments have apparently made an initial commitment. Crisis response can be an erratic lever for achieving and maintaining systemic change.

Accordingly, several less ephemeral devices have developed over the years. An important example is the role of the various State Offices of the

---

1   Nagle, J (1978) Report of an Inquiry into the New South Wales Department of Corrective Services, Sydney: State Government Printer.

2   Woolf, HK and Tumim, S (1991) *Prison Disturbances, April 1990: Report of an Inquiry, Cm 1456*, London: HMSO.

3   Johnson, E (1991) *Report of the Royal Commission into Aboriginal Deaths in Custody*, Canberra: AGPS.

4   "Evaluating Nagle 25 years on", in (2004) 16 *Current Issues in Criminal Justice* 108-111.

Ombudsman, each of which has jurisdiction and sufficient powers to inquire into individual complaints by prisoners. A problem with Ombudsman jurisdiction is that by its very nature it involves delay. In addition, although a ruling in favour of any given prisoner should in theory spill over into the general administration of the prison system for the benefit of all prisoners, in practice the impact tends to be restricted to the complainant. To compound matters, most Ombudsman systems have moved away from the model of direct and immediate investigation of a complaint to a position where they normally expect prisoners first to exhaust internal complaints or grievance mechanisms. Prisoners therefore tend to be cynical about the efficacy of Ombudsman offices.[5]

The context is, of course, that prisoners do not possess, in the Australian jurisprudential model, *rights* in relation to their treatment;[6] rather, the imprisoning authority possesses non-enforceable obligations. These may seem to be reasonably comprehensive – as in relation to the *Standard Guidelines for Corrections in Australia*[7] – but they are not legally binding in the sense of giving prisoners a right of action in court.

Nor indeed will they be taken into account in related matters. This point has been starkly illustrated in the case of *Bekink v The Queen*.[8] In that case the accused appealed against his sentence on the basis that its practical impact was far more repressive than the sentencing court could have anticipated or intended. This was so because the prison to which he had been sent, Casuarina Prison, had been subject to a 23-hour-a-day lockdown for many months following a major disturbance that had occurred before his conviction and sentence. The *Standard Guidelines*[9] prohibited collective punishment. Nevertheless, the court showed no appetite for going beyond the prison gatehouse and dealing with the day-to-day realities of prison conditions, and the appeal was rejected.

Those obligations that are enforceable at law, such as hygiene requirements under the applicable environmental health statutes, are only actionable by the regulatory authorities, not by prisoners. However, it has become clear

---

5   See, for example, Minogue, CWJ, "An Insider's View: Human Rights and Excursions from the Flat Lands" in Brown, D and Wilkie, M (2002) *Prisoners as Citizens: Human Rights in Australian Prisons*, Sydney: Federation Press.

     In the UK, a specialised Ombudsman office has been created to deal exclusively with complaints as to the administration of prisons and probation. This model appears to be more successful than the Australian approach where general Ombudsman jurisdiction includes prison matters.

6   See, for example, *Flynn v The King*, (1949) 79 CLR 1. This Australian case reflects the English approach, epitomised by *Arbon v Anderson* [1943] 1 KB 242.

7   This document, which is derived from the United Nations Standard Minimum Rules for the Treatment of Prisoners, was first produced in 1978. It amounts in effect to a voluntary code agreed upon by the Ministers and Administrators of Australian Correctional Systems. A revised version was adopted in August 2004. A comparable code, based on applicable international conventions and instruments, has been agreed by Juvenile Justice Ministers and Administrators.

8   [1999] WASC Appeals 160.

9   See the 1996 version, para 5.31.

that imprisoning authorities owe a common law duty of care to prisoners. This extends not only to ordinary negligence – for example, in the prison workplace – but also to such matters as placement of vulnerable prisoners with predators.[10] The drawback is that this right is one that only be identified and become legally active once it has been breached; it is not a positive part of everyday prison life. Prison authorities, for their part, have been adept at keeping cases out of court, by settling them on terms that include a confidentiality clause. Consequently, the jurisprudence in this area remains somewhat undeveloped.

In summary, the accountability arrangements that prisoners can attempt to activate constitute an unsatisfactory patchwork. The occasional "victory", whilst gratifying to the particular individual, typically has little or no impact across the system. Human rights activist groups, other lobbyists, periodically the media, sometimes professional politicians, trade unions when it suits their industrial purposes and other concerned citizens exert pressure from time to time. However, their efforts inevitably become diffused or tend to be event-driven, and in any case their access to accurate information is often restricted. Thus, in some democratic societies the ground is laid for the creation of a standing mechanism to achieve system-wide accountability.

The Inspectorate model

The original modern prison inspectorates is the UK one. It was established by statute[11] in 1982; the Scottish Inspectorate followed four years later. At the present time, comparable inspectorates exist in Ireland, South Africa, Norway and Western Australia. In addition, the European Convention against Torture[12] provides for a visits-based inspection system for closed custodial institutions in all 45 nations of the Council of Europe. The jurisdiction of the UK inspectorate has progressively been extended from prisons to Young Offenders' Institutions, Immigration Detention Centres, prison transportation arrangements and military prisons, as well as geographically to Northern Ireland.

For an Australian audience, the Western Australia model – setting up the Office of the Inspector of Custodial Services as from June 2000 – is the most informative. It is closely derived from the UK model. However, its statutory base[13] is much more explicit and detailed, reflecting what currently

---

10   See, for example, *Dixon v Western Australia* [1974] WAR 65.

11   Section 5A of the *Prisons Act* 1952, as enacted by s 57(1) of the *Criminal Justice Act* 1982.

12   The European Convention for the Prevention of Torture and Inhuman or Degrading Treatment or Punishment establishes the Committee for the Prevention of Torture, which is the inspection body responsible for applying the standards contained in the Convention.

13   Initially, the Office of the Inspector was created by way of the *Prisons Amendment Act* 1999. The statutory framework was clarified, consolidated and extended by the Inspector of *Custodial Services Act* 2003, which became law on 15 December 2003.

happens in the UK by way of "custom and practice"[14] and taking the matter somewhat further. Substantively, the jurisdiction relates to prisons, juvenile detention centres and other "custodial services", which for these purposes means prisoner transportation arrangements and court custody centres. Immigration detention centres, being a Commonwealth function, are not within the jurisdiction of the Office of the Inspector of Custodial Services, which is a State-based agency.

Autonomy

The Inspector's office is independent of the Department of Justice, which is operationally responsible for running the prison system. This is absolutely crucial. Prisons' Departments should have their own internal compliance auditing systems and groups, to ensure that the standards they have set for themselves are being met, and indeed that is the case with all Australian States. The inspection role should go further than this, however, concentrating on what the standards should be, how they can be developed and improved and whether they meet international standards.

The Inspector's office is also independent of the relevant government Minister, in the sense that the reporting line is direct to Parliament. The timing of the tabling of inspection reports is within the Inspector's control, and cannot be subjected to party political convenience.[15] Of course, in a functional sense the relevant Minister is a key player in terms of the potential effectiveness of the Inspector's office. The statute provides for the Minister to direct the Inspector to carry out an inspection in certain circumstances, though it also provides that the Inspector may refuse to do so. In either event the matter must be reported to Parliament.[16]

To date, two directed inspections have been carried out and none refused. The first was an inspection of the Special Handling Unit at Casuarina Prison – the prison within the prison – and the context was repeated allegations in the media and amongst lobby groups of brutality against prisoners in that area.[17] The second related to deaths at Hakea Prison, and in particular the deaths by suicide in quick succession in early 2003 of two

---

14 Section 5A of the *Prisons Act* 1952 is remarkably non-specific as to the powers and role of the UK Inspectorate, providing merely that "it shall be the duty of the Chief Inspector to inspect or to arrange for the inspection of prisons in England and Wales and to report to the Secretary of State … in particular on the treatment of prisoners and the conditions in prisons".

15 See ss 33-38 of the *Inspector of Custodial Services Act* 2003 (WA), and note in particular s 35(2) that enables the Inspector to activate the device of a deemed tabling if he considers the delay in formal Parliamentary tabling is not reasonable.

16 See *Inspector of Custodial Services Act* 2003 (WA), ss 17 and 33(2).

17 See Report No 1, Office of the Inspector of Custodial Services (2001), *Report of an Unannounced Inspection of the Induction and Orientation Unit and the Special Handling Unit at Casuarina Prison*. All reports can be accessed on the Inspector's website: <www.custodialinspector.wa.gov.au>.

young Aboriginal men.[18] In each case the Ministerial directive lent extra status to difficult and sensitive inspection tasks.

Access to prisons

"Free and unfettered access" to prisons and other custodial services is crucial to the inspection process. That means, at any time the Inspector chooses. An inspection that occurs by the leave and at the convenience of the inspected agency is no inspection at all. This is so whether it relate to drug testing for athletes or to weapons of mass destruction allegedly possessed by States or to environmental pollution by manufacturers or to any situation where the inspected persons may have something they prefer to conceal. There is no other way to carry out such functions.

In the case of the Western Australia Inspector, he may authorise whomever he selects to use the statutory powers. They extend not only to entering prisons but also to persons (ie, staff or prisoners) in the prison, vehicles used to transport prisoners and documents in the possession of the Department that relate to the prison or custodial service.[19]

This last provision is exceedingly important. It enables the Inspector to go behind the failures or gaps that are seen within the prison itself to the administrative or policy matters that may have contributed to the situation.[20]

In gaining access, the Inspector or authorised persons may take with him or her such equipment as he or she thinks is necessary. The most usual item in this regard is a camera. The reality of conditions in prisons that are predominantly occupied by Aboriginal prisoners has been revealed to Parliament and the public[21] far more graphically by way of photographs than could have been achieved by words.[22]

Incentives for co-operation

Operational Departments understandably do not always welcome inspections. There are many ways in which they can hinder or undermine the process. This may be direct – for example, by delays in facilitating entry or refusing access to required documentation – or indirect – for example, by conniving at or even tacitly encouraging non-co-operation by staff. The

18 See Report No 22, Office of the Inspector of Custodial Services (2004), *The Diminishing Quality of Prison Life: Deaths at Hakea Prison 2001-2003*.

19 See *Inspector of Custodial Services Act* 2003 (WA), ss 28, 29 and 30.

20 This approach is fortified by the fact that the Act defines custodial services as including "an administrative arrangement in relation to the management, control or security of a prison or the security, control, safety, care or welfare of prisoners committed to the prison": see s 3.

21 And even more importantly in the case of Roebourne, Broome and Eastern Goldfields prisons, to the then Minister.

22 See, eg, the photos on pp 21 and 22 of Report No 4, Office of the Inspector of Custodial Services (2001), *Report of an Unannounced Inspection of Eastern Goldfields Regional Prison*. These reveal the squalor of conditions there.

Western Australian inspection model uniquely provides for these possibilities by creating criminal offences of hindrance, victimisation and intimidation.[23]

There have been two occasions when the Inspector has contemplated the possibility of activating one of these provisions. However, the mere existence of such offences and the symbolic statement they represent as to the relationship between the Inspectorate and the Department has ensured that that no one has ever been charged. In practice, the culture that facilitates and supports full co-operation will not grow out of punitive sanctions but from mutual respect. A criminal prosecution would, except in the most extreme circumstances, represent a failure of communication rather than a successful assertion of authority.

Announced or unannounced inspections

Most inspections occur as part of an announced schedule. Indeed, the Inspector is required to set out his or her announced inspection program in his or her Annual Report.[24] The statutory obligation is to inspect each prison or other relevant custodial service no less than once every three years.[25] In practice, this sequence of announced inspections is also the most efficient way in normal circumstances of carrying out the inspection function. The Department can be given notice, documentation requested, a presentation about the prison and its issues made, a thorough inspection plan worked out, experts commissioned, and so on.

However, the notion of a planned, announced and highly structured inspection implies a degree of normality in the way the prison is functioning. The situation may be different if the prison is in some kind of crisis. Just as there must be free and unfettered access once the Inspector has decided to make an inspection, so also an element of surprise may be necessary if the purposes of inspection are to be achieved.

The UK inspectorate makes unannounced inspections quite frequently – usually but not invariably for short follow-up inspections of a prison that has revealed problems during an announced inspection. In Western Australia, this device[26] has been utilised exceptionally – on two occasions only in the first four years' operation. The first related to the inspection of the "prison within a prison" at Casuarina Prison;[27] obviously, if the prime objective is to try to ascertain whether the staff are involved in systematic brutality to prisoners, an unexpected and unimpeded arrival on the premises is essential. The conclusion was that systematic brutality was not occurring. There were many serious management problems in the Special Handling

---

23   See, *Inspector of Custodial Services Act* 2003, ss 32, 49 and 50.

24   See *Inspector of Custodial Services Act* 2003, s 33(2)(e).

25   See *Inspector of Custodial Services Act* 2003, s 19.

26   Section 25(1) of the *Inspector of Custodial Services Act* 2003 specifically empowers the Inspector to make unannounced inspections.

27   See n 17, above.

Unit, but that was not one of them.[28] The second related to Eastern Goldfields Regional Prison.[29] Information available to the Inspector led him to believe that this prison was the repository of serious structural racism in the sense that conditions were such as would never have been tolerated if the population had been predominantly non-Aboriginal, as well as positive racism in the sense of discriminatory advantage for non-Aboriginal prisoners. Such serious potential findings needed to be tested without any opportunity being given for concealment or obfuscation. In the event, both forms of racism were clearly established.

Liaison visits

The need for unannounced inspections mainly arises because a prison's performance has been allowed to drift and deteriorate. The sheer numbers of prisons within the remit of the UK inspectorate mean that it is virtually impossible to "keep an eye" on prisons between inspections. In Western Australia, the Inspector's strategy has been to allocate responsibility for particular prisons to nominated inspection officers, who then visit at regular intervals so as to keep a finger on the pulse of the prison. The decision to inspect Eastern Goldfields unannounced followed upon observations made at liaison visits. There were additional information sources – reports of the Independent Prison Visitors, whose activities are reported through the Inspector's office, and the Department's own intelligence reports, to which the Inspector's office has routine access.

Inspection standards

The most important single issue about inspection is that the inspectorate should have a clear philosophy as to what it is seeking and expects the operational Department to achieve. The UK Inspectorate has set the tone in this regard, with the development of its "healthy prison test". A healthy prison is one where safety, respect, purposeful activity and preparation for release and resettlement are achieved to an appropriate degree and balance. The Chief Inspector, Ms Anne Owers, has recently emphasised that "safety and respect above all must be found in prison systems. These are the bottom lines of any custodial environment; they should be expected and demanded as things in themselves, whether or not they are 'effective' in process terms or can be shown to prevent re-offending". The human rights agenda, or the "decency agenda" as it is sometimes called, is thus the paramount though not the exclusive focus of the healthy prison test as currently applied in the UK.

---

28 Note that the Department of Justice is one of the beneficiaries of this unannounced modus operandi. The confidence that an autonomous body was able to establish in relation to its conclusions crucially affected the subsequent debate in a way that the Department's own inquiry into its practices could never have done. More importantly, the public interest was best served by this approach to inspection.

29 See n 22, above.

The Committee for the Prevention of Torture conducts its inspections exclusively from a human rights point of view. Its remit is to "examine the treatment of persons deprived of their liberty with a view to strengthening, if necessary, the protection of such persons from torture and from inhuman and degrading treatment or punishment".

The Western Australian Inspectorate has proceeded on the basis that prisons should seek to achieve a balance between four values or cornerstones: custodial containment and safety; care and well being; rehabilitation; and reparation. What is an appropriate balance will vary somewhat with each prison, according to its profile and its role in the custodial continuum. In every case, however, the systems and resources must also be appropriate.

To this point, the suggested inspection standards are somewhat abstract. They could arguably lie too much in the eye of the beholder; the inspected parties could perhaps claim they have been ambushed if they receive an adverse finding. The UK Inspectorate has confronted this possible accusation with the publication in April 2004 of "Expectations: *Criteria for assessing the conditions in prisons and the treatment of prisoners*".[30] "Expectations" sets out the broad criteria, the detailed tests within those criteria, sources for each of those tests and the evidence base that will be explored in assessing whether the test has been satisfactorily met. The sources may be mandatory (binding international or regional conventions, domestic statute, case law) or normative; the evidence base documentary, observational or survey-based. It is no longer possible to claim uncertainty or lack of clarity. With this publication – which is the culmination of many years of evolving custom and practice – the inherent credibility of the inspection process has been consolidated.

The Committee for the Prevention of Torture has likewise spelled out exactly what meets its standards. These are derived and defined by previous inspections, by decisions of the European Court of Human Rights and by the Committee's own publications.[31]

The Western Australian Inspectorate has not yet brought its inspection standards together in a consolidated and succinctly expressed way. After 23 inspections they are reasonably well understood by the Department of Justice; but they are implicit rather than explicit. A document akin to "Expectations" will be prepared as soon as resources allow.

A big debate about inspection standards is whether they should be those of the operational Department or those that reflect the inspectorate's view of what prisons should be seeking to achieve. In other words, how independent should an inspectorate be? In the UK, "Expectations" has not been received with unbridled delight by the Prison Service. There is a feeling that HM Inspectorate is pushing the boundaries to an uncomfortable extent, particularly by its adoption of normative instruments as the basis for some of its expectations. This echoes an earlier debate sparked by Lord Laming in

---

30 London: HM Inspectorate of Prisons. See also <www.homeoffice.gov.uk/justice/ prisons/ inspprisons>

31 See generally <www.cpt.coe.int>.

2000. Criticising the Inspectorate, his report stated: "The time has come for the development of a set of standards *determined jointly by the Prison Service and the inspectorate and agreed by Ministers*. Prisons should be both managed and inspected against agreed standards".[32] This approach would turn an inspectorate into something very much akin to the internal compliance audit groups mentioned earlier. The leverage for change and improvement that an independent inspectorate provides would be eroded.

Thematic reviews

A problem with a continuing sequence of prison inspections is that the individual details can obscure the broad patterns. Some of the most valuable work of the UK inspectorate has been thematic – for example, on suicide and self-harm, on the conditions for "lifers", and on the imprisonment of women. The Western Australia statute specifically contemplates that thematic reviews will be carried out.[33] To date, three such reviews have been completed and a fourth is in train.

The first of these explored the immensely difficult problem, common to all prison systems, of how to handle predatory prisoners and those who are vulnerable to them. Whilst the primary objective was to log the situation in Western Australia accurately by way of fieldwork and documentation, to identify problems on the ground and to try to offer guidance on how best to address them, the intention in such a universal subject must also be to make some contribution to the literature. In other words, through the vehicle of thematic reviews and inspectorate should try to locate the local experience in the wider world of prison administration.[34]

The second such review related to Deaths at Hakea Prison.[35] This was thematic in the sense that the issues uncovered at Hakea were likely to have implications for the identification and management of at-risk prisoners across the whole of the Western Australian prison system. It was also prison-focussed, in the sense that viewing Hakea prison through the prism of a key aspect of its services was a way of evaluating the culture and processes of the prison as a whole. As with the Report on Vulnerable and Predatory Prisoners, this Report drew upon and attempted to contribute to international literature.

Much the same approach was taken to the Review of Cognitive Skills Training in the Western Australia Prison System.[36] The thematic review currently in progress relates to prisoner health services.

---

32   Lord Laming of Tewin (2000), Modernising the Management of the Prison Service, p 7. London: Home Office.

33   See *Inspector of Custodial Services Act* 2003 (WA), s 22.

34   See Report No 15, Office of the Inspector of Custodial Services (2003), *Vulnerable and Predatory Prisoners in Western Australia: A Review of Policy and Practice*.

35   See n 18, above.

36   See Report No 23, Office of the Inspector of Custodial Services (2004).

Reporting, acceptance of recommendations and implementation

The Western Australian protocol requires that draft reports should be sent to the Department (or other affected parties) to enable comments to be made. In practice, this has become an interactive process, with factual challenges and/or clarification and debates as to the thrust of the recommendations. Ultimately, however, the Inspector controls all aspects of the Report. The Department's responses to the recommendations are appended to the Report itself, and become the basis of an Implementation or Action Plan. With the subsequent tabling of the Report, these undertakings or intentions thus become public. In the UK, the Action Plan remains something between the Inspectorate, the Prison Service and the Minister.

The acceptance of recommendations has so far run at a high rate – more than 90 per cent. The Inspector has attempted to differentiate between categories of recommendation and his expectation that they will be accepted. For example, those relating to human rights or racism should be accepted in their entirety whilst those relating to staffing issues can quite properly be seen as falling to a considerable extent within managerial prerogative as to how and when to do something even if it is broadly accepted that it is a desirable initiative.[37]

Inevitably, there is some slippage between acceptance and on-the-ground implementation. This is not necessarily a symptom of bad faith; circumstances change, with the passage of time matters can become no longer relevant, policy and funding priorities have to give way to more pressing exigencies. Nevertheless, too great a disparity would be worrying. Progress can be monitored in various ways: through liaison visits, reports of Independent Prison Visitors, and above all in the second phase of announced (or if necessary unannounced) inspections.

In the UK, the 2003 Annual Report analysed implementation rates by checking the operational status of previous recommendations when returning to that site for a follow-up inspection. A total of 5,170 recommendations made in the course of 49 inspections had resulted in a 55 per cent achieved rate and a 15 per cent partially achieved rate – or a 30 per cent not achieved rate. It is too early in the cycle of inspections in Western Australia to confidently make a comparison with the UK.

The reporting line to Parliament provides an opportunity for the Inspector to be questioned as to the activities of his own office and, more significantly, the performance of the Department in response to recommendations. To date, the Estimates Committees of both Houses[38] have shown increasing interest in this matter; also during the debates preceding the passage of the 2003 legislation it was explicitly stated that Parliament was

---

37 This matter is fully discussed in the 2001/02 Annual Report of the Inspector of Custodial Services at pp 28-29 and the 2002/03 Annual Report at p 26.

38 In Western Australia these are known as the Legislative Assembly and the Legislative Council.

above all concerned with implementation of recommendations. The lever of Parliamentary concern has not yet been fully utilised, but would seem to be a factor that will in the future bear upon the Inspector's effectiveness.

Inspection in the other Australian States

In 1997 the New South Wales Parliament passed legislation establishing the office of the Inspector-General of Corrective Services.[39] The powers were extensive and the wide-ranging jurisdiction included, as a centrepiece, a prison inspection function akin to that described above. Somewhat oddly, the statute contained a sunset clause that the office would cease to exist on 30 September 2003, unless Parliament re-affirmed the legislation.

In February 2003 the Minister for Corrective Services set up an Inquiry to advise him as to the continuation of the office. The starting point of the Report of that Inquiry, it must be said, was that of scepticism as to the role of such bodies:

> The concept and function of the Office of the Inspector-General inevitably places that Office among the raft of monitoring organisations that, by their nature, take a problem-oriented approach.[40]

The fact that the Inspector-General had indeed done this was a source of concern:

> In major inspections of two correctional centres, the Inspector-General adopted a problem-oriented approach, seeking shortfalls and difficulties rather than basing his approach on maximising organisational strengths in a way that would lead to substantial change and best practice.[41]

Evidently, a good working relationship had not evolved:

> From the outset it appears that there was considerable tension between the Inspector-General and the Department of Corrective Services. The alleged aggressive, combative, adversarial approach adopted by the Inspector-General has entered into corrections folklore ... This is particularly disappointing when it is clear that the Government was anticipating a jointly collaborative, constructive approach and a positive role for the Inspector-General.[42]

In the light of these findings, the Office was not continued; it lapsed on 30 September 2003. A directorate of Probity and Performance Management, reporting to the Commissioner of Corrective Services and possessing no statutory autonomy, has now been set up in its place.[43]

---

39 See the *Correctional Centres (Inspector-General) Act* 1997.

40 See Review of the Office of Inspector-General, Department of Corrective Services, p 8.

41 Ibid, p 3.

42 Ibid, p 11.

43 The Inspector-General also possessed jurisdiction over individual complaints. This sat uneasily with the Ombudsman's jurisdiction and has now been transferred to that Office.

From this saga it is apparent that the inspectorate model can cause a lot of stress and resentment within operational organisations and that they are not without the resources to retaliate. One cannot possibly make a sensible judgment as to whose "fault" it was that the arrangement failed, but it is evident that even the most robust inspectorate can only go so far if it does not bring the inspected organisation along with it some of the way.

The inquiry also commented on the nature and process of organisational change:

It is generally accepted that change imposed externally on organisations does not have a high success rate. It is recognised that organisations can be influenced if they have some ownership of the change process, and it is for this reason that a shared approach would achieve greater results.[44]

An inquiry in Victoria in 2000 had taken up this theme:

External reviews, like outsourcing, do not serve to enhance organisational learning. Too often the response to external reviews is a defensive rebuttal of the ... recommendations, and allegations that they "got it wrong" or didn't fully understand the complexities of the situation.[45]

On this basis, it was recommended that Victoria should not adopt an independent inspection model but rather establish an in-house team reporting directly to the Secretary of Justice and by-passing the office of the Commissioner responsible in a day-to-day sense for running the prison system.

These two stories would suggest that the inspectorate model has not yet taken hold in Australia. The clear preference is for in-house compliance bodies, for reports that are not made public and for tight bureaucratic control mechanisms. The Western Australian model at this stage contradicts the received orthodoxy.

The future of the inspection model

On 23 March 2004, the Joint Standing Committee on Treaties of the Commonwealth Parliament tabled a report recommending that Australia should not adopt the Optional Protocol to the United Nations Convention against Torture and other forms of Cruel, Inhuman or Degrading Treatment or Punishment.[46]

The Convention represents internationally what the European Convention on Torture represents regionally.[47] The Optional Protocol provides for a visits-based inspection system. At the present time Australia, with its immigration detention system operating in breach of international

---

44 See op cit at n 40, above, at p 15.

45 See Kirby, P, *Independent Investigation into the Management and Operation of Victoria's Private Prisons*, p 43, Melbourne: Department of Justice.

46 See Report 58, Canberra: The Parliament of the Commonwealth of Australia.

47 See n 12, above, and the accompanying text.

standards,[48] was predictably reluctant to open up the possibility of autonomous inspection by a respected external agency. The government-dominated Committee was thus able to ensure that the recommendation was in line with current government policy.

However, the minority recommended that "binding treaty action be taken" to adopt the Optional Protocol. The significance of this is that, if a change of government occurs, the matter will be back on the agenda. Commitment to a visits-based inspection system will not simply bind the Commonwealth government but also the States and the Territories. There will be a strong political incentive in such circumstances for these governments to bring their inspection processes and mechanisms up to the international standard. International inspections agencies take note of the autonomy and efficacy of domestic arrangements in deciding upon their own programs. At the present time only Western Australia meets international standards.

Thus, international convention law could act as a lever to spread the autonomous inspection model throughout Australia. To say that is not to make a prediction[49] but simply to remind oneself that political arrangements are never fixed and, in particular, that the area of accountability for the management of closed institutions remains potentially dynamic.

---

48   See Human Rights and Equal Opportunity Commission (2004), *A Last Resort: Inquiry into the Condition of Children in Immigration Detention Centres*, Sydney: HREOC.

49   This chapter was written before the Australian General Election of 9 October 2004. It now seems virtually certain that the issue of adoption of the Optional Protocol is dead for at least the next three years. However, the comment in the text that political arrangements are never fixed in relation to prisons administration remains valid. In the UK, it was the Conservative Government of Mrs Thatcher that legislated for the creation of an independent inspectorate as concern about conditions in prisons and the managerial competence of the Home Office began to increase. Similarly, the Conservative Government of Mr Major created the office of Prisons Ombudsman as a consequence of 1990 prison riots and the recommendations contained in the Woolf Report. Finally, the establishment of an inspectorate in Western Australia came "out of left field", with a Coalition Government moving to establish it as part of a "deal" with a minor party in the Upper House of Parliament to enable legislation to be passed authorising private management of a new prison.

– CHAPTER 11 –

Causes and prevention of violence in prisons

Professor Ross Homel and Carleen Thompson
Griffith University

Prisons are not normal environments. They are, as Bottoms (1999) observed, not only "total institutions" in the sense that they encompass inmates' lives to an extent greater than other social institutions (Goffman 1961), they are physical places (mostly surrounded by high walls) with a specific history and ethos that are designed to be places of punishment. Prisons bring troubled human beings, often with a long history of violence as victim or offender, into confined spaces against their will. These scarred individuals are brought into close contact with staff whom they greatly outnumber but who also must, on a daily basis, maintain a peaceful and orderly routine. The wonder is there is not more violence in such an environment.

There are no over-arching theories of prison violence, but there are several influential schools of thought. In prison sociology two well-established but contrasting perspectives are the *deprivation* and *importation* models. The deprivation model states that the prison environment and loss of freedom cause deep psychological trauma. Consequently, for reasons of psychological self-preservation, prisoners create a deviant prison subculture that promotes violence (Farrington & Nuttal, 1980; Sykes 1958; Wortley 2002). The importation model (Cao, Zhao & Vandine 1997; Harer & Steffensmeier, 1996) emphasises what prisoners bring into the institution: their histories, personal attributes and social networks, including links to criminal groups.

The literature supports both these models but perhaps the most pronounced trend in recent literature is a growing recognition of the importance of very specific features of the social and physical environments of the prison and of the "minutiae of the average prison day" (Bottoms 1999: 212). Even in studies that are primarily focused on other factors, the details of how a prison is organised in time and space, how individuals interact with and help shape a dynamic environment, and the role of specific situational factors in precipitating or regulating violence emerge as crucial. Thus we should add, as two newer but influential theoretical positions, the *transactional model* (Bottoms 1999) and the *situational model* (Wortley 2002). The transactional model focuses on "the continual dynamic process of interaction between the prisoner, the staff, and the environment they both inhabit" (Bottoms 1999: 212). The situational model, as developed by Wortley, distinguishes *situational precipitators* and *situational regulators* in a two-stage model. Precipitators include environmental cues that may actively induce individuals to engage in conduct that they may not otherwise have performed (eg, drab institutionalised cells may trigger depression), while regulators are the more familiar opportunity-reducing strategies (such as camera surveillance). The key point from a prevention perspective is that many of the techniques of precipitation control conflict with the techniques of opportunity reduction that have been the traditional focus of prison administrators.

Factors found to be related to violence include pre-existing prisoner characteristics (eg, prisoner age and gender); structural or situational factors (eg, prison architecture and design; level of security); management practices (eg, staffing models, staff skills and training, prison culture and management style); and outside environmental influences (eg, political pressures on prison administrators; racial tensions). Poor prison management resulting in dysfunctional forms of control emerges as a major cause of interpersonal violence, and by implication modification of these practices (especially the removal of arbitrary coercive controls) is effective in reducing violence.

Other effective prevention strategies include a range of situational measures (eg, improved surveillance of high-risk locations, the manipulation of prisoner privileges, improvement of supervision of both staff and prisoners); some offender treatment and education programs (eg, in-prison therapeutic communities; college-level education programs); and some "social prevention" programs (eg, the Barlinnie Special Unit in Scotland).

The evidence for the violence-reduction effects of prisoner treatment and education tends to be weak and inconsistent, with situational factors such as time spent in programs away from unstructured recreational activities perhaps a more logical explanation for what effects were found than program philosophy or content. Situational factors also seem to be essential to the success of most social prevention approaches.

There is little Australian research of any kind in relation to prison violence, despite major problems with institutionalised violence being identified in Royal Commissions (Nagle 1978; RCIADIC 1992) and Reports of the National Committee on Violence (1990, 1994).

Prison management and accountability

Prison management practices are critically important for the control of violence. There is increasing evidence that poor prison management and control is the most significant factor in contributing to and even promoting both individual and collective prison violence (Ekland-Olson 1986; various studies cited in McCorkle et al 1995; Silberman, 1992). Bottoms' interactionist model is supported by Peteron-Badali & Koegl (2002), who show that correctional staff in Canadian juvenile institutions frequently not only allowed, but actually induced, juveniles to use force on other young offenders.

An important study by Reisig (1998) contrasted the *control, responsibility* and *consensual* models of prison management. According to the control model, rules should guide almost all areas of prisoners' lives and these rules should be rigorously enforced to control prison behaviour. According to the responsibility model, prisoners should be provided with a high degree of responsibility over the order of the prison and management should exercise the minimum required control over such order. The consensual model is an integration of the control and responsibility models. The findings indicated that in prisons adopting the responsibility and consensual models, prison personnel reported lower levels of all forms of disorder than in prisons adopting the control model.

A range of specific management factors related to violence are cited in the literature: security lapses, lack of prison officer discipline and morale, officers' inability or unwillingness to intervene in instances of victimisation and violence, poor grievance and dispute resolution mechanisms, the formation of gangs and cliques, prisoners relying on self-protection, staff violence for control of prisoners, deterrence and payback (especially where officers feel justified in taking matters into their own hands because the administration provides limited protection from attack).

Drug use and trafficking in illegal and prescription drugs by prisoners also relates to prison violence (Edgar & O'Donnell 1998; Inciardi et al 1993; Incorvaia & Kirby 1997). Echoing Bottoms' emphasis on legitimation, Silberman (1992, 1994) particularly stresses the importance of appropriate accountability and dispute resolution mechanisms, including mediation and ombudsmen, for defusing violence.

Architectural design

Neither overcrowding nor prison size have been shown to be causally related to violence (Farrington & Nuttal 1980, Wortley 2002). However, several studies indicate that group cell housing of prisoners contributes to interpersonal violence, especially where there are poor selection procedures and safeguards in place (O'Donnell & Edgar 1996). Individual cells greatly reduce the opportunities for prisoner-prisoner victimisation and violence, the only exception to this being self-inflicted violence (self-mutilation and suicide) which is more likely when prisoners are in single cells or segregation. The linear architectural design of most prisons is a factor that contributes to violence. The inherent design features of this architecture, in conjunction with the indirect staff supervision model that necessarily accompanies this kind of design, creates opportunities for both prisoner-prisoner and prisoner-staff violence (various studies cited in Jay Farbstein et al 1991; Wright & Goodstein; Zupan & Menke 1991).

"New generation philosophy, which espouses a podular design (that reduces unprotected spaces) and direct supervision of prisoners, is increasingly being implemented in the US and the UK. Although there are fewer studies and some mixed findings on the effectiveness of this new prison concept (Tartaro 2000), the literature generally indicates promising results for a reduction in prison violence and vandalism where new generation architectural design and staffing models have been implemented. Researchers warn, however, that successful implementation of this approach is heavily predicated on a commitment from management and the recruitment, selection, training and retention of appropriate prison personnel (Farbstein et al 1991; Zupan & Menke 1991).

Staff inexperience and training

There is no clear relationship between staff experience and prisoner-prisoner violence, but consistent evidence that staff inexperience is a factor influencing violence by prisoners against staff (Wortley 2002). Kratcoski (1988) found that work experience of officers, with trainees receiving a disproportionate number of assaults, was one of the four most important factors related to prisoner-staff assault. Munroe's study of aggressive and non-aggressive offender responses to an unknown prison officer suggest that "inexperienced prison officers are more likely to become involved in violent incidents, because they are perceived by aggressive prisoners as 'ambiguous'" (Munroe 1995: 245).

Vulnerability to violence

Research evidence suggests vulnerability to victimisation and violence in prison is associated with a number of factors (younger age, race, homosexuality, transexuality, status of offence) and that certain prisoners both feel, and in fact are more vulnerable to, victimisation and violence (Cooley 1993; Nacci & Kane 1984; Edgar & O'Donnell 1998; Edgar, O'Donnell & Martin 2003). Racial institutional violence is also well documented as influencing the extent of violence against Aborigines in the prison system (RCIADIC). However, Edgar, O'Donnell & Martin (2003) also found that while victimisation is pervasive in British prisons, there are many misconceptions about the nature of victimisation and that these are often counter-intuitive. For example, victims and victimiser are not discrete groups, with those who victimised others often likely to be victims themselves, making an understanding of the nature of conflict in prisons a matter of central importance. Prisoners rarely reported their victimisation to staff.

Programs and approaches to reduce prison violence

Historically, prison administrators have concentrated on the classification and segregation of different kinds of prisoners as one key tool for maintaining good order and promoting rehabilitation. Prisoner classification relied on methods for predicting violence and/or prison adjustment, looking to background prisoner characteristics (eg, age, race, offence) using various risk-assessment tools or inmate classification models, or to personality characteristics, using various mental health-psychopathology screening instruments (eg, the MMPI typology). A review of the literature reveals that many of these instruments do not predict violence reliably or accurately (Cooper & Werner 1990; Dictaldo et al 1995; Proctor 1994). This evidence accords with the general literature on prison violence, which suggests that importation factors alone are not sufficient for understanding the causes of prison violence.

Given the more sophisticated research and theoretical models that are now available, there are currently more good ideas in the literature about how to reduce prison violence than there are careful evaluations of well-designed interventions. Strategies may be classified into three broad categories: programs for prisoners, situational approaches, and institutional reforms and management practices. All strategies rely for their success, of course, on far-sighted management that is willing to act on the basis of evidence.

Programs for prisoners

A range of prison educational and rehabilitative programs are reported in the literature, although primarily these studies address post-release recidivism. Fewer studies directly consider the effectiveness of such programs for reducing interpersonal violence in prisons. Some program types (academic and vocational) may with reasonable confidence be expected to reduce prison violence, while other program types (such as violence alternatives) require far more rigorous research, particularly of different treatment modalities, in order to confidently predict outcomes. It is tentatively concluded from the literature that programs that implement violence alternative training or other forms of treatment such as drug rehabilitation within a supportive and "opportunity enhancing" environment of a specialist or rehabilitative unit are more likely to be effective in reducing prisoner violence (Bottoms et al 1995; Dietz 2003; Rucker 1994; Wolfus & Bierman 1996).

Several authors refer to program principles for ensuring effective offender rehabilitation to reduce recidivism (Gerber & Fritsch 1995; MacKenzie 1997). While no similar literature indicating program principles for reducing prison violence *per se* were found, several of the studies in this review discuss program strengths and limitations in light of the following program requirements. These include the need for programs to:

- Provide sufficient program integrity so that what is delivered is consistent with the planned design;
- Address offender characteristics that are capable of change and predictive of future criminal activities, such as anti-social attitudes and behaviour, drug use, anger responses;
- Allow sufficient intensity or time in view of the desired changes;
- Use treatment modes and delivery styles that take account of offender learning styles and abilities (cognitive and behavioural methods that provide positive reinforcement and privileges for pro-social behaviour are generally favoured).

Generally, the literature suggests that *prisoner academic and vocational education programs* help decrease prison rule violations and violence and are therefore one of the more useful management approaches for maintaining prison order (Gerber & Fritsch 1995). McCorkle et al's (1995: 325) study of 371 US State prisons found that "even after controlling for other institutional characteristics, prisons in which a large percentage of the prisoner population was involved in educational, vocational, and prison industry programs reported lower rates of violence against inmates and staff". Furthermore, their findings suggested that order was best promoted when prisoners were involved in meaningful programs that offered opportunities for self-improvement, and not just structure or "keep busy" assignments.

The evidence is not strong for the violence-reduction effects of *treatment programs, including cognitive-behavioural, violence alternatives, and anger management* (eg, Baro 1999; Walrath 2001). While a number of programs running in prisons both in Australia and the US are reportedly successful (Love 1994; Smith 1995; Report into Youth Violence in NSW 1995) a rigorous evaluation of their effects on prison violence and post-program prisoner behaviour was not always conducted or available. Howells and his colleagues (2002: 3) report the evaluation of well-implemented anger management programs in South Australian and West Australian prisons, concluding that, "[w]ith some consistency, the results demonstrate that the overall impact of the anger management interventions was small".

There is much wisdom in this paper about why offender populations are different from other populations for which anger management interventions are much more successful, and how programs can be made more effective in correctional settings (broadly consistent with the principles listed earlier). Promising approaches appear to be multi-modal methods that utilise a broad range of behavioural, cognitive-behavioural and psychological skills training (Morrisey 1997), or the siting of programs in a rehabilitation unit with an intensive dual program modality (group and individual sessions) (Wolfus & Bierman 1996).

Given the positive relationship between prison violence and prisoner drug taking, *substance abuse programs* in prisons may also be useful for reducing prison violence, particularly prisoner-prisoner assaults. The literature suggests that the most promising treatments are prison-based therapeutic communities operating as segregated facilities within the prison (Dietz et al 2003; Incorvaia & Kirby 1997; McKenzie 1997). Drug treatment as a stand-alone program is less promising (Kinlock et al 2003).

Situational prevention strategies

This is a field where rapid developments are taking place. A strong theoretical case has already been outlined for paying much closer attention to the fine-grained details of everyday routines and the minutiae of prison contexts when planning preventive interventions. The empirical research increasingly supports this perspective (eg, Jiang et al 2002; O'Donnell & Edgar 1996, 2003). Wortley's (2002) book contains comprehensive and up-to-date overviews of many promising (but in most cases not "proven") situational strategies for the reduction of prisoner-prisoner and other forms of violence, the details of which cannot be presented here. Some examples:

- Single-cell accommodation can reduce crowding and respect a prisoner's territory (precipitation-control), while "target hardening" a prisoner (opportunity reduction, or regulation-control);

- Increasing prisoner control over their environments can encourage compliance and reduce frustration (precipitation-control);

- Small or subdivided prisons can reduce anonymity (precipitation-control);

- Age-heterogeneous populations can reduce both inappropriate imitation and conformity (precipitation-control);

- Increasing women staff may encourage compliance and reduce frustration (precipitation-control), reducing assaults on staff;

- Elimination of blind spots may improve formal and natural surveillance (regulation-control).

Institutional reforms and management practices

Ultimately even the smallest features of prison life depend on management.

Recent research confirms that the control model of prison management, with its emphasis on highly formal or coercive managerial practises, is less effective at controlling disorder than practises based on the responsibility or consensual models (Reisig 1998: 2002).

Deprivation theory, with its emphasis on the formation of an oppositional subculture, suggests that management policies that minimise the deprivations of imprisonment by (for example) fostering links with families or improving the fairness of the application of rules will reduce disorder. Bottoms et al (1995) link such an approach with *social crime prevention*, distinguishing it sharply from situational prevention (Wortley 2002). In the prison context, social prevention approaches rely heavily on a changed role for prison officers and an "opportunity-enhancing" environment for prisoners. Bottoms argues that this approach improves the legitimacy of the prison regime in the eyes of prisoners.

One of the more successful examples of this approach reported in the literature is the *Barlinnie Special Unit* in Scotland for violent offenders (Bottoms 1999). This unit, while it operated, was characterised by a sense of community involving both prisoners and staff, greater than usual prisoner autonomy, and distinctive incentives and disincentives (such as unlimited rights to family visits, subject to good behaviour). The fact that prisoners often resided in this unit for several years may also have significantly contributed to its long-term success in reducing violence, as prisoners were socialised into new ways of thinking and behaving. Bottoms et al (1995) also contrast the success of the social preventive approach adopted by the Long Lartin maximum-security prison in England with the less positive outcomes of the more controlling but similar status Albany prison.

Allied to social prevention are *"whole-of-prison" approaches* to reducing violence. Such approaches are effective in other contexts such as schools

(Homel 1999), and are strongly endorsed in the research conducted on the British Prison Service by O'Donnell & Edgar (1996). This research highlighted the ineffectiveness of relying on anti-bullying policies without strong support for communication and implementation of the policies and concomitant intervention across a range of areas, including situational prevention, prisoner education programs, staff training, victim support, and ongoing research.

Staff recruitment and training are critical to any management policy, but little relevant evaluation literature on these topics is available. The Pennsylvania conflict resolution program that jointly trains officers and prisoners is reportedly successful in improving staff-prisoner relationships (Love 1994), and many authors endorse new approaches to recruitment and training in order to screen out inappropriate staff (eg, Peteron-Badali & Koegl 2002), to equip staff to recognise and deal with conflict (eg, Edgar & Martin 2002; Patrick 1998), or to improve supervision (eg, Zupan & Menke 1991).

Conclusion

Although the picture is complex and some inconsistent findings have emerged, generally the literature supports the notion that the more coercive the prison environment the greater the potential for violence. This is especially so where prison management and treatment of prisoners are perceived by prisoners as unfair or illegitimate, as this strengthens prisoner solidarity in opposition to the authorities. This in turn threatens the legitimacy of the regime and reduces prisoner compliance. Conversely, prisons that provide more opportunities for prisoner participation in education and vocational programs and promote self-efficacy, generally report reduced levels of rule violations and violence.

The literature also strongly supports the contention that situational strategies are among the most powerful weapons in our armoury, especially with the expansion of the theory to include situational precipitators as well as regulators. The prison environment is such a powerful influence, whether understood in physical, psychological, social or cultural terms, that it must become much more the focus of attention in devising prevention policies. Many possible strategies are now "on the menu", but each requires careful development and evaluation, with an eye to the broader dimensions of prison control discussed in this chapter. A whole-of-prison approach that thoughtfully combines situational and social prevention strategies, supported by appropriate management policies and research-based staff recruitment and training practices, is probably the most promising model for reducing interpersonal violence in prisons.

CHAPTER 12

The over-representation of Indigenous persons in custody

Bill Anscomb[1]
Charles Sturt University

Foley (2003) is critical of the academic discourse in Australia which constructs a Western perspective of Indigenous reality and which presents racially-biased constructions of the "truth". It needs to be acknowledged that this chapter has been written by a non-Indigenous person and the chapter needs to viewed with that "bias" taken into account. Professor Mick Dodson (2003: 8) says that he is "unable to give comfort to the view that a non-Indigenous person should leave public statements on these questions to Indigenous people alone. The tragic circumstances ... are not alone the business of those who suffer them."

A prominent historian considers the history of Indigenous people's relationship with Europeans as being the transition from "tribesman to prisoner". Whatever view one may take of the "history wars", colonisation or invasion and a host of other issues related to the relationship between Indigenous and non-Indigenous Australians, the fact is that many Indigenous Australians' lives are significantly impacted upon by crime, policing and corrections. Information, narratives and analysis emerging from the Gordon Inquiry, the *Bringing Them Home Report* ("Stolen Generations" Report), the Royal Commission into Aboriginal Deaths in Custody, and numerous coronial inquiries are evidence that Indigenous people are affected by criminal behaviour, welfare approaches, correctional organisations and law enforcement programs.

The facts

In 2004, 20 per cent of the Australian prison population was Indigenous. The 2001 ABS Census Reports indicated that the Aboriginal population was about 2 per cent of the Australian nation.

Nearly 55 per cent of all prisoners in 2004 were males aged between 20 and 34 years. The 25 to 29 year age group had the highest imprisonment rates

---

1   Bill wishes to acknowledge the initial research assistance of Bradley Callander.

for both males and females, with 659 male prisoners per 100,000 adult males (a 3% increase on the 2002 rate) and 53 female prisoners per 100,000 adult females (a 5% increase on the 2002 rate). Between 1993 and 2003 the female prisoner population has increased by 110 per cent, in comparison to a 45 per cent increase in the male prisoner population.

The Royal Commission into Aboriginal Deaths in Custody (RCIADIC), headed by Commissioner Elliott Johnson, handed down its findings on 15 April 1991. According to the Royal Commission:

> On an Australia-wide basis an Aboriginal was 27 times more likely to be in police custody than a non-Aboriginal, and the figure was 15 times in New South Wales, 13 times in Victoria and three times in Tasmania. Australia wide an Aboriginal was 11 times more likely to be in prison than a non-Aboriginal, and in New South Wales eight times and in Tasmania three times " (Wooten 1991: 21-22, cited in White and Perrone 1997)

> While it is recognised that prisoners in general tend to come from the young adult range, this tendency seems to be even more marked for Aboriginal prisoners" (Johnston 1991: 168)

The Royal Commission into Aboriginal Deaths in Custody was established in October 1987 and reported on 99 deaths of Indigenous people between the 1 January 1980 and 1 May 1989. The RCIADIC was a response to growing public concern that deaths in custody of Aboriginal and Torres Islander peoples were too common and public explanations were too evasive. There was an underlying theme that foul play may have been a factor. The conclusions reached in RCIADIC final report did not support the expectations of systemic and deliberate foul play. The Commissioners, however, did find that there appeared to be little appreciation of, and less dedication to, the duty of care by custodial authorities and their officers and found system defects, failure to exercise proper care and in general a poor standard of care.

The RCIADIC established that Aboriginal people in custody do *not* die at a greater rate that non-Aboriginal people in custody. However, the Commission concluded, *"what is overwhelmingly different is the rate of which Aboriginal people come into custody, compared to the rate of the general community"*. The report stated:

> [T]he conclusions are clear. Aboriginal people die in custody at a rate relative to the proportion of the whole population which is totally unacceptable and which would not be tolerated if it occurred in the non-Aboriginal community. But this occurs not because Aboriginal people in custody are more likely to die than other in custody but because the Aboriginal is grossly over represented in custody. Too many Aboriginal people are in custody too often.

Commissioner Johnson, in the overview of the National Report, highlights the importance of history and the consequences of that history. The clear tone of the report is upon reducing the number of Aboriginal people in custody with a focus upon Aboriginal empowerment and self-determination. The final National Report (p 27) says:

> [T]he principal thrust of the recommendations, as of the report, is directed towards the prime objectives – historically linked – of the elimination of disadvantage and the growth of empowerment and self-determination of Aboriginal society.

In the years since the publication of the RCIADIC, the situation has deteriorated in terms of over-representation of Aboriginal people in custody, rather than ameliorated.

Theoretical perspectives

1. Criminological perspectives

Criminologists from differing paradigms may have differing explanations for the over-representation of Indigenous people in correctional settings. Some criminologists, for example, will locate criminal behaviour from the structural criminology approach seeing the over-representation as a response to social injustice and inequalities. Those operating from a volitional perspective may well see the over-representation as a result of individual choice and individual behaviour.

2. Welfare perspectives

In explaining social phenomena, a wide range of perspectives can be used. Some will see the explanation of the existence of social welfare from a purely individual perspective while others will adopt a political or communitarian approach.

3. Discussion

Weatherburn et al (2003), in explaining the over-representation of Indigenous peoples in prisons and criminology, state:

> [T]he simplest explanation for the state of affairs is Aboriginal over representation in crime. The dominant focus of scholarly attention in relation to Aboriginal over representation in the criminal justice system, however, has been upon systemic bias of the law, the exercise of police discretion and operation of the criminal justice system.

This article highlights the contribution that Aboriginal offending makes to Aboriginal over-representation. The authors do not dispute the contribution of the history of colonisation and concede that prejudice and discrimination of Indigenous people at the hands of police and the criminal justice system has been substantial, but they underline that focusing on crime will highlight the limited value of diversionary policies as a way of reducing Aboriginal over-representation. The critical issue is to significantly impact on the under-lying causes of high crime rates in Aboriginal communities.

The causes of Indigenous over-representation in prisons are matters highlighted by the RCIADIC and include socioeconomic disadvantage, chronic unemployment, substantial substance abuse, family dissolution and alienation from economic, social and political structures. These have been most recently highlighted in the Indigenous section of the Australian Bureau of Statistics Year Book.

A second group of factors influencing over-representation is systemic biases at varying points of the criminal justice system. An analysis of police cautioning, police utilisation of summonses, Court Attendance Notices and court appearance rates for Aboriginal juveniles, for example, show that Aboriginal young people receive fewer cautions, fewer summonses and Court Attendance Notices but have higher rates of arrests and are signifi-cantly over-represented in the Juvenile Justice Centres when compared with non-Indigenous young people.

Weatherburn et al (2003) assert that:

> [A]ll discriminatory treatment of Aboriginal people by prison, police and the court system is an historical fact, the leading current cause of Aboriginal over representation in prison is not systemic bias but high rates of Aboriginal involvement in serious crime.

They conclude that the primary focus in reducing Indigenous over-representation must be upon reducing Indigenous crime – not changing the response of the criminal justice system. Significantly, much of the violent crime committed by Aboriginal offenders is committed against other Aboriginal people – often women and children (Harding et al 1995: 36-44). Logically, both perpetrators and victims are over-represented in the Indigenous community.

To sustain this view, systemic bias needs to be limited in definition to systemic bias of the justice and correctional authorities. There is over-whelming evidence of the social exclusion of Indigenous people from the mainstream of society. For example, the Australian Bureau of Statistics (ABS 4221.0) in describing schools in Australia indicated that the apparent retention rate in 2002 of full-time students from year 7 to year 12 is 75 per cent while for those full-time Indigenous students it is 38 per cent. The Indigenous population is much younger (median age 20 years) than the total Australian population (median age 34). The Indigenous population is predicted to grow at the rate of 5.3 per cent per year, which is much faster than the total Australian population with a growth rate of approximately 1.0 per cent in the 2003-04 financial year.

Of persons aged 15 years and over, 3 per cent of Indigenous people – compared with 5 per cent of non-Indigenous people – were at university. However, in the age range 18-24 years, 5 per cent of Indigenous people were at university compared to 23 per cent of non-Indigenous people.

The unemployment rate is higher for Indigenous people, being 17.6 per cent compared with 7.3 per cent for all Australians as at February 2000 (ABS 2000). This figure excludes the 26 per cent of "employed" Indigenous people in the Community Development Employment Program (CDEP) which is a "work for the dole" scheme operated through the Aboriginal and Torres Strait Islander Services (ATSIS). In the 2001 census, Indigenous people of labour force age were three times more likely than non-Indigenous people to be unemployed (20% compared with 7%).

In the 2001 census, 59 per cent of non-Indigenous people aged 15 years and over were employed compared to 42 per cent of Indigenous people; 32,000 Indigenous people are recorded for administrative purposes by the Aboriginal and Torres Straight Islander Services as CDEP participants. Significantly 55 per cent of Indigenous people are employed by the private sector compared to 82 per cent of non-Indigenous people.

At the 2001 census, the mean (average) gross household income for Indigenous persons was $364 per week, corresponding to 62 per cent of the income for non-Indigenous persons ($585 per week). The ABS indicates this disparity reflects lower household incomes received by households with Indigenous people. The tendency is for those households to have more inhabitants than non-Indigenous households. In the five years between the 1996 and the 2001 Census the average equivalised gross household income for Indigenous persons rose by approximately 11 per cent compared with a 13 per cent rise for non-Indigenous persons after making adjustments for inflation and using the consumer price index. In terms of income distribution, 40 per cent of the total Australian population was the in the lowest or second lowest income quintiles. Among Indigenous persons this figure was 72 per cent. Only 5 per cent of Indigenous people were in the top one-fifth (20%) of income distribution.

Indigenous people are much more likely to be renting homes (63%) than purchasing (19%) or owning their homes outright (13%). The Australian Housing Survey, reported in Edwards and Madden (2001) found that one-third of community-owned or managed permanent housing in discrete locations were found to be in need of major repair or demolition. Fifteen per cent of households with Indigenous persons were considered overcrowded, compared to 4 per cent of non-Indigenous households.

Aboriginal and Torres Straight Islander children are over-represented in child protections systems by an overall rate ratio of 3.2 to 1 (ABS 4704.0). The incidence of Indigenous children coming into the care and protection of the State is about six times of that of non-Indigenous children.

Aggregated data for 2000 and 2001 in relation to juvenile detention centres for Australian shows that 43 per cent of detainees (aged 10 to 17 years) were Indigenous.

The average age of an Indigenous mother in the two-year period prior to 2000 was 24.7 years compared with an average age for of 29.2 years for non-Indigenous mothers. Indigenous mothers were twice as likely to have children of low birth weight (13%) than non-Indigenous mothers (6%). The comparative rates of perinatal death in 1998-2000 indicated 20 stillbirths out of every thousand births for Indigenous mothers compared with ten stillbirths out of every thousand where the mother was non-Indigenous.

Hospitalisation rates are several times higher among Indigenous peoples. Hospitalisations attributed to assaults are eight times higher for Indigenous males and 28 times higher for Indigenous females when compared with their non-Indigenous counterparts.

Indigenous people aged 18 years and over were twice as likely to be current smokers (51%) compared with non-Indigenous people (24%).

Interestingly, Indigenous adults aged 18 years and over were less likely (42%) than non-Indigenous adults (62%) to have consumed alcohol in the week prior to the National Health Surveys. Of those Indigenous people who consumed alcohol their level of risky/high drinking was 29 per cent compared to 17 per cent of non-Indigenous consumers. There is repeated association between substance abuse and violence in Indigenous communities (Atkinson 1991; Fitzgerald 2001; Robertson 2000). According to Noel Pearson:

> Ours is one of the most dysfunctional societies on the planet: surely the fact that the per capita consumption of alcohol in Cape York is the highest in the world says something about our dysfunction. (cited in Robertson 2000: 71)

The ABS (4704.0) concludes, "after adjusting for different population compositions, Aboriginal and Torres Straight Islander peoples are shown to be dying at three times the total population rates".

These tragic national figures can often mask very real regional differences. According to data given to the Wilcannia Health Service Development Transitional Plan in 2000, the average life expectancy for an Aboriginal man living in Wilcannia was 36.7 years and for an Aboriginal woman 42.5 years. The estimates show the life expectancy in that particular location to be far lower than people living in NSW.

Given the demographic distribution of Indigenous people with a far heavier concentration in rural and remote areas, it would be significant to consider regional variations and regional figures as well as national statistics.

Summary and future directions

Tomison and Wise (1999) have shown the association between stressful, negative community conditions and maladaptive coping behaviours and social dysfunction. Memmott et al (2001) describe the pattern of some Indigenous communities as "dysfunctional community syndrome".

Indigenous over-representation in prisons has increased rather than decreased. Indigenous people continue to be disadvantaged in a range of areas including health, housing, employment and education. Aboriginal offenders offend (at least in the serious offence categories) at a higher rate than non-Indigenous people. Many of the victims (of Aboriginal offenders who end up in custody) are themselves Indigenous.

Robertson states:

Indigenous people generally have been profoundly affected by the erosion of their cultural and spiritual identity and the disintegration of family and community that has traditionally sustained relationships and obligations and maintained social order and control. (2000: xii)

In this authors view, the future approach to redressing the continuing and escalating over-representation of Indigenous people will need to be understood within a framework that acknowledges the past and takes account of multiple societal, family, community and individual factors in an holistic way. Understandings of oppression (possibly based on the work of Friere), passive welfare, racism, silence and denial (both within and outside of the Indigenous community), distorted development and a commitment to economic and social empowerment will be necessary pre-conditions for reversing the trend towards increasing over-representation of Indigenous people.

Models of intervention may have the following characteristics (modified from Blagg 2000 – in relation to family violence):

- Programs that are customised to meet the needs of specific locations;

- Programs based on community development principles and models of empowerment;

- Programs that are linked to health, housing, education etc in an holistic way;

- Programs (where possible) that employ and up-skill local Indigenous people;

- Programs that respect traditions and traditional law and custom;

- Programs that are linked to progressive education;

- Programs that employ a multi-disciplinary approach;

- Programs that emphasise partnerships between communities and agencies;

- Programs that focus upon working with men;

- Programs that emphasise healing;

- Programs that promote positive pro-social role models and whole family models;

- Programs that enhance existing functional community structures and groups;

- Community Corrections Services that are advocates for community change;

- Departments of Corrective Services that are involved in whole community change in alliance with the Indigenous communities; and

- Empowering correctional and justice programs that restrict and reverse the debilitating effect of crime and corrections within communities.

There are differing paradigms of corrections and criminology. There are differing paradigms of welfare intervention. These paradigms and approaches can be applied to the over-representation of Indigenous people. In the author's view, until the social and structural disadvantages of the Indigenous community are addressed from a basis of self-determination and self-governance and until the social conditions that promote crime and offending behaviour are addressed in a cooperative, reconciliatory and just way, then the future may be an escalating number and rate of Indigenous people in Australian prisons.

CHAPTER 13

Risk and responsibilities
in women's prisons

Professor Pat Carlen,
Keele University, UK

The risk: Growth of the women's prison business

Recently, women's prisons populations have soared. In response, many jurisdictions have developed in-prison programs, policies and strategies designed to address women's "needs". However, there is mounting suspicion among campaigners and professionals that the women's prison system is feeding off itself – with high numbers of recidivists on the one hand and, on the other, sentencers sending women to prison because they believe that in-prison programs and reforms can prevent future lawbreaking. Additionally, there is widespread belief among criminal justice professionals that there should be less emphasis on prison-regime reforms and programming, and more on resettling women in their own safe accommodation and then supporting them in struggles against addiction and abusive relationships. Anti-prison campaigners have research evidence on their side: studies of female ex-prisoners suggest that what happens outside prison in terms of housing, jobs and personal relationships is much more important than any brainwashing attempts made via prison programming (eg, Eaton 1993; Kendall 2002); while, from a different perspective, studies of women's prisons suggest that imprisonment may cause more psychological damage than any in-prison therapy can ever cure (eg, Comack 1996).

The "prison programming/increased prison population" syndrome is a by-product of the women's prison business. Typically, it is triggered when public inquiries into women's imprisonment result in recommendations for a three-pronged reform strategy: reformation of prison regimes; radical reduction in the numbers sent to prison; and increased community provision. What usually happens, however, is that only prison regimes are changed. New psychology-based programs are set-up in women's prisons and unfounded claims (or unfulfilled promises) are made that these psychology-based programs will reduce recidivism. The community provision and sentencing reforms are quietly let slide. (See Inspector of Custodial Services 2003 for a review of cognitive skills programs in Western Australia.)

In England, the in-prison programs have been provided by groups additional to the Prison Service. To implement the in-prison reforms, a range of organisations previously critical of the women's prison regimes have been tempted into forming lucrative "partnerships" with the Prison Service in order to develop "accredited" programs which will, so the rhetoric goes "empower" women, give them "choices" and result in women-centred regimes. The ideological justification for this emphasis on psychological re-adjustment in prison rather than the provision of citizen rights outside prison is effected by a translation of welfare need into psychological need. Whereas "need" was previously seen to mean "welfare need", it is nowadays translated into "risk of re-offending" which, in official jargon becomes "criminogenic need" requiring psychological re-programming in prison (see McMahon 2000; Hudson 2002).

Non-custodial programs holding to the notion that women suffer more from economic deficits than cognitive deficits, and which attempt to show women how to cope practically and lawfully with their daily problems outside prison, do not receive official accreditation; traditional in-prison programs (such as art and discussion groups) deemed to be without anti-criminogenic purpose are abandoned in favour of cognitive behavioural programs parachuted in from Canada and originally designed for *men*. A whole new language is developed to sell the product – which is now quite openly called "prison works".

Courts, impressed by claims about the efficacy of in-prison programs in meeting criminogenic need, and not hearing much about the community programs or the research which suggests that the claims of the psychological programmers are ill-founded, send more and more women "at risk" to prison. As more women prisoners are in poverty (and therefore "at risk") than male prisoners, the disproportionately increasing numbers of female prisoners has a knock-on effect in the men's prisons, leading to more over-crowding there. Overcrowding in the women's prisons results in a lack of fit between the locations of programs and the locations of prisoners and the gap between reform rhetoric and reform reality becomes wider than ever. Having been inappropriately imprisoned in increasingly crowded prisons, women go out of prison materially worse off than when they went in, they reoffend and the increasing female prison population together with programming propaganda suggests that there is a new type of female criminal who should be imprisoned, and the whole circle begins again.

That is the risk inherent in the prison business; that it results in what Stan Cohen (1983) famously called *"netwidening"*, and in this particular case, in a net-widening mistakenly based on an assumption that in-prison program provision can reduce recidivism and, concomitantly be assessed in terms of recidivism reduction. It is therefore argued that a *responsible* approach to imprisonment would *roll back the prison business* on the grounds that both these claims are false: first, because the essential nature of prison means there are insuperable limits to prison reform; and secondly, because the quality of life in prison is not reducible to a quantitative audit which can assess the claims of programs to reduce recidivism. Instead, the ways in which prisons are run should be initially evaluated according to a penal probity which will sometimes have to make moral decisions that certain ways of treating prisoners are *"good in themselves"*.

The second and related responsibility of governments, therefore, is the *quest for penal probity* (in terms of its of its dictionary meaning of honesty and moral integrity) about why prison populations and prison regimes take the forms they do.

The responsibilities

1. Rolling back the prison business

The prisons' business should be rolled back for two main reasons: first, because the nature of imprisonment necessarily limits the extent to which prisons can either reform themselves or their inmates; secondly, because recidivism audits cannot possibly provide evidence as to the efficacy of imprisonment in reducing recidivism.

Limits to in-prison reform

A necessary condition of imprisonment is that prisoners must be *kept in*, otherwise the prison would be no more. It follows, therefore, that (within legal limits) security arrangements must always have priority over other prison objectives including those of the various rehabilitative programs for prisoners. Take the following examples. One of the commonly described characteristics of women prisoners is "low self-esteem". Is it possible to believe that *any* person's self-esteem would be enhanced by the regular strip-searching that women in prison undergo in the name of security? Similarly, with programs designed to help women be more assertive or manage their anger better: if prisoners are not expected to answer back or question rules ... so much for self-assertion! As for anger: is it not hypocritical to offer anger management techniques in a situation where strip-searching and innumerable petty rules are such that they would be likely to try the patience of a saint?

Quality of life and the limits to audit

Ten years ago, the authors of a book entitled *How Organisations Measure Success*, (Carter et al 1992) pointed out that it is usually impossible to measure the impact on society of specific social policies for three main reasons: the problem of multiple objectives; the difficulties of specifying and understanding the relationships between intermediate outputs and output measures; and the inevitable time lag between input and impact, especially in programs "where the benefits only become fully apparent over decades". Attempts to measure the outputs of many in-prison and rehabilitation projects for women fall foul of all three strictures, while paper and other routine organisational outputs tell nothing about either the quality, or the relative importance, of their audited activities in reducing recidivism in the future or of improving the quality of life of project participants and their children.

The limits to the quantification of qualitative measures becomes most apparent when projects are explicitly committed to making and sustaining qualitative changes not amenable to measurement, and when the assessment of (at least some of) the success of those changes called for moral rather than quantitative evaluations – for example, the recent anti-suicide strategy at the Scottish women's prison, Cornton Vale. Many project workers there expressed the view that when they are faced with women on the edge of despair or even death, one prerequisite for the preservation of life and the maintenance of staff morale is official recognition – not only in life and death situations, but also in many of the other emotionally-draining experiences characteristic of work with women in trouble with the law – that qualitative inputs are called-for, the value of which are not amenable to measurement as *performances*. Moreover, time-consuming but life-supporting responses (*inputs*) involving listening, kindness and comfort, together with other *non-programmable* therapies may be *good in themselves*.

2. The quest for penal probity

There is no recipe for penal probity. In talking of the quest for penal probity I am talking about a desirable process: a conversation must go on between everyone involved in the criminal justice system about how prisons can be run according to moral principles. That is, principles which do not seek to justify imprisonment by dishonestly arguing that prisons can do something they can't – for instance, "win the war on drugs", or "reduce recidivism" – but instead aim to make prisons moral communities which limit the damage done to prisoners and the harm done to society. For it is in "penal probity" discourse and conversations about the limits to sovereignty, (and concomitantly, the resultant individual moral responsibilities of those employed by the state) that the possibilities for a more flexible, ameliorative penality are revealed. Though such an ameliorative penality would certainly not change either institutional or societal power relations, it might temporarily (ie, for the duration of their imprisonment at least) halt the damage being done to individual prisoners by the pains that imprisonment inevitably entail. Therefore, as part of the quest for penal probity the paper now outlines three principles which might inform strategies relevant to women's prisons today:

Minimal carceralism

Sentencing

As the opportunities for in-prison reform are so limited, programs of in-prison reform must be accompanied by a real reduction in the numbers of women being imprisoned. It is only with much smaller and more stable prison populations that prison staff have any chance of engaging in the quest for prison probity which may well be the hallmark of healthy penal policy. Maybe the term "healthy prison" is a contradiction in terms but a healthy penal policy, one which limits the damage which prisons do to prisoners, is much more possible of achievement.

Prison regimes

In relation to women's prisons, minimal carceralism refers to the desirability of an ongoing conversation questioning the security value-added of every prison practice that is justified in the name of prison order and security. This is especially important in relation to women. For, given that in many jurisdictions women prisoners have committed less serious crimes, are less of a risk to the public if they escape, and the public have less fear of women, it is doubtful whether constant strip-searching, humiliating drug testing and close surveillance is always as necessary on security grounds as is sometimes implied.

Cultural specificity (according to age, gender, ethnicity, sexual orientation)

The second principle refers to the desirability of constantly analysing prison organisation and process in the light of what we know about cultural differences, which the normal prison organisation does not allow for, and in not allowing for them, causes additional pain to particular groups. The pains of imprisonment which discriminate against women in prisons designed and organised for men, or ethnic minority women in prisons which cater primarily for white people, have nowadays been well-documented; but aging women also find their specific needs neglected in prisons organised primarily for young women (see Carlen 1998: 98); and sometimes lesbian women's talk about partners and home problems outside prison are not taken seriously by prison staff. In prisons geared to damage limitation the quest for penal probity would entail a constant questioning of the provision made for cultural difference of all kinds and the appropriate treatment of prisoners would be decided within a moral calculus of prisoner-need rather than a contractual one of prisoner-desert.

Remoralisation (of staff) rather than responsibilisation

For penal probity to be constructed through constant questioning about the morally appropriate ways to treat prisoners, there has to be a remoralisation of staff and staff discourse. I suggest two steps that might increase the levels of remoralisation – both of them suggested by the anti-suicide strategy developed at Cornton Vale Prison for women, Scotland, after the spate of suicides which occurred there in the mid-1990s.

Democratic ownership of innovation

The central strategy of organisational change employed at Cornton Vale was the democratisation of staff input into the programs to combat prisoner suicide-proneness. But it was not an individualisation of responsibility with its accompanying personalised blame and vulnerability to risk – the strategy favoured by states anxious to distance themselves from failures in crime control and which criminologists have called *responsibilisation* (O'Malley 1992) Instead, it was deemed that a *corporate* and more *democratised* structure of decision-making was required, together with a continuing debate about the probity of the rules and practices governing the life of the whole custodial community.

The new structuring of responsibility indicated that when confronted with a suicidal prisoner, custodial staff would be supported (and not blamed) if they used their discretion with intent to save life. Interestingly, this strategy did not involve a displacement of responsibility from more senior to less senior or even junior staff, but it did extend shares in the ownership and shaping of innovation to the staff who actually had to operationalise it. Thus, unlike the "responsibilisation" strategies whereby the state *distances* itself from responsibility for crime control by making communities responsible for crime prevention (Garland 2001), and prisoners responsible for their own reform and rehabilitation (Hannah-Moffat 2001), the Cornton Vale "corporate community" approach not only implicated state employees at all levels, it also opened up the way for them to sow the seeds of effective change from within (cf, Marks 2000). Therefore, in terms of governance, it might more appropriately be represented as a *remoralisation*, (in one sense, of penal discourse; in another, of penal personnel) than a *responsibilisation* (of either staff or prisoners) strategy.

According to the personnel interviewed, the extension of "problem-ownership" helped secure a very positive and "bottom-up" staff involvement in the regime innovations, as well as lifting morale after the critical and public hammering Cornton Vale had taken at the hands of its critics. However, such a change in prison culture had other consequences. It opened up a space where staff at all levels became more critical – of the sentencing practices of the courts and of the myth that all their prisoners are criminals in need of the strongest security.

Evolutionary development of process and structure

An evolutionary (rather than revolutionary) approach to the development of prisoner-need-responsive processes and structures was an inevitable concomitant of Cornton Vale management's commitment to sharing the shaping of policy innovation with staff at all levels and in all specialisations (eg medical, nursing, social work – as well as prison officers). It entailed an emphasis on process rather than rigid structures and an ongoing commitment to the creation of a caring community rather than a short-term commitment to programs, projects or fashionable penal "gimmicks". Although in line with official Scottish Prison Service Policy, the Governor had to ensure that regimes and programs were "accredited", "audited" and evaluated according to transparent criteria. Programs developed in other countries or for men (such as cognitive skills acquisition) were not parachuted into the prison as prisoner-processing packages with a universal application; instead, they were gender-assessed and adapted to the very specific needs and attributes of *Scotland's* imprisoned *women*.

Conclusion

If courts decide that the only *punishment* for a female offender is that she should be sent to prison, then let them at least be honest enough to say that women go to prison for punishment, to act with a penal probity that calls a women's prison a prison and does not pretend it can be something else: for example a hospital, an addictions rehabilitation centre, an educational establishment, or a women's refuge where the powerless can be "empowered" and the impoverished learn to take responsibility for their own impoverishment. Prison programming cannot provide the magic bullet that will reduce recidivism independently of a change in women's circumstances outside prison. Until governments committed to tackling the causes of women's crime fully accept this and put many more resources into addressing women prisoners' material necessities outside prison, female prison populations will steadily increase as courts continue to succumb to the promises of programming and ex-prisoners continue to succumb to the realities of poverty, homelessness and addictions.

– CHAPTER 14 –

Managing an ageing prison population

Dr John Dawes
Charles Sturt University

This chapter could easily be titled "growing old in prison" or transforming "swords into ploughshares",[1] that is, reconfiguring some prisons into nursing homes and some prisoners into aged "citizens" (see Drummond 1999: 62). For it is the special requirements of aged prisoners – their health care and social and environmental needs – that are likely to result in a major clash of cultures within our prisons: maintaining discipline versus providing health care; managing groups versus focusing on individuals (Norman & Parrish 1999; Willmott 1997; Scott 1997). Statistical trends reveal the developing issues in relation to ageing in the Australian population and provide the context for discussion of aged prisoners and their care.

The Australian population

By 2020 more that 1000 million people aged 60 years and over will be living in the world. Some of us are part of that world already! Over the past 50 years mortality rates in developing countries have declined dramatically, raising life expectancy at birth from around 41 years in the early 1950s to almost 62 years by 1990 and 70 years by 2020 (Resnick 2003; WHO 2003).

What about Australia? Over the past 100 years the proportion of the population aged 65 and over has risen from 4 per cent in 1901 to 12.5 per cent in 2001. It is projected to rise to about 18 per cent in 2020 (ABS 2003). The life expectancy for women in Australia is just over 80 years and for men near 79 years (except for Indigenous Australians whose life expectancy is about 20 years less than other Australians). South Australia has the highest median age in the country (37) and the Northern Territory the lowest at 28 (ABS 2002). The median age is not the average, but that point where half the population is above the age and half below that age. Adelaide has the highest median age of any Australian city (37). So Australia's population is ageing numerically, that is we are getting older and, structurally older people are making up an increasingly larger part of that community (ABS 2004).

---

1   *Isaiah* 2 verse 5.

Ageing and Australian prisoners

While the same dramatic community trends are not currently duplicated within our prisons, similar statistical trends are evident. The majority of prisoners in Australia, as measured by census on the 30 June 2003, are young adult males: 62 per cent are aged between 18 years (and under) and 34 years. The largest group, 4503, or 20.5 per cent, were between 25 and 29 years. At the other end of the life cycle are the elderly, 1970, that is, those prisoners aged 50 years and over. This group comprises 8.9 per cent of the total prisoner population (ABS 2004: 13).

Older prisoners

The most common definition of "elderly inmate" applies to those aged 50 years and older (Howse 2003; Grant 1999) and I will use that definition in the discussion to follow. Normally, a 50-year old person is not considered to be elderly. The ABS classifies those over 65 as older Australians (ABS 1999: 57). However, research has identified an apparent ten-year differential between the overall health of prisoners and that of the general population (Aday 2003: 88; Fazel, Hope, O'Donnell, Piper & Jacoby 2001: 406; Dawes 1997: 193-261). The majority of research studies have attributed this difference to the former lifestyles of prisoners, many of whom used drugs and alcohol to excess, had poor eating habits and a stressful life and commonly suffered economic disadvantage (Aday 2003; Dawes 1997; Kratcoski & Pownall 1989).

In 1987, prisoners older than 50 years of age comprised 4.1 per cent of the total Australian prison population of 12,113 persons. By 1997, this had risen to 7.4 per cent of 19,082 persons and in 2003, 8.9 per cent (1970 persons in a total population of 21,961) (ABS 2004: 13). The average age of prisoners in Australia shows a rise from 30 (30.1) years in 1987 to nearly 32 (31.9) years in 1997 to 33.8 in 2003 (ABS 2004). Since 1987, the number of prisoners in the older than 65 age group has risen from 50 in 1987 to 158 in 1997 to 266 in 2003 (ABS 2004: 13).

Most elderly prisoners (95%) are male, and the proportion of male to female prisoners older than 50 years of age has remained fairly stable over time. Almost 10 per cent (9.7) of prisoners older than 50 years are remanded, a figure that has also remained stable. Elderly sentenced prisoners are also more likely to be held in lower security prisons, which may be beneficial but at the same time present some difficulties in accessing services, as such prisons tend to be located away from major centres. Approximately 46 per cent of prisoners older than 50 are held in minimum-security prisons compared to 37 per cent of prisoners younger than 50. The majority of elderly prisoners are non-Aboriginal, although elderly Indigenous prisoners have increased from 2.9 per cent older than 50 years in 1993 to 4.3 per cent of prisoners older than 50 in 1997, both being disproportionately high numbers since Aboriginal people represent only 1.6 per cent of the total Australian adult population (Grant 1999).

Caring for elderly prisoners

This statistical discussion shows it is likely that all Australian correctional systems will face the challenge of caring for increasing numbers of elderly prisoners in the next few years (Dawes & Grant 2002), especially given the contemporary changes to sentencing regimes in Australia with longer sentences for more serious offences, the popularity of law and order issues in the media and their exploitation by State and Territory politicians, especially close to elections. A number of important policy and practice issues emerge when considering how elderly prisoners should be managed.

Differences among elderly prisoners

While the statistical summary presents elderly prisoners as all of those over 50, it is possible to differentiate among them for the purposes of planning, care and health management. Four groups of elderly prisoners have been identified by Aday (2003: 18) in a comprehensive study of elderly prisoners in the US and each group has different needs and will present different challenges to prison staff and administrators.

First time in prison/elderly new prisoners

People who comprise this group readily spring to mind. Prior to imprisonment such prisoners are often well known, notorious because of their offences (child sexual assault, murder, fraud). They usually find making the transition to prison life extremely difficult and can be at risk of serious self-harm or suicide in prison. Imprisonment can represent a dramatic change of status for members of this group and a final step in a series of humiliating experiences. Their offences may make them vulnerable to bullying, harassment or serious violence and even death. They may present with serious health issues including psychiatric morbidity (Aday 2003; Howse 2003; Fazel, Hope, O'Donnell & Jacoby, R. 2001; Specter 1994; McCarthy 1983).

Career or "chronic" offenders

This group of prisoners consists of those who return to prison regularly because of re-offending. They are often called recidivists. While some may "burn out", cease offending and re-establish themselves in the community, many will continue coming into prison until they become elderly.

"Lifers" who have grown old in prison

This group consists of those who increasingly find themselves serving natural life sentences without any real prospect of release. Prison is their home and, as they grow old, they will present many challenges to the authorities because of institutionalisation, loss of social skills, and dependency, as well as other more significant signs of ageing, such as chronic health issues, loss of mobility, senility, dementia, terminal illness and needing assistance with the activities of daily living (see Dawes 2002a). Family contact usually becomes less frequent or ceases with each passing year and, if release is considered, loss of family, lack of sponsors and the probable "cultural shock" of the world outside prison presents additional challenges to those involved in assisting such prisoners towards release.

Prisoners given shorter sentences later in life

This group, sometimes including some very high profile prisoners, can also present with serious health problems that require acute and on-going care.

So while chronological age (50 and over) provides the point at which we consider prisoners to be elderly, it may not always be the best indicator of ageing and health difficulties (Dawes 1997, 2002). This means that correctional authorities need to avoid the pitfall of ageism, which is "discrimination" against older people (Thompson 2002: 81) and be responsive to individual differences. Elderly prisoners "are not a homogeneous group" (Neeley, Addison & Craig-Moreland 1997).

Ageism might present itself in a prison setting if it was suggested that all prisoners 60 years and older should "retire" from active work, so that younger prisoners could take their place in the prison industries. If this view was rigorously applied no matter how fit, competent and committed to work such prisoners are, it would present as ageism. But it is also legitimate to consider the issue of "retirement" – of suggesting to a prisoner he or she does not have to work any more, but can pursue leisure and hobby activities. So to avoid "infantilisation", an aspect of ageism, older prisoners need to participate in the decision-making about their lives in prison. More will be said about this later when discussing health care.

Regimes

Prison regimes need to be constructed which take account of the total needs of elderly prisoners. Elderly prisoners are known to desire quiet living spaces with appropriate access to services, meals, recreation and work, with safety in all of these being a specific concern (Smyer, Gragert & La Mere 1997: 10).

The recognised policy/management issue here is whether "mainstreaming" or separating the elderly population from younger prisoners is appropriate (Aday 2003: 144 ff; Howse 2003: 30; Grant 1999: 5). Sometimes correctional administrators argue that mainstreaming the elderly approximates to the real world (normalisation). Additionally, it is argued that having elderly prisoners in the cell block or living unit may have a calming effect on other prisoners. However, while the elderly may not be segregated in the community, the reality for most of us is that we interact mainly with people of similar age, or at least in a similar point in the life cycle as ourselves. Victim surveys consistently demonstrate that older people are more fearful of being victims of crime than is supported by actual rates of victimisation (Grant, David & Cook 2002: 282; Smyer et al 1977: 10). This view also seems to apply to elderly prisoners. They are fearful of assault. Such prisoners see themselves as different to the newer, younger prisoners and can view them as "other". Just as some older people may not have the economic resources to fully participate in the community even if they wished to and were physically able so some older prisoners may have the personal and social skills to participate in the wider prison community, but choose not to for various reasons. It is difficult to be prescriptive therefore about mainstreaming or creating separate facilities for elderly prisoners, but the weight of evidence appears to support separate facilities where these are requested (Howse 2003: 30; Aday 2003: 144ff; Aday 1994: 52).

Prisoners' housing

Most prisons are designed for young energetic people. However, when elderly prisoners begin to show signs of ageing, re-configuring prisons to provide for their needs is desirable. Risk may be involved negotiating stairs and for some prisoners this may become physically impossible (Morton & Anderson 1982: 15; Kelsey 1986: 58; Aday 2003: 144). It may be desirable to house elderly prisoners on ground floors. Elderly prisoners with acute or chronic conditions, as well as the frail aged, may require ready access to the prison infirmary, as well as external specialist health care services.

The "way a facility treats its dead sends a powerful message to the survivors" (Bonifazi 1998: 52). Elderly prisoners will observe how their peers are cared for. Eventually hospice programs will be needed, either delivered to prisoners throughout the prison system (decentralised care) or within internal specialised units (see Dawes 2002a). Humane management of dying prisoners includes appropriate training in supporting and caring for dying prisoners for medical and nursing staff as well as correctional personnel. Prisoners who choose to become hospice volunteers will also need this (Dawes & Dawes 2004, forthcoming).

Health care

Australians are usually concerned about their health system and it often becomes an election issue. The ageing of the Australian population will place the health system under greater pressure in the future. Waiting times for some procedures in public hospitals can be many months and even years. In this environment of increasing pressure and demand on the health care system, the priority given to aged prisoners in need of expensive but very necessary interventions becomes problematic. While prisoners in Australia are not "civilly dead" and enjoy some form of limited citizenship (Brown 2002: 322), there is no absolute right for prisoners to obtain a publicly funded standard of health care. Some people may even see prisoners as "less deserving" – a view that could gain wider support in an environment of scarce health care resources. Research in some countries has pointed to neglect (Howse 2003). However, there is in Australia a common law tradition that makes it quite clear that the correctional and medical authorities have a duty of care to prisoners (Dawes 2002b: 125). There are also powerful "watchdogs", such as the Ombudsman, that can assist prisoners and correctional agencies in obtaining a decent level of service. Given the present reality in Australia's public health system of longer waiting lists, rationing of health care, and managed care for ordinary citizens, correctional agencies may struggle in the competition for resources to be able to provide adequate health care to prisoners. Many of the more expensive diagnostic and treatment methodologies simply cannot be provided within prisons. Prisoners need to attend clinics and hospitals in the community and this is dependent on the correctional agency being able to provide the escorting staff needed to ensure the prisoner's appointment is kept. It is also here that the clash between individual health care plans for prisoners and the budgetary constraints on correctional agencies may be manifest.

Imprisonment and release

One option for humane management of elderly prisoners is their early release. The arguments for and against early release are complex and are summarised in Howse (2003: 26) and Dawes (2002a: 195-197). Release triggered by failing health or because the prison system is unable to provide appropriate programs for elderly prisoners requires an act of "forgiveness" on the part of the community. Such acts of forgiveness may be more difficult to achieve in the current climate, including the appropriate need for governments to consult widely with victims' groups, specific victims and others who may be involved with the prisoner and plans for his or her release. Some community facilities have criteria that exclude persons with mental illness, no matter how well controlled. If the prisoner to be released is being transferred from prison to a nursing home, questions arise as to how many people need to know of the prisoner's status and criminal history. Placement of long-sentenced prisoners with serious criminal convictions in a community nursing home may cause anxiety for other residents and their families as well as for the staff. Over extended hospice and palliative care programs may resist having a prisoner to deal with among other dying people. Successful transfers take considerable skill and diplomacy to negotiate. The experience in the US shows that early release of such prisoners is resisted, even in high imprisoning States and States dealing with budgetary distress (Anderson 1994; Butterfield 2003).

Consent to medical and dental treatment

The practice issue for correctional personnel is what to do when a prisoner is not competent to make decisions about appropriate health care and to give informed or effective consent to any medical procedure that might be suggested by medical staff. In these situations a surrogate decision-maker may be needed (Dawes 2002b: 125). Competency is diminished usually as a result of "mental incapacity". The term "mental incapacity" is a legal concept, but in practice means any condition that prevents or impedes appropriate decision making by the person needing medical assistance. Mental incapacity can arise as a result of a stroke, senility, mental illness or, more commonly, amongst the aged because of dementia. All Australian States and Territories provide for a *responsible person* (usually a nominated relative) or an appointed guardian to make such decisions (see, for example, *Guardianship and Administration Act* 1993 (SA) and the *Guardianship and Administration Act* 1990 (WA)).[2] In the past departmental officials had the power to authorise medical treatment, but appropriately this now no longer applies. Such arrangements fail to adequately deal with the conflict of interest between the custodial authorities and the best interests and rights of the individual prisoner. State and Territory laws prohibit professional persons in a professional relationship with the person needing treatment or care from making such decisions (except medical staff in an emergency). Where the prisoner is unable to nominate a relative or another person to make such decisions an independent public official (Public Advocate or Public Guardian) can be appointed (see Dawes 2002a).

Release procedures for elderly prisoners

Releasing elderly prisoners at the end of their sentence may need careful attention to enable them to adapt to the particular challenges facing them in the midst of with the increasing demands on aged care services. There is a need to develop more comprehensive programs to assist long-term prisoners to integrate into the community, recognising that releasing elderly prisoners is a time consuming and resource intensive process (if it is done compassionately). A better understanding of the issues involved in the release of elderly long-term prisoners, could be enhanced by research – both records-based and by interviewing those returned to the community – and describing and analysing their experiences.

---

2   Section 5 of the *Guardianship and Administration Act* 1993 of South Australia is as follows:

    5. Where a guardian appointed under this Act, an administrator, the Public Advocate, the Board or any court or other person, body or authority makes any decision or order in relation to a person or a person's estate pursuant to this Act or pursuant to the powers conferred by or under this Act –

    (a) consideration (and this will be the paramount consideration) must be given to what would, in the opinion of the decision-maker, be the wishes of the person in the matter if he or she were not mentally incapacitated, but only so far as there is reasonably ascertainable evidence on which to base such an opinion;

    (b) the present wishes of the person should, unless it is not possible or reasonably practicable to do so, be sought in respect of the matter and consideration must be given to those wishes;

    (c) consideration must, in the case of the making or affirming of a guardianship order, be given to the adequacy of the existing informal arrangements for the care of the person or the management of his or her financial affairs and to the desirability of not disturbing those arrangements; and

    (d) the decision or order made must be the one that is the least restrictive of the person's rights and personal autonomy as is consistent with his or her proper care and protection.

    This decision-making framework (s 5) is often described as "substituted judgement" and requires that the decision-maker "stand in the shoes" of the person for whom the decision is being made. It contrasts with the common law framework of "best interests".

Conclusion

This chapter has provided a brief introduction to the policy and practice challenges of caring for elderly prisoners. While Australia is not facing proportionately the same numbers of elderly prisoners as the US or UK, the numbers of elderly prisoners in all Australian jurisdictions are trending upwards. Administrators should begin now to plan for the provision of adequate care, programs and residential accommodation for these people. In doing so the traditional custody-based approach to prison management may face some challenges. For example, the provision of decent health care for aged prisoners will require specialised personnel whose professional values may be in conflict with those of traditional prison staff (AMA, 1998), a dynamic already witnessed in Immigration Detention Centres.

– CHAPTER 15 –

Prisoner health

Michael Levy, Director, Centre for Health Research in Criminal Justice, Justice Health NSW
Tony Butler, Research Manager, Centre for Health Research in Criminal Justice, Justice Health NSW
Tony Falconer, Consultant, Health & Medical, Queensland Corrections

Any description of the health of prisoners needs to commence with the reiteration of the principle that a when a court of law sentences someone to imprisonment, "deprivation of liberty" should be the only punishment. Regrettably, in Australia at the turn of a new century, too many citizens are incarcerated because of the consequences of illness.

In reality the "punishment" is only the beginning of a complex and punitive criminal justice system – prisoners, their families and their partners experience a number of "losses". There are levels of punishment – loss of privacy and loss of intimacy are just two that directly impact on the health of Australian prisoners. Regrettably, we confine our prisoners in conditions of physical squalor and overcrowding with the consequent health risks. Australian prisoners lose their Medicare entitlement. While this merely shifts the responsibility of primary health care onto the States and Territories, it significantly reduces the option of "second opinions" that the prisoner may request (as this now needs to be paid for by the prisoner or their family). These health risks and consequent health outcomes are readily transferred from the prison environment back to the outside community.

Prison health services in Australia

There is an absence of uniform standards for the provision of health services to Australian prisoners. The federal Minister of Justice and Customs has a reporting role to Parliament on the state of the nation's prisons. However, neither that Ministry, nor the Commonwealth Ministry of Health and Ageing have identified a mechanism for monitoring State and Territory performance in custodial or prisoner health matters.

This leaves the States and Territories to develop systems in isolation from each other. Health services to prisoners in NSW are provided by the health department (through the Justice Health), in Queensland and Western Australia the custodial authority funds health services, in South Australia, the

Australian Capital Territory and Tasmania there are contractual arrangements between the health department and a health service provider, while in the Northern Territory and Victoria, health services are privatised. The Commonwealth does have responsibility for Immigration Detention Centres, but here too the services have been contracted out, so the federal government maintains its distance. Paradoxically, the area of Commonwealth interest for prisoner health remains the fate of Australians incarcerated in overseas prisons, where consular responsibility cannot be delegated. However, prisoner health is not an area of demonstrated concern.

The prison environment in Australia – implications for health

Because of the eight different jurisdictions operating custodial facilities there is no single characteristic of the Australian custodial system. Prisons range from less than 50 beds to over 1000; some have been operating continuously since the 19th century, some have been built recently, but have not yet been commissioned. All Australian facilities are single gender (or where there are males and females in close proximity, always segregated). All Australian jurisdictions separate adult from juvenile detainees in full-time custody. However, while in police custody, males and females, young and old might be held in the same facility for a number of days.

Prisoners are moved frequently between prison and court, between prisons themselves, and between the community and prison. This makes continuity of health services, and contact with family members difficult. In June 2003, there were 123 custodial institutions in Australia. With an official capacity of 22,000, the occupancy rate for Australian prisons was 106 per cent! Hardly conducive to privacy, intimacy and respect of the individual's rights, but conducive to the transmission of airborne, droplet spread and other infections.

Aboriginal health – the health priority

The proportion of prisoners who were Aboriginal and/or Torres Strait Islander rose from 14 per cent in 1992 to 20 per cent in 2002. In 1991 the Royal Commission into Aboriginal Deaths in Custody (RCIADIC) handed down its recommendations. RCIADIC made 29 recommendations specifically directed to the principle of imprisonment as a last resort. Since the handing down of the report, however, the level of over-representation of Aboriginal and Torres Strait Islander people in prison has increased unabated, from year to year.

Aboriginal and Torres Strait Islander citizens make up less than 2 per cent of the Australian population. Yet 20 per cent of the Australian prisoner population are identified as Aboriginal and/or Torres Strait Islander. The Australian Bureau of Statistics reported this as an incarceration rate of 1,806 prisoners per 100,000 adult Indigenous population – 16 times higher than for non-Indigenous Australians. This is the highest incarceration rate for Indigenous citizens of all Organisation of Economic Co-operation and Development

(OECD)[1] countries. The highest Indigenous incarceration rate is in Western Australia (2,414 per 100,000 adult Indigenous population); however, there has been a 20 per cent reduction in the Indigenous incarceration rate in that State between 2001 and 2002. Indigenous juveniles account for 42 per cent of juvenile detainees in Australia (Human Rights and Equal Opportunity Commission, 2002).

What is the socio-economic background of Australian prisoners?

The social and physical environment of prison has a great effect on health behaviours. Given that a person's perceived status in the world is dependent on education, income, employment and life satisfaction, it is clear that imprisonment strips each component away. Poor prior education, low income, meagre employment and poor self-esteem typify the prisoner entering the prison gate; and ever more so at the point of exit. Sexual abuse, physical maltreatment, emotional maltreatment, abandonment, and suicide attempts by significant others are common life experiences of prisoners (Blaauw et al, 2003). When asked about previous sexual abuse, 69 per cent of female inmates and 29 per cent of male inmates reported that they been victims at least once, with 35 per cent of female and 10 per cent of males being involved in two or more such incidents (Butler and Milner 2003).

Equity is a function of fairness and social justice (not to be confused with criminal justice) and is largely beyond an individual prisoner's control. Consider issues such as the over-representation of Aboriginals and Torres Strait Islanders, perpetual unemployment and entrenched social dislocation of Australian prisoners – and one readily appreciates the fatalism common around issues of incarceration and health – sexuality being a prominent example.

Prison is an environment of power relationships, low interpersonal trust, values touched by punishment and corruption, and deeply moralistic. For example, condoms are available in prisons in New South Wales, Western Australia, the Australian Capital Territory, and Tasmania; they should be available to inmates in South Australia (but this has been effectively blocked by the prison officers union) and Queensland (where they have been withdrawn for financial reasons). Prisoners in those States have no control over the level of protection afforded them *by the Crown* should they have successfully negotiated consensual penetrative sex.

The 1996 NSW Inmate Health Survey reported that a higher proportion of male prisoners who were survivors of childhood sexual abuse reported involvement in both consensual and non-consensual sexual activity in prison,

---

1   Australia, Austria, Belgium, Canada, Czech Republic, Denmark, Finland, Germany, Greece, Hungary, Iceland, Ireland, Italy, Japan, Republic of Korea, Luxembourg, Mexico, Netherlands, New Zealand, Norway, Poland, Portugal, Slovak Republic, Spain, Sweden, Switzerland, Turkey, UK and USA.

compared to those with no such history. No comparable conclusions could be drawn for females, as there were too few participants (Butler, 1997).

The 2001 New South Wales Inmate Health Survey reported on a broader range of sexual health issues, including sexual identity, gender of sexual partners, age of first intercourse, the number of life-time sexual partners and the number of sexual partners in the previous 12 months. Ninety-five per cent of men and 63 per cent of females self-identified as heterosexual. Four percent of male respondents, and 30 per cent of females, identified as bisexual, with the remainder identifying as homosexual.

The Inmate Health Survey was conducted in a prison system with virtually no restrictions on access to condoms (in the male system) and dental dams (in the female system). Yet only 12 per cent of male respondents and 18 per cent of female respondents stated that they had tried to obtain either condoms or dental dams. The researchers noted the impact of sexual assault in prison – both male and female. Protection scams among prisoners do include physical abuse, coercion and sexual favours as "currency".

Little is known about sexual activity in Australian prisons. One published report from NSW stated that 25 per cent of young offenders could expect to be raped in prison. In that study, the key causes of sexual assault in prison were stated as: (1) perpetrators seeking power through sexual assault: (2) the acquiescence of prison authorities; (3) overcrowding; and (4) the prior sexual experiences of perpetrators (Heilpern, 1998). Young prisoners, particularly those serving their first custodial sentence, are also at higher risk of sexual assault. The risks also increase in maximum-security facilities. The practice of remanding all offenders in maximum-security facilities exposes young offenders to more experienced criminals who have committed more serious offences, making remand centres particularly risky.

It is worth noting that there is a spectrum of sexual activity within correctional facilities. As in the general community, a proportion of prisoners will be homosexual and may choose to participate in consensual homosexual activity while in custody. Prisoners who identify as heterosexual in the community may choose to do the same. Other prisoners may participate in sexual activity, despite preferring not to, either as a form of protection or as currency. At the end of the spectrum is the risk of sexual assault within custodial settings.

There are other special features about sexual assault in the prison setting. Commonly, there is considerable reluctance to report sexual assault as this breaks the prison code and necessitates the victim going on protection, which is often viewed as worse than keeping silent. Partly because of this, victims can be the subject of repeated assault and may go to extreme measures, such as self-harm, to gain protection.

The different Australian jurisdictions have developed different models of screening and treatment for sexually-transmitted infections. Compulsory testing for HIV was introduced in New South Wales in 1991 following the malicious stabbing of a prison officer with a syringe filled with HIV-positive blood. It was replaced by voluntary testing in 1995. Compulsory testing for HIV is practised in the Northern Territory and Queensland. All jurisdictions would claim that testing, even if compulsory, is conducted with informed consent – such are the paradoxes of providing health care in the prison environment. All testing is carried out with pre- and post-test counselling. Screening for other sexually-transmitted and blood-borne viruses is conducted to a varying degree in the different jurisdictions. Aboriginal inmates can benefit from the Commonwealth-funded PCR screening program for *Chlamydia trachomatis*.

Access to health services

All prisoners have access to primary health services while in prison. Given the complex health problems of the prisoner population, access to services while in the outside community is often poor. It is not unusual for a new prisoner to have a backlog of dental health, mental health, drug and alcohol problems – and not unusually, sexual health problems. A measure of this deficit is that while over 40 per cent of NSW prisoners are infected with the hepatitis C virus, one-third of these people receive their first hepatitis C test while in prison. A recent report on hepatitis B immunisation among injecting drug users reported that the strongest predictor for immunisation was having been in prison (Day, 2003).

So how ill are Australia's prisoners?

The best assessment of the health of the prisoner population is, on a world scale, the New South Wales Inmate Health Survey – conducted in 1996 and repeated in 2001 (the 2001 survey was replicated with female inmates in Queensland). The results are truly amazing:

- 64 per cent of women and 40 per cent of men had been infected with hepatitis C (compared with approximately 2 per cent in the general community);
- 39 per cent of women, and 45 per cent of men had sustained a head injury so serious that there had been a loss of consciousness (no similar result is known for the general community);
- 95 per cent of women and 78 per cent of men have at least one chronic health condition – and most have more than one;
- 83 per cent of women and 78 per cent of men smoke tobacco – levels not experienced in the general community for over 40 years;
- 60 per cent of women and 37 per cent of men had been sexually abused before they had reached the age of 16 years of age.

Can prisons better reflect society?
Social norms ... better health

The issue of sexuality and sexual licence is rarely discussed in the Australian prison context. Yet consider the issue of conjugal visits for prisoners in Australia. Conjugal visits are sanctioned to a limited extent in some Victorian

(Loddon, Bendigo, Yarrawonga) and one Tasmanian (Hayes) prison. This is in contrast to some western European (Spain, Portugal, and Switzerland), Middle Eastern (Iran), central/South American (Peru) and Asia (Thailand) prison systems, where conjugal visits are arranged, regardless of the security classification of the prison inmate.

In no correctional centre in Australia can male and female inmates meet. However, in some Spanish prisons, male and female inmates intermingle. While residential areas are segregated, inmates can disclose a relationship to the Governor, and qualify for "intimate visits", with prior partners or with other inmates. These arrangements are available to inmates at each stage of incarceration – remand and sentenced, maximum to mini-mum security. Irrespective of the stage of sentencing and classification status, inmates are eligible for three intimate visits from family or friends, per month. A fourth visit can be "earned". Homosexual relationships are tole-rated, as are relationships that have been established within the prison. Prostitutes are not allowed to visit – although this is an arrangement tolerated in some South American jurisdictions. Doesn't this just reflect community standards?

Continuity of health care

Incarceration, apart from being "deprivation of liberty", is a major dislocation from the community – even if previous connections are judged dysfunctional. Health care provision in the community, and in prison, connects with great difficulty. Prisoners may have multiple health care providers in the community – some or none are the advisors on past or current health problems; some of these treatments may be complied with, others not; some may be in a functional health care provider/client relationship, others not. While this dynamic is simplified while in prison, with a single health care provider, and the capacity to supervise all treatments if necessary, the prospect of release once again brings with it the possibility of therapeutic chaos and poor compliance. No health care provider – in prison or outside – has yet overcome these seemingly insurmountable problems. The result of these failures is unnecessary reincarceration for the results of poor treatment compliance, and in the extreme, the high rate of immediate post-release mortality of drug-dependent former prisoners.

The impact of incarceration on inmates and on partners and children – the health of those left in the community

> [T]he prison indirectly produces delinquents by throwing the inmate's family into destitution. (Foucault 1977)

Lord Woolf in his report following the 1991 Stangeways (Manchester, United Kingdom) prison riots identified that domestic and employment prospects diminished drastically through the act of incarceration. A 2001 NSW report made the following observation – 62 per cent of females and 70 per cent males reported being in a stable relationship before coming to prison. Of these, only 69 per cent of females and 65 per cent of males expected to resume that relationship post-release. (Butler and Milner, 2003)

Partners face adversities such as the stress of partner loss, witnessing the arrest and accompanying violence, the rapid change from dependence to the "absence of dependable partner", multiple contacts with the criminal justice system, separation, coercive pressures to acquit the partners debt (in and out of prison), stigma and the impending release of a partner. Australian custodial authorities have demonstrated their incapacity to support equity initiatives – judging by the response of Australian authorities, sexuality is seen either as a threat to security, good order and management, or its deprivation as a suitable and just punishment.

Conclusion

Until the basic principles of incarceration are adhered to, Australian society will perpetuate inequity – beyond health. To achieve equity for prisoners, fewer citizens should be consigned to punitive incarceration. Those who are should reside in an environment that promotes principles of health, justice, fairness, safety, and respect. Three guiding principles could enhance the status of Australian prisoners, and their families.

First, once deprived of liberty, the detainee should be offered all the benefits and responsibilities of a citizen – accordingly, sexuality should be acknowledged as a fundamental quality of human life, which is important for health, happiness, individual development and preservation of the human race. Second, the correctional environment should respect the individuals' right to privacy and intimacy as a right, not a benefit. Finally, violence, including sexual violence, must not be tolerated – neither in the community, nor in prison.

The accepted principles of harm minimisation should guide policy development and application within Australia's prisons. Good sense should not be confused with leniency. Conjugal visiting rights for all Australian prisoners, and their partners, makes good sense. All prisoners, irrespective of the stage of sentencing and the crime of which they are accused of should have contact with partners – irrespective of disclosed sexuality. Operational considerations will modify this for some prisoners, but a sympathetic approach would preserve the principle of intimacy. Health differentials between prisoners and the outside community, deleteriously affect the general health of the community. Addressing health inequalities among prisoners will provide benefits to both prisoners and the Australian community.

CHAPTER 16

Managing mentally ill offenders released from jail – the US experience

Professor Dale K Sechrest, University of California, US
Associate Professor Don A Josi, Armstrong Atlantic State University, US[1]

Since the passing of legislation by the federal Congress in 1963 (*Mental Retardation Facilities and Community Mental Health Centers Act*) and by the California State government in the late 1950s and 60s, California's philosophy for dealing with the mentally ill[2] made a dramatic shift. The mental health deinstitutionalisation movement had begun. The old policy was to place those who were mentally ill into facilities called Institutes for Mental Disease (IMD). The combined ideals of civil rights groups, advanced psychiatry, and a conservative legislature felt they had a solution that would appease all sides. It was proposed that inmates[3] could be released from their confines in state hospitals and given greater personal freedom, along with appropriate medication.

It was thought that this change would produce an overall cost benefit for the California taxpayer, however, letting these patients out into the streets merely led to the creation of a new, large segment of the State population: the homeless mentally ill. Nationally, the number of people in mental institutions fell from a peak of 558,992 in 1955 to 275,995 in 1972, a decline of about 50 per cent (Brown 1973), and ultimately to about 72,000 in 1994 (Lurigio 2000; Center for Mental Health Services 1994). Probably the most drastic movement toward the deinstitutionalisation of mentally ill patients occurred in California during the governorship of Ronald Reagan (1966-74) when it was planned to phase out State mental hospitals. At that time, the main reason for treating the mentally ill in the community was motivated by fiscal considerations, and not by treatment considerations. Concern was for reducing the cost of managing the mentally ill population in institutions (Scull 1977).

This policy led to the closure of large numbers of mental institutions. The new medications touted by psychiatry were clearly an improvement in

---

1   This research was funded by the California Board of Corrections through a grant by the California Legislature. Jerry Dowdall, David Shichor, David Sechrest, and Shari Darling provided assistance in preparing this paper.

2   For the purpose of this paper and unless otherwise noted, the term mentally ill or mental illness includes the mentally ill substance abuser.

3   The terms clients, patients, and consumers refer to a participant who is released into the community while the term inmate refers to people who are still incarcerated.

treatment, but not to the extent as initially hoped. The initially proposed community programs were never funded. For many, the newfound civil liberties merely translated into becoming part of the new segment of California society – the homeless mentally ill, as many mentally ill took to the streets and began lives of crime and substance abuse.

Of an estimated 2.2 million Americans who went untreated for severe mental illness in 1997, close to 300,000 are homeless or in prison (Jacobs, 1998). Many, if not most, of these released individuals became frequent residents of local detention facilities and State prisons. These mentally ill offenders became a problem for the criminal justice system, leaving State prisons with the task of running psychiatric inpatient facilities. It is recognised today, as it has been since the early 1800s, that keeping mentally ill offenders in jail presents many problems. The majority of their crimes are "nuisance" offences, and they are more likely than other populations to recidivate upon release due to their greater need for support and aftercare. More than 75 per cent of mentally ill inmates incarcerated in 1998 had at least one prior conviction resulting in prison, jail, or probation (Ditton 1999).

According to the US Department of Justice report in 1999, approximately 16 per cent of inmates in jails and State prisons (267,157), 7 per cent of federal prisoners, 16 per cent of all local jail offenders, and 16 per cent of all probationers (Ditton 1999) were mentally impaired. These populations include the case of an inmate with schizophrenia in the Denver County Jail, who was incarcerated for the 100th time, charged with creating a nuisance in the community. In Memphis, Tennessee, a mentally ill woman was incarcerated for the 258th time on an assault charge. In 1998, in Orange County California, there were 300 mentally ill offenders who were rearrested three times and 119 were rearrested four times (Torrey 1999). Moreover, disciplinary problems are more common among mentally ill inmates. According to Gallemore (2000), on average, 24 per cent of inmates classified as mentally ill were charged with breaking jail rules compared with 16 per cent of the general population. Gallemore (2000) also found that only 41 per cent of mentally ill inmates in local jails report receiving some sort of treatment (counselling, medication, etc.). It is clear that in many cases of mentally ill or disturbed offenders, jails are only serving as a "revolving door" institution.

Some estimates of the mentally ill in jails and prisons are higher than those cited by Ditton (1999). McConville (1995) found that 37 per cent of men and 56 per cent of women serving more than six months in England were "suffering from diagnosable mental disorders" (McConville 1995). Based on our study, much depends upon the particular definition of mental illness or impairment used and the techniques used for evaluating the individual. One Federal Bureau of Prisons study used the definition of mental illness as "self-report data indicating either a mental condition or an overnight stay in a mental hospital" (Beck & Maruschak 2001).

Fazel and Danesh (2002) looked at the prevalence of serious mental disorders in their summary of patient surveys for 12 Western counties, and found 4 per cent of their sample diagnosed with psychotic disorders, 10 per cent with major depression, and 47 per cent with antisocial personality disorders.

Many mentally ill individuals demonstrate behavior patterns that are often referred to as "social maladjustment", as a general, but not very well defined, concept (Stark, 1975). One of the most important findings about mental illness is that it falls disproportionately upon the poorer segments of society. This may be an artifact of the reality that public agencies, which usually keep the statistics, serve mainly poor people, while middle- and upper-class individuals having similar mental problems can find treatment in private facilities.

Mental illness might be related to physiological, genetic, psychological, and social sources. Often several etiological factors may interact in influencing mental disorders. Generally, mental illness, and specifically schizophrenia, may very well be the product of a combination of a genetic predisposition and environmental experiences. Stressful events may rekindle or trigger an outbreak in an individual who is biologically predisposed (Goode 1994).

Public mental hospitals were not necessarily model institutions. Several social scientists have shown the underside of these institutions in their research (eg, Goffman, 1961). These studies contributed to the trend in the 1950s to treat the mentally ill in the community. Many psychiatrists, psychologists, and other mental health experts believed that deinstitutionalisation of mental patients is generally a good idea, but the implementation of this policy was flawed. Because of the lack of alternative treatment programs to deal with the mentally ill patients who were released from the closed institutions large numbers of them became homeless, creating a burden on and a public nuisance for communities.

The mentally ill in the criminal justice system

As deinstitutionalisation[4] increasingly became public policy, the number of patients in mental health institutions started to decline, and they began to appear in local detention facilities in large numbers. As Lurigio (2001) carefully documents, the process of criminalising the mentally ill began in the US more than 25 years ago. Persons with schizophrenia, bipolar disorder or major depression were referred to as persons with serious mental illnesses, or PSMIs, in the correctional system. They were seen as unable to function due to the chronicity of their illnesses. Many have co-occurring substance abuse and dependence disorders.

Jails and prisons do not provide the necessary treatment essential for the proper management of a mental illness. In addition to needing psychiatric and psychological care, this population is likely to abuse alcohol and/or illicit drugs. This condition is referred to in professional literature as a co-occurring disorder, which includes substance abuse and mental health disorders (Hills 2000). Research by the Bureau of Justice Statistics estimates that 38 per cent of mentally ill jail inmates exhibit a history of alcohol dependence as measured through the CAGE[5] diagnostic instrument (Ditton 1999). Statistics from the US Department of

---

4   Not sentenced to State prison, State mental hospital, or have a legal hold requesting transfer to another county.

5   CAGE is an acronym for four questions used by the diagnostic instrument to assess alcohol dependence or abuse.

Justice indicate that approximately 59 per cent of mentally ill offenders either used illicit drugs within 30 days of their current crime or were under the influence at the time of their most recent arrest (Ditton 1999).

According to the GAINS Center (Peters & Bartoi 1997), between 25 per cent and 50 per cent of all people with mental health disorders also have a substance abuse disorder. Abram and Teplin (1991) report both male and female detainees with severe mental disorders have a 72 per cent rate of co-occurring substance abuse disorders. In criminal justice populations, the rates are significantly higher than in the general population for both mental health disorders (four times higher) and alcohol/drug disorders (four to seven times higher).

Additionally, offenders with a mental illness and a substance abuse disorder experience a high rate of recidivism. Research conducted by the Federal Bureau of Prisons found that recidivism rates are higher among individuals who have a pre-prison history of drug or alcohol abuse (Harer 1994). These individuals then become part of a revolving door syndrome because they do not receive the proper services and support necessary to allow them to integrate successfully back into the community. The program described in this paper sought to address these needs in San Bernardino County. While the treatment of these individuals has not been realised as originally conceived, the large numbers of mentally ill persons who are held in county jails *should* be treated in the community, as envisioned.

The SPAN program

To address the issues related to serving the incarcerated mentally ill, homeless mentally ill, and dually-diagnosed mentally ill/substance abusers, in 1998 California Governor Pete Wilson signed a Bill establishing the Mentally Ill Offender Crime Reduction Grant Programs (MIOCRG). Administered through the Board of Corrections, the program was funded for the implementation and evaluation of locally developed demonstration projects designed to reduce crime, jail crowding and criminal justice costs associated with mentally ill offenders.

San Bernardino County[6] received funding to develop a local demonstration project that addressed the problems associated with mentally ill offenders. A local task force determined that aftercare planning was inconsistent; inmates were not released during times when services were available in the community; prescription medications were interrupted at the time of release; families lacked knowledge of community resources and ways of effectively supporting their family members to avoid re-incarceration; and clients were not linked to community treatment resources at the time of release.

---

6   Two "waves" of Mentally Ill Offender Crime Reduction Grants were funded across the State; this paper refers to the first study in San Bernardino County.

Program setting and philosophy

The SPAN clinic was housed next to the main county jail, holding over 3,000 inmates. The mental health staff was comprised of a program manager, a clinic supervisor, three clinicians, a public health nurse, an alcohol and drug counselor, a social worker, two mental health specialists, and two support staff. The Sheriff provided several administrative, management, and liaison staff. Mental health staff worked closely with the research staff from California State University at San Bernardino. The philosophy of the program was that mentally ill and dually-diagnosed inmates had been re-incarcerated due to a lack of mental health and community support. A key assumption was that at the time of release, the mentally ill needed assistance to successfully transition back into the community. The hypothesis was that with short-term case management services and linkage to community resources, the mentally ill would avoid re-incarceration and hence reduce detention and related justice system costs.

Program goals and objectives

The primary goal of the program was to provide mental health services in order to reduce additional incarceration and/or recidivism of mentally ill and dually-diagnosed inmates. Recidivism included reducing arrests, jail bed days, inpatient hospitalisations, court appearances, and mental health services provided while in custody.

Description of study population

The study employed an experimental and control group design in order to make comparisons for treated and non-treated clients and pre- and post-program intervention, while implementing random selection procedures. The target population[7] consisted of adult mentally ill and dually-diagnosed offenders. At the onset of the program, services were intended to assist the lower-functioning chronically and persistently mentally ill (clients who carry schizophrenia and major mood disorder diagnoses). Later, however, the program was expanded to include the dually diagnosed (mentally ill/substance abuser).

Findings

The major hypothesis was that with short-term case management services and linkage to community resources, the mentally ill would avoid re-incarceration and hence reduce detention and related justice system costs. Another hypothesis was that key variables would show statistically significant differences between the Enhanced Treatment group members who receive the continuum of services and members of the control group.

The following conclusions and findings of the SPAN program were drawn from input from research and clinical staff, the process evaluation and a review of this document.

---

7 Inmates were pre-selected and assigned to a group by a computer generated random number based on the inmate's date of birth.

The basic hypothesis that jail recidivism would be reduced as a result of clinical services was not supported. Seventy per cent of clients never used any mental health services regardless of what experimental group the clients were assigned. The explanation for this appears to be that instead of serving the persistently mentally ill, the program served substance abusers that were highly unwilling to change their drug related life styles. Eighty-eight per cent were substance abusers as defined by their own self-reports and crimes.

For the majority of clients, short-term case management augmented by additional DBH services had no remarkable impact on the outcome. Of the 30 per cent of clients who did follow-up with services after release, the experimental group faired no better than the control group clients. There was no positive correlation between being eligible for benefits and following up for services. For those who had benefits, just as many pursued after care services as those who did not.

Conclusions

The study cited here is but one of 28 funded by the California legislature. Other studies are being done with smaller populations using more intensive treatment modalities. While its successes were limited, findings from other programs may be more promising. Programs of long-term care appear to work better. Milwaukee's Community Support Program, for example, has been helping mentally ill offenders, half of whom have co-occurring disorders, meet their basic needs for over 25 years (McDonald & Teitelbaum 1994). The primary goal is to set realistic expectations and follow through with services. For those who accept the program, hospitalisation in psychiatric care unit has declined, and 90 per cent are maintained in independent or semi-independent housing; 10 per cent are involved in employment-related activities. At least 90 per cent of their clients remain arrest-free while participating in the program, and jail staff report reduced numbers of mentally ill offenders.

Programs of long term and intensive care receive support from other studies. As noted by Lovell, Gagliardi, and Peterson (2002: 1290), whether community mental health treatment levels affect recidivism cannot be assessed fairly in the absence of higher levels of service during the first months after release. They note that arrests may themselves have prevented service delivery and that many of these individuals lack interest in the programs available to them, as found in the study reported here. Examination of programs for parolees in California and Maryland find much higher success rates for mentally ill parolees who have stringent conditions for treatment that they must meet upon release (Lurigio 2001: 455). Far more evaluation of existing programs is needed to begin to understand how the criminal justice and mental health systems can assist these individuals and in doing so reduce their reliance on costly criminal justice alternatives within the context of public safety. Additional information on such programs can be obtained from the GAINS Center for People with Co-Occurring Disorders in the Justice System <www.gainsctr.com>.

CHAPTER 17

Offenders with drug and alcohol dependencies

Maria Kevin
Senior Research Officer, NSW Department of Corrective Services

Introduction

New South Wales houses 8,000 prisoners, which is more than one-third of all prisoners held in Australia. Offenders entering NSW prisons with drug-related[1] crimes represent more than three-quarters of the prison population. Similar rates of occurrence are recorded in prison populations in the UK, Europe, Canada and the US. On arrival to prison in NSW, half of all prisoners reportedly experience drug withdrawal syndrome and on any given day more than one in ten prisoners receives some form of drug substitution therapy for their drug problem. NSW provides the largest prison-based methadone maintenance service in the world.

Defining the drug-crime connection

In NSW over one-tenth of prisoners (13%) are sentenced for a drug-defined offence as their most serious offence (Corben 2003). Yet, the proportion of prisoners with drug-related crime burgeons to more than three-quarters of the population when the link is examined in terms of the reported influence that drug use brings to bear on offending behaviour (Kevin 2003). Drug intoxication or drug withdrawal, acquisitive intent and systemic drug use within criminal communities are all drug-crime links that are not identifiable by simple offence definition. Prevalence rates that include these additional links are generally derived from drug testing data collections on arrestees and interview based surveys on prison populations. Studies of this type consistently find an association between drugs and crime.

Given the magnitude of the problem, over the past decade more systematic data collections have evolved with collection programs increasing in scale and frequency. International data collections on drug-related crime record similar rates as those evident in Australia, showing that drug users are over-represented in offender samples (National Institute of Justice 1999; Makkai 1999; Kevin 2000; Correctional Service of Canada 2000; Home Office

---

1   Unless otherwise stated the term "drug" includes alcohol.

2001). The information arising from these drug use data collection programs is being used for policy, planning and control in the public health and criminal justices areas.

Though the association between drug use and criminality is a given, causality or quantifying the relationship has proved to be contentious. Is the relationship causal or due to a third factor or factors common to both, such as personality, socio-geographic location or unemployment. Reportedly, drug users have more extensive criminal histories. In NSW, prisoners whose current offences are drug-related are more likely to have prior imprisonment episodes when compared with those whose current offences are not drug related (Kevin 1992; Kevin 2000; Kevin 2003). Similarly, a study which examined the drug use patterns of "first-time" versus "repeat" prisoners in the UK found that about two-thirds of those who had been sentenced to prison before were using drugs, at least daily, before imprisonment compared with one-third of "first-time" prisoners (Liriano & Ramsay 2003).

A key question asked is "what occurs first in the lives of offenders, illicit drug using behaviour or criminal behaviour?" To date, most studies conducted on heroin or cocaine users support the argument that criminal activity pre-dates illicit drug use (Hawks 1976; Potteiger 1981; Dobinson & Ward 1984; Bertram & Gorta 1990; and Stathis 1990). Acquisitive criminal activity has been found to increase with illicit drug use (Chaiken 1983; Miner & Gorta 1986; Hammersley et al 1989; Stevenson & Forthsythe 1998; and Liriano & Ramsay 2003).

Further, reductions in drug use subsequent to treatment have been found to be associated with reductions in criminal activity (Inciardi, et al 1997; Pearson & Lipton 1999; Pelissier, et al 2000; Lightfoot 2003; Godfrey, et al 2004). This is a complex equation as the temporal relationship between illicit drug use and criminal activity may not necessarily be constant throughout a drug user's career. Faupel and Klockars (1987) found that at one point in time a drug user may be committing crime to pay for drugs and at another time it may be because criminal activity has become a livelihood for the drug user.

Some recent studies challenge the "physical need for drugs drives the crime" explanation. In these findings, levels of drug use were determined by success in procuring money from crime and associated disposable income (Grapendaal 1992; Parker 1996). In other words, the level of crime was more likely to predict drug use than drug use predicts the level of crime.

A second line of investigation has attempted to identify certain profiles of drug-related offender. The best evidence indicates an association between type of drug used and the type of crime committed. Illicit drug use, specifically heroin use, is more likely to be associated with acquisitive crime and alcohol intoxication with violent crime. Not all illicit drug users commit acquisitive crime. Similarly, not all alcohol-intoxicated individuals become violent. Violence results from alcohol consumption in some situations, under some circumstances, for certain people (Collins & Messerschmidt 1993).

A number of studies on offender populations question the simplicity of the model that links alcohol to violence and illicit drugs to acquisitive crime.

In 1990, the US Bureau of Justice Statistics reported that 60 per cent of parolees for violent crimes tested positive for at least one illicit drug. A NSW study on a representative sample of prisoners sentenced for violent crimes found that although more than three-quarters were reportedly intoxicated by alcohol at the time of offence, about one-third of the sample were also injecting drug users and had committed a property crime just prior to imprisonment (Kevin 1999). Further, systemic violence has been associated with illicit drug dealing (Dobinson & Ward 1984; De La Rosa et al 1990). Such findings highlight the polydrug and polycrime patterns of prisoners with violent offences.

Drug misuse is pervasive among prison populations. However, studies on the drug crime connection raise as many questions as they answer. Broadly speaking, it has been found that alcohol intoxication escalates violence in terms of frequency and level and that illicit drug use moderates the frequency and severity of criminal activity by facilitating and reinforcing criminal activity. The polydrug use and polycrime patterns of offenders present further challenges to understanding the processes involved. It appears that the relationship is a complex interplay in the lives of offenders. Arguably any offence would be caused by a number of factors – individual, situational, socio-economic and cultural.

Recovery from the inside: Knowing the population and responding

Prisoners often enter prison as regular drug users and, for some, prison represents a continuum in their drug-using behaviour. In NSW, a biennial data collection is conducted on a representative sample of sentenced prisoners about to be released to freedom on a range of drug-related measures. Drug-related criminal activity, patterns of drug use in the community and prison, treatment engagement and contextual themes around the prison drug trade continue to be investigated. The data provides a knowledge base for correctional management enabling the monitoring and review of drug-related crime and drug-use trends over time. More importantly, it provides an empirical basis for developing and targeting treatment, prevention and interdiction strategies.

The most recent data collection on 254 sentenced male prisoners found that half had experienced drug-withdrawal syndrome on reception to prison and more than three-quarters reported having a drug problem at some stage in their lives. The drug-related statistics for females in the most recent collection showed very similar levels of occurrence as those for the men. However, what the findings on women did suggest was a higher prevalence of emotional distress as measured by thoughts of self-harm (21%) or suicide (18%).

It is clear that most prisoners have experienced physical, psychological and social problems of a significant kind related to their drug use. Encouragingly for treatment providers, most of the prisoners with a problem history had spent at least six months abstaining from drugs in the past (Kevin, 2003). It was common for those with a problematic drug history to have engaged in some form of drug treatment in the past. More than one-quarter of male prisoners had received methadone maintenance treatment at some time in their past and three-quarters of those with a drug problem history had participated in non-medical drug treatment in the past. This information on the nature and level of prior treatment engagement is an important consideration in service planning and delivery. Recovery from drug addiction is long term and frequently requires multiple episodes of treatment (National Institute on Drugs and Alcohol 1999).

A sizeable proportion of drug users in the NSW prison system seek treatment (Kevin 2003). Accounts from prisoners who have discontinued opiate use in prison have them quoted as saying, "it's a chance to get clean" and "a chance to get fit". The most recent data collection found that half of all male prisoners interviewed had used counselling-based services, either individualised, group based or residential during their current prison term. In addition, one-quarter reportedly received methadone maintenance therapy from the health service during their current prison term.

The role of providing drug treatment services in NSW prisons falls under the administration of two government agencies: the NSW Department of Corrective Services and NSW Justice Health– an Area Health Service of the NSW Health Department. NSW Corrective Services (DCS) employs counsellors and offers non-medical treatment based on education and psychological principles. NSW Justice Health provides medically-based services to prisoners, including medicated detoxification, drug-overdose management and drug-substitution therapy with their associated procedures. This demarcation of treatment provision has resulted in some benefits for prisoners. Given that drug-substitution therapy has been the jurisdiction of the medical service over the past decade, DCS has concurrently produced a dedicated program of non-medical treatment alternatives and adjuncts to drug-substitution therapy.

The outcome for prisoners has been a comprehensive range of both medical and non-medical treatment options. The non-medical options are well placed to meet the treatment challenges arising from the growth of polydrug use by offenders. The treatment options are also not necessarily mutually exclusive. A prisoner may be receiving methadone maintenance (Justice Health) and concurrently attending a methadone support group (DCS) or residing in a drug treatment wing program (DCS).

Current treatment strategies adopted in the NSW correctional system are underpinned by harm-reduction principles and tend to draw on social learning and addiction theory in the management and treatment of drug users. Social equivalence is addressed through matching the range of programs offered in the greater community (with the exception of syringe exchange). Pro-social lifestyle skills are addressed in drug treatment programming, disease prevention and health promotion campaigns. Individual health, vocational and social needs are also addressed. Additional funding through a bipartisan NSW Parliament Drug Summit has enabled NSW to trial a number of innovative strategies including a drug-free wing and a therapeutic community program to serve as intensive treatment options for prisoners at high risk of drug-related harm.

As an adjunct to these programs a "differential sanctions scheme for cannabis use" has been trialled. Detection of cannabis does not mean automatic termination from a treatment program whereas heroin use would. Those terminated from the program are encouraged to enrol in a more suitable form of drug treatment. The scheme differentiates between illicit drugs on the basis of the harm associated with the particular type of drug. The rationale behind the scheme was to prioritise strategies aimed at reducing high-risk injecting drug use and maintaining prisoners in drug treatment.

Drugs in prison

It has been said that prison acts as a modifier of drug-using behaviour (Shewan et al 1994). In drawing on the NSW data and that of other jurisdictions it would seem that drug use prevalence rates decline with imprisonment (with the exception of tobacco). Further, with the exception of cannabis, drug use frequency levels (how often) decline sharply during imprisonment. It is interesting to note that positive behaviour change of this kind is an outcome of imprisonment.

The NSW data (Kevin 2000; Kevin 2003) observed a majority of "soft" drug users (cannabis) and a small minority of high-risk drug users (injecting drug users) in prison. Similar rates of both drug use and injecting drug use among prisoners have been observed internationally (Shewan et al 1994; Bird et al 1997; Keene 1997; Koulierakis et al 1999). It appears that this prison-based drug use has more to do with the nature of the population and their pre-prison behaviour than the prison environment.

In prison, even though the kind of drugs used remains the same, drug use is not sustained on a regular or consistent basis reportedly due to the lack of availability. When compared to the community, drug use practices are reportedly less safe in prison. Drug use in prison is seen as more harm inducing in terms of the potential for transmission of blood-borne viruses, such as hepatitis C and HIV.

A substantial majority of the NSW prisoners who shared injecting equipment reportedly cleaned the equipment with water and bleach. That injecting drug use drops significantly on imprisonment, that prisoners are spatially confined and that drug-substitution therapy is provided would, to some extent, account for the very low HIV sero-conversion rates among prisoners in NSW.

As evident in the risk-assessment profiles that are currently implemented with offenders in many correctional jurisdictions, the best predictor of current behaviour is past behaviour. Across two data collections the factor most significantly associated with injecting drug use in the current prison episode was injecting drug use in a previous prison episode (Kevin 2000; Kevin 2003). Further, just over half of those who shared injecting equipment in the community went on to share injecting equipment in their current prison episode. The importance of such information is that it can be factored into risk assessment criteria to identify prisoners at risk of injecting drugs in prison with a view to establishing contact and providing access to a variety of treatment services.

Drug use in prison, as in the community, occurs in a social context. Findings on the prison social system as defined by prisoners indicated that "lack of trust" was the defining marker of the code of conduct among prisoners in NSW (Kevin 2000). This finding accords with that of the Dutch study (Grapendaal 1990) in which isolationism was identified as the dominant aspect of prisoner social system. For drug users in NSW prisons, debt avoidance and the necessity to maintain secrecy from other prisoners about possession were identified as the most salient considerations (Kevin 2000). To this end, financial cost and the associated dire consequences of defaulting on any loans would be a major deterrent to ongoing drug use in prison. These risks associated with the prisoner drug trade would further account for the reduction in the use of "heavy-end" drugs on confinement to prison.

Prison drug strategy

Correctional administrators are continually faced with the challenge of identifying better ways of preventing drug-related problems in the prison population and drug-related re-offending on release. In accepting that behavioural change is an ongoing process, it is both rational and humane to prioritise harm-reduction responses that are augmented by a range of hierarchical treatment options and *Throughcare* services. Reductions in the level and frequency of drug use and criminal activity by offenders would be key indicators of drug treatment effectiveness in a process of behavioural change. Consistent with the principles of social learning theory, positive behaviour change in prisoners can only be promoted through the use of management and legal responses, including privileges and sanctions for behaviour which maximise therapeutic effects and minimise anti-therapeutic consequences rather than punishment.

Drug treatment effectiveness is a complex interplay between the participant and the treatment process. Research and evaluation is crucial to unravelling these processes. Those aspects of the treatment program that work need to be identified as do characteristics of the participant that are associated with retention in treatment and post-treatment success. At a minimum, a thorough assessment of the participant's drug-related background prior to treatment needs to be conducted as baseline information and also program structure and process should be thoroughly documented. NSW Corrective Services is continuing to examine its programs through the lens of program evaluation methodologies. Effective programs need to be precisely identified in order to be successfully operationalised and replicated.

CHAPTER 18

A framework for minimising the incidence of self-harm in prison

Dr Greg Dear
Edith Cowan University

In this chapter I have adopted the nomenclature outlined by Dear (2001), adapted from O'Carroll et al (1996), in which *self-harm* refers to any deliberately enacted behaviour that is intended to physically harm oneself, no matter how slight the intended injury. Self-harm is first categorised into either *with or without any degree of suicidal intent,* and both are further divided into three categories: without resultant injury, with non-fatal injury, and with fatal injury. Suicide and suicide attempts are therefore clearly defined as subcategories of self-harm.

The rate of suicide and other self-harm is higher among prisoners than among the general population, even when basic demographic factors (eg, age, sex, race) are controlled. Two main explanations have been provided. The importation model posits that the individuals who are imprisoned are a high-risk group. The deprivation model posits that prisons are high-risk environments in that they create the types of intolerable circumstance that lead to self-harming. However, current thinking in the field is that both personal vulnerability factors (importation) and situational factors (deprivation) interact to result in self-harm (Bonner 2000; Dear, Thomson, Howells & Hall 2001; Liebling 1992). According to this view, prison administrators who seek to prevent self-harm must address those individual vulnerability factors that are associated with it and minimise the incidence of those situations that appear to precipitate it.

In this chapter I outline a theoretical framework to guide administrators in developing comprehensive self-harm prevention programs. Given the space limitations of this chapter, I am unable to provide a critical review of the research that informs this framework. Instead I present a small number of key assumptions that one can make on the basis of the research literature. As I have sought to reflect in the title, while we must strive to prevent all self-harming behaviour in our prisons, it is likely that we can only minimise the frequency and severity of such behaviour.

Key assumptions about self-harm

The following assumptions can be made on the basis of the existing research literature. Some of these assumptions are consistently supported by research findings and can be regarded as facts (eg, item 1 on the list) while others have more limited empirical support. Given the limited space in this chapter, I have not critically reviewed the research behind these assumptions; the references given at some points in the list refer the reader to appropriate starting points to examine that research (eg, articles in which the relevant literature is reviewed). These are assumptions that, in my mind, carry important implications for preventing self-harm in prison.

1. People who enact non-fatal self-harm have a significantly increased risk of suicide (Hawton & Catalan, 1987; van Heeringen, Hawton & Williams, 2000). A history of self-harm is consistently found to be the best distal predictor of subsequent suicide.

2. While self-harm that involves no suicidal intent is epidemiologically distinct from self-harm that involves some degree of suicidal intent, they are best regarded as parts of one overall suicidal process (Shneidman 1985; van Heeringen et al 2000).

3. The central psychological feature of all self-harm, regardless of degree of suicidal intent, is psychological pain (Shneidman 1993; Williams 1997).

4. Self-harm is an expression of several, sometimes seemingly contradictory, motives rather than an act that serves a single function. For example, an act of self-harm can be an attempt to influence one's social environment (so-called manipulative self-harm) and at the same time involve a high degree of suicidal intent (Dear, Thomson & Hills 2000; Hawton & Catalan 1987).

5. The lethality of a self-harm incident (the likelihood of the act resulting in death) is only weakly to moderately correlated with the level of suicidal intent (Dear et al 2000; Hawton & Catalan 1987; Shneidman 1993).

6. Major psychiatric disorders such as depression and psychosis are implicated in most suicides in the general community (van Heeringen et al 2000), but in fewer than half of those in prison (Dear et al 2001; Liebling 1992). According to Shneidman (1985, 1993) it is not the psychiatric condition itself, but the pain of that condition combined with a loss of hope, that leads to a suicidal crisis.

7. While events that occur outside prison (eg, traumas experienced by members of the prisoner's family, a spouse deciding to end his or her relationship with the prisoner) impact on prisoners' lives and can precipitate self-harming behaviour, most precipitating events occur within the prison setting (Dear et al 2001; Liebling 1992; Liebling & Krarup 1993).

8. The most common precipitants of self-harming behaviour in prison are events that involve conflict and aggression among prisoners, sometimes referred to as bullying, (see, eg, Liebling 1992), conflict between prisoners and staff, and the routine deprivations of imprisonment (regime restrictions, prison disciplinary procedures, separation from family and other supports, etc) and the wider justice system (Dear et al 2001; Liebling 1992; Liebling & Krarup 1993).

9. Studies have consistently identified the following categories of prisoner as high self-harm risk: unsentenced prisoners, female prisoners, young prisoners (18-24), those subjected to specific punishment regimes (particularly those placed in separate confinement cells), and prisoners who are in their first few weeks of incarceration or are at critical transition points such as sentencing or parole review (Bonner 2000; Dear et al 2001; Liebling 1992).

Implications for preventing self-harm

The principal implication that arises from the assumptions outlined above is that prison staff must take every self-harm incident seriously and treat the prisoner who enacted it with genuine respect and concern. This applies to even minor self-harm that involved no risk to life and that appears to have been enacted without any degree of suicidal intent (eg, the prisoner denied any intention to die). Such behaviour is an expression of emotional pain and an overtaxing of coping resources. Prisoners who self-harm have a significantly elevated risk of suicide and should be recognised as the most easily identified high-risk group requiring specialised preventive interventions. The principles just listed apply to all self-harm regardless of the degree to which the behaviour appears manipulative, attention-seeking, or simply a seemingly effective strategy for venting frustration and anger. Given the clear role of prison-based stressors in self-harm, preventing self-harm requires prison staff to attend to the overall quality of life in prisons and not just to focus on identifying and managing high-risk prisoners. Those particular times in the incarceration process (eg, reception) and particular categories of prisoner (eg, remandees) that indicate elevated risk require closer monitoring of prisoners' distress and greater resources dedicated to ameliorating any distress that is detected. Being in a high-risk group should not increase one's chances of being placed into a strip cell (suicide-proof cell that is bereft of any stimulation or social interaction) but it should increase one's chances of having people take an interest in one's current adjustment and psychological and welfare needs.

Theoretical perspectives on self-harm

The following theoretical principles provide a framework to guide any self-harm prevention program. In my mind they are essential ingredients for developing successful strategies for preventing self-harm in prison. My intention in this chapter is to provide a framework that can be applied in prisons around the world, rather than describe one or other example of a sound self-harm prevention system or provide a set of strategies that should work in the type of prison with which I am familiar, but might not work in another prison system.

Shneidman's concept of psychache

Shneidman (1985, 1993) conceptualised the suicidal crisis as one of intolerable psychological pain, which he termed psychache. He conceptualised that pain in terms of unmet psychological needs, adopting Murray's (1938) motivational theory of personality. According to Murray's theory, there are a number of psychological needs that all people possess (eg, need for affiliation, need for achievement, need for autonomy, need for order), but that individuals vary in how strongly each need is felt. One person's need for order and predictability will be stronger than another person's, and the person with the stronger need will be the more inclined to enact behaviour that leads toward greater order and structure in his or her life. The person with the stronger need for order will be more distressed than the other person when circumstances prevent the attainment of orderliness, neatness and predictability. More importantly, an individual will feel particular needs more strongly than other needs, with a small number of needs (usually only one or two) being vital to the person's psychological functioning. When the person is unable to meet those most vital needs and sees no hope of meeting them, the consequential distress will be so severe that it might exceed the person's threshold for tolerance. This is the essential ingredient for a suicidal crisis: an inability or unwillingness to tolerate the level of pain that one is experiencing.

People who commit suicide are not committed to the goal of dying but are ambivalent about living (Shneidman 1985 1993). They are unwilling to tolerate their current level of psychological pain and cannot see any means by which to change the circumstances that they find so painful (hopelessness and helplessness). If the intensity of their pain is reduced, even a little, they can choose to tolerate that pain and thereby choose to live (Shneidman 1993). Reducing the person's pain necessarily involves assisting the person to meet, in even a small degree, whatever vital need is unmet. For example, if the unmet need is shame-avoidance, then one must reduce the person's sense of shame. If the unmet need is affiliation, then one must assist the person to feel even the slightest bit connected with another person and even the slightest bit hopeful about achieving some limited sense of belonging. If the unmet need is for succorance, then one must enable the person to feel loved and cared for even to the slightest degree (if not loved then at least not shunned, neglected and despised).

Environmental press

The other half of Murray's (1938) needs-press theory of personality involves the concept of environmental press. An environmental press is any aspect of the environment, whether real or perceived, that activates a psychological need. For example, two female prisoners become engaged in a fight in the art room and the room is somewhat trashed in the process. For one prisoner and fellow art student onlooker with a high need for order, this event will press upon that need and she will be upset by the mess and disorder and will move to clean and tidy her work area and reinstate a sense of order. The next person with a high need for harm-avoidance will be more distressed by the sense of danger and risk that the event suggests. The next person has a very high need for nurturance (a need to nurture others) and will express concern at what might have happened to cause the two prisoners to "go off", and will also go about checking on how others in the art room are coping with the event. The prisoner with a very high need for achievement will be angry at the two fighters for disrupting her work schedule and will be frustrated at needing to put her work area sufficiently in order to resume work. The same event will press on numerous psychological needs and different individuals will be motivated to act in ways that fill their most vital need that is pressed.

To the extent that each person is able to enact the required behaviours in a competent manner, each will successfully meet the need that is pressed and will experience emotional relief and satisfaction, although possibly with some residual anger for the fact that the troubling event occurred. To the extent that one's environment consistently presses on one's most vital needs and one is unable to competently act in a manner to respond to those presses, one will be chronically upset (angry, anxious, depressed, or all of the above). For example, the prisoner above who has the high need for achievement might also have high needs for aggression and counteraction and in addition to the anger described above will be personally affronted by the event and will be motivated to "right the wrong" and "punish the wrong-doer". This prisoner might physically assault one of the fighters and consequently be banned from the art room, which provides her with her only avenue for meeting her need for achievement. While one can correctly say that she created that problem for herself, it might, in combination with other factors that frustrate her ability to meet her most vital needs, lead to self-harming behaviour including suicide attempts. It is all very well to act in a manner that is intended to meet one's needs, but if one is unable to do so in a competent and socially acceptable manner, then one's efforts will be in vain and emotional pain (psychache) will be the cost.

Psychogenic needs linked to suicidal behaviour

While any of the 20 psychological needs identified by Murray (1938) can be implicated in a suicidal crisis when chronically unmet, or perceived to be unable to be met, Shneidman (1998) argued that a small subset of those needs are involved in most suicidal crises. Shneidman summarises his discussion thus: "In general, we are talking about thwarted love, fractured control, assaulted self-image, excessive anger, a surfeit of shame, ruptured key relations and the attendant grief" (1998: 249). Shneidman is writing on the basis of research and clinical experience of suicide attempters who present to health services and to community suicide prevention services. It is as if he is trying to provide a caricature of the prison experience. When I reflect on typical prison settings I do not sense social or physical environments that strongly facilitate prisoners to meet their need to belong to a socially esteemed group and to be loved and emotionally nourished, their need to avoid humiliation and indifference, or their needs for autonomy and control. On the contrary, the environmental presses that characterise the typical prison environment frustrate the fulfilment of the very needs that Shneidman identifies as suicide-related.

Applying Murray's theory, the prisoners most likely to develop suicidal crises are those who have strong needs for affiliation, succorance ("to feel loved and safe, and certainly *not* to be neglected, scorned, criticised, abused, beaten, or molested", Shneidman 1998: 248), shame-avoidance, counteraction ("to obliterate a past humiliation by resumed action", Shneidman 1998: 248), privacy, autonomy, or control. That is, those who are most vulnerable to suicide are those who feel the greatest psychological need for those psychological goods that the prison environment typically does not provide. There are no data to indicate whether the same needs are implicated in the majority of self-harm incidents that do not involve any degree of suicidal intent, although it appears from the types of precipitating factor reported (eg, Dear et al 2001; Liebling 1992; Liebling & Krarup 1993) that these same needs are highly relevant to self-harm incidents more generally than just to suicide attempts.

Toch's concept of prison preferences

Toch (1977) adopted Murray's (1938) needs-press model to guide his original research into prisoners' adaptation and maladaptation to the prison environment. On the basis of thematic analyses of over 400 interviews with prisoners in New York, Toch identified eight environmental concerns that prisoners commonly express. In essence, he identified broad categories of environmental press. These are:

1. Privacy (avoiding overstimulation and unwanted social involvement);

2. Activity (a need for stimulation and diversion);

3. Support (a need for reliable, tangible assistance);

4. Freedom (meeting one's autonomy needs);

5. Safety (a need to be physically safe);

6. Social stimulation (meeting one's affiliation needs);

7. Structure (stability and predictability); and

8. Emotional feedback (a concern about being loved, appreciated and cared for).

While the taxonomy is somewhat different, one can see Murray's list of needs embedded in Toch's broader categories. Toch's message is the same as that delivered by Shneidman (1993; 1998) – maladaptive behaviour in prisons will be minimised to the extent that prison systems can place prisoners into those settings that match their environmental preferences (profile of psychological needs). This assumes that prison systems contain various types of housing in which prisoners can be placed. For example, prisoners with high needs for safety and structure relative to other needs would adjust well in a unit in which safety and structure are well provided even though this is achieved at the expense of activity and freedom. Toch explicitly recognises that it might be impossible to design environments that address all eight environmental concerns simultaneously.

Psychological vulnerabilities

Decades of psychological research has identified a myriad of risk factors and other variables that are associated with self-harming behaviour. In recent years, researchers have been able to integrate many of these findings and identify the key psychological mechanisms that underlie self-harm (Williams 1997; Williams & Pollock 2000). These vulnerabilities include aspects of temperament (personality factors that are largely genetically determined and have clear biological substrates) such as impulsivity and emotional instability; distorted cognitive processes (most likely learned rather than innate) such as dichotomous thinking and pessimism (hopelessness); and deficient competencies (variously related to both biological factors and social learning history) such as poor problem-solving skills, inadequate coping skills in general and specific memory deficits.

Those same vulnerabilities that have been found in studies conducted in health settings and in the general community have been found to be associated with self-harm in prison (eg, Dear, Slattery & Hillan 2001; Dear, Thomson, Howells & Hall, 2001; Liebling & Krarup 1993). Moreover, many of these vulnerabilities are quite prevalent among prisoners (eg, impulsivity, poor problem-solving, impaired affect-regulation). It is clear that these vulnerabilities limit the degree to which a person will be able to work toward effective fulfilment of his or her vital psychological needs if the environment is persistently pressing those needs.

Criminogenic factors and self-harm

In addition to the types of psychological vulnerability outlined in the previous section, criminogenic factors (psychological factors related to re-offending and other antisocial behaviour) are likely to be related to the risk of self-harm in prison because they preclude the person from enacting need-fulfilment strategies that will be tolerated by the controlled institutional environment. Criminogenic factors that are likely to increase self-harm risk include: an inflated sense of entitlement (a sense of oneself as special and that the normal rules and restrictions don't apply); misattribution of hostile intent (the tendency to misperceive hostile intent and threat and the contingent hypervigence and proneness to attack them before they attack me); and basic criminal sentiments (eg, that damaging others in order to meet your own needs is an acceptable means to an ends). Such antisocial strategies are clearly unlikely to be successful in meeting needs for affiliation, succour and safety, and in the controlled environment of a prison they are also unlikely to meet needs for autonomy and power because they will incite an over-powering response from an unforgiving, security conscious system. It goes without saying that such criminogenic factors are common among prisoners.

A theoretical framework for understanding self-harm in prison

The following framework offers an integration of the various theoretical principles outlined above. When vital needs are pressed the individual needs to apply his or her coping resources and competencies to the task of meeting those needs. If the person's competencies don't match the setting or are more generally deficient, then those needs won't be met and the person will experience ongoing emotional pain. Depending on other vulnerabilities (biological factors, cognitive style, emotional regulation competencies, etc), this could result in mental health problems such as depression or anxiety disorders. A suicidal crisis ensues when vital needs are unmet, the person sees no hope of being able to meet those needs, and the emotional pain exceeds that person's threshold for what is tolerable. The only two exit points from that suicidal crisis are death (escape from the intolerable pain) and a reduction in the intensity of the pain such that life becomes tolerable.

Shneidman (1993) is very clear that the goal of suicide prevention is not to eliminate the pain by setting the person's life to some ideal, but to reduce the pain just enough to make it bearable by meeting that person's vital needs just a little. Assistance in meeting needs must involve facilitating the person to enact his or her own competencies and assisting him or her to develop appropriate (pro-social, flexible) competencies. However, at times the helper needs to directly act on meeting those needs because the suicidal person is not currently capable, or the need pertains to the connection with and responses from others.

Implications for prevention: The concept of the healthy prison

The implications that flow from the theoretical principles outlined in the previous section are:

1. Prison systems need to be sensitive to and responsive to the psychological needs of prisoners;

2. Different prisoners have different needs and the system therefore needs to be flexible in how prisoners are managed and what types of psychological resources are provided;

3. Prison administrators need to focus more on creating prison environments that press minimally on prisoners' psychological needs than on identifying high-risk prisoners;

4. Prisons must have well-functioning systems for detecting and ameliorating prisoners' distress;

5. Prison administrators need to provide interventions (to all prisoners) aimed at reducing those vulnerability factors that are common among prisoners; and

6. Reducing criminality (psychological factors that lead to re-offending) will assist in reducing self-harm.

These implications are contained within the concept of the healthy prison, as described by Her Majesty's Chief Inspector of Prisons (HM Inspectorate (1999)). These implications are also addressed in the context of the US prison system by Toch (1997), and in the context of Australian prisons by Dear et al (2001a, 2001b) and McArthur, Camilleri and Webb (1999). As I have stated above, the limited space of this chapter precludes a comprehensive discussion of specific prevention strategies. Instead, I discuss below the concept of the healthy prison and how that might guide self-harm prevention initiatives. In doing so I unashamedly adopt a moral rather than an empirical stance, although I would argue that my stance is entirely consistent with the empirical data.

What is a healthy prison?

The essence of a healthy prison is that staff and prisoners are "enabled to live and work in prisons in a way that promotes their well-being" (HM Inspectorate 1999: 59). HM Inspectorate discusses four principles that provide a test of whether or not a prison is healthy: "the weakest prisoners feel safe; all prisoners are treated with respect as individuals; all prisoners are busily occupied, are expected to improve themselves and given the opportunity to do so; and all prisoners can strengthen links with their families and prepare for release" (1999: 60).

Healthy prisons as inoculations against self-harm

In a healthy prison, individual prisoners' vulnerabilities (eg, poor coping skills, mental health problems, criminogenic factors) are addressed, their external coping resources (eg, access to valued social supports) are enhanced, and the types of situation that are known to be associated with self-harming behaviour (eg, bullying, boredom) are minimised. Healthy prisons minimise the incidence of distress among prisoners, but cannot eliminate it (no environment can be free of stress). Healthy prisons provide meaningful avenues for distressed prisoners to manage their distress, and accurately detect and humanely respond to prisoners' distress. A humane response to intense psychache is not to isolate the person in a strip cell, although there might be occasions where it is necessary to place a prisoner into such a suicide-proof cell for a brief period (minutes, not days) while appropriate resources are assembled to assess and assist the prisoner.

Healthy prisons not only facilitate staff to act in a consistently respectful manner toward prisoners but they protect prisoners from each other. Not all prisoners have a great concern and respect for their fellow inmates, particularly for those who are emotionally or physically vulnerable and can be abused for personal gain. Prison officers and other staff who work in healthy prisons acknowledge such realities but do not tolerate them.

In essence, healthy prisons are those in which prisoners' real psychological needs are anticipated and catered for as much as is possible within the legislative restrictions of the day. This does not mean that prisoners are pampered and excused from being responsible for their own behaviour and its consequences, indeed to do so would run counter to the aim of meeting real psychological needs. As HM Inspectorate stated, "It is the very opposite of creating an easy life for prisoners; rather it is helping prisoners to face up to and overcome problems and prepare for a useful life on release" (1999: 63). However, not every prisoner with an inflated sense of entitlement will come to appreciate that it is quite reasonable that other people will not accommodate that inflated sense of entitlement but will be affronted by it. Healthy prisons contain clear boundaries that reflect and reinforce the mainstream values of society, and they enforce those values without betraying them. Developing a healthy prison environment will not magically shape prisoners' behaviour and eliminate self-harming and other dysfunctional behaviour, but it does provide the necessary context for behaviour-change strategies to function effectively.

Healthy prisons recognise and respond to the diverse needs of prisoners (including diverse cultural needs). As Toch's (1977) work suggests, it is unlikely that any given environment can provide for all psychological needs at the same time. It is therefore important that prisons contain diverse psychological environments such as cell blocks in which particular needs are not pressed, but in order to achieve this, other needs might be pressed. For example, cell blocks that effectively protect privacy might not be effective in providing activity and freedom (autonomy). To the extent that alternative environments are constructed within prisons, prisoners' individual psychological needs can be catered for; prisoners can be placed in those settings that most closely match their psychological profile.

Healthy prisons, like healthy communities, are an ideal that one strives toward rather than a standard that one easily achieves and effortlessly maintains. The people who are imprisoned by the courts have already demonstrated that they are not society's high achievers in establishing healthy communities. It is therefore incumbent upon the prison staff to establish the health of the prison environment, although prisoners also have a responsibility to enhance the health of their environment. The staff who work in healthy prisons will appreciate the benefits of their workplace, but they must also accept that some prisoners will not reciprocate the respect that they are given and that those prisoners might also feel intense emotional pain when their psychological needs are unmet and that those lives, no matter how flawed they might seem to the prison staff, also deserve to be saved. To think otherwise would be to betray the very ideals that one is supposed to be reinforcing.

I offer one final observation on the nature of a healthy prison. The various staff groups (psychologists, nurses, medical practitioners, prison officers, social workers, administrators, chaplains, etc) form an integrated whole that is greater than the sum of its parts. Information about prisoners' needs, vulnerabilities, strengths and distress is shared among these parts of the system in appropriate ways. It is impossible to work toward preventing suicide and other self-harm when some parts of the system withhold information that other parts require in order to perform their functions. There are few greater risks to the task of suicide prevention than an overdeveloped sense of obligation to maintain confidentiality.

– CHAPTER 19 –

Beyond what works: A retrospective of Robert Martinson's famous article

Associate Professor Rick Sarre,
University of South Australia

Robert Martinson in 1974

In the late 1960s in the US a large number of rehabilitation evaluations were reviewed by the New York sociologist Robert Martinson in the company of two research colleagues, Dr Doug Lipton and Ms Judith Wilks. His interpretations of the results were published in a now famous article under his name alone in the journal *The Public Interest*, entitled "What Works? Questions and Answers About Prison Reform". The 1974 article is historically regarded as debunking the idea that it is possible to rehabilitate custodial inmates, indeed, to reform prisoners at all. Many authors have noted that it is probably the least frequently read but most frequently quoted and cited article in the rehabilitation literature (Cousineau & Plecas 1982; Gendreau & Ross 1987).

Martinson is often misquoted. What did he *actually* say? He wrote:

> With few and isolated exceptions, the rehabilitative efforts that have been reported so far have had no appreciable effect on recidivism. Studies that have been done since our survey was completed do not present any major grounds for altering that original conclusion. (1974: 25)

Moreover,

> It may be simply that our programs aren't yet good enough, that the education we provide to inmates is still poor education, that the therapy we administer is not administered skillfully enough, that our intensive supervision and counseling do not yet provide enough personal support for the offenders who are subjected to them. If one wishes to believe this, then what our correctional system needs is simply a more full-hearted commitment to the strategy of treatment. It may be, on the other hand, that there is a more radical flaw in our present strategies that education at its best, or that psychotherapy at its best, cannot overcome, or even appreciably reduce, the powerful tendencies of offenders to continue in criminal behavior. (1974: 49)

These conclusions were not dissimilar to his earlier expressed views on the subject. In 1972 he had concluded, in a four part series in the liberal *New Republic,* that correctional treatments has no appreciable effect "positive or negative" on rates of recidivism of convicted offenders (Martinson 1972).

Martinson's scepticism of the ability of prisons to rehabilitate offenders derived from his participation in a survey of American evaluations of rehabilitative programs. From 1968 to 1970 the research team reviewed 231 evaluations that had been conducted in the USA from 1945 to 1967. The programs under scrutiny included intensive supervision, psychotherapy, group therapy, vocational training, educational approaches and medical interventions. In each case the three researchers had to be satisfied that the program had been systematically evaluated. At this time, rehabilitative notions dominated penal philosophy, and had done so for at least a century and a half. Rehabilitation had grown out of a humanistic tradition that demanded that the individual be the focus of sentencing, not the crime itself. Thus, in 1974, many people considered rehabilitation to be the main aim of imprisonment (Hall 1996). Martinson's summary of the review, however, was entirely pessimistic and appeared to undermine this traditional faith in the rehabilitative ideal. It was not long before his article became nicknamed, "Nothing Works!" His conclusions were soon treated as fact by researchers, policy-makers and the public alike (Lipton 1995, 1998) and gave rise to heated debates in the contemporary literature (Palmer 1975; Wilson 1980).

Paradoxically, the idea that nothing worked in rehabilitating offenders appealed to Left and Right alike (Cullen & Gendreau 1989). The Left was concerned with the injustices of sentencing that accepted the idea that those pushing rehabilitative ideals had forsaken the notion of commensurate "desert" in favour of indeterminate lengths of incarceration and forced treatment (von Hirsch 1976). The Right favoured anything that did not discourage retribution in sentencing. Indeed, if nothing worked, then longer prison terms and capital punishment became easier for the Right to sell. To a nation emerging from the Vietnam War and faced with an unruly youth and drug culture, "nothing works" became a slogan for the times (Cousineau & Plecas 1982). Indeed, there is a view that Martinson was able to provide the fuel for those keen to justify a scaling back of rehabilitation. Most correctional systems had few, if any trained psychiatrists, psychologists, or social workers, and a full-scale commitment to rehabilitation would have crippled corrections budgets, especially as prison numbers began to rise with the coming of age of the "baby-boomers" (Miller 1989; DiIulio 1991). It should have surprised no one, then, that few observers doubted that Martinson was correct, and that the article's conclusions received widespread publicity and acclaim.

"What Works?" in context

It is important, however, to put "What Works?" in context. As stated above, Martinson was only one of three researchers to undertake the survey, which was published as *The Effectiveness of Correctional Treatment* (Lipton et al 1975). It had been finished in 1970 but was not publicly released until five years later. Although the survey came to be essentially identified with Martinson's name alone, he had joined the other two only after they were well into their work. Unknown to Lipton and Wilks, Martinson published the now famous article peremptorily and without their specific consent (Lipton 1998).

In fact, the final 735-page report, published just six months after the appearance of "What Works?" concluded that "the field of corrections has not *as yet* found satisfactory ways to reduce recidivism *by significant amounts*" (Lipton et al 1975) (my emphasis). This was, of course, a far more guarded conclusion, and left open the door for further rehabilitative optimism. The three authors appeared keen to emphasise that one should not shut the door on rehabilitation without first developing better diagnostic evaluative tools and collecting better data.

The 1975 findings were then reviewed by the National Academy of Sciences in the form of an assessment by a Panel on Research on Rehabilitative Techniques. In their judgment, "Lipton, Martinson and Wilks were ... accurate and fair in their appraisal of the rehabilitation literature" (Sechrest et al 1979: 5, 31). The Panel (and therefore the Academy) appeared to temper Martinson's 1974 opinion by stating, "we do not now know of any program or method of rehabilitation that could be *guaranteed* to reduce the criminal activity of released offenders" (Sechrest et al 1979: 3) (Lipton's emphasis). Academics were not universal in their praise of the 1975 report, however. Cousineau and Plecas (1982) noted that it contained methodological weaknesses. They concluded that the evidence used to support the conclusions of the report was taken at face value rather than being subjected to what they refer to as "organized scepticism"(Cousineau & Plecas 1982).

Be that as it may, the Martinson report of 1974 is the one that most people remember. It was well written. It cleverly incorporated a "devil's advocate" style of presentation, where issues were presented as questions and then debated using the evidence presented by the researchers' interpretations of the evaluations. However, with the value of hindsight, Martinson's approach had a number of flaws, principally in his providing insufficient qualification for the conclusions he alone had reached. For example, many rehabilitative programs reviewed and regarded as failures by Martinson (if not the other researchers as well) were simply those that were starved of funds and which could never have provided the services they purported to provide (Cullen & Gilbert 1982).

How one assesses the "failure" of any program is a topic that has been the subject of much celebrated debate more recently too (Sherman 1992; University of Maryland 1998). The 1974 appraisal simply tested programs against recidivism (re-arrest and re-conviction) rates (Martinson 1974), and did not consider, for example, the winding down of an offender's criminal activity or how sentences are administered (Mair 1991). Nor did it consider the difficulty posed by a lack of custodial choices. It is possible, of course, that the debilitating aspects of prison life would always outweigh any "aversive" rehabilitation programs effects (Vito and Allen 1981). In other words, rehabilitation effects may be easily subverted by the criminogenic effect of their place of delivery (Sarre 1984).

Moreover, Martinson's report did not consider the possibilities revealed by meta-analysis as a tool of prediction (Gendreau et al 1996). It did not test the growing field of psychologically-based treatment methods focusing on "offence behaviour" (McGuire & Priestley 1985). In all, Martinson had drawn his conclusions selectively from the broader study, and drew only from the evidence that was unduly pessimistic (Lipton 1998).

Three years later, in an article co-authored with Judith Wilks, Martinson showed signs of softening his stance, re-affirming the value of probation as a rehabilitative method (Martinson & Wilks 1977). And then, a year before his death in 1980, he recanted substantially in an article published in the *Hofstra Law Review*. In that piece, he pointed to a plethora of rehabilitative models that had proved effective with offenders. He wrote that:

> [C]ontrary to my previous position, some treatment programs do have an appreciable effect on recidivism. Some programs are indeed beneficial; of equal or greater significance, some programs are harmful. (1979: 244, emphasis in the original)

Furthermore, he wrote that:

> [T]he most interesting general conclusion is that no treatment program now used in criminal justice is inherently either substantially helpful or harmful. The critical fact seems to be the conditions under which the program is delivered … Such startling results are found again and again in our study, for treatment programs as diverse as individual psychotherapy, group counseling, intensive supervision, and what we have called individual/help (aid, advice, counseling). (1979: 254-255, emphasis in the original)

The man who had started it all had come almost full circle. But by now, no one appeared to be listening. This later article is probably the most *infrequently* cited article on rehabilitation (Gendreau & Ross 1987) notwithstanding its importance in the literature at the time, and since.

The past decade

In 1987, Gendreau and Ross published a survey of over 200 studies on rehabilitation conducted from 1981-1987, many of which used data more reliable than the data available to their predecessors. They concluded:

> Our reviews of the research literature demonstrated that successful rehabilitation of offenders had been accomplished, and continued to be accomplished quite well. … Reductions in recidivism, sometimes as substantial as 80 percent, had been achieved in a considerable number of well-controlled studies. Effective programs were conducted in a variety of community and (to a lesser degree) institutional settings, involving predelinquents, hard-core adolescent offenders, and recidivistic adult offenders, including criminal heroin addicts. The results of these programs were not short-lived; follow-up periods of at least two years were not uncommon, and several studies reported even longer follow-ups. (1987: 350-351)

In short, many things "worked". However, the policy legacy for rehabilitation in the US was already being etched in stone. Despite any rear-guard action, rehabilitation appeared to be doomed in the face of official mistrust of its effectiveness. The same year of the Gendreau and Ross publication, and a full 13 years after the article's publication, then Attorney-General Edwin Meese referred to the "substantially discredited theory of rehabilitation" (cited in Cullen & Gendreau 1989: 25). His views echoed those of the Director of the Office of Juvenile Justice and Delinquency Prevention, Alfred Regnery, who had spoken two years earlier of the "folly of rehabi-litation", adding, "since [Martinson], rehabilitation has sunk further in esteem ... the criminal justice system has all but given up on the concept. Virtually no successful juvenile programs – those that reduce recidivism to an appreciable degree – rely on rehabilitation" (Regnery 1985: 3).

Moreover, on 18 January 1989 – a full 15 years after the publication of "What Works?"– the demise of rehabilitation in corrections was confirmed by the US Supreme Court. In *Mistretta v United States* (1989) 488 US 361, the court upheld federal sentencing guidelines that had been challenged on consti-tutional grounds. These guidelines removed the goal of rehabilitation from serious consideration when sentencing offenders. Defendants could hence-forth be sentenced strictly for the crime – a 'deserts-based' approach – with no recognition given to such factors as amenability to treatment, personal and family history, or previous efforts toward rehabilitation. The court summarised the history of the debate as follows: "Rehabilitation as a sound penological theory came to be questioned and, in any event, was regarded by some as an unattainable goal for most cases" (at 365). The court cited a Senate Report that referred to the "outmoded rehabilitation model" for federal criminal sentencing, and stated that the efforts of the criminal justice system to achieve rehabilitation of offenders had failed. Arguably this reference provides another legacy of the Martinsonian "conclusion". As Gendreau and Ross note, "All too often, in the face of all contrary empirical evidence, we adhere to theories for political or ideological reasons ... or cavalierly switch ideologies depending upon transient political developments ..." (1987: 395).

The present and the future

In Australia today, similar themes prevail. For, while lip service is paid to the goal of rehabilitation in many of the official sentencing policies of this nation, much of the terminology is ambiguous. For example, even though s 5 of the Victorian *Sentencing Act* 1991 states that one of the purposes for which sentences may be imposed is to "establish conditions within which it is considered by the court that the rehabilitation of the offender may be facilitated", the legislation speaks in passive rather than active terms (Tomaino 1999). In other jurisdictions, other factors (eg, protection of the community) are given pre-eminence in sentencing guidelines. In South Australia, for example, the *Criminal Law (Sentencing) Act* 1988 states that one purpose of sentencing is "the rehabilitation of the offender" (s 10(m)), but it is the thirteenth consideration. In Tasmania's *Sentencing Act* 1997 rehabilitation is mentioned (s 3(e)(ii)), but it is secondary to deterrence as a goal. In the Commonwealth *Crimes Act* 1914, the "prospects of the rehabilitation of the person" (s 16A(n)) is again a lowly consideration. In Western Australia (*Sentence Administration Act 1995*) and New South Wales (*Sentencing Act 1989* and *Sentencing Amendment (Parole) Act* 1996), the only mention of rehabilitation is in relation to parole decisions. Queensland's *Criminal Law (Rehabilitation of Offenders) Act* 1986 contains provisions, which for the most part, deal not with rehabilitation at all, but rather with the treatment of "spent" convictions.

Hence, while rehabilitation has never completely faded as a justification for punishment, "deserts"-based approaches hold a pre-eminent place in contemporary Australian sentencing practices (Braithwaite & Pettit 1990). Freiberg and Ross reiterate this theme when they state:

> Harshness has replaced hope, retribution has replaced rehabilitation, and prevention has eroded proportionality. (1995: 138)

Even the literature on the newly-emerging paradigm of restorative justice appears keen to establish restorative notions as new concepts rather than ones aligned with, (infer "tainted by:), rehabilitation (Sarre 1999a). For example, Albert Eglash, the psychologist who coined the term "restorative justice", advised that restoration must extend beyond rehabilitation, "[b]eyond what a court orders us to do, beyond what family or friends expect of us, beyond what a victim demands of us, beyond any source of external or internal coercion ..." (1977: 95).

Having said that, there are some signs of a "new rehabilitation-ism"(Zdenkowski 2000) apparent in at least two recent justice trends. The first is the creation of specialist courts such as the drug courts currently operating in, for example, New York and NSW (Makkai 2000) where treatment and rehabilitation are given a primary focus. The second new trend is prison privatisation. Although it has been suggested that it is "not entirely without significance that the era of the development of private prisons has coincided with the decline of the 'rehabilitative ideal' within prisons" (Bottomley et al 1996), it is also the case that private contractors are, for the most part, required to set and sustain certain performance indicators regarding rehabilitation. This is in stark contrast to the position in the 1970s (at which time one might assume the rehabilitative zeal had reached its zenith) when few, if any, prison systems would have regarded reduction of recidivism as a specific performance indicator (Harding 1997).

Be that as it may, the fact remains that rehabilitation, as an aim of sentencing in Australia, if not elsewhere, appears now to have assumed second-class status. It is arguable that the Martinsonian legacy must take some of the blame. Yet the zeal of those anxious to entomb rehabilitative initiatives sits awkwardly next to those presenting reasons for contemporary optimism (Gendreau & Ross 1987; Cullen & Gendreau 1989; McGuire & Priestley 1992; Pitts 1992; Holland & Mlyniec 1995; Lipton 1996; Dowden & Andrews 1999). In the words of McGuire and Priestley:

[S]ome years ago there was a widely quoted dictum, a flat and dismissive assertion that "treatment is dead". Given the accumulation of evidence since, the reverse case can now be made. (1995: 25)

Yet in the minds of those commentators and politicians anxious to push politically popular "desert"-based themes, the idea that "nothing works" has become difficult to dislodge.

Conclusion

The story of the reification of "nothing works" should send an important message to researchers that their responsibility in qualifying their findings and tempering their conclusions can never be overstated. Notwithstanding the substantial body of evidence that the doctrine of "nothing works" was and is little more than a socially-constructed reality rather than a scientific truth, Martinson's famous article remains in the forefront of the minds of many contemporary Australian policy-makers, politicians and administrators alike. In this context, researchers should keep in mind the cautions expressed by Barnes (1990) that our thinking is really little more than models and interpretations, together with a minimally interrelated array of empirical findings, brought into the public arena for further debate. It is worth reflecting on that caution as we remember and acknowledge the 25th anniversary of the publication of the article. Such acknowledgment provides a good opportunity for researchers to review the evidence, enliven the debate, sharpen the diagnostic tools and search anew for evidence of "what works".

– CHAPTER 20 –

Bridging the gap between prison and the community: Post-release support and supervision

Dr Stuart Ross
Centre for Criminological Research & Evaluation,
Melbourne University Private

Between prison and the community

Most prisoners look forward to the day they leave prison. Release brings an end of the restrictions and deprivations of imprisonment. It means returning to family and friends, having the autonomy to choose how to live, being free of petty rules. Ideally, release is an opportunity to start life again with the hope of not repeating the mistakes that led to prison. However, release can also present a new set of problems and threats. Releasees may find relationships are difficult to re-establish. Without money, a job, or somewhere to live, releasees may have little real autonomy over how they live. Old problems of drug or alcohol dependence may re-emerge, bringing with them the threat of illness or death. This chapter examines what goes wrong when prisoners fail to make a successful transition back to the community, some of the problems that released prisoners must overcome, and what can be done to assist the process of transition and re-integration.

The failure to make a successful transition from prison back into the community can have serious consequences for the individual, their family and their community. The most obvious form of post-release failure is when the releasee re-offends or fails to comply with parole requirements and is returned to prison. The probability of re-imprisonment is highest in the weeks and months immediately following release (Maltz 1984). While there are significant jurisdictional variations in the way that recidivism is defined and counted, in the US, UK, New Zealand and Australia, roughly one-quarter of all prison releasees will be returned to prison within one year, and one-third within two years (Table 20.1). These high failure and re-imprisonment rates mean that the pool of released prisoners includes large numbers of those who have previously failed to make the transition back to the community (Lynch & Sabol 2001).

Table 20.1: Recidivism by released prisoners: US, UK, Australia

	US[1]			UK[2]		Australia[3]
	Any recon-viction	New prison sentence	All returns to prison	Any recon-viction	All returns to prison	All returns to prison
6 months	11%	5%	–	25%	–	–
1 year	22%	10%	–	43%	–	–
2 years	36%	19%	–	58%	37%	37%
3 years	47%	25%	52%	62%	–	–

Sources: 1. (Langan & Levin 2002); 2. (Home Office 2001); 3. (Productivity Commission 2003)

Release from prison can also involve hazards to the releasee's health and even life. Ex-prisoners experience extremely high rates of drug-related accidents, overdose and death. In the first week after release, UK prisoners are 40 times more likely to die than the general population and drug overdoses are the main cause of death (Singleton et al 2003). In Australia, ex-prisoners have death rates ten times that of the general community, and over half of all these deaths are heroin related. In the period 1990-1999, ex-prisoner heroin-related deaths accounted for one-quarter of all heroin-related deaths (Graham 2003).

Prisoners themselves are not the only ones who suffer the adverse consequences of release. Families experience strain when a member is imprisoned and again during the process of transition back to the community. Up to 40 per cent of UK sentenced prisoners say that they have lost contact with their families while they were in prison (Social Exclusion Unit 2002), and the longer someone is in prison, the greater the extent of this breakdown (Travis & Waul 2003). Children in particular can experience great emotional stress from losing a parent and then months or even years later resuming contact.

Prisoners tend to come from communities that already experience high levels of socio-economic deprivation, and the problems that accompany them when they are released can have a deleterious impact on the neighbourhoods, suburbs or communities to which they return (Lynch & Sabol 2001). Releasees require high levels of social and economic support and their needs add to the demands on programs that service disadvantaged populations (Cadora et al 2003; Baldry et al 2003). The high rates of imprisonment and return of young males in these communities can lead to health and crime problems, social disorganisation and a loss of social capital (Rose & Clear 1998; Travis et al 2001).

Problems of transition

In order to make a successful transition back to the community, ex-prisoners need to deal with the problems like drug or alcohol dependence, criminal associates and the mental disorders that lead them to offend in the first place.

However, they must also find ways to rebuild the components of a normal life. In doing so, they face three kinds of problems. These are:

- Problems of material security (food, clothing, accommodation and income);
- Problems of personal relationships (family, spousal, parental and friendships);
- Problems of personal identity and psychological adjustment (self-image, institutionalisation).

Material security

Typically, prisoners are released with little in the way of material supports. They may receive some kind of transitional payment to tide them over the first few days, and some may have modest savings from prison employment. The first priority is likely to be finding somewhere to live. Releasees who are able to find stable, secure accommodation have a higher likelihood of remaining free than those who are homeless or in transient or emergency housing (Baldry et al 2003; Rodriguez 2003). However, there are a number of barriers facing released prisoners looking for accommodation. Private rental housing is likely to require a security deposit, rent in advance and references, while finding public housing may mean spending long periods on waiting lists. The preferred option for many will be to return to live with family, although post-release stresses in family relationships can mean that these arrangements break down in the weeks and months after release.

Income security is a second material factor that is strongly associated with post-release success (Nelson et al 1999; May 1999; Webster et al 2001). Even those prisoners who were employed before they went to prison are likely to have difficulties finding work after they are released. Employers are reluctant to employ ex-prisoners, there may be laws that prohibit ex-prisoners from some forms of employment, and parole reporting requirements may severely limit releasees' employability (Petersilia 2000). Unemployment benefits or some other form of pension are an alternative source of legitimate income. Releasees may face delays until their applications have been processed and they may need to satisfy compliance requirements (job-seeking or training programs). A common problem for prison releasees is that they do not have the identity documentation (birth certificates, citizenship papers) or financial documentation (bank accounts, credit cards) necessary to apply for or receive benefit payments. As with employment, released prisoners may be prevented from accessing some forms of social support (Travis & Waul 2003).

Personal relationships

Strong relationship networks are another of the keys to post-release success. Families and friends can provide accommodation and other material support, and their emotional support can be critical in making the psychological re-adjustment to living in the community (Ditchfield 1994). While the loss of an imprisoned family member may impose financial and emotional stresses on the family, over time families adjust to life without the prisoner, and the releasee may not be able to simply step back into his or her former roles as parent, spouse or breadwinner. Returning home is likely to impose additional financial strain on the family – at least in the short term. Releasees may bring with them prison behaviours that are not acceptable to the family, and may find themselves unable to readjust to the structures, compromises and responsibilities of family living. Problems like drug dependence or family violence that were suppressed but not resolved by imprisonment may resurface. The result can be conflict within the family leading to rejection of the releasee or breakdown of the family (Travis & Waul 2003).

Women released from prison can find the process of returning to their children particularly difficult. In most cases, relatives care for children of imprisoned mothers, although a substantial minority go into some form of state care. Only about half of imprisoned mothers continue to receive visits from their children when they are in custody (Mumola 2000). While regaining custody of their children is likely to be a high priority for mothers when they are released, there are a series of institutional and emotional problems that need to be addressed before this can happen. Where children are in state care, it is usual for the care agency to make transfer of custody conditional on the mother establishing a stable home, demonstrating that she is free from drugs or alcohol and satisfying all parole requirements. Relatives who have taken responsibility for children may also want to see evidence of a stable lifestyle and absence of offending. The children themselves may have found their mother's imprisonment hurtful and shameful, and may be anxious, angry or resentful when she returns (Conly 1998).

Personal identity and psychological adjustment

Psychological distress is a common experience of prisoners' returning to the community. This distress may involve finding it hard to relate to other people, difficulty in making decisions, thinking and behaving as if they were still a prisoner and can extend to depression, anxiety or even panic. Adjusting to prison life involves a variety of psychological changes that are sometimes referred to as "institutionalisation" or "prisonisation" (Clemmer 1940). These changes include becoming dependent on institutional structures and routines, being generally distrustful and suspicious of others, social distancing, and adopting the informal rules and standards of prisoner culture (Haney 2003). While these ways of adapting to prison can serve to protect the prisoner's physical safety and personal identity while in prison, they are maladaptive if they continue to frame the way the releasee interacts with others in the outside world. For many releasees, the process of making the psychological transition back to the community is further hampered because the person has unrealistic expectations about the problems he or she will face, and is unwilling to consider how these post-release problems will be overcome. Even those releasees who have been released before tend to believe that it will be relatively easy to re-connect with their family, find accommodation and get a job (Visher et al 2003). This lack of preparedness to plan for release is a major obstacle in improving success rates of released prisoners (Nelson et al 1999).

Managing re-entry through post-release supervision

It is clear that prisoners being released back to the community face a range of material and psychological barriers that they are unlikely to overcome without assistance, and that failure to overcome these problems is likely to lead to further offending and ultimately the return of the offender to prison. The primary institutional mechanism that has been developed to manage prisoner re-entry to the community is parole. Under the parole system, a prisoner is released prior to the expiry of his or her full sentence, and subject to a range of reporting and other requirements. There are three main elements to the system of parole. First, prison sentences passed by the courts are indeterminate. That is, the court sets a maximum period of imprisonment, but the actual period served in prison is determined by a non-judicial releasing authority – usually titled a Parole Board. Secondly, a prisoner released to parole is not "free" but rather continues to serve his or her sentence in the community. A requirement of this arrangement is that the parolee must satisfy conditions sets by the Parole Board. These include reporting to a parole officer at specified intervals, undertaking programs, being prohibited from drugs or alcohol, notifying the Parole Board of any changes of address or employment, being subject to curfews, and a host of other requirements that the Parole Board may see as necessary to prevent further offending. The third element of parole is that the parolee may be returned to prison if he or she is found to be in breach of any of the conditions set by the Parole Board without recourse to judicial appeal or review.

In the late 1970s, the system of parole came under increasing attack, especially in the US. It was argued that indeterminate sentences were inherently unjust, and that the rights of the community to be protected from offenders outweighed the needs of offenders for supervised release (Travis & Lawrence 2002). In the past two decades, the proportion of prisoners released to parole has fallen, but the very large increases in imprisonment rates have meant that the total number of parolees has risen substantially.

More recently, there has been renewed attention on the place of parole in the corrections system. A variety of post-release programs have been developed around specialised post-release program or surveillance components. These include work release, day-reporting centres, post-release hostels, intensive parole, home detention and electronic monitoring programs. All these programs retain the basic structure of parole: the release decision is administrative rather than judicial, the releasee remains subject to supervision and other controls, and breach of release conditions results in return to prison. Greater attention has been given to parole as the basis for more effective management of prisoner re-entry (Lynch & Sabol 2001; Seiter & Kadela 2003), with some arguing for increases in the proportion of prisoners released to parole and the funding given to support re-entry (Petersilia 1999).

However, the evidence to support the effectiveness of parole as a way of assisting releasees to make the transition back to the community is weak. There is no evidence that some of the "new" post-release surveillance options like intensive parole or home detention are more effective at preventing further offending than convention parole or even no parole at all (McKenzie

1997). Part of the problem is that increasingly stringent enforcement of parole conditions results in releasees being returned to prison for breaches of parole conditions (eg, failing to notify of a change of address) or for minor offences that would not otherwise lead to a prison sentence (Austin 2001). Between 1980 and 2000, the number of parole violators who were returned to prison in the US increased seven-fold, from 27,000 to 203,000 (Travis & Lawrence 2002).

On the other hand, there is evidence that some forms of re-entry support programs that address specific causes of offending do work. Seiter and Kadela (2003) reviewed 32 US programs that were designed to support prisoner re-entry. They found positive results for work release and training programs, drug treatment and rehabilitation, halfway houses and pre-release programs, and weaker but still positive results for programs targeted at sex offenders and violent offenders. They argued that the effectiveness of re-entry programs is constrained because they must be delivered in a political and administrative environment that is dominated by the avoidance of risk.

Social support for released prisoners

Many of the problems that releasees face are problems of gaining adequate access to the social support network that services disadvantaged groups in the general community. Traditionally, voluntary or charitable organisations have been key providers of these services to ex-prisoners. Groups such as the National Association for the Care and Resettlement of Offenders (NACRO) in the UK and the Womens' Prison Association in the US have provided material aid, counselling and family support, acted as service brokers and advocated on behalf of prisoners' rights. The relationship between these voluntary organisations and criminal justice agencies is complex. Some voluntary agencies will not enter into support arrangements where there is mandatory involvement by the releasee. However, increasingly voluntary agencies are becoming involved in the delivery of treatment or support services to released prisoners who are under some form of post-release supervision.

Lack of access to mainstream social services is a systemic problem for offenders. A review of re-offending by released prisoners carried out by the Deputy Prime Minister's Office in the UK (Social Exclusion Unit 2002) found that many prisoners had been effectively excluded from access to social services before they went to prison, and that imprisonment only worsened their social exclusion. The review team argued that the corrections system is being asked to "remedy a lifetime of combined service failure" (2002: 9), and called for a co-ordinated, multi-agency response that begins in prison and continues until long after release. This response would take the form of a "Going Straight" contract entered into by the releasee that would specify the areas of need to be addressed on release, the services and programs to be provided, and the releasee's obligations.

Similar programs aimed at securing better access to existing resources for releasees and improving the co-ordination between criminal justice and social service agencies have been developed in the US and Australia. The US Department of Justice has funded the Re-entry Partnership Initiative (Taxman et al 2002) in eight States. This program seeks to engage releasees' families, community-based service providers, the faith community and other sources of formal and informal support in reintegrating offenders. The program model is flexible to take account of the differences in release policies across the eight participating States and involves in-prison preparatory activities as well as post-release support and supervision. The Bridging the Gap program in the Australian State of Victoria (Ross 2004) seeks to engage releasees with outreach workers in one of five community-based support agencies. The program involves direct service provision by the support agencies as well as service brokerage.

The resurgence of interest in re-entry programs and transitional support for releasees marks a dramatic turn-around from the emphasis on punishment and control that has characterised the past two decades. There are those that argue that the problem of the transition between prison and the community would be better served by imprisoning fewer people for shorter periods and under more humane regimes (Morgan 1997; Austin 2001). Nevertheless, since there is no prospect of any fundamental change in penal policy, it is important that we make use of the lessons learned from the new re-entry programs. At the risk of reducing the current complex variety of programs to overly simplistic principles, let me propose that these lessons are:

1. Programs for released prisoners must be based on the principle of through-care. That is, they should begin while the prisoner is still in custody and continue through the post-release period.

2. Material and social service support needs to be backed up with programs designed to address the causes of offending. Providing releasees with stable accommodation or vocational training is unlikely to be of value if their drug or alcohol dependence remains untreated.

3. While it may be critical to provide specialised, intensive support in the period immediately after release, the ultimate goal of re-entry programs should be to engage releasees in mainstream support services. Engaging families in the transitional process is a critical element in this normalisation.

4. The process of re-integration is likely to take a long time. Prison typically lies at the end of a long pathway of social deprivation, stunted life options and emotional and physical abuse, and the process of building a new life after prison necessarily involves tackling issues that have previously been unresolved. The need to take a long view of re-entry is especially important when we are dealing with individuals who have long custodial histories.

5. Post-release success depends fundamentally on the commitment and perseverance of the person being released. Participants in post-release support programs must see themselves as actively involved in their own re-integration rather than as passive recipients.

CHAPTER 21

Prison industries in a time of science-based prison programming

Judy McHutchison,
Senior Research Officer, NSW Department of Corrective Services

Introduction

It may seem old fashioned in these times when inmate programs are discussed in terms of "strategic frameworks" and "accreditation systems" to be writing on prison/correctional industries. However, prison-based work either in the form of prison industries or work that assists in the operation or maintenance of the prison remains the major activity for a significant number of prisoners in western countries.

Part of the support for prison employment programs has emanated from the notion that people could be reformed through work (Hawkins 1981). Such beliefs have had broad appeal and a long tradition, possibly emanating from the importance placed on work within society. Additionally, there has long been an association between unemployment and crime. A number of Australian studies have found that offenders, particularly those sentenced to full-time custody, have experienced higher unemployment than the general population (Bates & Nun 1989; Gilchrist et al 1989; Broadhurst et al 1988). A Canadian study by Gillis et al (2001) investigated the impact of post-release employment on re-offending and found that offenders who were employed within the first six months of release had fewer convictions than those who had not obtained work during this period.

Despite the existence of this association between unemployment and crime, evidence concerning causality is inconclusive. It may be that unemployment has some influence on crime rates but it is clear also that some offenders eschew legitimate employment in favour of criminal activities (Bossler et al 2000). Most of the unemployed do not commit crimes and female unemployment rates have been found to not influence female crime rates (Naffine & Gale 1989).

As almost all offenders sentenced to a period of full-time custody will eventually be released into the general community, it is crucial that prison administrators undertake initiatives aimed at ensuring offenders are not made worse by their incarceration. The time offenders spend in custody also provides an opportunity to address those factors which lead to offending in the hope that the offender will not commit further crimes on release.

Reducing reoffending

Finding the magic formula that would convert offenders into ex-offenders is a longed-for goal of corrections professionals. This interest in re-offending is understandable, as crime causes considerable harm to the victims and their families, offenders and their families, and communities generally. In addition the financial/economic costs of crime pose a significant burden on public expenditure.

For example, Mayhew (2003) using police and victim survey data sought to answer the question, How much does crime cost the Australian economy? Mayhew included in his calculations not only property losses, medical expenses and the costs of the criminal justice system but also the intangible costs of crimes such as pain and suffering and lost quality of life and the cost of preventive efforts made to reduce the future incidence or severity of such crimes.

Mayhew concluded that an overall estimate of crime in Australia was $32 billion per annum – 5 per cent of the country's GDP (Mayhew, 2003). Clearly communities could achieve large financial savings if offenders could be circumvented from continuing with their criminal activities. The interest in reducing re-offending led to the development of the "what works" literature.

"What works" literature

Re-offending by released offenders can only come to official notice once further charges, convictions, or revocation or breach of parole occur. Due to the importance placed on it, the level of re-offending (commonly referred to as recidivism) is often used as an outcome measure in program evaluation. International research developments have used meta-analysis to evaluate the effectiveness of a range of interventions on post-release outcomes such as recidivism. Meta-analysis involves the compilation and analysis of relevant studies that have employed methodologies which meet set criteria concerned with scientific rigour. This literature concerned with identifying factors within interventions that have a positive effect on re-offending came to be known as the "what works" literature.

After Martinson's (1974) pessimistic announcement that "nothing works" (see Chapter 19), greater knowledge has become available. There is now recognition that treatment programs with certain characteristics can be effective in reducing recidivism. Most success has been found with cognitive behavioural programs, that is, programs aimed at producing a change in the thinking of prisoners with the intention that this would have a corresponding influence on offending behaviour (Vennard et al 1997; Kennedy & Serin 1997).

The push to turn the "what works" research into effective practice saw the development of systems to accredit programs (Ellis & Winstone 2002). Program accreditation involves establishing standards with regard to content, design and delivery and assessing prospective programs against those standards. So accreditation vets and monitors the implementation of programs to ensure resources are directed at programs effective at reducing reconvictions.

International bodies such as the Campbell Crime and Justice Group have been established to systematically and continuously review evaluations of inmate programs (Farrington et al 2001). This development is occurring at a time when more and more jurisdictions are incorporating an inmate's program participation into computerised tracking systems, thus making answering the question of *What works for what offenders?* more amenable to large scale analysis. With these two developments, the "what works" knowledge base is poised to rise greatly.

Part of the support for prison employment programs, such as prison industry, has emanated from the belief that such programs are beneficial in reforming offenders. However, historically much of the support for prison employment programs relies on anecdotal evidence. With the developments described above regarding the pursuit of excellence in program development how will prison industries fare? The available empirical evidence is looked at in the following section.

Empirical evidence of employment programs and re-offending

Although research into the influence of prison industries on re-offending is growing. there is not a large body of empirical research into this area. Some studies such as McGuire et al (1988) and Basinger (1985), did not find evidence that prison industry employment lead to a reduction in re-offending. However, other studies, that is, Wirth (1993, 1995) Motiuk & Belcourt (1996) the Ohio Bureau of Planning and Evaluation (1995) and Canestrini, (1993) have found some evidence that employment experience in prison industries can lead to a reduction in re-offending. A 1995 study investigated the long-term outcome, that is, eight to ten years after release, and found that male offenders who had been employed in prison industries had a lower rate of re-conviction for new offences (Saylor & Gaes 1992).

Some of the findings in the above studies support a hypothesis that employment in prison industries can lead to a reduction in recidivism. However, with the exception of Saylor & Gaes (1992, 1995) there are serious deficiencies in the methodology of the studies and/or lack of information in the respective reports.

In the NSW jurisdiction, two studies have been undertaken to determine if prison industry employment reduces re-offending (McHutchison 1991 & 1995). However, in NSW all sentenced prisoners are expected to work in either prison industries (furniture, textiles, engineering, electronics and printing etc) or services involved in maintaining the prison (cleaning, kitchen, garden, maintenance, laundry and clerical). Therefore there was no suitable control group of non-working prisoners against which the post release outcomes on employment and re-offending of prison industries offenders could be compared. The NSW studies found the rates of recidivism between offenders employed in *prison industries* and offenders employed in *services* were not significantly different. There was anecdotal evidence that both these areas of employment provide experience which could be later used in obtaining employment after release.

Clearly more research needs to be conducted before definitive conclusions can be made about the effect of prison industries on recidivism. Even then there may be limited value in generalising the research conducted in one jurisdiction to other jurisdictions not included in a study.

Limitations of empirical evidence

Prison industry planners have many factors to take into account in their decision-making. A variety of local factors affect the type of product or service that is viable. Consideration of business opportunities needs to be balanced with work which is meaningful but also routine enough to accommodate the general low level of skills of prisoners. Pressure can arise to increase prisoner staffing levels beyond that desirable for optimum production thus detracting from an industry's ability to replicate "real world" work. In establishing markets, skill is required to navigate around the sensitivities of private employers and employees in the general community.

Thus far from being some packaged program, prison industries is not a standardised intervention and the nature and type of industry vary. The importance placed on the vocational training within a workshop and the opportunity to receive formal accreditation with post-release utility would vary between workshops as well as jurisdictions. Prison environments differ due to security classification and many other reasons and this also could influence post release outcomes.

The social environment into which prisoners are released varies between jurisdictions and within jurisdictions, affecting an offender's ability to locate employment. The immediate post-release period is a critical time for offenders and as with other interventions the availability of post release services can be crucial for successful reintegration.

It is problematic to determine the value of prison industries as a global program. Studies undertaken in one jurisdiction may be valid for that jurisdiction but have little relevance to other jurisdictions. To claim widespread integrity as an evidenced-based program, prison industry may need to resort to other sources of evidence. The principles flowing from the "what works" literature do provide some support.

Prison industries as a cognitive behavioural program

Referring to the "what works" literature, it would appear that prison industries, by its very nature, would have some generic utility with regard to a positive impact on re-offending. This is because many of the characteristics of successful rehabilitation programs, particularly programs that address pro-social values and crimnogenic factors within a social learning model appear to be present in prison industry employment (McHutchison 1999). The main components of the social learning model are that learning takes place in a social setting, is interactive, and has components of role playing, behaviour modelling and rewards from positive reinforcement.

Prison industries workshops are social settings in which prisoners interact with fellow workers and work supervisors while taking on the role of worker; in this setting pro-social values are prescribed. These pro-social values provide an alternative to the criminogenic anti-social attitudes and include cooperative behaviour, accepting of responsibility, complying with instructions and operating as a member of a team. Prison industries provide an opportunity for prisoners to be habituated towards employment and to gain general employment competencies such as planning and organising activities, communicating and ability to follow instructions, working in teams, solving problems etc (McHutchison 2000; Mayer 1992). These basic employment competencies are transferable and independent of the nature of the work and therefore assist offenders to be employable.

Behaviour is learned, not only through one's own actions, but also by observing the actions of others and the consequences that stem from those actions (Bandura 1986). Modelling of behaviour is one of the most powerful means of transmitting values. There is evidence that in prison industries, work supervisors can operate as positive role models for prisoners (McHutchison 1991; Hawkins 1983). Prisoners given the responsibility for instructing fellow prisoners can also operate as positive role models (McHutchison 1991).

The literature on cognitive behavioural therapy states that the greater the range of positive reinforcers, the more powerful the learning experience. Due to the range of reinforcements available to prisoners employed in prison industries the learning experience should be a more powerful one both in terms of the learning of pro-social values as well as generic and specific employment skills. Employment in prison industry is positively reinforced by a range of actual and potential reinforcers such as wages and bonus payments, extra visits, employment reports which assist in gaining lower security classification and parole, by a sense of achievement from seeing the results of ones productivity, and positive feedback from work supervisors and fellow workers.

Prison industries, in contradiction to accredited programs, do not usually target prisoners for employment on the basis of risk but on the basis of other factors related to the demands of the production process. However, responsivity should be high due to prison industries consistency with social learning, as discussed above.

Another factor that can affect responsivity is the characteristics of the program leader. Prison work supervisors often come from similar socio-economic backgrounds to the offenders and the imperatives of the production process require the forming of good working relationships and effective communication. McHutchison (1999) found that prisoner workers held work supervisors in high regard due to both an admiration for their skills and because they treated the prisoner workers with respect. While programs which address specific offending behaviour (eg, sex offences, drug related offences, etc) are essential, prison industries, by its very nature, appears to have generic utility with regard to instilling pro-social values.

Essentials of good prison management

While the "what works" literature predominantly focuses on finding interventions which reduce re-offending, there are additional factors which are important to the operations of modern correctional systems. Cost-effective strategies are needed for managing prisoners during the period of their incarceration

There is a substantial amount of anecdotal literature that prison industries employment positively contributes to effective prison management (Edgar 1995; Verdeyen 1995). This anecdotal evidence is supported by empirical evidence from North America. In these studies, prisoners employed in prison industries received fewer misconduct reports than prisoners who were largely idle (Flanagan et al 1988; Maguire 1996; Saylor & Gaes 1996).

A study conducted in NSW surveyed the Governors of 25 prisons to ascertain their views on the effect of prison industries on inmate management (McHutchison 1999). There was universal agreement among the Governors that prison industries contributed to the good management of prisons. This was principally due to the role prison industries played in keeping prisoners occupied and alleviating boredom. All Governors reported that if employment in prison industries was not available, there would be a negative effect on the operation of their centres. This included an increase in tension with more inmate misbehaviour and subsequently greater pressure on prison staff.

Through reducing boredom, prison industries not only positively contribute to the management of prisons, it also contributes to prisoner well being. It has long been an overriding concern of prison administrators that incarceration does not leave offenders in a worse state than when they commenced their sentence. Idleness is one of the worst aspects of incarceration. While the principal aim of programs may be a reduction in re-offending, they also keep prisoners occupied. Program participation can operate as a form of dynamic security by keeping prisoners active and involved and thus reducing threats to security and control (Smartt, 1999).

Prison industries are unique in terms of inmate programming in that the flow of money is not simply one way. Like all programs, prison industries require expenditure but unlike other programs they also receive revenue. In some cases this revenue may exceed the costs of operating the prison industry –resulting in a profit. If an industry operates at a loss, that loss could conceptually be viewed as the cost of operating the prison industry program.

While generating revenue appears to give prison industries a head start in the efficiency stakes, other factors need also to be taken into account. If prison industries incur a loss on its production activities, this cost may be greater than the cost of operating alternate programs. However, to determine the economic efficiency of programs the cost of operating the programs would need to be balanced against the benefits for those programs.

If prison industries employment has a positive impact on the behaviour of prisoners during their incarceration, it is likely that the general operating costs of prisons will be lower. Cost savings to prisons would include a reduction in supervision costs, less costly containment because of increased numbers of prisoners qualifying for lower security classification, and also the early release of prisoners due to good behaviour (McHutchison 1999).

Conclusion

While the knowledge base of "what works" is only in its infancy, it is poised to develop greatly in the years ahead. Programs based on well-meaning assumptions, intuition, or on what *appears* to work are no longer appropriate. All programs should be evidenced based. However, all change, particularly when there is so much at stake, needs to be tempered with caution and an open mind. The primary role of prisons is to confine prisoners humanely and this often has to occur within very limited budgets. As science-based programming proceeds, prison industries still retain integrity as a prison-based program. This is because there are features of prison industries that suggest that they may have some utility for inculcating pro-social values and addressing criminogenic needs. Prison industry employment may also increase the employability of offenders after release. Additionally, the evidence that prison industries assists in the good management of prisons is strong. That prison industry offers these benefits, while simultaneously contributing to its own cost through the revenue it generates, makes it a very worthwhile program.

CHAPTER 22

The effect of post-release housing on prisoner re-integration into the community

Dr Eileen Baldry
University of New South Wales

Introduction

Article 25 of the *Universal Declaration on Human Rights*, adopted by the UN General Assembly in 1948, states: "Every person has the right to a standard of living adequate for the health and welfare of himself (sic) and his family, including food, clothing, housing and medical care and necessary social services." These rights apply to all people, including prisoners and ex-prisoners.

Without adequate housing in Australia, it is impossible to participate fully in society. Those who suffer inadequate housing – a form of social exclusion – in its most extreme form are homeless. Homelessness has a number of forms: primary homelessness in which persons are living on the street or in squats or cars; secondary, in which persons are transient, having to move often; and tertiary, in which persons may have accommodation but without the security of a lease (Chamberlain & MacKenzie 1992). The evidence internationally is that ex-prisoners are over-represented in all forms of homelessness and that homeless persons are more likely to be imprisoned than those with housing (Belcher 1988; Benda1991; NACRO 1992; Paylor 1995; Aderibigbe 1997; Craig & Hodson 2000; SEU 2002).

This chapter rehearses briefly international information on ex-prisoners and housing and outlines results of a recent study in Australia on the matter.[1]

---

1   For a detailed literature review on ex-prisoners, housing and allied social issues see Baldry, E, McDonnell, D, Maplestone, P & Peeters, M, (2003), "Australian Prisoners' Post-release Housing" *Current Issues in Criminal Justice*, vol 15, no 2.

Ex-prisoners

Data on persons flowing through the prison system during a year rather than census data is required to understand the scope of post-release issues. Persons released from remand should be considered in this data collection also, as many spend weeks or months in prison (Thompson 2001): long enough to seriously disrupt social connections and lose their housing. Release data is inconsistently gathered; for example, most jurisdictions do not count remand prisoner releasees in their figures and others do not count releasees who have spent less than 14 days in prison, and there is little information routinely gathered on the housing situation of releasees. There is some information available nevertheless.

In the US, the number of persons released from State and federal prisons increased threefold over the two decades to 2001 (US General Accounting Office 2001), and in 2002, 650,000 sentenced persons were released from State and federal prisons alone (this excludes those in county gaols) (US Department of Justice 2003). In the UK over 90,000 persons were released from prison in 2001 (SEU 2002). All ex-prisoners are likely to be socially excluded with little prospect of suitable housing, employment, family reconnection or good health (SEU 2002).

In Australia, the Commonwealth Department of Family and Community Services estimated that, in the 1999-2000 financial year, some 43,200 persons (some possibly appearing more than once) were released from Australian prisons. Over one-quarter of these (11,900) had served less than and 31,300 had served more than 14 days (Anderson 2000).

There are tens of thousands of people released from prison each year in Australia. A majority of these ex-prisoners appear to suffer a number of forms of social exclusion including inadequate housing.

Factors that increase the risk of homelessness for prisoners/ex-prisoners

Pathways (usually combined) into homelessness for releasees identified in studies (Banks 1978; Corden & Clifton 1983; Paylor 1995; Carlisle 1996; Hamlyn & Lewis 2000, Social Exclusion Unit 2002; Baldry et al 2003) are:

- Going to prison and having been in prison before;
- Poor or no release arrangements;
- No support immediately upon, or for two or three months after release;
- Poverty;
- Having no option but to return to the negative environment from which they came;
- Having no stable housing upon release/lack of availability of affordable housing;
- Worsening drug use;
- Deteriorating relationships with family and /or friends;

- Increasing debt, especially housing debt;
- Worsening mental health problems;
- Being a woman;
- In Australia, being an Indigenous person.

Losing housing

UK evidence suggests that prison releasees suffer deteriorated housing circumstances compared to prior to imprisonment, and women ex-prisoners suffer worse housing than men (Paylor 1995). Short sentence prisoners are more likely than those who served longer sentences to be homeless and then reincarcerated post-release (Banks 1978). Social isolation is strongly associated with being homeless post-release (Corden & Clifton 1983). One-third of prisoners lose their housing, two-thirds lose their job, more than one in five experience an increase in financial problems and more than two-fifths lose contact with their family (SEU 2002: 7). One in three prisoners in the UK are in impermanent accommodation prior to imprisonment with one in 20 sleeping rough (SEU 2002: 95).

Mental and intellectual disability

Researchers in the US estimate that between 30 to 40 per cent of mentally ill persons facing court or in prisons having been homeless and that homeless mentally ill persons are up to 40 times more likely to be arrested and 20 times more likely to be imprisoned than mentally ill persons with stable, suitable accommodation (see Benda 1991, 1993; Caton et al 1993; Martell et al 1995; Aderibigbe 1997; Lamb & Weinberger 1998; Solomon & Draine 1999; Desai et al 2000). A higher proportion of those who are homeless with a learning disability are arrested and incarcerated, compared to those without any other problem than their homelessness (Lyall et al 1995; Winter et al 1997).

Similar observations are made in Canada (Vitelli 1993; Zapf et al 1996) and the UK (James et al 1999; Craig & Hodson 2000). No such data are available in Australia.

Poor pre-release planning

Reception and pre-release interviews in the UK and US regularly fail to prepare prisoners for post-release life in the community. It is common for release prisoners to receive no information on housing, social security, employment or on drug and alcohol support services (Greater London Authority 2000; Travis 2000).

Indigenous Australians

Keys Young (1998) reported that Indigenous persons are over-represented among the homeless and that there was a lack of effective pre- and post-release programs for Indigenous releasees often resulting in homelessness.

Barriers to ex-prisoners accessing housing

Lack of affordable and suitable housing for ex-prisoners is a barrier to gaining housing in the UK (SEU, 98: 2002). This problem is worse in the US where social housing is much scarcer than in the UK & Europe. Private landlords are unwilling to rent to an ex-prisoner and/or ex-prisoners just do not have enough money to rent (Travis 2000). As noted earlier, prison releasees with a mental or intellectual disability are unlikely to find suitable housing, are likely to end up homeless and be quickly reincarcerated (Aderibigbe 1996).

In Australia, a Victorian Homelessness Strategy Report (Department of Human Services Victoria 2001) highlighted critical problems faced by ex-prisoners including no post-release support for the majority, no housing exit, poor information dissemination in prisons and the fact that the homeless service system responds only once a person is homeless.

Strategies to address ex-prisoner homelessness and poor housing

In Europe and the UK, cross-jurisdictional approaches to combating ex-prisoner social exclusion that promote housing-related support services are being developed (Rough Sleepers Unit 2000; Office of the Deputy Prime Minister 2001; European Social Fund 2002; Best 2003).

The US faces more severe problems due to the massive numbers of persons released each year. Most programs have been employment or drug rehabilitation based but new approaches suggest prison-based preparation, transition programs and community-based support with housing (Office of Justice Programs 2003).

In Australia, apart from the few established "halfway house" schemes, the best documented of recent approaches is the Victorian *Transitional Housing Management Correction Pathways Initiative* which uses caseworkers pre-release and increased provision of supported accommodation post-release to address housing problems (Aktepe & Lake 2003).

Summary

Literature and studies suggest that just being homeless increases the chance of being arrested and imprisoned. Barriers to ex-prisoners gaining stable housing post-release include poverty, lack of affordable and suitable housing, stigma and poor social functioning often due to a mental or intellectual disability. Responses are characterised by attempting to address social exclusion in the UK and Europe and taking an integrated, whole of government approach. In the US, approaches have been uncoordinated but a more holistic strategy is being contemplated. Some Australian States are taking similar approaches. None of these initiatives has been going long enough to provide reliable results.

Recent Australian research:
Ex-prisoner housing in NSW and Victoria

No empirical study of a general sample of ex-prisoners' post-release experiences and outcomes had been conducted in Australia prior to 2001, therefore almost nothing was known of ex-prisoners' housing and other social integration. An Australian Housing and Urban Research Institute funded study was begun in late 2001 and completed mid-2003 (Baldry et al 2002, 2003, forthcoming). One hundred-and-ninety-four prisoners in NSW and 145 in Victoria were interviewed just prior to release over a three-month period (consecutive sample) and then were sought for interview at three, six and nine months post-release. Of these participants, 145 from NSW and 93 from Victoria were re-interviewed or followed up in some way; therefore 70 per cent of the original sample was included in the final analysis. The profile of that 70 per cent was not significantly different from the original sample. Of the total original sample:

- 75 per cent were male, 25 per cent female;

- 16 per cent were Aboriginal or Torres Strait Islander;

- 66 per cent had been imprisoned previously;

- 82 per cent had just served sentences of 12 months or less with 53 per cent having served 6 months or less;

- 75 per cent had not completed secondary school with most not completing Year 10.

Staying out of prison post-release was chosen as the only readily available and fairly reliable measure of ex-prisoners' progress. At nine months, 34 per cent of the original sample had been re-incarcerated, 32 per cent in Victoria and 35 per cent in NSW.

Findings

Of the original sample, 73 per cent in NSW, and 58 per cent in Victoria were given no information on accommodation or support pre-release. Also notable was that participants came from, went back to, and called home, a small number of disadvantaged suburbs and towns. This was particularly marked in NSW.

Returning to prison

Two factors emerged as the strongest predictors of return to prison:

- Worsening problems with heroin use; and

- Moving house often (in this context, two or more times in a three-month post-release period).

Participants associated worsening drug use with poor housing and moving often.

Half of those interviewed post-release were highly transient, moving two times or more between interviews. Upon release, many ex-prisoners hoped they would live with their parents, partners or other family members. This proved impossible for most, especially in NSW where, by three months post-release, 60 per cent of that group were on the move and without stable accommodation. These ex-prisoners moved from friend to friend, sleeping on a couch, and often to the street and maybe to a hostel.

These chaotic living arrangements made drug rehabilitation, employment or social connections virtually impossible. A majority of these participants therefore were living in a state of homelessness, and were re-incarcerated by nine months post-release, as the following table shows.

Table 22. 1 Number of moves post-release

Moves	0 or 1	2 or more	Total
Not returned prison	89 (78%)	46 (41%)	91
Returned prison	25 (22%)	66 (59%)	135
Total	114	112	226

Statistical analysis showed significant associations between returning to prison and a number of factors. These were:

1. **Being homeless**. At nine-months post-release there were clear differences in the rate of primary homelessness between the two States. For NSW participants' homelessness increased from 20 per cent to 28 per cent, while in Victoria the rate was reduced (12% to 8%).

2. **Not having accommodation support or the support offered being assessed as unhelpful.** Two-thirds said they received some support, mainly social, with other forms being financial and counselling. Their assessment of whether the support was helpful was highly correlated with recidivism with 14 people (18%) who said the support was helpful returning to prison compared with 52 (69%) of those who said it was unhelpful.

3. **An increase in the severity of alcohol and other drug problems**. With time, the total numbers rating their drug use as a problem increased significantly, and many said their alcohol or other drug use was a significant factor in their return to prison.

4. **Being an Aboriginal or Torres Strait Islander**. Of the 57 Indigenous participants 29 (51%) were reincarcerated at nine-months post-release with Indigenous women, at 68 per cent, significantly more likely than the men to be returned. None of the Indigenous participants had lived in a family home post-release and many relied on public and publicly

assisted housing. There was a strong trend towards poorer housing in disadvantaged areas in NSW. Of those still out of prison 80 per cent were living alone and half were homeless at the nine-month interview.

5. **Being a woman**. Of the men in the sample 78 (31%) returned to prison whereas 37 (43%) women returned. Women had greater problems securing suitable accommodation and far fewer were living with parents, partners or close family than the men.

6. **Debt**. 116 (51%) said they had a debt of some sort and were more likely to return to prison (50%) than those who had no debt (30%). Of those with a debt, 35 (30%) had a State Housing Authority debt. Of these people, 22 (63%) returned to prison compared with 45 per cent of those with other forms of debt.

Staying out of prison

Three factors were significant in staying out of prison. They were:

1. **Living with parents, partner or close family**. Of the 41 per cent of those living with their parents, partner or other family member only 23 per cent returned to prison. Of those living alone or with friends or acquaintances, 52 per cent returned to prison. In Victoria, a much larger percentage (44%) than in NSW (18%) was still living with parents at nine months post-release.

2. **Having employment or being a student**. Of the 227 participants who answered the question about employment post-release, only 36 (16%) had employment of any kind or were full-time students. Of those who had employment or were full-time students only 3 (or 8%) returned to prison, whereas 46 per cent of those who were unemployed returned to prison. None of the five students had returned.

3. **Helpful agencies**. Ex-prisoners' own assessments of the helpfulness of support agencies proved to be highly reliable in indicating whether they were returned to prison.

There were major differences between NSW and Victoria highlighted in this study. The higher concentration in NSW in areas of disadvantage and the higher number staying in stable family accommodation in Victoria have been mentioned. Only 5 per cent in NSW, compared with 25 per cent in Victoria, had employment or were students. The lack of affordable housing in NSW compared to Victoria was a consistent problem. This study has also shown that moving often post-release is a predictive factor in a person's return to prison. When stable housing is combined with helpful support that assists in addressing issues such as drug problems, family relations and employment, the evidence from this study is that ex-prisoners are much less likely to return to prison.

– CHAPTER 23 –

Ethics and the role of the Correctional Officer

Anna Grant,
Crime Prevention Officer,
Queensland Crime and Misconduct Commission

Prisons remain relatively inaccessible to the majority of researchers and the methodological difficulties involved in conducting research within such environments are becoming well established (Liebling 1999). When such difficulties are combined with the general community indifference to the conditions of imprisonment, the attention given to the issues of prison staff, their role and ethical workplace behaviour is frequently negative and typically either the result of accumulated concerns over an extended period of time or the outcome of an immediate and well-publicised crisis. The irregular nature of prison organisational reviews, combined with the sensitive nature of personnel misconduct in such closed and controlled environments, increases the difficulty in undertaking a systematic study of the role of correctional officers and the dynamics of prison workplace behaviour (McCarthy 1981).

By virtue of the design and nature of prison environments, staff control the majority of prisoner movement and, consequently, much of their behaviour (McCarthy 1981). Prisoners have little to no discretion regarding potential employment, exercising, eating or the times at which they are locked in their cells. Visits, recreation and education are all part of controlled daily regimes (Bryans & Wilson 2000).

There is very little prisoners can do to prevent the consequences or seek effective redress when power and authority is misused by staff. The impact of this was described in a report by the Independent Commission Against Corruption (ICAC) which stated, "[w]hile other forms of corrupt conduct might be regarded undesirable because they impact on the fairness, efficiency and effectiveness of the machinery of executive government, corrupt conduct in a prison environment may, because of the peculiar vulnerability of prisoners to abuse, lead to a denial of basic human rights" (ICAC 1998).

This chapter briefly examines the role of the correctional officer and examines how organisational influences specific to prisons have the potential to influence staff behaviour. This is followed by a discussion on ethical behaviour within correctional environments and the potential for misconduct by prison staff. It concludes with a brief examination of some possible prevention mechanisms and the challenges surrounding the promotion of an ethical work climate within prison environments.

Occupational role

Correctional officers are a group of people who have a particular employment role with a unique level of responsibility. The occupational role of prison officers involves interpersonal exchanges with people who are physically restrained within an artificially constructed environment. Features of this environment for staff include hierarchical personnel structures, constant exposure to personal physical risk and mental strain, management of difficult inmate attitudes and behaviour and the ever-present threat of violence (ICAC 2004). In undertaking their work they have a duty of care towards, and must provide for and manage, people judged and sentenced by the criminal justice system, which the community expects to be securely contained. Correctional officers, similar to police officers, must always conduct themselves during the execution of their workplace duties with due consideration of the unique demands of their role, responsibilities and environment (Kennedy 1988).

The role of the correctional officer continues to change with the evolution of the prison environment. This includes the advent of different theoretical and practical frameworks for the management of prisoners, new technology, different architectural prison designs, changing organisational structures and increasing external scrutiny of the role and function of prisons. In part, this environmental change has manifested itself in recent decades in the increasingly multi-faceted role of the correctional officer. In addition to their traditional security and containment role, officers are required to assess, monitor and assist prisoners in issues of health, welfare and safety (Josi & Sechrest 1998).

Officers are also required to understand complex legislative and regulatory frameworks in the execution of their own duties. They are required to liaise with and assist a range of other professional staff within the prison environment – such as nurses, counsellors, teachers and psychologists. They must also deal with organisational administrative requirements and changing ideas of prisoner and prison management (Josi and Sechrest 1998).

Despite the considerable changes in the role of prison officers, there remains a deficit in the literature investigating the psychological functioning and organisational pressures which shape and influence the execution of this important role within prisons. Literature continues to highlight the conflicting nature of many of the responsibilities undertaken by officers (ie, counsellor versus regulator) (Kauffman 1988; Lombardo 1989; Josi & Sechrest 1998). The literature, however, does not investigate how such task and role conflicts manifest themselves in the workplace behaviour of front-line staff, or the resulting implications for the execution of their duties. McCarthy (1981) believes it is because "of an underlying assumption by correctional researchers that prison guards and other staff were malleable components of the correctional process and hence could be moulded to fit whatever role or design administrators had in mind". Other more recent perspectives, drawing on the sociology of occupations literature, suggest that occupational role demands for correctional officers are so encompassing that, regardless of individual background, they tend to develop common attitudes and behaviours in the execution of their workplace role (Jurik 1985; Kamerman 1998; Chan et al 2003).

Much of the research on prison officers, with strong ethnographic methodologies, has highlighted cohesiveness as a central feature in this occupation (see Kauffman 1988; Lombardo 1989). Cohesiveness has important implications for the behaviour of a group. Members of a cohesive group tend to be highly motivated to remain in the group. Groups that are cohesive also tend to exhibit strong norms and require compliance to the norms to ensure group continuation (McKnight & Sutton 1994).

Many of the existing studies of staff within prisons outline loyalty, compliance and conformity to a range of identified occupational norms which appear to be specific to prison staff and prison environments and may potentially be at odds with the ethical environment. For instance, research surveys of staff in correctional environments have found one of the main influences upon correctional staff behaviour is the fear for personal or physical security. Kauffman (1988) found that such fears influenced officer behaviour: "More important in shaping officers attitudes than the actual numbers of assaults (whatever that number may have been) were officer perceptions of the threat against them". Kauffman (1988) found that informal sanctions existed among the staff regarding inmate violence towards officers. One of the primary justifications used by staff for their use of violence against inmates was that they believed it deterred inmate violence against them.

Organisational culture and corrections

The operation of organisations in developing norms regarding staff behaviour is often called the organisational "culture". Schein (1988) defines culture as a "learned product of group experience" and believes it is based upon a series of shared assumptions by staff regarding values, attitudes and beliefs regarding the organisation and the ways in which they carry out their role as staff in that organisation. While it is often commonly assumed that there is a link between an organisation's culture and staff behaviour, the actual nature of this link has not been adequately examined (Chan, in Dixon 1999).

It has been argued that the development of a strong organisational culture comes from the formation of a strong identifiable character for the group of individuals concerned. The existence of an inmate culture within correctional centres has long been recognised. As Kauffman (1988) identifies, "much of the research conducted within corrections has concentrated on the unique features of that culture: the beliefs, values and 'code' of behaviour that characterises it". The same cannot be said of the research surrounding custodial officer culture.

Goffman's (1961) pioneering work on the concept of "prisonisation" and "institutionalisation" in total institutions attempted to measure the extent to which staff may also be exposed to these processes as a part of working in closed and inaccessible environments. Over time, however, these concepts have largely only been applied to inmates and not to staff. This is despite the fact that staffing issues and the impact of these processes on staff and workplace behaviour were specifically addressed.

Part of the problem is that "culture" itself is not a useful concept unless there is a good understanding of what it is, how it is formed, how it is transmitted, how it affects organisational practices and how it can be changed (Chan, in Dixon 1999). Staff members develop particular ways of perceiving understanding and responding to their occupational environment, distinctive cognitive tendencies which result from factors unique to each occupation (Bessant et al 1995). It is evident from the continuing lack of in-depth examinations of prison staff that the concept of a prison officer "culture" has not been clearly articulated or investigated. It remains unclear what features such a culture may have on ethical behaviour, or what processes are involved in its formation and how this may operate in affecting an individual's workplace behaviour within correctional environments.

Despite a lack of attempts to describe and map what this looks like, it is obvious that a prison is made up of many subcultures including, but not limited to, prisoner culture. Any reference to organisational culture in a prison context should therefore be describing the sum of all the various sub-cultures within most prisons. Mapping the complex interaction of these subcultures within a prison is an important part of understanding the overall manifestation of prison culture and the implications for those living and working in these environments. Any research in this area should recognise the existence of a range of subcultures, understand the power balance between these and how these are manipulated by their members and external influences to achieve certain goals (Bryans & Wilson 2000).

One feature that is immediately clear is that there is no homogeneity among prison subcultures. This is certainly the case with regards to staff culture, despite ideas to the contrary regarding staff being similar in nature and malleable elements of the organisation. Even within a prison staff culture, different groups of staff have different cultures. There may be a management culture, a custodial officer culture and a professional staff (psy-chologists, teachers, counsellors etc) culture. Some staff cultures may be more dominant than others due to their respective power over decision-making and daily operations, the specific functions of their role in the prison, the closeness of their working relationships and the operational constraints within the prison.

The prison officer subculture is generally accepted as being parti-cularly strong compared to the others (Bryans & Wilson 2000). Strong subcultures are often dominant because they have certain elements and norms that tend to be learnt through the work environment and everyday occupational tasks. Prison officer cultures would appear to have such features and can overcome any organisational instruction that takes place during initial training and induction.

For instance, research has noted that staff frequently perceive their authority as jeopardised by changes in inmate management or other correctional reforms. Individual officers may feel that they lack the power necessary to do their jobs and to ensure their own safety as well as the safety of the inmates and thus resort to certain ways of behaving in order to gain the power they feel is required (Ben-David et al 1996). Lombardo (1989) also identified the difficulties faced by officers in the exercise of their authority. Lombardo found that many officers recognised that complex power dynamics existed and it was perceived that authority over inmates could only be gained from recognition of that authority by inmates themselves.

While many investigations of prison officer culture have viewed these tendencies as negative, the elements of these socialisation processes can also be harnessed and used for positive cultural change. This idea is supported by a growing body of research which suggests that culture can be viewed as a distinct organisational feature which can be manipulated and managed in such a way as to improve organisational or staff performance, attitudes and values (Bryans & Wilson 2000; Grantiz & Ward 2001).

Often decision-making, ethical or unethical, takes place within an organisational context which structures and supports such decisions and subsequent behaviours (Bessant et al 1995). Organisational culture is believed to influence how ethical decision-making occurs, in both process and content. The provision of norms and behavioural cues can produce pressure for individuals to adapt their behaviour to unethical norms which may then lead to unethical behaviour. Conversely, when ethical behaviours are reinforced by norms and cues provided by an organisational culture, ethical behaviour may increase (Key 1999).

Organisational influence on staff behaviour

There remains a strong attachment among commentators to the idea that decisions to behave either ethically or unethically are individual choices upon which the organisation has little bearing. Theories and research in this area argue that individuals bring tendencies to behave unethically with them into the organisation and have the ability to then influence other staff behaviour. Similarly, importation theories of socialisation have argued that people import their own ideas and norms into any organisational setting. More recently, however, these theories have gained less support with research studies suggesting that ethical workplace behaviour is more closely related to the attributes of organisational culture than to the characteristics of individual employees (Chen et al 1997).

There is an increasingly rich literature and research base which has investigated concepts, such as the effects of larger groups on individual compliance and conformity. This literature has noted that there is a tendency for groups to influence the behaviour of their members in such a way that the larger group dynamic may affect individual compliance. This research notes that an individual member of a group often acts in a way as a member of that group that he or she would not act as an individual (Alderfer & Thomas 1988; Kamerman 1998).

While there have been only a few corrections specific empirical studies in this area, what has been articulated from the research is that many prison staff feel it necessary to identify and use (to varying extents) certain value and belief structures in undertaking their occupational role. In one example, participants in the Standford Prison Experiment playing the role of guards allowed them a feeling of group cohesion and sense of anonymity which then afforded a sense of protection from prosecution and identification as an individual. These participants used the argument that they were acting in a certain ways due to their role as a guard and believed that they would not otherwise act in such ways as an individual (Lombardo 1989).

Furthering this line of research has been the idea that individuals use particular cognitive processes to define stereotypes about the attributes of a group, including beliefs, attitudes, feelings and behaviour. These may be applied to groups of which they are members as well as other external groups they may have contact with (Grantiz & Ward 2001). It is argued that these psychological processes allow individuals to function as part of a group and provide them with certain scripts regarding acceptable group behaviour.

Not surprisingly, this type of influence is often found in organisations that require a high degree of regulation of employee behaviour in order for the organisation to function cohesively. In these types of organisations, individuals are more likely to join or form groups to reduce uncertainty. A fundamental need to feel certain about their world and their place within it gives people confidence about how to behave and what to expect from the physical and social environment (Allen & Meyer 1990).

Empirical research examining peers and groups on the formation of shared values and norms has also examined the effect of these processes on individuals' ethical reasoning and behaviour. Such research has demonstrated that the conduct of peers and wider workplace groupings are reliable predictors of individual group members' ethical behaviour (Granitz & Ward 2001). When an individual perceives that their peers expect them to behave in a particular way, this perception induces compliance in the individual to conform their behaviour in certain ways (Patterson 2001).

Informal or formal mentoring may also reinforce the homogeneity of a group in highly regulated environments. Newly trained staff are placed into what they perceive to be an uncertain organisational environment and look toward more experienced staff members to provide certainty. These more experienced staff members may, in turn, introduce them to their own personal views, values and guidelines for the job as well as values and guidelines of existing staff subcultures. In an attempt to find certainty and security, newcomers are then more likely to follow the lead of the more experienced member and learn a certain view or perception of the organisational roles and guidelines from them (Allen & Meyer 1990).

In many cases, the prison officer culture could possibly conflict with other individual norms or societal norms concerning the behaviour expected of people working in such bodies of public administration. Kauffman (1988) found that many officers "characterised problems that they faced within prisons as moral dilemmas, ones involving discrepancies between their own ethical standards and behaviour expected of them as officers".

Non-conformity can come at great expense to a new staff member. In correctional environments, expulsion from the staff culture is the ultimate sanction that can be imposed for the violation of the norms the group imposes upon staff behaviour. The safety of the staff culture can be very effective sanction for the reason that officers are operating within a potentially dangerous and violent environment. Staff members often argue that they rely heavily upon fellow staff members for their own safety and as such cannot be seen to go against staff norms for fear of being abandoned in a dangerous situation where they require assistance (Kauffman 1988).

While broader organisational structures and frameworks provide a context for ethical decision-making by organisational members, these processes can be overridden by especially strong attitudes of peer work groups. Because members share in common values, functional/operational working contexts and environments they may also frequently develop common inter-group biases (Granitz & Ward 2001). The nature of the correctional environment can make this uniformity of biases, not just behaviour, seem essential to survival. As a result, correctional centres would appear to be one environment of adult socialisation in which the acculturation of values and biases takes precedence over adherence to behavioural norms (Kauffman 1988).

Misconduct and unethical behaviour may therefore be an example whereby organisational process and social pressures have induced conformity and compliance to deviant norms among workplace members. However, espoused organisational values (which may be very different from the demonstrated organisational norms) can still strongly affect the behaviour of staff by determining certain frameworks within which members perceive problems and make decisions (Stevens 1999).

Ethical workplace behaviour

In the only published study directly examining misconduct by custodial staff in correctional systems, McCarthy (1981) uses the categories of misfeasance, malfeasance and nonfeasance to define the types of behaviour involved.

McCarthy defines misfeasance as situations where there is misuse by staff of their occupational role, authority and duties. In large organisations, responsibility is diffused through the fragmentation of various tasks that the organisation performs and the sharing of various tasks among large numbers of staff. The division of labour operates to make no one officer or office wholly responsible for organisational actions (Kamerman 1998). In the case of correctional staff, the large amount of discretionary power with which they are vested can be dangerous as decision-making within centres is often of low visibility and there is limited accountability. Correctional officers for instance have large amounts of discretion concerning the daily movements and regimes of prisoners and are often required to make such decisions quickly. Given the structure of the organisation, these small daily decisions are rarely accountable as part of the larger daily management of the prison/organisation as a whole.

Malfeasance, on the other hand, refers to actions involving illegal or improper behaviour rather than the improper use of lawful authority. Practices involving malfeasance are probably the most easily identified unethical behaviour as they are primarily criminal acts (McCarthy 1981). Staff engaging in malfeasance are more likely to be careful regarding the commission of these acts due to their visibility and ease of identification as misconduct. However, in closed environments such as prisons, the function of group norms and psychological processes previously identified can serve to protect those engaging in such actions. Research in policing organisations identifies such protection of in-group members as a "code of silence" (Chan 2003).

Finally, there is the category of nonfeasance referring primarily to negligent behaviour. Rather than direct acts, nonfeasance is the failure to act, or the failure to properly undertake various duties and tasks associated with a role. Traditional definitions of official misconduct tend to neglect this category. Nonfeasance is particularly notable in relation to misconduct within correctional centres due to the encompassing nature of its role and environment. Omissions by correctional staff in their duties can have significantly more serious ramifications than in other organisations as the health and safety of inmates can depend upon action by staff. McCarthy (1981) identifies two particular types of such conduct within correctional centres "selectively ignoring inmate violations of institutional rules and the failure to report or stop other employees involved in misconduct".

Implementing an ethical workplace culture

One of the most popular methods of implementing and promoting ethical behaviour in organisations is through the use of codes of conduct. Codes of conduct attempt to publicly define what the required standards of ethical behaviour are for members of that organisation. It is frequently used by organisations to encourage self-regulation among employees, act as a supporting reference framework against internal and external pressures to behave inappropriately and is also used by organisations as a method of adjudicating disputes regarding employee conduct (Higgs-Kleyn & Kapelianis 1999).

Codes of conduct serve an important function in assisting the development of ethical behaviour in organisations. It is important they are considered as part of a wider system promoting ethical workplace behaviour. (Higgs-Kleyn & Kapelianis 1999).

Numerous studies (Murphy 1988; Raelin 1991; Knouse & Giacalone 1992) cite the important role that organisational culture plays in the implementation of ethical standards for staff. Many of the studies have found that the role of management and supervisors is particularly important in this process. In order to develop organisational cultures conducive to ethical behaviour, management and senior staff must ensure that they themselves rigorously exhibit the required standard of behaviour as well as facilitating discussion of ethical issues specific to that workplace. They can do this by identifying shared ethical values common across the organisation and through the use of organisational narratives which clearly provide employees with what are appropriate and acceptable standards and types of behaviour.

The research also stresses the importance of staff involvement in these processes. There must be bottom-up as well as top-down implementation and development of ethical standards. To implement a broader ethical culture among employees requires, a significant organisational commitment must articulate, apply and enforce standards of ethical behaviour, and also requires the provision of sufficient governance and transparency of process among all employees at all levels of the organisation (Higgs-Kleyn & Kapelianis 1999).

If, for instance, existing security measures and monitoring arrangements in relation to staff behaviour are inadequate, officers may perceive that the risk of detection is lessened and that the rewards of engaging in unethical behaviour outweigh the risks (ICAC 2004). Correctional administrators must therefore investigate ways to ensure that an ethical organisational culture, including counter-measures, is implemented.

Conclusion

The influence of organisations upon the behaviour of staff can be significant. Nowhere has this been the subject of more interest in recent times than the area of ethical workplace behaviour. Ethical behaviour within prisons is of particular importance given that the role of a correctional officer involves the exercise of significant amounts of discretion and authority over people confined against their own wishes within a closed physical environment. While research in the area of ethics has shown that the organisation and peer work groups have the potential to greatly influence individual's behaviour through the development of organisational and workplace specific cultures.

Unfortunately, there has been a dearth of research in the area of staff subcultures within prisons and a lack of attempts to gain an understanding of what prison culture, not just prisoner culture, is, how it forms and how it affects a prison operationally as well as any effect it may have upon behaviour by staff members. The investigation and implementation of ethical workplace cultures in prisons is an important goal in protecting the rights of prisoners and staff as well as ensuring the effective administration of criminal justice.

– CHAPTER 24 –

Measuring prisons and their moral performance

Alison Liebling
Director Prisons Research Centre, Cambridge University, UK

> As for the question of what in fact are the values which we regard as
> universal and "basic" – presupposed by the very notions of morality and
> humanity ... this seems to me a question of a quasi-empirical kind. (Berlin
> 2002: 45)

Dramatic transformations have occurred in the organisation and management of prisons, and other traditionally public sector institutions, over recent
decades. Performance measurement, for example, has become a refined and
complex art. Technology has ensured that there is a management reach
into institutions which was unimaginable 20 or 30 years ago. We live in an
audit society, according to Power and other critics (Power 2001; Pollitt and
Bouckaert 2000; Clarke and Newman 1997). Our generation has invented
performance improvement planning, performance testing, market testing and
private sector competition. These new techniques of quality measurement,
and new forms of accountability, form the cornerstone of modern approaches
to management. This is a sociologically significant development, with
implications for the nature and quality of our institutions, for the staff who
work in them, and inevitably, for those on the receiving end of the so-called
services delivered.

There is much critique of this process of transformation, and there are
some risks, like the substitution of trust in organisations with "rituals of
verification" (Power 2001; O'Neill 2002). Other complaints include the
instrumental reasoning inherent in managerialism, the impatient demands
being made for continual improvement, a future-oriented, or always forward-
looking approach to work and people wanting to be treated as individuals
rather than aggregates (see Feeley & Simon 1992, 1994; Bottoms 1995). This
forward-looking approach to work is contrary to how prison officers go
about their work, grounded as they necessarily are in "what worked
yesterday" (Liebling & Price 2001). On the other hand, in the prisons context,
and in other corrections fields and beyond, modernisation was long overdue.
One of the difficulties with this kind of progress, a difficulty often expressed
in the form of a general dissatisfaction with performance measurement, is

that the mechanical techniques are often more developed than the deliberation is. There has been insufficient reflection on what it is that should be measured, and why, or about what measures might be appropriate. The concept of safety in prison is highly complex, for example, and may not be reflected adequately by rates of assault, and so on. There has been little dialogue between those responsible for the development of performance measures and scholars of prison quality (Liebling 2004; Saylor 1984).

The research question we should pose, in the light of the above developments, is: what *matters* when evaluating the quality of a prison? Our research suggests that the answer seems to be, "how *just* is it?"[1]

I want to outline briefly in this chapter, how a research team at the Cambridge Institute of Criminology approached this question of "what matters" and how we arrived at this answer. I shall show whether such a concept can be meaningfully measured, outline where this research is taking us, and discuss what some of the implications are. One of the aspects of this research I will not be raising here, but is of interest in the recent history of corrections, is the problem of what goes wrong when important terms like 'care', 'justice', 'respect' and 'humanity' are misunderstood (Liebling 2002a, 2004).[2] The original rationale for the study was to deliberate and reflect on what these important words might mean in the penal context, and to find some way of measuring them appreciatively or positively. Prisons found to have a "culture of brutality", still contain some examples of good practice, in places, and among some staff. It is important to reflect in official performance measurement of that prison, precisely how much respect exists there, despite this culture, and to reflect what it looks like and where it can be found (see, eg, Braithwaite and Makkai 1994; Braithwaite 2002). Failure to do this can lead to further losses of legitimacy.

The research began as a Home Office *Innovative Research Challenge Award*, in 2001. The nature of the award meant that considerable freedom to innovate was built into the project from the start. We wanted to explore ways of putting words to that "feeling" people talk about when they spend time in a prison. A senior manager might say, for example, as one did about one of the establishments we selected for our research, "it is meeting all its targets, but there's something not quite right about its staff-prisoner relationships". We adopted an "appreciative inquiry" approach, which meant we used specific, creative exercises aimed at identifying peak or best experiences (Ludema et al 2001; Liebling 2004). This included a three-day workshop with staff in each of five prisons, and more limited group exercises with prisoners,

---

1   This begs the question of whose views should inform the answer. Here, I am proposing that the views of prisoners, prison staff, political philosophers, and the results from empirical research, should be taken into account. There seems to be a degree of consensus about "what matters" from these different sources. The importance of justice is less surprising in the light of other recent work on prison life (see Home Office 1991; Sparks et al. 1996).

2   Barbara Hudson has suggested, likewise, that the terms "security" and "justice" in particular have quite recently lost "half of their traditional connotations" (Hudson 2003: 203).

during which we invited them to tell us stories about the prison. They drew a history wall of its peaks and troughs, in groups, reporting back and discussing significant events: a suicide, a disturbance, a change of Governor, a new wing, a change of function, and so on. They identified headwinds and tailwinds, and finally, imagined the prison if all its best experiences were brought together and the headwinds vanished. They were then asked to identify the values underlying this vision and, eventually, we reached a consensus about these values and the words that should be used to describe them. These exercises generated considerable consensus, between prisons, but also between prisoners and staff. We were able to proceed, at a much earlier stage than we had originally intended, with a single version of the questionnaire arising from the dimensions. This meant we were able to make comparisons between prisons much sooner than we had expected, and so on.

The dimensions were as follows: Respect, Humanity, Trust, Support, Relationships, Fairness, Order, Safety, Personal Development, Family Contact, Well being, Decency, Social Relations among Prisoners, Distribution of Power, and Meaning.

This is a sort of "legitimacy-plus" formula of prison life (Sparks 1994; Sparks and Bottoms 1995; Liebling 2004). We spent considerable time discussing what these words meant in the penal context, using scenarios and examples, and exploring each concept further in individual appreciative interviews. So we might ask, for example, "tell me about a time when you have felt treated with respect in here". We digested as much as we could of the literature on each of these concepts. We solicited suggestions and came up with several statements or items thought to reflect each dimension. These were randomly distributed in a 100-item questionnaire, which were administered with 100 randomly selected prisoners in each prison, during the course of a long appreciative interview about the meaning of these terms and each individual's experience of them in each prison. The reliabilities were high. A mean score was calculated on each dimension to reflect prisoners' overall rating. We remain interested in individual item scores, as prisons can have similar dimension scores on safety, for example, but very different forms of safety. One prison's *form* of safety might be based on lack of movement, or situational control, and another's might be based on activity, or social control (Liebling 2004; Bottoms et al 1991). In a recent longitudinal development of the study, there are specific questions, or items, where we shall look in detail for movement over time in the answers, in the light of specific initiatives. One of the key questions in a longitudinal evaluation of a new set of suicide prevention measures, for example, is the question, "did you feel cared about when you came into this prison?" Between 12 per cent and 43 per cent of prisoners agreed or strongly agreed with this statement in 12 prisons at Time 1. We are hoping to find increases in most of the establishments (especially the low scoring prisons) in the program two years later, at Time 2 (Liebling 2002; Liebling et al, forthcoming).

We found statistically significant differences between prisons in these important areas of prison life (see Liebling & Arnold 2002; Liebling 2004). The five prisons in the study had relatively high levels of safety and order, and relatively low levels of (especially) trust, but also respect, humanity, and staff-prisoner relationships. We found some dramatic differences between the public prisons and the one private prison in our sample, which have been replicated in other prisons. In our deliberations about the work, we have been attracted to some work by Valerie Braithwaite on security and harmony values (Braithwaite 1994, 1998). Prisons differ, and they emphasise each value orientation to different degrees over time. But it also seems that the private sector has some significant strengths in relation to "harmony values", on the whole, while the public sector's strengths seem to lie in the area of "security values", including safety (see further Liebling, forthcoming).

The results for each establishment seem to "ring true" with our (and others') instincts, so that the prison mentioned above emerged as hypothesised, with good performance on regime activity and family contact, but relatively low performance on respect. The fact that it went on to have a major disturbance during the year following our fieldwork made good theoretical sense (see Bottoms 1999; Sparks et al 1996). A second prison that scored relatively high on trust and respect went on to have two escapes, so it is not the case in our framework that more of everything is better. Staff can be too accommodating (Home Office 1994). As Isaiah Berlin said, certain basic values are always in tension, this is a "permanent characteristic of the human predicament" (Berlin 2002: 43). The measuring process, and our discussions of the results with the field, is intended to generate serious and on-going reflection about what a good prison is.

So this measuring exercise is essentially a deliberation and thinking exercise and it helps us to understand the nature of prisons, as well as the particular characteristics of any individual prison. The survey can be used to compare prisons longitudinally (we have done this once, and we are currently doing so more systematically in an evaluation I shall mention below). Numerous prisons requested the survey, for example, if they were suffering from a particular problem, or if they were about to undergo a performance improvement process. We have entered into a partnership with the Prison Service's Standards Audit Unit, whereby they do most of the "measuring" (that is the conducting of the surveys during routine audit visits) and we do more of the detailed analysis.

We have used the scores above three (the neutral score) to identify the *value cultures* of each prison (see Liebling 2004). Low scoring prisons are not all alike, and negative cultures can be distinctive. The best use of this kind of data is clearly when it is used in tandem with other information and extended familiarity with a single establishment. We have explored, rather more tentatively, the *emotional climates* of the five prisons in the original study, based on the qualitative data. This tells us a great deal about how and why establishments might go wrong; for example, when staff and prisoners inhabit an opposite emotional climate.

Finally, we can investigate the relationships of the dimensions to each other, so we found, for example, that fairness is predicted by relationships and respect, as Bottoms and colleagues would have predicted, but fairness is also significantly related to well being (see Liebling 2004, Figure 9.1; Liebling et al, forthcoming). This is an important finding, and an illustration of the vulnerability of individuals (MacIntyre 1999), especially in the face of *unfairness*.

Where is the research taking us?

This research has taken us in several new directions. First, we are currently completing an evaluation of the pilot phase of the Prison Service's new suicide prevention strategy, using these quality of life measures, and measures of prisoner distress, in order to see whether considerable investments in five establishments in particular, make a significant impact on levels of distress. These levels of distress are, in turn, significantly related to institutional suicide rates. The findings so far indicate that levels of fairness, perceived safety and assistance for the vulnerable, significantly affect levels of distress (Liebling et al, forthcoming). We are hoping that some of the establishments in the pilot phase of the strategy have achieved significant improvements in these areas of prison life. One of the intriguing questions here is how far physical improvements to the built environment, and new practices at the reception and induction stage, bring about broader cultural changes in some establishments, and if so, why this is the case. We have developed a detailed staff survey, with its own dimensions, to help us disentangle more about what is going on in each of the 12 establishments in the overall study. The staff data suggest that communication, relationships with senior management, and work culture and climate, are significantly associated with good suicide prevention effectiveness and low suicide rates, taking population and other institutional differences into account. For uniformed staff only, communication is replaced by safety and security in the model. Safety is clearly important to both prisoners and staff. This need for safety is sometimes overlooked by liberal models of justice (see Liebling 2004; Hudson 2003).

Secondly, some interesting differences are emerging between the public and the private sector in specific areas of "moral performance", with the public sector outdoing the private sector in important security and safety dimensions, but the private sector apparently outdoing the public sector in relational dimensions, at least in those prisons we have studied. These findings are consistent with emerging research results from elsewhere (National Audit Office 2003; Camp et al 2003; and see Perrone & Pratt 2003), although there are some important exceptions (see, eg, Coyle et al 2003, passim; HMCIP 2003). This exploratory work is telling us a great deal about the complexity of prison life, culture and management in the new world of 'contestability'.

Thirdly, the Prison Services in England and Wales have adopted a version of our quality of life survey (using a more efficient small group administration method) as part of its routine audit procedure. This is a paradoxical outcome, since a measure we devised to offset the worst excesses of managerialism has been enthusiastically adopted by those in charge of performance measurement. We have mixed feelings about this but, in general, cannot be fundamentally unhappy that prisons are coming under pressure if their scores on "respect", "fairness" and "relationships" are low.

One of the purposes of the exercise is to explore the extent to which there is a fit between performance on audit, generally and in specific areas like sentence planning or suicide prevention, and our measures. That is, what is the relationship between processes intended to achieve specific aims, and outcomes for prisoners? There seem to be several areas where this relationship is weak. So, for example, establishments might be achieving good audit scores for sentence planning, but prisoners do not feel their time in prison is being planned or that constructive use is being made of it. We are providing an oversight role in this process, and are currently, in collaboration with the in-house MQPL team, developing some new dimensions, such as race relations, healthcare and procedural fairness. We take a particular interest in those prisons where there is a particularly wide gap between performance on audit and our moral performance measures. The original spirit of the exercise was exploratory, and therefore we are continuing to develop the tool, and explore the data, in ways that help us to understand more about the prison.

The implications

There are several implications arising from this research. The first is that human beings, including offenders, need to be in environments that treat them with dignity and permit their development (MacIntyre 1985, 1999). Prisoner well being (human well being) is dependent on fair and respectful treatment. Several philosophers have said this before, but we have some empirical data that demonstrates this to be true. We are inclined to ask "what works" more often than we ask "what is just", yet there may be sound instrumental reasons, as well as moral reasons, why what is just works better than what is unjust.[3]

Secondly, we need to understand cultures (and therefore values) in establishments and institutions. It might be wise to include more emphasis in future research on the role of senior managers in establishing, changing or shaping cultures. We need to move beyond the public good, private bad character of much recent penological debate, and look instead at the role of values in different organisations, including the infusion of instrumental and business values into the public sector and its effects.

Thirdly, we need to re-evaluate the prison, and use of the prison, against these "dimensions-that-matter". On the one hand, our hypothesis would be that high scoring prisons will both implement programs and initiatives more effectively, and individual prisoners reporting respectful and fair treatment in a safe prison will do better on release. On the other hand, when we consider these results, the prison looks like a more precarious place than sentencers or the public think, a place where decency is inherently difficult to achieve.

---

3   Hudson suggests, following Habermas, that we should introduce a "legitimation filter" into (senior and policy) administrative decision-making processes. See further, Hudson 2003 (p 170) and Habermas 1996.

CHAPTER 25

Professionalising the Correctional Officer: The US perspective

Professor Don A Josi, University of California, US
Associate Professor Dale K Sechrest, Armstrong State University, US[1]

The changing role of the prison guard: Historical antecedents

Historically, employment in corrections has been viewed as an occupational field, not a profession. The correctional institution was referred to as a penitentiary, a facility designed to punish; correctional officers' were called guards, their duty was strictly custodial, their role was principally that of "turn key." Without demand for additional skills, little attention was paid to upgrading the position.

In the US, for example, employment as a penitentiary guard attracted white males from rural areas or small towns, many with a limited education and a history of unemployment (Irwin 1980). These "guards" frequently began their careers in their mid to late twenties, after having tried a variety of other occupations. Many were retired enlisted military personnel who frequently reported an interest in police work and chose corrections because it appeared somewhat related (Philliber 1987). A primary employment motivation factor was job security. The prison system provided the promise of steady work, with little fear of layoffs. These individuals frequently were not able to identify with this occupation as a profession; the common tendency was to view their work as "just another job" (Lombardo 1980).

The past 35 to 40 years of research and correctional activity has created an increasingly complex, and somewhat contradictory, body of knowledge regarding the changing role of the correctional officer. In a 1947 article on the selection process of prison personnel, Lundberg stated, the "methods of selection of the prison guard are generally loose and have little empirical validity"(p 38). As recently as 1981, Toch wrote, "the correctional officer is a residue of the dark ages. He requires 20/20 vision, the IQ of an imbecile, a high threshold for boredom and a basement position in Maslow's hierarchy" (p 20). On the other hand, another view has it that the correctional officer can

---

1   Research assistance for this paper was provided by Shari Darling.

be the single most important person in terms of influencing the inmate and having the potential for enhancing or minimising, through his or her actions, the effectiveness of the various treatment programs (Glaser 1969; Teske and Williamson 1979; Wicks 1980).

With the involvement of social workers, psychologists, and psychiatrists in the late 1940s came marked civil service classification and pay scale preference. Prison guards were not classified as "professionals." Higher education was not required and the caste system was strengthened. In-service training programs for guards were rare and did not give a "professional" aura. Clemmer, writing in the 1940s, observed that guards had a "retaliatory spirit" toward their charges. This theme was supported some 12 years later by Barnes and Teeters (1952) who referred to guards developing "lock psychosis," the result of continual "numbering, counting, checking, and locking."

During the last half of the 20th century the penal environment changed dramatically as penitentiaries gradually became less severe and more humane "correctional institutions". Since the 1950s humanitarian reforms designed to lessen the pain of imprisonment and provide constructive inmate "programs" replaced the more repressive penitentiary setting.

Starting in the early 1960s, the role of the prison guard expanded to include the idea that the guard might have some influence on the inmate. In fact, inmates, when polled, more often cite officers than treatment staff as influential (Josi and Sechrest 1996). This is not surprising, considering that inmates spend more time with custodial staff than treatment staff. With an expanded role came a different title – correctional officer. Some old-timers refused the offer, preferring to continue calling themselves guards. Even today, one hears correctional officers use the term guard as often as correctional officer. There is a definite split between the custody-oriented officer and the "professional" officers who welcomes a more diverse agenda and role (Freeman 1997).

A rehabilitative philosophy dominated corrections through the early-1970s. It offered a humanistic approach and corrective action to lead offenders to a law-abiding lifestyle. This was the era of the "rehabilitative ideal" (Morris 1974; Sechrest and Reimer 1982) when treatment supplanted custody as the theme in many prisons and older methods of control were challenged and abandoned. Crouch (1995), in a discussion of the changes that affected correctional officers during this era, noted that three factors combined to change the prison world for inmates and officers alike. First there was a new emphasis on rehabilitation that led to a loosening of the tight controls that characterised prisons in early years, as well as an expectation that officers would do more than just "lock and unlock" doors. The second factor was a change in the size and composition of the inmate population. There were more inmates entering the system and more of them had serious drug problems. Finally, judicial intervention eventually affected every policy and procedure, leading to a belief that "the courts ruled the prison" (p 184).

By the early 1980s, court holdings requiring due process protections for prisoners eliminated the unquestioned authority of correctional officers. Other prisoners' rights, such as to send and receive legal mail, to practice their religion, and to receive medical care, were recognised. Prison administrators rescinded strict rules of inmate movement and there were more privileges and freedoms granted, either as a result of court cases or in anticipation of a legal challenge.

Ironically, curtailing "official oppression" opened the door to gangs and inmate cliques who filled the power vacuum and used violence to get what they wanted. By the late 1980s, inmates had less to fear from guards but more to fear from each other as racial gangs and other powerful cliques or individuals solidified their control over prison black markets. By the end of the 1990s, most observers noted a dramatic lessening of violence (similar to the rise and fall of criminal violence in our cities). Analysts propose that the prisons were brought under control by able administrators, good management skills and the increasing "professionalism" of the correctional officers (Josi and Sechrest 1998; Lin 2000).

Throughout these periods of change, the role of the correctional officer evolved. The rapid growth of "prison systems" into departments of corrections, and "prison guards" into correctional officers, heightened interest in the role of the correctional officer as a more stable, career-oriented profession. Although legislation in several States has emphasised punishment as the primary role of incarceration the negative and stereotypical connotations associated with corrections employment have been offset by substantial pay increases and a professionalised work environment. Increased training and organisation within the field has brought status and readily marketable skills to the work force.

The new model: Correctional officers today

The new millennium marks a turning point for correctional systems throughout the world. For some time, there has been an intensive effort by corrections to gain the confidence of the public. With increased urbanisation, more timely electronic news media reports and renewed emphasis on human rights, corrections has more and more become the target of a wide variety of attacks. These have included questions on departmental and officer effectiveness of treatment efforts, cost effectiveness of operations, bureaucratic ineptitude, violations of civil rights of offenders, and institution overcrowding, among others. To combat this backlash, correctional agencies have devised a plan that has worked very well for law enforcement, a plan best summed up by a single word – professionalisation. This movement has been led by an articulate and tactful group of correctional officials who have stressed a new ideology of the correctional officer occupation.

Historically, policy makers and managers in the criminal justice system have viewed "professionalisation" as a favored solution to escalating organisational problems – a panacea used to silence occasional opposition. It is generally assumed by management that a "professional staff" will do what is necessary to ameliorate a crisis and better serve the community. While mandating the professionalisation of front-line officers, top correctional officials often ignore deeper organisational problems and fail to consider the compatibility of personnel development with the organisational realities of work in contemporary correctional institutions (Josi and Sechrest 1998).

Professional development for the correctional officer should be characterised by a concern for departmental performance through higher standards. Moreover, improvement in a number of personnel-related areas need to be addressed. Newer technologies, more sophisticated reporting procedures, and increased legal demands have made it necessary to reconsider the role of the correctional officer. In addition to maintaining the safety and security of the institution, the modern correctional officer must be able to communicate with inmates, supervisors, and the administration in order to avoid minor issues from escalating into major disturbances or riots. Moreover, the officers must be able to interface with a host of ancillary professionals employed by the institution, which include, psychologists, counselors, educators, and social workers.

Recruitment and selection

The recruitment and selection process is generally acknowledged as a key event in the operational effectiveness of a correctional agency. All jurisdictions necessarily differ in a variety of unique and important ways regarding personnel selection. Nevertheless, basic principles exist for the development of an efficient, effective, and fair selection process that results in the appointment of those individuals who best possess the skills, knowledge, and abilities necessary for an effective respected correctional agency. Knowledgeable, highly skilled, motivated, and professional correctional personnel are essential to fulfill the purpose of corrections effectively. Improved recruitment and selection standards of entry-level correctional officers can make a positive contribution to the overall performance and operation of the organisation.

As the numbers of correctional personnel expand to keep pace with growing inmate populations, it is also sometimes difficult to keep in mind that every number on every agency's table of organisation represents an individual employee – a person with strengths and weaknesses; capabilities and limitations; satisfactions and frustrations. The field of corrections spends a tremendous amount of money on recruitment and selection of its corrections staff. It seems prudent, therefore, to be concerned about the quality of this expensive investment.

Training

Pre- and in-service training has often been cited as one of the most important responsibilities in any correctional agency (Grabow, Sevy and Houston 1983; McKenna and Pottle 1985; Wahler and Gendreau 1985; Craig 1987; Humphery 1990; Johnson 1990; Morton 1991; Carter 1991). Training serves three broad purposes. First, well-trained officers are generally better prepared to act decisively and correctly in a broad spectrum of situations. Second, training results in greater productivity and effectiveness. Third, it fosters cooperation and unity of purpose. Furthermore, agencies are consistently being held legally accountable for the actions of their personnel and for failing to provide initial or remedial training (ACA Training Standards 1990, 1992).

Historically, correctional organisations have been slow to recognise the value of training and the impact it can have on the total organisation (Carter 1991). Poorly trained officers with no prior experience can be a threat to themselves and to other staff. New officers with no prior training have no idea of the proper role or job responsibilities of correctional officers. And yet most new correctional officers have no prior experience in working with inmates, and almost none have any experience that applies to the prison setting (American Correctional Association 1999).

To carry out their security and supervision responsibilities, correctional officers need to understand their agency's correctional philosophy and their institution's regulations and procedures. All officers must be security technicians, with expertise in search, supervision, and inmate management. They must know the limits of their responsibility and authority, as well as how to work as team members with other staff. Finally, they must understand the judicial and legislative decisions that affect most of their activities. To know all of these important facts, well-developed training programs are necessary.

These concerns are the reasons why training is so critical. In fact, in the 1970s, the American Correctional Association (ACA) Commission on Accreditation for Corrections specified the first national training standards. ACA not only identified specific standards for new officers, but also established requirements identifying essential training topics and the number of hours for pre-service orientation, academy, and in-service training. Other organisations such as the National Sheriff's Association, the American Jail Association (AJA), and the International Association of Correctional Officers (IACO) have contributed to the training standards for correctional officers in the US. These standards have contributed to the development of individual officer certification criteria for these organisations.

Training also received an additional boost in the late 1970s when federal judges began ordering correctional agencies to implement or to improve existing training programs. By the mid- to late-1980s there was less emphasis on merely requiring training programs and more on the effectiveness of the training provided (Johnson 1990).

Although the overcrowding problem of the past two decades limited and slowed the trend toward professionalism through training, most jurisdictions now have extensive pre- and in-service training academies. In these academies, officers experience training somewhat similar to law enforcement, a combination of practical how-to courses and a sampling of sociological and psychological offerings such as communication, cultural sensitivity, criminology, and legal rights of prisoners. A list of subjects in a typical training curriculum includes relevant legal knowledge, institutional rules, administrative policies and procedures, elementary personality development, methods of counselling, self-defence tactics and use of firearms, report writing, inmate rules and regulations, inmates' rights and responsibilities, race relations, basic first aid and CPR techniques, radio communications, substance abuse awareness, and how to deal with special inmate problems like the mentally ill offender (Josi and Sechrest 1998).

Continued education

Does today's correctional officer need a college education? A primary role of education is to instill in individuals the desire, capability, and ability to continue learning throughout life. The world is which the corrections professional operates is continually changing. New discoveries are made, new laws passed, new judicial rulings issued, and new technology is developed on a continuous basis. Adequate development of all skills – technical, human and conceptual – requires increased amounts of education as society changes and the complexity of the profession and its knowledge base increases. Because higher order skills require more education than lower order skills, those who wish to compete adequately and rise to higher-level positions must continue to pursue continuing education opportunities conscientiously.

Despite the increased importance of the correctional officer, little attention has been directed to the fundamental issue of education. Current research studies on the relationship between continued education and correctional officer career development and professionalism are methodologically deficient. This is possibly because the job of correctional officer over the years has not been seen as a job requiring education at even the high school level, much less beyond.

Sample data that strive to predict a relationship between higher education and job satisfaction, turnover, attitudinal variables, and substance abuse are relatively small in number and often do not include a significant subset of the target population (Josi and Sechrest 1998). For these reasons, any examination of correctional officer education begins with two assumptions. First, that there is a need for increasing the educational levels of correctional officers, and second, that increased levels of officer education will improve overall correctional operations, including planning, management and supervisorial duties and services.

Career path development

The burgeoning offender population in the US draws attention to the need for more corrections facilities, programs and personnel. The current demand of correctional systems for well-trained employees is unprecedented in correctional experience. Simultaneously, the competition for resources to address facility and operational needs is unsurpassed. However, when correctional managers are forced to make the hard choices between providing funds for security and custody staff or to training the decision frequently is made in favor of custody requirements. Unfortunately, such circumstances and the lack of training which results can leave members of the corrections community handicapped in their ability to address their performance in an efficient, effective, and lawful way.

It is essential that correctional officers receive adequate preparation for their jobs. This preparation should include appropriate training and orientation to job assignments, and on-going in-service training to enable them to assume increasing responsibilities. Moreover, training should go beyond pre-service orientation and provide an opportunity for the organisation to impart its mission, values, vision, and culture. Too often in corrections only worker skills are targeted for training, and the organisation misses a significant opportunity to communicate its vision and mission.

Correctional agencies cannot expect to have a top-notch workforce without having made an investment in career development education and training programs. Organisations clearly communicate how they value training, education and job development by the resources directed toward staff preparation, both at the pre-service and in-service levels and by upper level management's involvement in the entire process.

Career planning is critical to the success of correctional management. Effective career planning is essential to hiring and retaining the most talented employees available and is useful in helping employees avoid career plateaus and obsolescence. From the individual's perspective, career planning is essential if employees are to maintain some self-determination with regard to their own careers. Career planning helps employees make better decisions about their careers, when to seek job mobility and more challenging job assignments and when to stay put. Most importantly, career planning assists employees in adjusting to the changing personal needs and job demands they face as they pass from one career stage to another.

Summary

Many correctional systems are trying to meet this broad range of needs in the continuing effort to upgrade the performance of their correctional officers. Scarce resources in the face of increased inmate populations often work to defeat these goals. Nonetheless, the profession has a voice through its various national and international organisations. Standards of performance have been developed for institutions and certification programs for individual officers are now being used widely. More training is available through associations and private organisations, most of which can be made part of formal departmental certification programs. Clearly, the "guard" has been replaced by the correctional officer. This officer has learned how to motivate inmates to improve and how to be proactive in addressing the daily problems of institutional operations.

Perhaps the biggest challenge in the future for correctional managers is to create a social climate within an institution where officers feel valued and trusted. Once that is achieved, then the trickle-down effect will be that officers will treat inmates with respect. Only in this atmosphere can anything positive come out of the prison experience. It should be noted that prisons are different. In some institutions, enthusiastic staff members are given the support necessary to create an environment where change can occur. Unfortunately, even with all the gains made by the corrections industry during the past 50 years, too many institutions are simply warehouses, where disgruntled staff and uncaring supervisors consider it a good day when there are no serious incidents or assaults during their watch.

CHAPTER 26

Human resources analysis of the Australian corrections industry

Sean O'Toole
Assistant Director, Learning and Staff Development
NSW Department of Corrective Services

Corrections as a human services industry

Corrections is now viewed strategically as a labour intensive "human service" industry. Analysis of the various annual reports from each of Australia's correctional agencies indicates that about three-quarters of the operating budgets of corrections agencies is spent on human resources. It is only logical that considerable efforts are devoted to ensure the quality and growth of this investment. A successful career in corrections clearly requires a greater commitment to professionalism than was evident even as recently as 15 years ago. Never has there been a greater demand for a professionally competent and motivated staff. Although entry standards are still comparatively low in some Australian States, career advancement requires a record of achievement in secondary education, a commitment to professional values and a record of exemplary performance.

The role of the prison officer

Historically, the role of prison officer has been observed to be at the base of the criminal justice pyramid. Consequently, the notions of education, training and career development have not been central to the role. Sechrest and Josi (1998) report that the typical prison guard comes from a rural area, has limited education and begins his or her career aged in their mid-20s after having tried a variety of other occupations. Many are retired military personnel who are motivated to select the occupation for "job security". While this profile is based on the American correctional system, research on the experience of officers in Australia (Myers 1989; O'Toole 1999) reveals a strikingly similar profile. Australia differs from the US, however, in the structure and focus being applied to the professional development of correctional officers.

Lombardo (1981) described the work environment of the prison officer as laden with fear, mental tension, uncertainty, isolation, inconsistency and boredom. This study of prison officers in New York is generally regarded as the seminal examination of the role of the prison officer. On the subject of job security and pay, Lombardo concluded that most officers were satisfied with their work to the extent that it fulfilled the need they had when they accepted their positions. Most felt that the prison business was a very stable field and that as crime rates always seemed to be increasing they had plenty of job security.

Recruitment

As recently as the 1980s the primary considerations in recruiting prison officers were physical fitness, size and strength (Biles & Morgan 2002). Big strong men, who had an elementary grasp of reading and writing, and who could count, were the ideal candidates for work in prisons. Prison officers make up the greatest percentage of all staff in the corrections industry (see Table 26.1 which displays staffing figures for all Australian jurisdictions for 2003). The corrections industry has made a distinct shift away from the military or para-military model of management that was common 25 years ago. Consequently, most jurisdictions have adopted psychological, psychometric and attitudinal testing in addition to cognitive tests such as literacy and numeracy. Interviews with psychologists to assess suitability are also now commonplace. That situation has changed dramatically in recent years as the job profile has changed. Women now have equal opportunities within the industry and their numbers are growing, while the physical attributes that were once prized are now not as important as cognitive skills and the right psychological profile.

Staff from Indigenous or minority backgrounds

Indigenous people are grossly over-represented in the Australian correctional system. This may be the reason it has been difficult to attract the right levels of Indigenous staff, which are integral to the delivery of culturally appropriate programs to these offenders. Countries such as New Zealand and Canada have been far more successful in recruiting Indigenous staff than Australia. Recruitment of the right mix of female staff has also proved problematic throughout Australia. In the Asia Pacific region it is China with 25 per cent of female corrections staff who is the leader in this area. Scandanavian jurisdictions like Norway and Sweden boast upwards of 35 per cent female prison staff.

Most Australian corrections organisations have between 15 and 20 per cent female staff despite setting higher targets for recruitment of this kind and having a range of strategies to address this imbalance. The problem with recruiting higher numbers of females and other minorities begins with the psychological, psychometric and attitudinal testing that is based on discriminatory and out of date workforce models. Potential recruits who manage to negotiate these hurdles then face a panel interview where experienced officers tend to recruit in their own image – an image which is also now out of date. Extensive marketing campaigns that aim to lure these minorities are often highly successful but ultimately those whose interest in the occupation is aroused cannot get past the barriers presented at the recruitment stage.

Table 26.1. Staffing numbers by jurisdiction (June 2003)

NSW	Prison officers	3,975
Total staff	5,672	
WA	Prison officers	1,232
(Dept of Justice) Total staff	4,296	
Victoria	Prison officers	1094
Total staff	2,069	
Northern Territory	Prison officers	309
Total staff	469	
Australian Capital Territory	Prison officers	115
Total staff	223	
Queensland	Prison officers	1,718
Total staff	3,537	
South Australia	Prison officers	806
Total staff	1,352	
Tasmania	Prison officers	300
Total staff	375	
Australia (combined)	Correctional officers	9549*
	Total staff	17,993*

* NB: The private sector provides an estimated 2000 staff and 1200 prison officers to Australian corrections.

Education levels for recruits

New South Wales is the only Australian jurisdiction that specifies a minimum standard of entry for correctional staff, although most jurisdictions now require potential recruits to have completed a recognised level of secondary schooling or an equivalent trade qualification. The entry-level standard of education may begin to gain greater scrutiny as corrections shifts its focus away from the traditional security oriented model to adopt a human services approach. Most jurisdictions also apply a probationary period to newly recruited officers to ensure their suitability under workplace conditions. There are workplace assessments that usually continue for the entire probationary period after the initial classroom training is completed.

One result of a failure to increase entry-level standards for the occupation is the inability of correctional agencies to attract and retain officers in today's highly competitive job market. Corrections officials are conscious they must guard against the job of prison officer being regarded as a second-class occupation open to anyone with more than a minimum education, average intelligence and good health. In recent years, correctional agencies have been guilty of not upgrading their basic standards for employment in line with similar occupations like policing and the other emergency services. Upgrading the education level of correctional officers and maintaining a strong focus on succession planning are key challenges. It is easier to attract people with undergraduate degrees into the community corrections field and most jurisdictions have a degree qualification as mandatory for entry to these roles.

Remuneration – comparisons with other professions

The base salaries of correctional staff in Australia are, on average, well below those for similar occupations such as police, firemen and ambulance officers. Interestingly, in neighbouring jurisdictions in the Asia Pacific Region this is not the case and could be a reason the profession there is held in higher regard. In China, Hong Kong and Pacific Island nations, prison officers are remunerated at the same level as police and are considerably higher than their civilian public service equivalents with similar academic qualifications.

Table 26.2. Salary comparisons with similar occupations 2003

Prison officer	The commencing salary for a prison officer in Australia in their first year of service based on averages from all States and Territories is $31,600.
Probation and Parole officer	The commencing salary for a probation and parole officer in Australia in their first year of service based on averages from all States and Territories is $37,700.
Australian Protective Service	APS officer grade one commences on a salary of $32,000 in their first year.
Fire Services	A trainee firefighter remains on probation for 6 months at a salary of $633 per week. After that time trainees progress to a level 1 fireman at $722 per week. This represents an annual salary of approximately $36,000 in their first year of service.
Police	A probationary constable in the NSW Police Service earns approximately $44,000 in their first year of service.
Federal Police	A federal agent with the Australian Federal Police commences on a salary of $34,346 while undergoing initial training and this salary can rise up to $44,350 (depending on qualifications and experience) within the first year of service.
Ambulance officer	A trainee ambulance officer commences at a salary of $32,356 per year ($34,834 if a registered nurse).
Customs officer	A customs officer who joins the Australian Customs Service at age 18 commences on a salary of $19,612. The rate varies each year until someone who joins at age 21 commences on a salary of between $28,018 and $30,967.

HR and organisational culture

As the role of the prison officer is transformed, the correctional organisation is confronted by the division in the workforce between the newer officers who have been trained in the context of modern correctional philosophies and more experienced officers with different work practices. These experienced officers often form the nucleus of the dominant culture within the corrections workplace and set the tone for work practices. Training programs that aim to create a unified common culture and to break down these barriers are one way of addressing these problems. Clearly the greatest challenge for corrections organisations is the need to create an integrated and supportive corporate culture where there is "one team one dream", while at the same time recognising that individual "professional cultures" co-exist within the specialist workgroups. Quite often these distinctive sub-cultures, which define work functions, are so influential they impede the organisation's ability to achieve its corporate goals. An effective learning and development strategy can ensure the experienced officers keep pace with the new generation in relation to correctional philosophies and changing organisational priorities and goals.

Employee health and safety

Working with offenders both in institutional settings and in the community promotes high levels of stress and anxiety. Most Australian jurisdictions have now implemented a range of programs to improve the physical and mental well-being of their staff (see Table 26.3 and 26.4 below). Most agencies have staff psychologists, who co-ordinate a range of pro-active services. However, external counselling services, which offer a confidential and voluntary early intervention and assessment for staff, are also increasingly being utilised. Peer support programs are also common and involve a volunteer network of staff who are suitably trained and then bound by a peer support code of conduct. These officers do not act as mediators, counsellors or therapists but simply listen to issues, provide practical advice and support, assist families and provide referrals where necessary to the other services.

Corrections, like many justice and emergency service occupations does have a high incidence of alcohol and drug dependency problems and many officers are reluctant to seek help for these addictions because of the possibility adverse action will be taken against them. The introduction of random or targeted drug or alcohol testing is an emerging challenge in all jurisdictions. The promotion of a healthy lifestyle and physical well-being is also an important trend in the industry and takes many forms including voluntary staff health assessments. The advent of anti-smoking legislation has been a catalyst for the industry to introduce structured smoking cessation programs. Other legislation in the area of workplace safety also places pressure on the industry to ensure the corrections workplace is safe. Although the greater proportion of corrections work is sedentary, those who are operational must be capable of performing all essential physical tasks. This, in turn, promotes a safer workplace, influences productivity and meets organisational "duty of care" obligations.

Table 26.3. Counselling services for correctional employees in Australia

	WA	SA	Qld	Vic	Tas	NT	NSW
Post-incident counselling/ debriefs?	√	√	√	√	√	√	√
EAP counselling for staff?	√	√	√	√	√	√	√
Number of sessions available?	6 (is)	5-6	10	4 (is)	3	5	3
Staff counsellor/psychologist?	√	√	x	x	√	X	√

Table 26.4. Other staff support services for correctional employees in Australia

	WA	SA	Qld	Vic	Tas	NT	NSW
Peer support program for staff?	√	√	x	√	x	X	√
Healthy lifestyle programs for staff?	x	√	x	√	√	√	√
Drug & alcohol testing and support?	x	√	x	x	x	X	√
Staff climate/ satisfaction surveys?	√	√	x	√	x	√	√
Psychological testing of recruits?	√	√	√	x	√	√	√

The emergence of the training academy and other educational delivery strategies

Over the past decade there has been a distinct trend emerging in relation to learning and development in correctional organisations. With the expansion of specialist training academies for staff, Australia's correctional jurisdictions are no exception. While these academies allow the corrections organisation to induct new members, skill and re-skill the existing workforce they also have a much more pervasive function. They effectively impact on every aspect of the life of the organisation by motivating, informing, developing and supporting its human resources. They reinforce organisational standards, values and practices and ultimately they position the organisation, through its people, to achieve optimum performance and productivity.

NSW has enjoyed such a facility since 1989, Queensland have also had a small Training and Development Centre for some years and the West Australian Department of Justice has recently floated plans for the development of an academy which would serve that State's corrections staff. Against that trend and with the advent of large-scale privatisation in Victoria's prison system in the mid 1990s, the Loyola staff training college was closed. Elsewhere in the Asia Pacific Region, training academies have been an integral feature of correctional systems in all major countries. China boasts numerous academies, the largest being its Central Institute for Correctional

Police, which boasts 5000 students and 260 academic staff. Japan has a training institute with eight branches, each boasting its own professor. Korea and Hong Kong also have notable and well established learning institutions for their prison officers.

In the absence of funding to build training academies, a second trend has occurred among the smaller jurisdictions, which have formed partnerships with private and tertiary providers for the provision of their learning and development services. Indeed, some Australian jurisdictions have entirely handed over the provision of their training and development function to private providers. In Tasmania, TAFE has been contracted to provide the corrections training package and other short courses. In Victoria, the entire Department of Justice, which includes the Office of the Correctional Services Commissioner, has formed a partnership with the Swinburne University of Technology for the delivery of a range of short courses and the government-training package. ACT Corrections also contracts the delivery of some of its programs to the Canberra Institute of Technology.

Tertiary education for prison officers

The debate surrounding training versus education for prison officers continues to gather momentum. Education implies a less structured approach to learning with an emphasis on research, analysis, debate and collection and assessment of evidence. Training is more formulaic – with an emphasis on explanation, demonstration, practice, correction and confirmation. Prison officers who can analyse a situation and find solutions to problems and persuade others to assist with their implementation are what the occupation desires. The ambiguous nature of what is both a "hands on" and a "dirty hands" occupation requires a high level of understanding.

These attributes are encouraged by education and more generally, tertiary qualifications provide an effective antidote to the claim that prison officers should be on the bottom of the criminal justice pyramid. Today we need prison officers who graduate from more than just the school of hard knocks. The dilemma about the need to provide tertiary education for prison officers has existed for some years, particularly as the complexity and knowledge base of the occupation increases and the skills – technical, human and conceptual – needed by the corrections professional change.

Myers (1989), conducted research into prison officer education in the mid-1980s focusing on Bathurst gaol in NSW. He examined the results of the first decade of the Associate Diploma in Justice Administration offered by the then Mitchell College of Advanced Education (now Charles Sturt University). That course was among the first to specialise in the field of corrections for corrections practitioners. Unfortunately, of the total number of graduates in the first decade of the course, 105 were police and only six were correctional officers. There were continuing difficulties filling the corrections strand of the course and it was finally abandoned.

Myers concluded that prison officers only saw a tertiary qualification as useful in relation to promotion to executive rank. However, most officers expressed no desire to proceed beyond the (non-executive) rank of senior prison officer. Furthermore, they saw no reason to have to study to get there. Tertiary education was seen primarily as a means of attaining skills for an alternative career. Officers interviewed by Myers in Sydney claimed enrolment in tertiary studies actually worked against them in interviews for promotion to non-executive positions, as officers interested in academic theory were thought to be unsuitable for corrections work.

Myers found that those who were engaged in tertiary studies complained that they had difficulties meeting tertiary commitments due to rostering arrangements and the sheer emotional exhaustion of the job. They also said they had trouble getting time off to study. On the positive side they said that study alleviated the "lonely boring hours at work" and gave them mental stimulation. A study conducted in the US (Regoli, Poole & Shrink 1979), expressed the view that moves to professionalise the role of prison officer would increase the already high levels of cynicism in the occupation and may actually serve to divide the workforce, as standards such as tertiary qualifications were said to be beyond the average officer. At the same time in Australia, a demographic study of the education levels of police and prison officers (Braithwaite & Cass 1979) revealed that less than half of 1 per cent of prison officers had any tertiary qualifications.

A review of the literature on this subject (Philiber 1987) concluded that increased education among prison officers actually led to increased job dissatisfaction. Studies on this subject cautioned that, as corrections administrators placed increasing importance on enhanced education as a rationale for recruitment or for in-service training, such moves could have an overall negative effect. Given this was the climate just 15 to 20 years ago, much has happened right across the spectrum of corrections in the past two decades to establish the foundations of a learning and development culture. Undoubtedly the role of the corrections worker has changed remarkably in that time. However, it is arguable that the increased emphasis on training and career development has been the catalyst for some of the greatest reforms. By the end of the 1990s, most of the larger States had formed educational partnerships with universities. No fewer than 12 universities now offer a combined total of more than 40 courses with a corrections component. Charles Sturt University leads the way with the only corrections specific Masters Degree.

Career development

The latest views of career development use what is termed a "systems approach" to an individual's career management. This approach presents the organisation, its environment, and the people within the environment, as part of a complex open system. All parts of the system are constantly subject to change. According to Kramer et al (1998), the challenge for the individual is to synchronise their career path with these changes. The organisation needs to see the development of its human resources beyond mere in-service training programs that allow them to assume greater responsibilities. Staff must be trained to understand the core values, strategic aims and ethical underpinnings that ultimately result in a close correlation between the needs and values of the individual officer and those of the organisation. This is commonly known as career development.

All Australian corrections organisations have well-established programs and provide ready access to public sector management courses, leadership development programs and other succession planning initiatives. The most innovative have blended several strategies. The NSW Department of Corrective Services Career Development Program is based on an assessment centre approach and has provided a range of opportunities such as job placements, financial support, coaching and mentoring for about 250 of that department's identified future leaders over a three-year period. NSW corrections also provides a number of scholarships and a range of management and leadership-based programs for all staff.

Northern Territory corrections has also opted to invest in the development centre approach, with work-related activities mapped against national executive competencies. Individuals are then audited by the organisation's executive against the competencies so professional development programs can be mapped out to suit their needs. The Victorian corrections system runs a "leadership impact system" on license through a private consultancy. Every person in the organisation undertakes performance management based on 360-degree feedback, which culminates in personalised management plans. Queensland corrections has qualifications from the national training package linked to salary increments. This strategy has ensured large numbers of staff have now obtained qualifications. Similarly, in Western Australia there is a link between the prison officer promotions system and the notions of career development and enhancement, providing a structure for genuine challenges and responsibilities and not just seniority.

The role of human resources in the success of the organisation

Corrections agencies throughout Australia have accepted the challenge to offer innovative multi-dimensional learning opportunities to a workforce that has historically viewed education and personal development with suspicion. The rapid growth of prison systems in departments of corrections and the evolution of prison guards into correctional officers have heightened interest in corrections as a worthy career.

Training and career development programs represent some real answers to the problems of poor job performance, negligence and related legal actions, as well as public concern over the effectiveness of the prison system. This is embodied by the practical application of the notions of lifelong and "lifewide" learning and represents a move from traditional training to more broadly-based education which embraces a range of learning methods and styles. Ultimately, the result should be a more relevant correctional system and a workforce more able to adapt to change. The human resources of a corrections organisation are its greatest assets. From the recruit who is sitting in their first day of pre-service training to the head of the department, the systems that select, train and then ultimately retain these resources determine the humanity and effectiveness of the punishment systems by which our society is measured.

CHAPTER 27

Towards crime prevention

Professor David Biles
Charles Sturt University

A criminal justice system is such a complex, and yet delicate, structure that developments or issues in any aspect of criminal justice will almost certainly have consequences for the other components of the system. Thus, increases in police numbers, for example, or changes in sentencing practices, will rebound on to corrective services, and so too will the efficiency or otherwise of corrective services in reducing re-offending have consequences for the police and the courts, as well as for the community at large.

Prisoner numbers

Whether we like it or not, one can confidently predict that short of a miracle prisoner numbers in Australia will continue to increase. Governments continue to promise more prisons, and the public demand for harsh penalties for offenders shows no sign of abating. The assumption by governments that the more offenders that are put into prison the safer the community will be is misconceived. That misconception is fairly easily demonstrated. There are two different ways of demonstrating the falsity of the assumption that increasing the use of prisons reduces the incidence of crime.

First, the assumption is challenged by known data on the relative use of imprisonment in the eight Australian jurisdictions. A glance at the figures for just two jurisdictions is enough to prove the point. For the past 30 or 40 years the imprisonment rate of NSW has constantly been almost exactly twice as high as the equivalent rate for Victoria. If there were any truth to the assumption, then the crime rate in NSW would have to be markedly lower than the crime rate in Victoria, but there is simply no evidence to support that expectation. Also, one would expect the Northern Territory and Western Australia to be especially safe as they lock up even higher proportions of their populations, but, again, that expectation cannot be met.

One could use the same data base to pose the historical question: do you think NSW is significantly safer now that it has over 8000 prisoners, at a rate of nearly 160 per 100,000 adults, compared with early 1987 when it had under 4000 prisoners, at a rate of about 100 per 100,000 adults? Has the doubling of the number of prisoners brought about a measurable reduction in burglary, motor vehicle theft, robbery or rape? The answer is self-evident.

The second method of demonstrating the fallacy of the assumption of more prisons means less crime is to examine the known facts about attrition in criminal justice. We know from crime victims surveys that only about 30 to 35 per cent of serious crime is reported to police, and we know from police reports that only about 10 per cent of reported crime is solved or cleared by the police. Of the cases that are cleared, for a variety of reasons, many do not go to court, and of those that do go to court, a significant number result in acquittals but, more importantly, the overwhelming majority of convictions result in the imposition of fines or non-custodial orders. A conservative estimate suggests that where a serious crime has been committed only in about one case in 100 does the offender go to gaol, and some analysts have suggested that a more accurate estimate would be one case in 1000. Whatever the true probability of a serious offence resulting in a prison sentence, the fact is that even if we doubled the number of prisoners the odds would still be so overwhelmingly in favour of the offender that it would be naive to expect a reduction in criminal behaviour.

A responsible conclusion from these two sets of data is that we should use the expensive resource of imprisonment as sparingly as possible, as we do know that the more money we spend on prisons the less money we have for schools, hospitals, and programs directly focusing on crime prevention.

Prisoner programs

There is good news from many parts of the world about what is happening inside prisons. After many years of trying to do justice by treating all offenders equally, today all progressive correctional administrations provide a range of programs that aim to address the underlying causes of the behaviour and attitudes that led to arrest and imprisonment. These programs include cognitive skills in anger management and personal relationships, sex offender treatment, drug and alcohol treatment, as well as a wide range of educational and vocational activities.

This development is to be encouraged, but a major deficiency is the fact that there has been virtually no research in Australia into what programs really work, with what offenders, and with what specific outcomes. It is true that some small pilot studies have been conducted and there is plenty of anecdotal evidence of prisoners appreciating what is offered, but if we look for hard evidence that is both reliable and valid, and is based on sample sizes sufficient to achieve significant results, we have no option but to look to Canada, Great Britain and the US.

The time has well and truly come when we in Australia should be conducting serious research to find out what really works in this country. It should be noted that major evaluative research projects of this type should not be as costly as they were in the past, now that all inmate records are held in readily retrievable electronic form.

It is relevant to note here that a major study by the Home Office in England (Falshew 2003), found no difference in the two-year reconviction rates for 649 prisoners who had participated in cognitive skills programs during 1996 to 1998 compared with a matched group of 1,947 prisoners who had not participated in these programs. This contrasts with the reduction in reconviction shown in previous evaluations of cognitive skills programs in England, and it suggested that the negative result of the recent study might be due to staff and prisoners being less motivated than was the case in earlier studies.

The most important conclusion to be drawn from this research is that all prisoner programs must be constantly and rigorously evaluated to ensure that money and effort are not being wasted on programs that are ineffective.

Alternatives to imprisonment

Australia, together with New Zealand, is one of the few nations in the Asia and Pacific region that has many times more offenders serving community-based, or non-custodial, correctional orders than we have in prison. Over twice as many offenders are serving probation, parole, community service, periodic detention, home detention and other orders than are serving prison sentences. This shows we are tolerant enough to deal with many offenders in a relatively non-retributive way while at the same time addressing their criminogenic needs.

The only significant argument in this area is whether we can call these correctional options "alternatives to imprisonment". The legislative debates that accompanied the introduction of non-custodial correctional options nearly always contained the argument that the more offenders that were placed on these options, the fewer would be the numbers sentenced to prison. As community-based options are always significantly less expensive than prison, this is a powerful argument, but it is simply not true. If it were true, one would reasonably expect that those Australian jurisdictions that had higher numbers of offenders serving community-based orders would have correspondingly lower rates of people in prison, and vice versa.

The facts do not support that proposition. In five of the eight Australian jurisdictions (NSW, Vic, Queensland, WA and Tasmania) the number of people serving community-based correctional orders is almost exactly twice the numbers of prisoners, regardless of whether the imprisonment rate is high or low. In the ACT and in South Australia there are much higher numbers in community-based corrections than in prison, while in the Northern Territory there are only slightly more offenders in the community than there are in prison. The graph below illustrates this picture. More research is needed on this subject as the details are rather more complex than indicated here, but enough is known to suggest that we should be cautious about using the term "alternatives to imprisonment".

A study of deaths in community corrections in Victoria by Biles et al (1999) found that the probability of an offender under a correctional order dying was much higher than the probability of death for an offender in prison. It is certainly true that the death rate in prisons is considerably higher than the equivalent rate for the same age and gender group in the general community, but it is difficult to make a useful comparison. What we need to compare is the rate of death for law-breakers in prison and law-breakers in the community, and that is what was done in this study. For all of the major causes of death (suicide, homicide, accidents and natural causes) the rates are significantly higher for community corrections clients than they are for prisoners. The bottom line is that for people who live law-breaking lifestyles, prisons are not dangerous, they are protective.

Correctional staff education and training

I believe that we are at the beginning of a quiet revolution in the education and training that is required of people who decide to make their careers in corrections. That revolution may take many years to fully develop, but it will eventually result in corrections being seen for the first time as a professional calling with its own body of knowledge, codes of conduct and ethical standards.

Until now, entry to work in custodial corrections has been by way of a few weeks training in a college or academy, followed by on-the-job training and then short courses and examinations leading to promotional grades. In sharp contrast, people starting work in community-based corrections had generally completed university degrees in social work or welfare studies and were not required to undertake further studies for promotion. Thus we have had, and we still have, two distinct types of correctional workers who have little contact with each other even though they are often dealing with the same people at different stages of their treatment by the criminal justice system.

If the revolution that I have mentioned does develop, I believe we will eventually see an integrated correctional profession with the two types of workers coming together. Thus a well-educated correctional worker could spend some of her or his career working in institutions and then spend time running programs in the community. Career paths would be more varied and interesting and the total correctional enterprise would be unified rather than bifurcated as it is today. Also, along the way to that goal, it would seem to me to be highly likely that sound qualifications in correctional theory and practice would be required for all persons in charge of institutions or specific programs. I think that the days of any university degree being acceptable are coming to an end. Correctional administrators of the future will be people who really know the subject and will be able to communicate their ideas clearly and effectively. They will have no trouble distinguishing between: repatriation, restitution, restoration, rehabilitation, retribution, and all of those other R-words which seem to flourish in the correctional literature.

Correctional through care

One of the recently emerging themes in corrections is the notion of correctional through care. This could be seen as related to the vision of correctional staff education and training which I outlined above as it is essentially concerned with the seamless continuity of influence or pressure on offenders as they move from one stage to another along the criminal justice continuum. To achieve this goal, efforts must be made to reduce the dislocations that may occur when an offender leaves prison and comes under parole supervision, for example, resulting in breaks in treatment programs for drugs or alcohol, anger management or sex offender treatment. Similarly, if an offender fails on a community-based program, such as community service or home detention with treatment or training obligations, and is ordered into full-time custody, efforts must be made to ensure that the treatment of training activities continue as smoothly as possible.

To achieve this end, short of having the sort of integrated correctional service outlined above, it would be necessary for those who offer treatment and training programs in institutions to be the same people who offer parallel programs to offenders in the community. This is a tall order and would create many different organisational difficulties, but the ultimate goal is one that is well worth pursuing in the interests of creating a more effective correctional system.

A crime prevention orientation

I would like to conclude on a fairly radical note by suggesting that correctional professionals must start to see themselves as crime prevention managers as well as administrators. Community-based crime prevention is a rapidly growing movement that many facets and includes a wide range of different activities. It includes such diverse notions as environmental design, street lighting, target hardening, aspects of parenting, programs for the responsible serving of alcohol, needle exchange outlets, the training and registration of crowd control marshals, various counselling services, youth clubs and summer camps, special activities designed for people at risk, and much more.

All crime prevention action aims to reduce either motivation or opportunity for criminal behaviour, and it is generally seen as the broad responsibility of the total community, rather than the police alone. The best known and most obvious manifestation of the crime prevention movement in Australia is seen in Neighbourhood Watch, and related organisations such as Safe House and the Big Brother and Sister Movement.

Correctional workers, whether they are working in institutions or in the community, use quite different language when they are asked to describe what they do, but they are essentially concerned with taking every reasonable step available to them to reduce the motivation and opportunity for criminal behaviour of the persons in their care. Corrections workers are in effect specialists in crime prevention, albeit in a fairly narrow area of the criminal justice system, but I believe there is the potential for mutually valuable exchanges of views if corrections specialists started talking with crime prevention experts in the broader community. After all, there is nothing to lose, and none of us would want to argue that we have all of the answers and therefore have nothing to learn from other people in the field.

CHAPTER 28

What future for the prison?

Paul Wilson
Professor of Criminology, Bond University

It is now 300 years since the creation of the first prisons, as we now know them. There remains, however, a deep confusion in society about what the prison, in general, is for. Why do we send people there? Who should be there and for how long? How many prisons is enough? What does it take to make a prison useful punishment? The questions seem endless and agreement upon the answers seems as far away as ever.

The place of the prison in society

The traditional, supposed, aims of imprisonment – punishment, retribution, rehabilitation and deterrence – have been transcended in recent years by the prevailing goal of incapacitation. Politicians have espoused that "prison works" as a crime prevention method as criminals in prison are prevented from further victimising innocent citizens. Most people should see this argument as simplistic and short sighted at best. The reality, despite the introduction of punitive legislation such as mandatory sentencing and "three strikes" laws, is that most offenders will be released back into the community.

The "prison works" mantra sounds increasingly pyrrhic as alienated, and often brutalised, men and women return to their communities with scant hope of avoiding crime.

Nobody now regards imprisonment in itself as an effective means of reform for most prisoners. The British government stated in 1990 that "prison can be an expensive way of making bad people worse", while last year their government reported, "the belief that imprisonment and punitive regimes will cure crime and make society safer misjudges the impact of custody".

It seems paradoxical then that while admitting to this misplaced faith in the curative powers of prison, governments increasingly continue to rely upon imprisonment as the sanction of choice. Around the world imprisonment is on the rise. Estimates put the global prison population as standing at around 8 million.

However, as staggering as this figure is, the true picture of how punitive a country is and how keen to imprison, is evidenced by their rate of imprisonment. This is where we in Australia, with a comparatively small prison population, need to be concerned.

In recent years our imprisonment rate has been increasing in tandem with global trends. The Australian national rate of imprisonment has risen from 114.8 per 100,000 in 1994-95 to 139.1 in 1998-99, with the average daily population increasing 94 per cent since 1980. However, in 1998, the then Director-General of Queensland Corrections observed, "in the context of world experience, which is typified by rapidly expanding rates of imprisonment, the situation in Queensland is far more dramatic than anywhere else. No country or state has experienced a rate of increase which has occurred in Queensland" (Apsey 1999).

Queensland has moved from a rate of 109.2 per 100,000 in 1994-95 to 191.5 per 100,000 in 1998-99. This has led to a 116 per cent increase in prisoners since 1993. This increase has taken place in the context of a 2 per cent rise in the adult population and a 4 per cent increase in recorded crime so it cannot be easily explained as a result of more people or more crime.

Characteristics of prison populations

Aside from the sheer numbers of people incarcerated around the globe and in Australia, and the confusion surrounding the purposes of prison, we face more immediate critical issues arising from disparities in sentencing and the particular characteristics of those found in our prisons.

While our national imprisonment rate should be a source of shame, there should be acute political embarrassment at the highest level when taking even the most cursory of glances at the over-representation of our Indigenous population in our prisons. This problem is highlighted throughout this book. Their rate of imprisonment nationally is three times greater than even the Californian or Russian rate of imprisonment. If we break this figure down by states it becomes even more alarming with the Western Australian aboriginal imprisonment rate standing at 2856.7 per 100,000 in contrast to their non-Indigenous rate of 133.1 per 100,000.

These rates go some way to explain why Aboriginals and Torres Strait Islanders are so over-represented in our prisons, particularly young Aboriginals. It is apparent that they are now also the primary targets of the mandatory sentencing laws of the Northern Territory and punitive sentencing legislation in Western Australia. What effect will the predilection for imprisoning of our Indigenous population have on the future? The situation has been characterised as "effectively amounting to a new forced separation of Aboriginal, and Torres Strait Islander children and young people from their families" (Cunneen 1993).

Also of concern in Australia and many countries around the world, is the increasing imprisonment of women – one of the recurring themes about imprisonment in this book. The number of women in prison has been increasing at an even greater rate than that of men in a number of countries. Since early 1996, the average daily number of female prisoners has more than doubled in the UK, US and Australia. Although again the absolute numbers of female prisoners in Australia remains low, the population has been rising at an alarming rate. Yet, we know that the majority of women do not commit serious or violent offences and do not pose a risk to public safety. Of perhaps even greater concern, recent research in the NSW prison system found that 73 per cent of the female prison population were suffering from a psychiatric illness while 40 per cent had attempted suicide.

We know that a term in prison is almost always extremely disruptive for women and their families with nearly half of women in prison with dependent children. It is well known that the costs of imprisonment for women can be significantly higher when adding into the equation the costs of caring for their children, housing mothers with their babies, and later dependency on welfare. Such welfare dependency and need for social services is a cost not often factored into equations of prison costs but when we look at the known outcomes of a term in prison for both males and females, we see that unemployment, homelessness, substance abuse and other health problems can be a costly side effect. This is on top of the unquantifiable cost of their attitude hardening and their alienation from society, their dislocation from friends and family and their propensity to get caught in the prison revolving door.

The imprisonment of women poses particular problems, both operationally and financially for corrections administrators. The imprisonment of older offenders is also a growing problem for administrators, highlighted in the text in Chapter 14 by John Dawes. Australia's prison population, like its general population and prison populations internationally, is ageing. The number of prisoners over 50 is increasing, either because they are growing old in prison with increased sentence lengths and the reduction of early release mechanisms, or because they are entering prison later in life.

These offenders need a high standard of care and have particular needs in terms of health care and their adaptation to prison life. These add significantly to correctional costs, being estimated to be in the order of three times more expensive than the care required by younger inmates and second only to caring for HIV and AIDS sufferers. They also present significant problems for the community post-release with many homeless, unemployed with no work prospects and having no family or friends, leaving them in the lap of social services.

Private prisons

So if we know that prison is costly, ineffective at reforming offenders and potentially the cause of greater long-term problems, why then do we continue to send increasing numbers to prison? Who stands, if anyone to benefit from imprisonment? This question of benefit has taken a dramatic turn in recent years. Debate over the advantages of imprisoning convicted offenders has always focused on the supposed benefits to victims, offenders and society at large. Now we can add to the list private enterprise.

Since the opening of Borallon prison in Queensland in 1990, private prisons have spread dramatically through the nation with Victoria now housing 40 per cent of its prisoner population in private prisons, more than any other state or country in the world. This at a time when increasing numbers of private corrections companies are coming under investigation either for corruption, financial irregularities, prisoner suicides and abuses, or simple inefficiency and incompetence. Indeed the market leader, Corrections Corporation America, sister to the Corrections Corporation Australia, which has recently lost its bid to keep the Borallon contract, has faced bankruptcy and expensive legal actions in America.

It may well be that the growth of private corrections, although still a prospering enterprise in some countries, including our own, is slowing or being blocked in others. New Zealand's Minister for Corrections has said that the solution to the failing public prison system was "not private but resourcing the New Zealand system to do its job properly" (PPRI no 34). Confidence in the private sector to provide correctional services in this country seems undiminished however, with increasing numbers of private beds planned.

Inviting the private sector to take responsibility for running our prisons, or some of them at least is recognition of the increasing financial burden that prisons represent for governments and the unpopularity of spending taxpayer's money on prisoners. Prisons are extremely costly. If the balance sheet of a public company evidenced such poor returns as out correctional system there would be cries for immediate restructuring.

Costs of imprisonment

There is little to justify the exorbitant sums spent on the correctional system when we are surrounded by evidence pointing to alternatives that are not only cheaper but more effective at preventing crime, more humane and satisfying more of the objectives of our criminal justice system. We must be cautious, however, not to be seen to be saying "don't punish". What we need to stress is that where punishment is necessary, let us use the right punishment.

Community punishments, while they don't satisfy the incessant calls to "get tough" on criminals, mainly espoused by ambitious politicians, can work, can protect the public from further victimisation and can reform offenders. They are also significantly cheaper. A non-custodial sentence in Queensland costs $4 a day compared with $116 a day for a custodial sentence.

This remarkable disparity however, is telling of another crisis in corrections. The number of offenders serving sentences in the community has also risen dramatically in Queensland, with the result that community corrections can now be said to be "overcrowded" just as prisons are. The outcome of this overcrowding is that while we spend comparatively little on these offenders, they are also receiving little attention from over-stretched and under-resourced community corrections departments. While these sentences have the potential to be a positive influence in offender's lives, at this time they are in danger of simply exacerbating the problems faced by corrections. Unless those sentenced to community sentences are challenged and attended to in a constructive manner, then we are wasting the potential of such opportunities to address the problems faced by these offenders.

Non-custodial options and diversion from prosecution and prison at every opportunity is of particular importance when the offender is young. Few subjects attract so much media attention and sensationalist reporting as youth crime. This media agenda and political attitude or approach towards youthful offenders is dangerous and counter-productive. The Chief Inspector of Prisons in England and Wales recently completed a review of young people in custody and reminds us that "Young offenders may have lost their way in society, but that does not mean that there are without talents which can be turned to advantage – theirs and the nation's given proper encouragement". It is clear that the receipt of such encouragement and nurturing once past the prison gates is a lottery dependent on too many variables.

Prison programs as a rehabilitative tool

A starting point for any debate about prisons must be recognition that a prison sentence can never be a neutral experience; it will always be either a positive or negative experience. It is imperative that those young people who are sent to prison, experience an environment that is challenging, constructive and needs based. Education, training and care are essential if we are to prevent their further decline into a life of crime and destitution. These young people must be equipped to deal with the problems they face and motivated to avoid re-offending on their return to society. Until this happens, any prison sentence will be counterproductive.

While it is vital for young offenders in our prisons to be treated with special attention, it must be reiterated that the larger problems must not be lost sight of. Young offenders should be diverted from prison at every opportunity. Prison is not a place for children.

We must ask why is it that we find ourselves, tackling the same problems year after year, indeed, decade after decade. One of the most obvious problems with prison and one that should be easily agreed upon is that it has to achieve many different objectives at once for very different groups of prisoners. It has to hold those awaiting trial. It has to keep juveniles, adolescents and the elderly; it has to keep men and women, boys and girls, the mentally ill, the addicted and drug dependent, the meek and pathetic and the domineering and violent, the illiterate and uneducated as well as the intelligent. Most importantly, it has to keep the alienated, alone and suicidal. With such a wide ranging population base it would seem impossible that the product will suit all of these variants and can effectively assist all of these people to lead useful and law abiding lives upon release.

The Pope recently called upon governments around the world to reduce prisoner numbers as a gesture of clemency. His message that prison sentences should contribute to the reduction of crime and the rehabilitation of criminals, not simply to their punishment, is an important one. He stated his belief that "prison should not be a corrupting experience, a place of idleness and vice, but instead a place of redemption".

We must have in the back of our minds the omnipresent problem of our reliance on prison. It is peculiar that many take solace in the rising prison populations, seeing them as evidence that something is being done about crime. I wonder if the same would be said about disease if our hospitals were filling up rapidly? We must attack the false assumption that a large prison population is a source of pride and a victory for those onboard the "tough on crime" gravy train.

Bibliography

Books, chapters, articles and reports

Abbott, J (1981) *In the Belly of the Beast*, Random House.

Abram, KM, & Teplin, LA (1991) "Co-Occurring disorders among mentally ill jail detainees", *American Psychologist*, 46(10).

Achieng, C (2004) "Introduction to International Human Rights Law", paper delivered at the Seminar for Senior Officers, Deputy Commissioners of Prisons, Assistant Commissioners on Human Rights and Administration of Justice, February 2004, Nairobi, Kenya.

ACT Department of Justice and Community Safety (2003) *Annual Report 2002-2003*, ACT Government.

ACT Department of Justice and Community Safety (2001) *ACT Prison Project Newsletter, Nos 1&2* ACT Government.

Aday, R (1994) "Golden years behind bars: special programs and facilities for elderly inmates", *Federal Probation* 58(2).

Aday, R (2003) *Aging Prisoners: Crisis in American Corrections*, Praeger.

Aderibigbe, YA (1997) "Deinstitutionalization and criminalization: tinkering in the interstices", *Forensic Science International* 85(2).

Aebi, M, Barclay, G, Jehle, JM, & Killias, M (2000) *Key Findings: European Sourcebook of Crime and Criminal Justice Statistics, 1999*, Council of Europe. Available: <http://www.europeansourcebook.org/esb/key_findings.pdf>.

Akatsuka, K (1998) "Diversity of Prison Problems in Asia", Paper presented at the "Beyond Prisons" Symposium, Kingston, Ontario, March 1998.

Aktepe, B & Lake P (2003) "The THM – Corrections Pathways Initiative", *Parity* 16(5).

Alderfer, C & Thomas, D (1988) "The significance of race and ethnicity for understanding organisational behaviour in organisational behaviour" in CL Cooper & I Robertson (eds), *International Review of Industrial and Organisational Psychology*, John Wiley and Sons.

Allen, N & Meyer J (1990) "Organisational Socialisation Tactics: a longitudinal analysis of links to newcomers' commitment and role orientation" *Academy of Management Journal* 33 (4).

Allen, J, Chilvers M, Doak, P, Goh, D, Painting, T & Ramsay, M (2002) *New South Wales Recorded Crime Statistics 2001*, NSW Bureau of Crime Statistics and Research.

American Correctional Association (1966) *Manual of Correctional Standards*, American Correctional Association.

American Correctional Association (1981) *Standards for Adult Correctional Institutions*, American Correctional Association.

American Correctional Association (1990), *Standards for Adult Correctional Institutions* 3rd edn, American Correctional Association in cooperation with the Commission on Accreditation for Corrections.

American Correctional Association (1992), *Standards for Adult Correctional Institutions*, 3rd edn American Correctional Association.

American Correctional Association (1999), *ACA Correctional Officers Resource Guide* (rev), American Correctional Association, Laurel, MD.

Andersen, J (2000) *Crisis Payment & Prisoner Statistics*, Commonwealth Department of Family and Community Services.

Anderson, G (1994) "Growing old behind bars", *America* 171(1).

APCCA (2002) *Correctional Statistics for Asia and the Pacific, 2002,* prepared for the 22nd Asian and Pacific Conference of Correctional Administrators, Dempasar, Indonesia, October 2002.

APCCA (2001) "Corrections in Asia and the Pacific", Record of the 21st Asian and Pacific Conference of Correctional Administrators, Chang Mai, Thailand, 21-26 October.

Apsey, B (1999) "Corrections in the new millennium: plan control or perish", 3rd National Outlook Symposium on Crime, Australian Institute of Criminology.

Atkinson, J (1991) "Stinkin Thinkin: Alcohol, Violence and Government Responses" *Aboriginal Law Bulletin* 2 (51).

Austin, J (2001) "Prisoner Re-entry: Current Trends, Practices and Issues", *Crime & Delinquency* 47(3).

Austin, J & Coventry, G (2001) *Emerging Issues on Privatised Prisons*, Bureau of Justice Association.

Australian Institute of Criminology (2004) *Australian Crime: Facts and Figures 2003*, Commonwealth of Australia.

Australian Bureau of Statistics, (2001) *Corrective Services, March Quarter*, Commonwealth of Australia.

Australian Bureau of Statistics (1995) *National Aboriginal and Torres Strait Islander Survey 1994: Detailed Findings*, Australian Bureau of Statistics.

Australian Bureau of Statistics (2001) Corrective Services Australia, September Quarter Australian Bureau of Statistics.

Australian Bureau of Statistics (1998) *Census of Population and Housing, Aboriginal and Torres Strait Islander People*, (Cat No 2032.0), Australian Bureau of Statistics.

Australian Bureau of Statistics (1999), *Australian Social Trends*, Australian Bureau of Statistics.

Australian Bureau of Statistics (2001) *AusStats: Prisoners in Australia*, (accessed online 5 April 2001).

Australian Bureau of Statistics (2003) *Year Book Australia, Income and Welfare, An Aging Australia* (accessed online 18 November 2003).

Australian Bureau of Statistics (2003) *Corrective Services Australia, June Quarter*, Commonwealth of Australia.

Australian Bureau of Statistics (2002) *AusStats: Prisoners in Australia*.

Australian Bureau of Statistics (2004) *AusStats: Prisoners in Australia*.

Australian Medical Association (1998) *Health Care of Prisoners and Detainees: AMA Position Statement*, AMA.

Bacon, C (ed) (1974) *Prison Reform*, Ams Press.

Baldry, E, McDonnell, D, Maplestone, P & Peeters, M (2003) *Ex-offenders' accommodation and social integration*, Australian Housing and Urban Research Institute, Melbourne.

Baldry, E, McDonnell, D, Maplestone, P & Peeters, M (2002, December 12 – last update) *Ex-offenders, accommodation and social integration Positioning Paper*, available at <http://www.ahuri.edu.au>.

Baldry, E, McDonnell, D, Maplestone, P & Peeters, M (forthcoming) "Ex-prisoners, accommodation and the state in Australia", *Australian and New Zealand Journal of Criminology*.

Baldry, E, McDonnell, D, Maplestone, P & Peeters, M (2002, December 12 – last update) *Ex-offenders, accommodation and social integration Positioning Paper*, available at <http://www.ahuri.edu.au>.

Bandura, A (1986) *Social foundations of thought and action: A social cognitive theory*, Prentice-Hall, Inc, New Jersey.

Banks, C (1978) "A Survey of the South East Prison Population", *Home Office Research Bulletin 5*.

Barnes, J (1990) *Models and Interpretations*, Cambridge University Press.

Barnes HE & Teeters, NK (1952), *New Horizons in Criminology*, Prentice-Hall.

Baro, AL (1999) "Effects of a cognitive restructuring program on inmate institutional behaviour", *Criminal Justice and Behaviour* 26(4)

Basinger, A (1985) *Are Prison Work Programs Working? The impact of prison industry participation on recidivism rates in Ohio*, School of Public Administration, Ohio State University.

Bates, M & Nunn, J (1986) "Educational Survey conducted at HM Prison, Woodford", *Literacy Link* (6)1.

Beck, AJ, & Maruschak, LM (2001) *Mental health treatment in state prisons, Bureau of Justice Statistics Special Report*, US Department of Justice.

Belcher, JR (1988) "Are jails replacing the mental health system for the homeless mentally ill?" *Community Mental Health Journal* 24(3).

Bell, C & Newby, H (1972) *Community studies: an introduction to the sociology of the local community*, Praeger.

Benton, D & Gesch, B (2003) "Vitamin and fatty acid supplements may reduce antisocial behaviour in incarcerated young adults", *Evidence-Based Mental Health* 6(2).

Berk, B (1977), "Organizational goals and inmate organization", in RG Leger & JR Stratton, *Sociology of corrections: a book of readings*, John Wiley & Sons.

Ben-David S, Silfen, P & Cohen, D (1996) "Fearful Custodial or Fearless Personal Relations: Prison Guards' Fear as a Factor Shaping Staff-Inmate Relation Prototype," *International Journal of Offender Therapy and Comparative Criminology* 40(2).

Berlin, I (2002) "Introduction" in H Hardy (ed) *Five Essays on Liberty*, Oxford University Press.

Bertram, S & Gorta, A (1990) *Views of Inmates about the Prison Methadone Program and Problems Faced on Release from Gaol*, NSW Department of Corrective Services.

Bessant J, Carrington, K & Cook, S (eds) (1995) *Cultures of Crime & Violence: the Australian experience*, La Trobe University.

Best, P (2003) *Resettlement Strategy South West Region*, National Probation Directorate, Home Office.

Beyens, K & Snacken, S (1996) "Prison Privatisation: An International Perspective", in R Matthews, & P Francis (eds), *Prisons 2000: an international perspective on the current state and future of imprisonment*, MacMillan Press.

Biles, D & Morgan, N (2002) "Corrections in Asia and the Pacific", Report of the 22nd Asian and Pacific Conference of Correctional Administrators, Bali, Indonesia, 13-18 October 2002.

Biles, D, Morgan, N & McDonald, A (2000) *Corrections in Asia and the Pacific*, Record of the Twentieth Asian and Pacific Conference of Correctional Administrators, Sydney, Australia, 5-10 November 2000.

Biles, D & Dalton, V (2001) "Deaths in Private and Public Prisons in Australia" *The Australian and New Zealand Journal of Criminology* 34 (3).

Biles, D, Harding, R & Walker, J (1999) *The Deaths of Offenders Serving Community Corrections Orders Trends and Issues No 107*, Australian Institute of Criminology.

Biles, D & McDonald, D (1992) *Deaths in Custody Australia 1980-1989*, Australian Institute of Criminology.

Bird, G, Gore, S, Hutchinson, S, Lewis, S, Cameron, S & Burns, S (1997) "Harm reduction measures and injecting inside prison versus mandatory drugs testing: results of a cross sectional anonymous questionnaire survey", *British Medical Journal* 315.

Blagg, H (2000) *Crisis Intervention in Aboriginal Family Violence: Summary Report Partnerships against Domestic Violence*, Commonwealth Office of the Status of Women.

Blaauw, E, Arensman, E, Kraaij, V, Winkel, FW & Bout, R (2002) "Traumatic life events and suicide risk among jail inmates: the influence of types of events, time period and significant others", *Journal of Trauma Stress* 15.

Boeij, K (2002) "Developments in the Netherlands Penitentiary system", *Corrections Today*, February 2002, pp 50-53.

Bonner, RL (2000) "Correctional suicide prevention in the year 2000 and beyond", *Suicide and Life Threatening Behaviour* 30.

Bonifazi, W (1998) "Final acts: the way a facility treats its dead serves as a powerful message to survivors", Contemporary Long term Care, May.

Borowski A & O'Connor, I (1997) *Juvenile Crime, Justice and Corrections*, Longmann.

Bossler, A, Fleisher, M, & Krienert, K, (2000) "Employment and crime: revisiting the resiliency effect of work on crime", *Corrections Compendium*, 25(2).

Broadhurst, R, Maller, R, Maller, M & Duffecy, J (1988) "Aboriginal and Non-aboriginal recidivism in Western Australia: A failure rate analysis", *Journal of Research in Crime and Delinquency*, 25(1) February.

Bottomley, K, James, A, Clare, E & Liebling, A (1996) *Evaluating Private Prisons: The Criminological Challenge*, Paper presented to the annual conference of the ANZ Society of Criminology.

Bottoms, AE (1995) "The Philosophy and Politics of Punishment and Sentencing", in C Clarkson & R Morgan (eds) *The Politics of Sentencing Reform*, Clarendon Press.

Bottoms, AE (1999) "Interpersonal Violence and Social Order in Prisons" in M Tonry & J Petersilia (eds), *"Prisons", Crime and Justice: A Review of Research*, The University of Chicago Press.

Bottoms, AE, Hay, W & Sparks, R (1991) 'Situational and Social Approaches to the Prevention of Disorder in Long-Term Prisons', *The Prison Journal*, 70.

Bottoms, AE (2001) "The Relationship between theory and research in criminology", in RD King and E Wincup (eds) *Doing Research on Crime and Justice*, MacMillan Press.

Borchardt, DH (1986) *Checklist of Royal Commissions, Select Committees of Parliament and Boards of Inquiry: Commonwealth, New South Wales, Queensland, Tasmania and Victoria, 1960-1980 and South Australia, 1970-1980*, La Trobe University Library.

Bureau of Justice Statistics (1990) *Criminal victimisation in the United States 1988: A national crime survey report*, US Government Printing Office.

Burton, F & Carlen, P (1979) *Official Discourse*, Routledge Kegan Paul.

Butler, T (1997) *Preliminary Findings from the Inmate Health Survey of the Inmate Population in the New South Wales Correctional System*, NSW Corrections Health Service.

Butler, T, Donovan, B, Levy, M, Kaldor, J (2002) "Sex behind the prison walls", *Australia and New Zealand Journal of Public Health*, 26.

Butler, T, Milner, L (2003) 2001 *Inmate Health Survey*, Corrections Health Service.

Braithwaite, J (2002) *Restorative Justice and Responsive Regulation*, Oxford University Press.

Braithwaite, J & Pettit, P (1990) *Not Just Deserts: A Republican Theory of Criminal Justice*, Clarendon Press.

Braithwaite, V (1994) "Beyond Rokeach's Equality-Freedom Model: Two-Dimensional Values in a One-Dimensional World", *Journal of Social Issues*, 50(4).

Braithwaite, V (1998) "The Value Balance of Political Evaluations", *British Journal of Psychology*, 89.

Braithwaite, J & Makkai, T (1994) "Trust and Compliance", *Policing and Society*, 4.

Broadhurst, RG, Maller, RA, Maller, MG & Duffecy, J (1998) "Aboriginal and Non-Aboriginal Recidivism in Western Australia: A Failure Rate Analysis", *Journal of Research in Crime and Delinquency* 25(1).

Brown, D (2002a) "Legislative Council Select Committee on the Increase in Prisoner Population, Interim Report, July 2000; Final Report, November 2001: A Review", *Current Issues in Criminal Justice* 14(1).

Brown, D & Wilkie, M (eds) (2002b) *Prisoners as Citizens: Human rights in Australian prisons*, The Federation Press.

Brown, D (2004) "The Nagle Royal Commission 25 years on", *Alternative Law Journal* 29(3).

Brown, D (2005) "Continuity, rupture or just more of the "volatile and contradictory"?: glimpses of New South Wales' penal practice behind and through the discursive" in J Pratt, D Brown, M Brown, S Hallsworth and W Morrison (eds) *The New Punitiveness*, Willan.

Bryans, S & Wilson, D (2000) *The Prison Governor: Theory and Practice*, Prison Service Journal.

Buergenthal, T (1988), *International Human Rights*, West Publishing Co.

Butterfield, F (2003) "With cash tight, states reassess long jail terms", *New York Times*, 10 November.

Brockway, Z (1969) *Fifty years of prison service: an autobiography*, Patterson Smith.

Brown, D (2002) "Prisoners as citizens", in D Brown, & M Wilkie (eds), *Prisoners as citizens: Human rights in Australian prisons*, Federation Press.

Cadora, E, Swartz, C & Gordon, M (2003) in J Travers & M Waul (eds) *Prisoners Once Removed: The Impact of Incarceration and Re-entry on Children, Families and Communities*, The Urban Institute Press.

Camp, SG, Gaes GG, Klein-Saffran J, Daggett DM & Saylor W (2003) "Using Inmate Survey Data in Assessing Prison Performance: A Case Study Comparing Private and Public Prisons", *Criminal Justice Review* 27(1).

Canestrini, K (1993) *Wallkill Optical Program Follow-Up*, Department of Corrective Services, State of New York.

Cao, LQ, Zhao, JH & Vandine, S (1997) "Prison disciplinary tickets: A test of the deprivation and importation models", *Journal of Criminal Justice* 25(2).

Carcach, C & Grant, A (2000) "Imprisonment in Australia: The Offence Composition of Australian Correctional Populations, 1988 and 1998", *Trends and Issues in Crime and Criminal Justice*, 164, July, Australian Institute of Criminology.

Carlisle, J (1996) *The Housing Needs of Ex-offenders*, Centre for Housing Policy, University of York.

Carroll, L (1998) *Lawful order: a case study of correctional crisis and reform*, Garland Publishing.

Carter, KW (2001) "The Casuarina Prison Riot: Official Discourse or Appreciative Inquiry?", 12(3) *Current Issues in Criminal Justice* 363.

Caton, CLM, Wyatt, RJ, Felix, A, Grunberg, J & Dominguez, B (1993) "Follow-up of chronically homeless mentally ill men" *American Journal of Psychiatry* 150(11).

Carlen, P (1998) *Sledgehammer: Women's Imprisonment at the Millennium*, Macmillan.

Carlen, P (2001) "Death and the triumph of governance: Lessons from the Scottish Women's Prison", *Punishment and Society* 3(4).

Carter, H, Klein R & Day P (1992) *How Organizations Measure Success: The Use of Performance Indicators*, Routledge.

Carter, D (1991), "The status of education and training in correct ions," *Federal Probation*, 55.

Centre on Juvenile and Criminal Justice (2002) "Texas Tough?: An Analysis of Incarceration and Crime Trends in The Lone Star State", Press Release (accessed online 20 March 2004), available: <http://www.cjcj.org/pubs/texas/texas.html>.

Chaiken, M (1986) "Crime rates and substance abuse among types of offenders", in Johnson B & Wish E (eds) *Crime rates among drug-abusing offenders*, Final report to the National Institute of Justice.

Chamberlain, C & MacKenzie, D (1992) "Understanding Contemporary Homelessness: Issues of Definitions and Meaning" *Australian Journal of Social Issues* 27(4).

Chan J, Devery, C & Doran, S (2003) *Fair cop: learning the art of policing*, University of Toronto Press.

Chen A, Sawyer, R & Williams, P (1997) "Reinforcing Ethical Decisions Through Corporate Culture", *Journal of Business Ethics* 16.

Clark, J & Newman, J (1997) *The Managerial State: Power, Politics and Ideology in the Remaking of Social Welfare*, Sage.

Clear, T (1994) *Harm in American Penology*, University of New York Press.

Clemmer, D (1958) *The Prison Community*, Rinehart.

Clifford, W (1979) "Criminal Justice Innovations in Australasia", in W Clifford & S Gokhale (eds) *Innovations in Criminal Justice in Asia and the Pacific*, Australian Institute of Criminology.

Clokie, HM & Robinson, JW (1937) *Royal Commissions of Inquiry, The Significance of Investigations in British Politics*, Stanford University Press.

Cohen, S (1979) Guilt, Justice and Tolerance, in D Downes & P Rock (eds) *Deviant Interpretations*, Martin Robertson.

Cohen, S (1983) *Visions of Social Control*, Polity.

Cohen, S & Taylor, L (1972) *Psychological survival: the experience of long term imprisonment*, Pantheon.

Colson, C (1976) *Born again*, Chosen Books.

Conference group on correctional organization 1956-57 (1960) *Theoretical studies in the sociology and organization of the prison*, Social science research council.

Comack, E (1996) *Women in Trouble*, Fernwood.

Collins, J (1990) "Summary thoughts about drugs and violence", in M De La Rosa, E Lambert & B Gropper (eds) *Drugs and Violence: Causes, Correlates and Consequences*, NIDA Research Monograph 103.

Collins, L (2002) *Deaths in Custody in Australia: 2001 National Deaths in Custody Program (NDICP) Annual Report*, Australian Institute of Criminology.

Commonwealth of Australia (1991) *Royal Commission into Aboriginal Deaths in Custody*, Commonwealth of Australia.

Cooley, D (1993) "Criminal victimization in male federal prisons. (Canada)", *Canadian Journal of Criminology*, 35(4).

Cooper, RP & Werner, PD (1990) "Predicting violence in newly admitted inmates; A lens model analysis of staff decision making", *Criminal Justice and Behaviour* 17(4).

Corben, S (2004) *NSW Inmate Census 2003 Summary Characteristics*, NSW Department of Corrective Services.

Correctional Service of Canada (2000) *The Safe Return of Offenders to the Community*, Statistical Overview Research Branch.

Corrothers, HG (1992) *Career vs job: Why become a correctional officer?*, The Effective Correctional Officer American Correctional Association.

Cousineau, F & Plecas, D (1982) "Justifying Criminal Justice Policy with Methodologically Inadequate Research", *Canadian Journal of Criminology* 24.

Coyle, A, Campbell, A & Neufeld, R (2003) *Capitalist Punishment: Prison Privatisation and Human Rights*, Clarity Press.

Coyle, A (2002) *A Human Rights Approach to Prison Management: A Handbook for Prison Staff*, International Centre for Prison Studies.

Coyle, A (2002) "The restorative prison project: the myth of prison work", *Prison Services Journal*, 144(2), November.

Corden, J (1983) "Persistent Petty Offenders: Problems and Patterns of Multiple Disadvantage" *The Howard Journal*, 22.

Cowen, D & Fionda, J (1994) "Meeting the Need – The Response of Local Authorities' Housing Departments to the Housing of Ex-Offenders", *British Journal of Criminology* 34(4).

Craig, TKJ & Hodson, S (2000) "Homeless youth in London: II. Accommodation, employment and health outcomes at 1 year", *Psychological Medicine* 30(1).

Craig, RL (1987), *Training and Development Handbook*, 3rd edn, McGraw-Hill.

Cressey, D (ed) (1961) The prison: studies in institutional organisational change, Holt, Rinehart & Winston.

Cressey, D (1977) "Prison organizations", in RG Leger & JR Stratton (eds), *Sociology of corrections: a book of readings*, John Wiley & Sons.

Crouch, B (1995) "Guard work in transition" in K Hass & G Alpert (eds), *The Dilemmas of Corrections*, Waveland Press.

Crouch, B (ed) (1980), *Keepers: prison guards and contemporary corrections*, Charles C Thomas.

Crouch, B & Marquart, J (1980) "On becoming a prison guard," in B Crouch (ed), *Keepers: prison guards and contemporary corrections*, Charles C Thomas.

Cunningham, D (1999) *Public strategies for private prisons*, Private Prisons Workshop, Institute of Criminal Justice.

Cullen, FT & Gendreau P (1989) "The Effectiveness of Correctional Rehabilitation: Reconsidering the 'Nothing Works' Debate", in L Goodstein & DL MacKenzie (eds), *The American Prison: Issues in Research and Policy*, Plenum.

Cullen, FT & Gilbert, KE (1982) Reaffirming Rehabilitation, Anderson Publishing.

Cunneen, C (2001a) *Conflict, Politics and Crime: Aboriginal Communities and the Police*, Allen & Unwin.

Cunneen, C (2001b) *The Impact of Crime Prevention on Aboriginal Communities*, Report to the NSW Aboriginal Justice Advisory Council.

Cunneen, C & McDonald, D (1996) *Keeping Aboriginal and Torres Strait Islander People Out of Custody*, Aboriginal and Tones Strait Islander Commission.

Cunneen, C (1993) "Aboriginal and Criminal Justice Issues in the Wake of the Royal Commission", *Law Society Journal* 31(5).

Daley, D (2003) "Reinvigorating Community Corrections: A View from Down Under", *Corrections Today* 65(1).

Dawes, J (2002) "Dying with Dignity: Prisoners and Terminal Illness", *Illness, Crisis & Loss* 10(3).

Dawes, J (2002) "Institutional perspectives and constraints", in D Brown & M Wilkie (eds) *Prisoners as citizens: Human rights in Australian prisons*, Federation Press.

Dawes, J (1997) "Dying in Prison: A study of deaths in correctional custody in South Australia 1980-1993", Unpublished PhD thesis, Flinders University.

Dawes, J & Dawes J (forthcoming), "End-of-life care in prisons", in Berzof, J & Silverman, P (eds) *Living with Dying: A Handbook in End-of-Life care for Practitioners*, Columbia University Press.

Dawes, J & Grant, A (2002) "Corrections", in A Graycar & P Grabosky (eds) *The Cambridge Handbook of Australian Criminology*, Cambridge University Press.

Day, A & Howells, K (2002) "Psychological treatments for rehabilitating offenders: evidenced based practice comes of age", *Australian Psychologist*, 37(1).

Day C, White B, Ross J & Dolan K (2003) "Poor knowledge and low coverage of hepatitis B vaccination among injecting drug users in Sydney", *Australian and New Zealand Journal of Public Health*, 27.

Dear, GE (2001) "Further comments on the nomenclature for suicide-related thoughts and behaviour", *Suicide and Life Threatening Behaviour* 31.

Dear, GE, Slattery, JL, & Hillan, RJ (2001) "Evaluations of the quality of coping reported by prisoners who have self-harmed and those who have not", *Suicide and Life Threatening Behaviour*, 31.

Dear, GE, Thomson, DM, Hall, GJ, & Howells, K (2001) "Non-fatal self-harm in Western Australian prisons: Who, where, when and why", *Australian and New Zealand Journal of Criminology* 34.

Dear, GE, Thomson, DM & Hills, AM (2000) "Self-harm in prison: Manipulators can also be suicide attempters", *Criminal Justice and Behaviour* 27.

Dear, GE, Thomson, DM, Howells, K & Hall, GJ (2001) "Self-harm in Western Australian prisons: Differences between prisoners who have self-harmed and those who have not", *Australian and New Zealand Journal of Criminology* 34.

De La Rosa, M, Lambert, E, Gropper, B (1990) *Drugs and Violence: Causes, Correlates and Consequences*, National Institute on Drug Abuse.

Dix, D (1845) *Remarks on prisons and prison discipline in the United States*, J Kite.

Dixon, D (ed) (1999) *A Culture of Corruption: Changing an Australian Police Service*, Hawkins Press.

Department of Human Services Victoria (2001) *VHS Focus Group on Homelessness and Pre and Post-release Services – Outcomes Paper – Representatives of Prison Providers and Sentence Management*, The Victorian Homelessness Strategy Ministerial Advisory Committee.

Desai, RA, Lam, J & Rosenheck, RA (2000) "Childhood risk factors for criminal justice involvement in a sample of homeless people with serious mental illness", *Journal of Nervous & Mental Disease* 188(6).

Dicataldo, F, Greer, A & Profit, WE (1995), "Screening prison inmates for mental disorder: An examination of the relationship between mental disorder and prison adjustment", *Bulletin of the American Academy of Psychiatry and the Law* 23(4)

Dietz, EF, O'Connell, DJ & Scarpitti, FR (2003) "Therapeutic communities and prison management: An examination of the effects of operating an in-prison therapeutic community on levels of institutional disorder", *International Journal of Offender Therapy and Comparative Criminology* 47(2).

Ditchfield, J (1994) "Family Ties and Recidivism: main findings from the literature". *Home Office Research Bulletin* 36.

Ditton, PM (1999) *Mental health and treatment of inmates and probationers*, Bureau of Justice Statistics, US Department of Justice.

DiIulio, J (1991) *No Escape: The Future of American Corrections*, Basic Books.

Dobinson, I & Ward, P (1984) *Drugs and Crime: A survey of NSW Prison Property Offenders*, NSW Bureau of Crime Statistics and Research.

Dodson, M (2003) *Violence and Dysfunctional Aboriginality*, Presentation to the National Press Club, 11 June.

Dolan, K (1997) "Aids, drugs and risk behaviour in prison: state of the art", *The International Journal of Drug Policy* 8(1).

Dolan, K, Shearer, J, White, B & Wodak, A (2002) *A randomised controlled trial of methadone maintenance treatment in NSW prisons*, National Drug and Alcohol Research Centre.

Doohan, J, Mowbray, W, Rowlands, S & Taylor, G (1999) "Contracting out: the French experience", *The Prison Service Journal*, International edition, February.

Dowden, C & Andrews, DA (1999) "What works in young offender treatment: A meta-analysis", *Forum on Corrections Research* 11(2).

Drummond, T (1999) "Cellblock seniors: they have grown old and frail in prison. Must they sill be locked up?" *Time* 28 June.

Dunn, A (1994) "Flood of prisoner rights suits brings effort to limit filings" *New York Times*, section A-1, 12 March.

Eaton, M (1993) *Women After Prison*, Open University Press.

Edgar, N (1995) *As Survey of inmates*, Prison Employment Project, Criminal Justice Policy Group, New Zealand Ministry of Justice.

Ellis & Winstone (2002) "Halliday, Sentencers and the National Probation Service" *Community Justice Matters* 46.

Edwards RW & Madden R (2001) *The Health and Welfare of Australia's Aboriginal and Torres Strait Islander Peoples*, Australian Bureau of Statistics.

Edgar, K & Martin, C (2002), "Conflicts and violence in prison", Available: <http://www1.rhul.ac.uk/sociopolitical-science/VRP/Findings/rfedgar.PDF>

Edgar, K & O'Donnell, I (1998) "Assault in prison: The victim's contribution", *British Journal of Criminology* 38(4).

Eglash, A (1977) "Beyond Restitution: Creative Restitution", in J Hudson & B Galaway (eds) *Restitution in Criminal Justice*, Lexington Books.

Ekland-Olson, S (1986) "Crowding, social control, and prison violence: Evidence form the post-Ruiz years in Texas", *Law and Society Review*, 20(3).

European Social Fund (2002) *Working with ex-offenders*, available: <http://www.esf.gov.uk/goodpractice/websheets/exoffenders.shtml>.

Falshew, L (2003) "Searching for 'What Works': an evaluation of cognitive skills programs" *Home Office Findings* 206.

Farbstein, J & Associates & Werner, R (1991), "A comparison of direct and indirect supervision correctional facilities", *Forum on Corrections Research* 3(2).

Farrington, D, Petrosino A & Welsh B (2001) "Systematic reviews and cost-benefit analyses of Correctional interventions", *The Prison Journal* 81(3).

Farrington, DP & Nuttal, CP (1980) "Prison size, overcrowding, prison violence, and recidivism", *Journal of Criminal Justice* 8.

Fattah EA (1997) *Criminology – Past Present and Future*, Macmillan Press.

Faupel, C & Klockars C (1987) "Drugs-Crime Connections: Elaborations from Life Histories of Hard Core Heroin Addicts", *Social Problems* 34(1).

Fazel, S, & Danesh J (2002) "Serious mental disorder in 23,000 prisoners: a systematic review of 62 surveys", *The Lancet*, 359.

Fazel, S, Hope T, O'Donnell, Piper M & Jacoby R (2001) "Health of Elderly Male Prisoners: worse that the general population, Worse than younger prisoners", *Age and Ageing* 30.

Fazel, S, Hope T, O'Donnell I & Jacoby R (2001) "Hidden Psychiatric Morbidity in Elderly Prisoners", *British Journal of Psychiatry* 179.

Feeley, M & Simon J (1992) "The New Penology: Notes on the Emerging Strategy of Corrections and its Implications", *Criminology* 30.

Feeley, M & Simon J (1994) "Actuarial justice: The Emerging New Criminal Law", in D Nelken (ed) *The Futures of Criminology*, Sage.

Findlay, M, Odgers S, & Yeo S (1999) *Australian Criminal Justice*, Oxford University Press.

Findlay, M (1982) *The State of the Prison*, Michellsearch.

Finnane, M (1997) *Punishment in Australian Society*, Oxford University Press.

Fitzgerald, T (2001) *Cape York Justice Study*, 3 Volumes, Queensland Government.

Flynn, E (1972) *Alderson story: my life as a political prisoner*, International Publishers.

Fogel, D (1971) *... we are the living proof*, Anderson Publishing.

Foley, D (2003) "Indigenous Epistemology and Indigenous Standpoint", *Theory Social Alternatives* 22(1).

Foucault, M (1980) *Power/Knowledge*, Pantheon Books.

Foucault, M (1977) *Discipline and Punish*, Penguin.

Fox, R & Freiberg, A (1999) *Sentencing: State and Federal Law in Victoria*, 2nd edn, Oxford University Press.

Franklin, B (1978) *The victim as criminal and artist: literature from the American prison*, Oxford University Press.

Freeman, R (1997) "Correctional officers: Understudied and misunderstood," in J Pollock (ed) *Prisons: Today and Tomorrow*, Aspen Publishers.

Freiberg, A & Ross, S (1995) Change and Stability in Sentencing: a Victorian Study, in A Karpardis (ed) *Sentencing: Some Key Issues, Special Edition of Law in Context*, 13(2).

Friere, P (1975) *Pedagogy of the Oppressed*, Penguin.

Gaes, GG (1994) "Prison crowding research reexamined", *Prison Journal* 74(3).

Gallagher P & Poletti P (2000) *Sentencing Disparity and the Ethnicity of Juvenile Offenders*, Judicial Commission of NSW.

Gallemore, J (2000) "Strategies for success: Addressing the needs of mentally ill inmates", *American Jails* (March/April).

Garland, D (1990) *Punishment and modern society*, University of Chicago Press.

Garland, D (2001) *The Culture of Control: Crime and Social Order in Contemporary Society*, Oxford University Press.

Garland, D (2001) "Introduction: The Meaning of Mass Imprisonment", in D Garland, (ed) *Mass Imprisonment*, Sage.

Gaultung, J (1961) "Prison: the organisation of dilemma", in D Cressey (ed), *The prison: studies in prison organisation and change*, Holt, Rinehart & Winston.

Gelfand, E (1983) *Imagination in confinement: women's writings from French prisons*, Cornell University Press.

Gendreau, P & Ross, RR (1987) "Revivification of Rehabilitation: Evidence from the 1980s", *Justice Quarterly* 4(3).

Gendreau, P, Little, T & Goggin, C (1996) "A Meta-Analysis of the Predictors of Adult Offender Recidivism: What Works!", *Criminology* 34(4).

Gerber, J & Fritsch, EJ (1995) "Adult academic and vocational correctional programs: A review of recent research", *Journal of Offender Rehabilitation* 22(1-2)

Giallombardo, R (1966) *Society of women: a study of a women's prison*, Wiley.

Gilchrist, A, Young, K & Elliot, R, (1989) *The young offenders project*, Research Publication No 18, NSW Department of Corrective Services.

Gillies, C (2000) "Women offenders and employment", *Forum on Corrections Research* 11(3), September.

Gillis, C, Motiuk, L, & Belcourt, R, (2001) "Prison work program CORCAN participation: Post–release employment and recidivism, (R-69, 1998") *Forum on Corrections Research*, 13(2), May.

Gilligan, G (2002) "Royal Commissions of Inquiry", *Australian and New Zealand Journal of Criminology* 35(3).

Gilligan, G & Pratt, J (eds) (2004), *Crime Truth and Justice* Willan.

Glaser D (1969) *The Effectiveness of a Prison and Parole System*, Bobbs-Merrill Publishing.

Godfrey, C, Stewart, D & Gossop, M (2004) "Economic analysis of costs and consequences of the treatment of drug misuse: 2 year outcome data from the National Treatment Outcome Research Study (NTORS)", *Addiction* 99(6).

Goffman, E (1961) *Asylums*, Anchor.

Gonsa, H (1995) "Introduction to the European Prison Rules", *Penological Information Bulletin*, 19 & 20.

Goode, E (1994) *Deviant behavior*, 4th edn, Prentice-Hall.

Gowing, L, Cooke, R, Biven, A, Watts, D (2002) *Towards Better Practice in Therapeutic Communities*, Australian Therapeutic Communities.

Grabow KM, Sevy, BA & Houston, JS (1983) *Statewide Job Analysis of Three Entry-level Corrections Positions for the California Board of Corrections Standards and Training for Corrections Program*, Personnel Decisions Research Institute.

Graham, A (2003) "Post-prison mortality: Unnatural deaths among people release from Victorian prisons", *Australian and New Zealand Journal of Criminology* 36.

Grapendaal, M (1990) "The inmate subculture in Dutch prisons", *British Journal of Criminology* 30(3).

Gray D, Saggers S, Sputore, B & Bourbon, D (2000) "What Works? A Review of Evaluated Alcohol Misuse Interventions Among Aboriginal Australians" *Addiction* 95(1).

Granitz, N & Ward, J (2001) "Actual and Perceived Sharing of Ethical Reasoning and Moral Intent Amongst In-Group and Out-Group Members" *Journal of Business Ethics* 33.

Grant, A (1999) "Elderly Inmates: issues for Australia", *Trends and Issues, No 115*, Australian Institute of Criminology.

Grant, A, David, F, & Cook, B (2002) "Victims of Crime", in A Graycar & P Grabosky (eds) *The Cambridge Handbook of Australian Criminology*, Cambridge University Press.

Graycar, A (2001) *Crime in Twentieth Century Australia-Yearbook Australia 2001*, Australian Bureau of Statistics.

Graycar, A (1997) "Probation and Parole 2000", South Australia Department for Correctional Services Conference 9 July 1997, Australian Institute of Criminology.

Greater London Authority (2000) *Blocking the Fast Track from Prison to Rough Sleeping*, GLA.

Grubb, RW (1977) *Report of Inquiry into Prison Administration*, Tasmania Government Publishing Service.

Habermas, J (1996) *Between Facts and Norms*, (trans, W Rehg) Polity Press.

Hall, G (1996) "Corrections", in KM Hazlehurst (ed), *Crime and Justice: An Australian Textbook in Criminology*, LBC Information Services.

Hamlyn, B & Lewis, D (2000) *Women Prisoners: a survey of their work and training experiences in custody and on release*, Home Office.

Hammersley, R, Forsyth, A, Morrison, V & Davies, J (1989) "The Relation Between Crime and Opoid Use", *British Journal of Addiction* 84.

Hancock, N & Liebling, A (2004) "Truth, independence and effectiveness in prison inquiries", in G Gilligan & J Pratt (eds) *Crime, Truth and Justice*, Willan.

Haney, C (2003) in J Travis & M Waul (eds) *Prisoners Once Removed: The Impact of Incarceration and Re-entry on Children, Families and Communities*, The Urban Institute Press.

Hannah-Moffat, K (2001) *Punishment in Disguise*, Toronto University Press.

Harding, R (1994) "Privatising prisons: principle and practice" in D Biles & J Vernon (eds), *Private Sector and Community Involvement in the Criminal Justice System*, Australian Institute of Criminology.

Harding R, Broadhurst, R, Ferrante, A & Loh, N (1995) *Aboriginal Contact with the Criminal Justice System and the Impact of the Recommendations of the Royal Commission into Aboriginal Deaths in Custody*, Federation Press.

Harding, R (1997) *Private Prisons and Public Accountability*, Open University Press.

Harding, R (1999) "Prison privatisation: the debate starts to mature", *Current Issues in Criminal Justice* 11(2).

Harding, R (1998) "Private prisons in Australia: The second phase" in *Trends and Issues, No 84*, Australian Institute of Criminology.

Harer, MD (1994) *Recidivism among Federal prisoners released in 1987*, Federal Bureau of Prisons, Office of Research and Evaluation.

Haas, KC (1977) "Judicial politics and correctional reform: An analysis of the decline of the "hands-off" doctrine" *Detroit College of Law Review* 4.

Haas, KC (1981) "The 'new federalism' and prisoners' rights: State supreme courts in comparative perspective" *Western Political Quarterly* 34.

Haas, KC & Alpert, GP (1995) "American prisoners and the right of access to the courts" in KC Haas & GP Alpert (eds) *The Dilemmas of Corrections*, 3rd edn, Waveland Press.

Hawkins, G (1997) "Prison Labour Prison Industries", *Crime and Justice: an annual review of research* 5.

Hawkins, G (1976) *The prison: policy and practice*, University of Chicago Press.

Hawks, D (1976) "The Evaluation of Measures to Deal with Drug Dependence in the United Kingdom" in G Edwards, M Russell, D Hawks & M McCafferty (eds) *Drugs and Drug Dependence*, Saxon House.

Hawton, K & Van Heeringen, K (eds) (2000) *The international handbook of suicide and attempted suicide*, Wiley.

Hawton, K & Catalan, J (1987) *Attempted suicide: A practical guide to its nature and management*, 2nd edn, Oxford University Press.

Hazelrigg, L (ed) (1968), *Prison within society*, Anchor.

Henry, RW (1979) *Report of Inquiry into Allegations of Misconduct by Prison Officers at Goulburn Gaol*, NSW Government Printer.

Her Majesty's Inspectorate of Prisons (1999) *Suicide is everyone's concern: A thematic review by HM Chief Inspector of Prisons for England and Wales*, Home Office.

Higgs-Kleyn, N & Kapelianis, D (1999) "The Role of Professional Codes in Regulating Ethical Conduct", *Journal of Business Ethics* 19.

High Commissioner for Human Rights (2000), *Human Rights Training: A Manual on Human Rights Training Methodology, Professional Training Series No 6*, Centre for Human Rights, United Nations, New York and Geneva.

Hills, HA (2000) *Creating effective treatment programs for persons with co-occurring disorders in the justice system*, The GAINS Centre.

Hillsman, S (1998) "Best Practices along the criminal justice process: Criminal fines as an intermediate sanction", Paper presented at the "Beyond Prisons" Symposium, Kingston, Ontario, March.

Hirst, JB (1983) *Convict Society and its Enemies*, Allen and Unwin.

HMCIP (2003) *Report on a full announced inspection of HMP and YOI Ashfield 1-5 July 2002 by HM Chief Inspector of Prisons*, Home Office.

Holland, P & Mlyniec, WJ (1995) "Whatever Happened to the Right to Treatment? – The modern quest for a historical promise", *Temple Law Review* 68(4).

Home Office (1991) *Prison Disturbances April 1990: Report of an Inquiry by the Rt Hon Lord Justice Woolf (Parts I and II) and his Honour Judge Stephen Tumim (Part II)*, HMSO.

Home Office (1994) *Report of an Enquiry into the Escape of Six Prisoners from the Special Security Unit at Whitemoor Prison, Cambridgeshire on Friday 9th September 1994 by Sir John Woodcock*, HMSO.

Howells, K, Day, A, Bubner, S, Jauncey, S, Williamson, P, Parker, A & Heseltine, K (2002) "Anger management and violence prevention: Improving effectiveness", *Trends and Issues in Crime and Criminal Justice* 227.

Howse, K (2003) *Growing old in prison: a scoping study on older prisoners*, Centre for Policy on Aging and Prison reform Trust.

Hudson, B (2003) *Justice in the Risk Society*, Sage.

Hudson, B (2002) "Gender Issues in Penal Policy and Penal Theory", in P Carlen (ed) *Women and Punishment*, Willan.

Human Rights Committee (2001) *General Comment 16: The Right to Respect Privacy, Family, Home and Correspondence and Protection of Honour and Reputation*, HRC/GenI/Rev 5, 26 April, Geneva.

Humphrey, V (1990) "Training the total organization", *Training and Development Journal* 44.

Ilgnatieff, M (1978) *A just measure of pain*, Columbia University Press.

Independent Commission Against Corruption (ICAC) (1998) *Investigation into the Department of Corrective Services: first report: the conduct of Prison Officer Toso Lila (Josh) Sua and matters related thereto*, ICAC.

Inciardi, JA, Lockwood, D & Quinlan, JA (1993) "Drug use in prison: Patterns, processes, and implications for treatment", *Journal of Drug Issues* 23(1).

Incorvaia, D & Kirby, N (1997) "A formative evaluation of a drug-free unit in a correctional services setting", *International Journal of Offender Therapy and Comparative Criminology* 41(3)

Independent Commission Against Corruption (ICAC) (2004) *Report on investigation into the introduction of contraband into the High Risk Management Unit at Goulburn Correctional Centre*, ICAC.

Ingstrup, O (1999) "Keynote Speech", Presented at the International Indigenous Symposium on Corrections: Effective Corrections through Indigenous Wisdom, Vancouver, BC, Canada, 23-25 March.

Ingstrup, O & Crookall, P (1998) *The Three Pillars of Public Management*, McGill-Queen's University Press.

Ingstrup, O (1998) "Opening address', "Beyond Prisons" Symposium, Kingston, Ontario, March.

Inspector of Custodial Services (2003) *Cognitive Skills Programs in Western Australian Prisons*, Office of the Inspector of Custodial Services.

Irwin, J (1980) *Prisons in Turmoil*, Little Brown & Co.

Irwin, J & Cressey, D (1962) "Thieves, convicts and the inmate culture", *Social Problems* 10 (Fall).

Jackson, G (1970) *Soledad brother*, Coward-Mccann.

Jacobs, C (1998) *Not As It Seems To Change Before Tragedy*, A Paper presented to the Washington State AMI Forensic Conference, 26 June.

James, DV, Farnham, F & Cripps, J (1999) "Homelessness and psychiatric admission rates through the criminal justice system", *The Lancet* 353.

Jenkinson, KJ (1972/73/74) *Reports of Board of Inquiry into several matters concerning HM Prison Pentridge*, Victorian Government Publisher.

Jiang, S & Fisher-Giorlando, M (2002) "Inmate misconduct: A test of the deprivation, importation, and situational models", *Prison Journal* 82(3).

Johnston, LFT (1975/76) *Report of the Royal Commission on allegations made by prisoners at Yatala labour prison,* SA Government Printer.

Johnston, E (1991) *National Report of the Royal Commission into Aboriginal Deaths in Custody,* Commonwealth Government.

Johnson, EH (1990) *Preliminary Survey of Personnel Training in American State Prison Systems,* Southern Illinois University (Mimeographed).

Johnson, R (1987) *Hard time: understanding and reforming the prison,* Brooks-Cole.

Jones, K & Fowles, A (1984) *Ideas on institutions: analysing the literature on long-term care and custody,* Routledge & Kegan Paul.

Josi DA & Sechrest, DK (1996) "Treatment vs security: The adversarial relationship between treatment facilitators and correctional officers in an institutional environment" *Journal of Offender Rehabilitation,* 23(1 & 2).

Josi, DA & Sechrest, DK (1998) The Changing Career of the Correctional Officer: Policy Implications for the 21st Century, Butterworth Heinemann.

Joutsen, M (1998) *Why have alternatives not been adopted more fully and what needs to be done? The European experience,* Paper presented at the "Beyond Prisons" Symposium, Kingston, Ontario, March.

Jurik, N (1985) "Individual and Organizational Determinants of Correctional Officer Attitudes towards Inmates" in Criminology, 23 (3)

Kitada, M (2001) *Prison population in Asian countries: Facts, trends and solutions,* Paper presented at the United Nations Programme Network Institutes Technical Assistance Workshop. Vienna, Austria, May 10.

Kamerman, J (ed) (1998) *Negotiating Responsibility in the Criminal Justice System,* Southern Illinois University Press.

Kaplan, C (1992) "Resisting autobiography: out-law genres and transactional feminist subjects", in S Smith & J Watson (eds), *De-colonising the subject: the politics of gender in women's autobiography,* University of Minnesota Press.

Kauffman, K (1988) *Prison Officers and their World,* Harvard University Press.

Keene, J (1997) "Drug Misuse in Prison: Views from Inside: A Qualitative Study of Prison Staff and Inmates", *The Howard Journal* 36(1).

Keene, J (1997) "Drug use among prisoners before, during and after custody", *Addiction Research* 4(4).

Kelsey, O (1986) "Elderly inmates: building safe and humane care", *Corrections Today,* May.

Kendall, K (2002) "Time to think again about cognitive behavioural programmes", in P Carlen (ed), *Women and Punishment: The Struggle for Justice,* Willan.

Kennedy, J (1988) *Commission of Review into Corrective Services in Queensland,* Queensland Department of Corrective Services.

Kennedy, S, & Serin, R, (1997) *Treatment responsively: Contributing to effective correctional Programming, Research Report SR-54,* Corrective Services of Canada.

Kenya National Commission on Human Rights and Kenya Prisons (2004) *Human Rights for Correctional Institutions in Kenya – Resource and Training Manual for Correctional Institutions,* The Raoul Wallenberg Institute of Human Rights and Humanitarian Law.

Kerr, JS (1988) *Out of Sight, Out of Mind, Australia's places of confinement, 1788-1988,* SH Ervin Gallery, National Trust of Australia.

Kevin, M (1992) *Drug & Alcohol Exit Survey. Part 1: Drug & Alcohol Background of Inmates*, NSW Department of Corrective Services.

Kevin, M (1999) *Violent Crime, Alcohol & Other Drugs: A survey of inmates imprisoned for assault in Drug & Alcohol Exit Survey. Part 1: Drug & Alcohol Background of Inmates*, NSW Department of Corrective Services.

Kevin, M (2000) *Addressing the Use of Drugs in Prison: A survey of prisoners in New South Wales*, NSW Department of Corrective Services.

Kevin, M (2000) *Addressing the Use of Drugs in Prison: A survey of inmates in New South Wales*, NSW Department of Corrective Services.

Kevin, M (2002) *Redressing issues of social inequality for drug misusers in prison: Patterns of drug use, service provision, differential sanctions and reducing re-offending*, Paper presented at conference on Offender Rehabilitation in the 21st Century, Hong Kong.

Kevin, M (2003) *Addressing the Use of Drugs in Prison: prevalence, nature and context, 2nd collection of a biennial survey of prisoners in New South Wales*, NSW Department of Corrective Services.

Key, S (1999) "Organisational Ethical Culture: Real or Imagined?" *Journal of Business Ethics*, 20.

Keys Young (1998), *Homelessness in the Aboriginal and Torres Strait Islander context and its possible implications for the Supported Accommodation Assistance Program. Final Report*, Commonwealth of Australia.

Kindred, H (1993) *International Law: Chiefly as Interpreted and Applied in Canada*, Edmond Montgomery Publications Ltd.

King, R (1995) "Woodcock and after", *Prison Service Journal* 102.

Kinlock, TW, O'Grady, KE & Hanlon, TE (2003) "Effects of drug treatment on institutional behaviour", *The Prison Journal* 83(3).

Kirby, P (2000) *Report of the Independent Investigation into the Management and operations of Victoria's Private Prisons*, Government of Victoria.

Knouse, S & Giacalone, R (1992) "Ethical Decision Making in Business – Behavioural Issues and Concerns", *Journal of Business Ethics*, 11.

Koulierakis, G, Agrafiotis, D, Gnardellis, C, Power, K (1999) "Injecting drug use amongst inmates in Greek prisons", *Addiction Research* 7(3).

Kratcoski, PC (1988) "The implications of research explaining prison violence and disruption", *Federal Probation* 52(1).

Kratcoski, P & Pownall, G (1989) "Federal Bureau of Prisons programming for older inmates ", *Federal Probation* 53(2).

Lamb, HR & Weinberger, LE (1998) "Persons with severe mental illness in jails and prisons – a review", *Psychiatric Services* 49(4).

Langan, PA & Levin, DJ (2002) In Bureau of Justice Statistics Special Report, Bureau of Justice Statistics.

Lappi-Seppala, T (2003) Papers (3) presented to the 121st International Training Course "Enhancement of community-based alternatives to incarceration at all stages of the criminal justice process", Annual Report for 2002 and Resource Material Series No 61, UNAFEI.

Latessa, EJ (1996) "Correctional technology", in M McShane & FP Williams (eds) *Encyclopedia of American Prisons*, Garland Publishing.

Lee, JJ (2003) *Resolving overcrowding: The enlargement of community-based treatment in Korea,* Paper presented to the 121st International Training Course "Enhancement of community-based alternatives to incarceration at all stages of the criminal justice process", Annual Report for 2002 and Resource Material Series No 61, UNAFEI.

Liebling, A, assisted by Arnold, H (2004) *Prisons and their Moral Performance: A Study of Values, Quality and Prison Life,* Clarendon Press.

Liebling, A (2002a) "A 'liberal regime within a secure perimeter'? Dispersal prisons and penal practice in the late twentieth century" in M Tonry & AE Bottoms (eds) *Ideology, Crime and Justice: A Symposium in Honour of Sir Leon Radzinowicz* Cambridge Criminal Justice Series.

Liebling, A (2002b) "Suicides in and the Safer Prisons Agenda", *Probation Journal* 49(2).

Liebling, A (forthcoming) "Prisons, Privatisation and the Problem of Moral Values" *British Journal of Criminology.*

Liebling, A & Arnold, H (2002) *Measuring the Quality of Prison Life Research Findings* 174, Home Office.

Liebling, A & Price, D (2001) *The Prison Officer,* Prison Service and Waterside Press.

Liebling, A with Durie L, van den Beukel, A & Tait, S (forthcoming) "Legitimacy, Prison Suicide and the Moral Performance of Prisons", *European Journal of Criminology.*

Liebling, A (1999) "Doing research in prison: Breaking the silence?", *Theoretical Criminology* 3(2).

Liebling, A (1992) *Suicides in prison,* Routledge.

Liebling, A & Krarup, H (1993) *Suicide attempts and self-injury in male prisons,* Cambridge Institute of Criminology.

Lin, A (2000) *Reform in the Making: The Implementation of Social Policy in Prison,* Princeton University Press.

Lipton, DS (1995) "CDATE: Updating 'The Effectiveness of Correctional Treatment' 25 Years Later", *Journal of Offender Rehabilitation* 22(1).

Lipton, DS (1996) "Prison-based Therapeutic Communities: Their success with drug-abusing offenders", *National Institute of Justice Journal* 230.

Lipton, DS (1998) "The Effectiveness of Correctional Treatment Revisited Thirty Years Later: Preliminary Meta-Analytic Findings from the CDATE Study", Unpublished paper presented to the 12th International Congress on Criminology, Seoul Korea, August.

Lipton, DS, Martinson, R & Wilks, J (1975) *The Effectiveness of Correctional Treatment: A Survey of Treatment Valuation Studies,* Praeger Press.

Liriano, S & Ramsay, M (2003) "Prisoners' drug use before prison and the links with crime", in M Ramsay (ed) *Prisoners' drug use and treatment: seven research studies, Home Office Research Study 26,* Development and Statistics Directorate, Home Office.

Lokdam, H (2000) "An Overview of Various Human Rights Standards for Prisons and Prisoners: Implementation of Human Rights Standards in Daily Front Line Work", in Workshop on Human Rights and Corrections: ICPA Conference, 27-31 August, Cape Town, South Africa.

Lombardo, L (1989) *Guards Imprisoned,* 2nd edn, Anderson Publishing Co.

Love, B (1994) "Program curbs prison violence through conflict resolution", *Corrections Today* 56(5)

Lovell, D, Gagliardi, GJ & Peterson, PD (2002) "Recidivism and use of services among persons with mental illness after release from prison", *Psychiatric Services*, 53(10).

Ludema, J, Cooperrider, D & Barrett, F (2001) "Appreciative Inquiry: The Power of the Unconditional Positive Question", in P Reason and H Bradbury (eds), *Handbook of Action Research*, Sage.

Luke, G & Cunneen, C (1995) *Aboriginal Over-representation and Discretionary Decisions in the NSW Juvenile Justice System*, Juvenile Justice Advisory Council.

Lurigio, AJ (2000) "Persons with serious mental illness in the criminal justice system: Background, prevalence, and principles of care", *Criminal Justice Policy Review* 11(4).

Lurigio, AJ (2001) "Effective services for parolees with mental illnesses", *Crime and Delinquency* 47(3).

Lundberg, DE (1947) "Methods of selecting prison personnel," *Journal of Criminal Law and Criminology* 38.

Lyall, I, Holland, AJ & Collins, S (1995) "Offending by adults with learning difficulties – identifying need in one health district", *Mental Handicap Research* 8(2).

Lynch, J & Sabol, W (2001) *Crime Policy Report No 3*, The Urban Institute Press.

Lynch, T (2000) "Population bomb behind bars," *The Washington Post*, 20 February.

Lynd, R & Lynd, H (1937) *Middletown in transition*, Harcourt Brace.

MacDonald, JM (1999) "Violence and drug use in juvenile institutions", *Journal of Criminal Justice* 27(1).

MacKenzie, DL (1997) "Criminal justice and crime prevention", *Preventing Crime: What Works, What Doesn't, What's Promising – A Report to the United States Congress*. University of Maryland, National Institute of Justice

MaGuire, K, Flanagan, T & Thornberry, T (1988) "Prison Labour and Recidivism", *Journal of Quantitative Criminology*, 4(3).

Martinson, R (1974) "What works? Questions and answers about prison reform", *The Public Interest*, Vol 35.

Mayer, E (1992) *The key competencies report- putting general education to work*, The Australian Education Council and Ministers for Vocational Education, Employment and Training.

Mayhew, P, (2003) *Counting the costs of crime in Australia, Trends & issues in crime and criminal justice, No 247*, Australian Institute of Criminology.

McGuire, J (2000) Defining prison programs, *Forum on Corrections Research* 12(2), May.

McHutchison, J (1991) *NSW Corrective Service Industries and Offender Post Release Employment*, Research Publication, No 14, NSW Department of Corrective Services.

McHutchison, J (1995) *Working Towards a Better Future: A study into inmate employment in NSW Correctional System*, Research Publication No 34, NSW Department of Corrective Services.

McHutchison, J (1999) *The Social & Economic Benefits & Costs of Commercial Industries: A foundation study*, Research Publication No 40, NSW Department of Corrective Services.

Mair, G (1991) "What works – nothing or everything?", *Home Office Research and Statistics Department Research Bulletin* 30.

Maltz, M (1984) *Recidivism*, Academic Press.

Makkai, T (2000) "Drug Trends and Policies" in D Chappell & P Wilson (eds) *Crime and the Criminal Justice System in Australia: 2000 and Beyond*, Butterworths.

Makkai, T (1999) *Drug Use Monitoring in Australia 1999 Annual Report on Drug Use Among Adult Detainees*, Australian Institute of Criminology.

Malcolm X (1989) *Autobiography of Malcolm X*, Ballentine.

Martell, DA, Rosner, R & Harmon, RB (1995) "Base-rate estimates of criminal behaviour by homeless mentally ill persons in New York City", *Psychiatric Services* 46(6).

Marshall, T (1999) *Restorative Justice: An Overview*, Home Office Research Development and Statistics Directorate.

Martinson, R (1972) "Paradox of Prison Reform", *The New Republic* 166.

Martinson, R (1974) "What Works? – Questions and Answers About Prison Reform", *The Public Interest* 35.

Martinson, R (1979) "New Findings, New Views: A Note of Caution Regarding Sentencing Reform", *Hofstra Law Review* 7.

Martinson, R & Wilks, J (1977) Save Parole Supervision, Federal Probation, 41.

Marks, M (2000) "Transforming Police Organization from Within: Police Dissident Groupings in South Africa", *British Journal of Criminology* 4.

Matthews, R & Francis, P (eds) (1996) *Prisons 2000: An international perspective on the current state and future of imprisonment*, Macmillan Press.

Massey, D (1989) *Doing time in American prisons: a study of modern novels*, Greenwood Press.

Matsheza, P & Zulu, L (2001) *Human Rights Enforcement and Implementation Mechanisms*, Human Rights Trust of Southern Africa.

Mauer, M (1995) "The international use of incarceration", *The Prison Journal* 75(1).

May, C (1999) *Drugs* statistics, Home Office, Research Development and Statistics Directorate.

McGuire, J & Priestley, P (1985) *Offending Behaviour: Skills and Stratagems for Going Straight*, Batsford Academic and Educational.

MacIntyre, A (1999) *Dependent Rational Animals: Why Human Beings Need the Virtues*, Duckworth.

McArthur, M, Camilleri, P & Webb, H (1999) "Strategies for managing suicide and self-harm in prisons" *Trends and Issues in Crime and Criminal Justice, No 125*, Australian Institute of Criminology.

McCartney, C, Lincoln, R & Wilson, P (2003) *Justice in the Deep North*, Bond University Press, Gold Coast, Queensland.

McCarthy, M (1972) *Medina*, Wildwood House.

McCarthy, M (1983) "The health status of elderly inmates", *Corrections Today* February.

McCarthy, B (1981), *An Exploratory Study of Corruption in Corrections*, PhD thesis, Florida State University.

McGiven, (1988) *Report of the Inquiry into the Fire and Riot at Fremantle Prison on 4 January 1988*, WA Government Printer.

McLaren, K (1996) *Dazed and Confused: New Evidence on What Works in Reducing Offending* Paper presented at Criminology Conference, Victoria University of Wellington.

McConville, S (1995) "Local justice: The jail", in N Morris & DJ Rothman (eds), *The Oxford history of prisons: the practice of punishment in Western society*, Oxford University Press.

McCorkle, RC, Miethe, TD & Drass, KA (1995) "The roots of prison violence: A test of the deprivation, management, and not so total institution models", *Crime and Delinquency* 41(3).

McDonald, DC & Teitelbaum, M (1994) *Managing mentally ill offenders in the community: Milwaukee's Community Support Program*, Program Focus, US Department of Justice, National Institute of Justice.

McGuire, J & Priestley, P (1992) "Some Things Do Work: Psychological Interventions With Offenders and the Effectiveness Debate", in F Losel, D Bender & T Bliesener (eds), *Psychology and Law: International Perspectives*, Walter de Gruyter Publishers.

McGuire, J (1995) (ed) *What Works: Reducing Offending: Lessons from Research*, Wiley.

McGuire, J & Priestley, P (1995) "Reviewing 'What Works': Past, Present and Future", in J McGuire (ed) *What Works: Reducing Re-offending: guidelines from research and practice*, John Wiley and Sons.

McKenna, DD & Pottle, C (1985) *Development of Training Standards, Standards Project: Training Phase Technical Report*, Personnel Decisions Research Institute.

McKenzie, DL (1997) in L Sherman, D Gottfredson, D McKenzie, J Eck, P Reuter & S Bushway, *Preventing Crime: What Works, What Doesn't, What's Promising. A Report to the US Congress*, University of Maryland.

MacIntyre, A (2000) *After Virtue: A Study in Moral Theory*, 10th edn, Duckworth.

McKnight, J & Sutton, J (1994) *Social Psychology*, Prentice-Hall Australia.

McMahon, M (2000) "Assisting Female Offenders: Art or Science?: Chairperson's Commentary" in M McMahon (ed) *Assessment to Assistance Programmes for Women in Community Corrections*, American Correctional Association.

Memmott P, Stacy R, Chambers, C & Keys, C (2001) *Violence in Indigenous Communities*, Commonwealth of Australia.

Miller, JG (1989) "The Debate on Rehabilitating Criminals: Is It True that Nothing Works?" *Washington Post*, March.

Miner, M & Gorta, A (1986) *Drugs and Women in Prison*, NSW Department of Corrective Services.

Mitford, J (1973) *Kind and usual punishment: the prison business*, Alfred A Knopf.

Moore, A (2002) *Private Prisons: Quality Corrections at a Lower Cost*, Policy Study No 240, Reason Public Policy Institute.

Morgan, R (1997) in M Maguire, R Morgan & R Reiner (eds) *The Oxford Handbook of Criminology*, 2nd edn, Oxford University Press.

Morgan, R (1991) "Woolf: in retrospect and prospect", *Modern Law Review* 54(3).

Morgan, R (1992) "Following Woolf: the prospects for prisons policy", *Journal of Law and Society* 19(2).

Morris, N & Rothman, DJ (eds) (1995) *The Oxford History of the Prison: The Practice of Punishment in Western Society*, Oxford University Press.

Morris, N (1988) "International Trends in the Treatment of Offenders" in D Biles, (ed), *Current international trends in corrections: Selected papers from the Australian Bicentennial International Congress on Corrective Services*, Sydney, January, Federation Press.

Morris, N (1974) *The Future of Imprisonment*, The University of Chicago Press.

Morton, JB (ed) (1991) *Public Policy for Corrections*, 2nd ed, American Correctional Association.

Morton, J & Anderson, J (1982) "Elderly offenders: the forgotten minority", *Corrections Today* December.

Morris, N (1974) *The future of imprisonment*, University of Chicago Press.

Morrisey, C (1997) "A multimodal approach to controlling inpatient assaultiveness among incarcerated juveniles", *Journal of Offender Rehabilitation* 25(1/2).

Motiuk, L & Belcourt, R, (1996) *Prison work programs and post-release outcomes: A Preliminary investigation*, Research Division, Correctional Service of Canada.

Moyle, P (2000) *Profiting from Punishment*, Pluto Press

Mumola, C (2000) *Bureau of Justice Statistics Special Report*, US Department of Justice.

Munroe, FM (1995) "Social skills differences in aggressive and non-aggressive male young offenders within an unfamiliar social situation", *Medicine Science and the Law* 35(3).

Murphy, P (1988) "Implementing Business Ethics" *Journal of Business Ethics*, 7.

Murray, HA (1938) *Explorations in personality*, Oxford University Press.

Myers, SL (1980) "The Rehabilitation Effects of Punishment, *Economic Inquiry* 18.

Nacci, PL & Kane, TR (1984) "Inmate sexual aggression: Some evolving propositions, empirical findings, and mitigating counter-forces", *Gender Issues, Sex Offences & Criminal Justice.*

NACRO (1992) *Revolving Doors: Report of the Telethon Inquiry into the Relationship Between Mental Health, Homelessness and Criminal Justice*, NACRO.

Nafine, N & Gale, F (1987) "Testing the nexus: Crime gender and unemployment", *British Journal of Criminology*, 29(2).

Nagle, J (1978) *Report of the Royal Commission into NSW Prisons*, NSW Government Printer.

NSW Legislative Council Select Committee on the Increase in Prisoner Population, (2000) *Interim Report: Issues Relating to Women*, NSW Government Printer.

National Audit Office (2003) *The Operational Performance of PFI Prisons Report by the Comptroller and Auditor General HC Session 2002-2003: 18 June 2003*, The Stationary Office.

National Institute of Justice (1999) *1998 ADAM: Annual Report on Drug Use Among Adult and Juvenile Arrestees*, Home Office.

Neeley, C, Addison, L & Craig-Moreland, D (1997) "Addressing needs of elderly offenders", *Corrections Today* 59(5).

Nelson, M, Deess, P & Allen, C (1999) *Post-incarceration experiences in New York City*, Vera Institute of Justice.

New South Wales Department of Corrective Services, (2001) *Annual Report 2000-2001*, NSW Government.

New South Wales Task Force on Women in Prison, (1985) *Report*, NSW Government Printer.

Norman, A & Parrish, A (1999) "Prison Health Care: Work Environment and the Nursing Role", *British Journal of Nursing* 8(10).

Northern Territory Correctional Services, (2003) *Annual Report 2002-03*, Northern Territory Government.

Northern Territory Correctional Services, (2003) *Strategic Directions 2002-03*, Northern Territory Government.

NSW Department of Corrective Services (2004) *Inmate Census Series (1993-2003)*, Research and Statistics Unit, NSW Department of Corrective Services.

NSW Law Reform Commission (2000) *Sentencing: Aboriginal Offenders Report 96*, October, NSW Law Reform Commission.

NSW Legislative Council, Select Committee on the Increase in Prisoner Population, (2001) *Final Report*, NSW Government Printer.

Ntuli, RN & Dlula, SW (2003) *Enhancement of community-based alternatives to incarceration at all stages of the criminal justice process in South Africa*, Paper presented to the 121st International Training Course "Enhancement of community-based alternatives to incarceration at all stages of the criminal justice process", Annual Report for 2002 and Resource Material Series No 61, UNAFEI.

Nurco, DN, Ball J, Shaffer, J & Hanlon, T (1985) "The Criminality of Narcotics Addicts", *The Journal of Nervous and Mental Diseases* 173.

O'Carroll, PW, Berman, AL, Maris, RW, Moscicki, EK, Tanney, BL, & Silverman, MM (1996) "Beyond the Tower of Babel: A nomenclature for suicidology", *Suicide and Life Threatening Behavior* 26.

O'Donnell, I & Edgar, K (1996) *The Extent and Dynamics of Victimisation in Prison*, Centre for Criminological Research, Oxford University.

O'Donnell, I & Edgar, K (1998), "Routine victimisation in prisons", *The Howard Journal*, 37.

Ohio Department of Planning and Evaluation, (1995) *Evaluation of the impact of participation in Ohio Penal Industries on Recidivism*, Ohio Department of Rehabilitation and Correction.

O'Malley, P (1992) "Risk, Power and Crime Prevention", *Economy and Society*, 21.

O'Neill, O (2002) *A Question of Trust, The BBC Reith Lecture Series*, Cambridge University Press.

Osborne, T (1916) *Society and prisons: some suggestions for a new penology*, Yale University Press.

Owen, B (1988) *The reproduction of social control: a study of prison workers at San Quentin*, Praeger.

Palmer, T (1975) "Martinson Revisited", *Journal of Research in Crime and Delinquency* 12(2).

Patrick, S (1998) "Differences in inmate-inmate and inmate-staff altercations: Examples from a medium security prison", *The Social Science Journal* 35(2).

Patterson, BL (1992) "Job experience and perceived stress among police, correctional, and probation/parole officers", *Criminal Justice and Behavior* 19.

Patterson, D (2001) "Causal Effects of Regulatory, Organisational and Personal Factors on Ethical Sensitivity" *Journal of Business Ethics* 30.

Paylor, I (1995) *Housing Needs of Ex-Offenders*, Ashgate.

Pearson, F & Lipton, D (1999) "A Meta-Analytic Review of the Effectiveness of Corrections-Based Treatments for Drug Abuse", *The Prison Journal* 79(4).

Penal Reform International (1995) *Lack of Implementation of United Nations Standard Minimum Rules for the Treatment of Prisoners*, Penal Reform International, The Hague.

Penal Reform International (1995) *Making Standards Work: An International Handbook on Good Prison Practices*, Penal Reform International and the United Nations, The Hague.

Penal Reform International (1997) "Prison Conditions in Africa" in *A Report of a Pan-African Seminar, 19-21 September 1996* Penal Reform International and the United Nations, The Hague.

Perrone, D & Pratt, TC (2003) "Comparing the Quality of Confinement and Cost-Effectiveness of Public Versus Private Prisons: What We Know, Why We Do Not Know More, and Where To Go From Here", *The Prison Journal* 83(3).

Peteron-Badali, M & Koegl, CJ (2002) "Juveniles' experiences of incarceration: The role of correctional staff in peer violence", *Journal of Criminal Justice* 30(1)

Peters, RH, & Bartoi, MG (1997) *Screening and assessment of co-occurring disorders in the justice system*, The GAINS Center.

Petersilia, J (1999) in M Tonry & P Joan (eds) *Prisons*, University of Chicago Press.

Petersilia, J (2000) *US Department of Justice Office of Justice Programs*, National Institute of Justice.

Philliber, S (1987) "Thy brother's keeper: A review of the literature on correctional officers" *Justice Quarterly* 4(1).

Pitts, J (1992) "The End of an Era", *The Howard Journal of Criminal Justice* 31(2).

Pollitt, C & Bouckaert G (2000) *Public Management Reform: A Comparative Analysis*, Oxford University Press.

Potteiger, A (1981) "Sample Bias in Drugs/Crimes Research", in Inciardi J (ed) *The Drugs-Crime Connection*, Sage.

Potter, F & Connolly L (1991) *AIDS: The Sexual & IV Drug Use Behaviour of Prisoners*, NSW Department of Corrective Services.

Posmakov, P (2002) "From a totalitarian prison system in Kazakhstan to a system based on human rights', *Corrections Today* February.

Power (2001) *The Audit Society*, Oxford University Press.

Powers, G (1828), *Report of Gershom Powers Agent and Keeper of the State Prison at Auburn*, Croswell & Van Benthuysen.

Pratt, J (2000) "Emotive and Ostentatious Punishment: its decline and resurgence in modern society" *Punishment and Society* 2.

Pratt, J (2002) *Punishment and Civilisation*, Sage.

Pratt, J (forthcoming 2005) *The New Punitiveness: Current Trends, Theories, Perspectives*.

Pratt, J (2002) "The globalisation of punishment", *Corrections Today*, February.

President's Commission on Law Enforcement and the Administration of Justice (1967) *Task force report: corrections*, Government Printing Office.

Priestly, P (1985) *Victorian prison lives: English prison biography 1830-1914*, Methuen.

"Prison crowding 'linked to suicides" (2002) BBC News, 10 December, available: <http://news.bbc.co.uk/1/low/uk/2561625.stm>.

Prison Policy Initiative (2002) "Overview: trends in the crime control industry-private prisons'", Prison Index-Overview of private prisons, Prison Policy Initiative.

Proctor, JL (1994) "Evaluating a modified version of the federal prison systems inmate classification model: An assessment of objectivity and predictive validity", *Criminal Justice and Behaviour* 21(2).

Public Services International Research Unit, University of Greenwich (2000) *Prison Privatisation Report International No 34*, March 2000, Prison Reform Trust.

Queensland Department of Corrective Services, (1999) *Prisoners in Queensland: Crime Statistics Bulletin No 5 April 1999*, Queensland Government.

Queensland Department of Corrective Services, (2003) *Strategic Plan 2002-03*, Queensland Government.

Queensland Department of Corrective Services, (2003) *Annual Report 2002-03*, Queensland Government.

Queensland Department of Corrective Services, (1999) *Corrections in the Balance – A review of Corrective Services in Queensland*, Queensland Government.

Querry, R (1973) "Prison movies: an annotated bibliography 1921-present", *Journal of popular film*, 2(2).

Raelin, J (1991) *The Clash of Cultures: Managers Managing Professionals*, Harvard Business School Press.

Ramcharan, BG (1988) "Human Rights and the Law", in P Davies (ed) *Human Rights*, Routledge.

Ramsay, M (1986), "Housing for the homeless ex-offender: key findings from a literature review", *Research Bulletin No 20*, Home Office.

Ramsay, M, Baker, P, Goulden, C, Sharp, C & Sondhi, A (2001) *Drug Misuse Declared in 2000: Results from the British Crime Survey*, Home Office.

Reid, ST (1982) *Crime and Criminology*, CBS College Publishing.

Regnery, AS (1985) "Getting Away with Murder: Why the justice system needs an overhaul", *Policy Review* 34.

Report on Government Services (2004), Productivity Commission, Steering Committee for the Review of Government Service Provision, 2.

Reichel, P (2002) *Comparative criminal justice systems: A topical approach*, 3rd edn, Prentice Hall.

Reisig, MD (1998) "Rates of disorder in higher-custody state prisons: A comparative analysis of managerial practices", *Crime and Delinquency* 44(2).

Reisig, MD (2002), "Administrative control and inmate homicide", *Homicide Studies* 6(1).

Resnick, B (2003) "Health promotion practices of older adults: testing an individualised approach", *Journal of Clinical Nursing* 12(1).

Rhodes, L (2004) *Total confinement: madness and reason in the maximum security prison*, University of California Press.

Ridley-Smith, M & Redman, R (2002) "Prisoners and the Right to Vote", in D Brown & M Wilkie (eds) *Prisoners as Citizens: Human rights in Australian Prisons*, Federation Press.

Ritchie, J (1976) "Towards Ending an unclean Thing: The Molesworth Committee and the Abolition of Transportation to New South Wales, 1937-40", *Historical Studies* 17(67).

Robinson, C (2003) *Understanding iterative homelessness: The case of people with mental disorders. Final Report*, Available: <http:/www.ahuri.edu.au>.

Rough Sleepers Unit (2000) *Blocking the fast track from Prison to Rough Sleeping*, Office of the Deputy Prime Minister.

Robertson, B (2000) *The Aboriginal and Torres Strait Islander Women's Task Force on Violence Report*, Department of Aboriginal and Torres Strait Islander Policy and Development.

Rodriguez, N (2003) in B Brown (ed) *Vol 1 Issues in Brief*, Vera Institute of Justice.

Rose, D & Clear, T (1998) "Incarceration, social capital and crime: Implications for social disorganisation theory", *Criminology* 36.

Ross, DL (1995) "A twenty-year analysis of section 1983 litigation in corrections," *American Jails* 9.

Rothman, D (1971) *The discovery of the asylum*, Little, Brown.

Ruback, RB & Carr, TS (1993) "Prison crowding over time: The relationship of density and changes in density to infraction rates", *Criminal Justice and Behaviour* 20(2).

Rucker, L (1994) "Coercive versus cooperative environments: The collateral effects in prison", *The Prison Journal* 73(1).

Rutherford, A (1991) "Penal reform and prison realities', in D Whitfield (ed), *The state of the prison – 200 years on*, Routledge.

Ryan, M & Ward, T (1989) "Privatisation and penal politics" in Justice R Matthews (ed) *Privatising Criminal Justice*, Sage Contemporary Criminology Series.

San Bernardino County Criminal Justice/Mentally Ill Offender Crime Reduction Strategy Committee (1999) San Bernardino Partners for Aftercare Networking (SPAN), Proposal to the California Board of Corrections.

Sarre, R (1984) "The Orwellian Connection: A Comment on Recent Correctional Reform Literature", *Canadian Criminology Forum* 6 (2).

Sarre, R (1999a) "Restorative Justice: Translating the Theory into Practice", *University of Notre Dame Australia Law Review* 1(1).

Sarre, R (1999b) "Destructuring and Criminal Justice Reforms: Rescuing Diversionary Ideas from the Waste-paper basket", *Current Issues in Criminal Justice* 10(3).

Saylor, WG (1984) *Surveying Prison Environments*, United States Federal Bureau of Prisons.

Saylor, W & Gaes, G (1992) "Federal Prisons: Work Experience Linked with Post-Release Success Research Forum", *FBI Law Enforcement Bulletin*, June.

Saylor, W & Gaes, G (1996) "Evaluation of Post-release Performance for Federal Prisoners in Industry and Vocational Programs", *Detention Reporter*, No 149, March.

Schein, EH (1988) *Organizational Psychology*, 3rd edn, Prentice-Hall.

Scott, E (1997) "A Prison and a Nursing Home: any Similarities", *International Journal of offender Therapy and Comparative Criminology* 41(3).

Scull, AT (1977) *Decarceration*. Prentice-Hall.

Sechrest, L, White, S & Brown, E (eds) (1979) *The Rehabilitation of Criminal Offenders: Problems and Prospects*, National Academy of Sciences Press.

Sechrest, DK & Reimer, EG (1982) "Adopting national standards for correctional reform" *Federal Probation* 46 (6).

Seiter, R & Kadela, K (2003) "What works, what does not and what is promising", *Crime & Delinquency*, 49.

Sherman, LW (1992) "Book Review of Herman Goldstein Problem-Oriented Policing, NY McGraw-Hill 1990", *The Journal of Criminal Law and Criminology* 82(3).

Sherman, M & Hawkins, G (1981) *Imprisonment in America: Choosing the Future*, University of Chicago Press.

Shewan, D, Gemmell, M, & Davies, J (1994) "Prison as a modifier of drug using behaviour", *Addiction Research* 2(2).

Shewan, D, Macpherson, S, Greenwood, J (2001) "Injecting risk behaviour among recently released prisoners in Edinburgh: The impact of in-prison and community drug treatment services", *Legal and Criminological Psychology* 6.

Shichor, D & Sechrest, DK (1996), *Three Strikes and You're Out: Vengeance as Public Policy*, Sage Publications.

Shneidman, E (1985) *Definition of suicide*, Jason Aronson.

Shneidman, E (1993) *Suicide as psychache: A clinical approach to self-destructive behaviour*, Jason Aronson.

Shneidman, E (1998) "Further reflections on suicide and psychache", *Suicide and Life Threatening Behaviour* 28.

Simpson, J, Martin, M & Green, J (2001) *The Framework Report*, Intellectual Disability Rights Service.

Singleton, N, Pendry, E, Taylor, C, Farrel, M & Marsden, J (2003) *Research Findings*, Home Office Research, Development and Statistics Directorate.

Silberman, M (1992) "Violence as social control in prison", *Virginia Review of Sociology* 1.

Smartt, U (1999) "X industries in Europe, Corrections Compendium", *The National Journal for Corrections* 24(11).

Smith, A, Rissel, C, Richters, J, Grulich, A & de Visser, R (2003) "Sex in Australia: Rationale and methods of the Australian Study of Health and Relationships", *Australian and New Zealand Journal of Public Health* 27.

Smith, L et al, (1999) *Report of the Inquiry into the Incident at Casuarina Prison on 25 December 1998*, WA Ministry of Justice.

Smith, R (1995) "The alternatives to violence project", *Social Alternatives* 14(1).

Smyer, T, Gragert M, & LaMere S (1997) "Stay safe! Stay healthy! Surviving old age in prison", *Journal of Psychosocial Nursing* 45(9).

Solomon, P & Draine, J (1995) "Jail Recidivism in a Forensic Case Management Program", *Health and Social Work* 20(3).

South Australia Department for Correctional Services, (2002) *Annual Report 2001-02*, South Australian Government.

South Australia Department for Correctional Services, (2003) *Annual Report 2002-03*, South Australian Government.

Sparks, R (1994) "Can Prisons Be Legitimate?" in R King & M McGuire (eds) *Prisons in Context*, Clarendon Press.

Sparks, R & Bottoms, AE (1995) "Legitimacy and order in prisons", *British Journal of Sociology* 46(1).

Sparks R, Bottoms, AE & Hay, W (1996) *Prisons and the Problem of Order*, Clarendon Press.

Specter, D (1994) "Cruel and unusual punishment of the mentally ill in California's prisons: A case study of a class action suit", *Social Justice* 21(3).

Stathis, H (1990) *Drug Use Amongst Offenders: A Literature Review*, NSW Department of Corrective Services.

Strang, J, Heuston, J, Gossop, M, Green, J, & Maden, T (1998) *HIV/AIDS Risk Behaviour Among Adult Male Prisoners*, Home Office.

Stark, R (1975) *Social Problems*, Random House.

Stevens, B (1999) "Communicating Ethical Values: A study of employee perceptions" *Journal of Business Ethics* 20.

Stevenson, R & Forthsythe, L (1998) *The Stolen Goods Market in New South Wales: An interview study with imprisoned burglars*, NSW Bureau of Crime Statistics and Research.

Sydney Morning Herald (2004) "Revolving doors at LA jails", 28 March, p 21.

Sykes, G (1958) *The society of captives*, Princeton University Press.

Tartaro, C (2000) "The impact of jail design and supervision strategies on jail violence", *Dissertation Abstracts International* 61(5).

Tartaro, C (2002) "Impact of density on jail violence", *Journal of Criminal Justice* 30(6).

Tasmanian Department of Justice and Industrial Relations, (1998) *Submission to the Legislative Council Select Committee on Correctional Services and Sentencing in Tasmania*, Tasmanian Government.

Tasmanian Department of Justice and Industrial Relations, (2003) *Annual Report 2002-03*, Tasmanian Government.

Taxman, F, Young, D, Byrne, J, Holsinger, A & Anspach, D (2002) *Bureau of Governmental Research Report*, University of Maryland.

Telfer,J (2003) *Duty of Care*, South Australian Institute of Justice Studies.

Tewksbury, R and Mustaine, E (2001) "Where to find Corrections Research: An Assessment of research Published in Corrections Specialty Journal, 1990-1999", *The Prison Journal* 81(4).

Thomas, JE & Stewart, A (1978), *Imprisonment in Western Australia: Evolution, Theory and Practice*, UNIWA Press.

Thomas, CW (1997) *Private Adult Correctional Facility Census*, 10th edn, University of Florida.

Thompson, N (2002) *People Skills,* 2nd edn, Palgrave Macmillan.

Thompson, B (2001) *Remand Inmates in NSW – Some Statistics*, Research Bulletin No 20, NSW Department of Corrective Services.

Toch, H (1977) *Living in prison: The ecology of survival*, The Free Press.

Toch, H (1997) *Corrections: A humanistic approach*, Criminal Justice Press.

Tomaino, J (1999) "Punishment Theory", in R Sarre & J Tomaino (eds) Exploring Criminal Justice: Contemporary Australian Themes, Adelaide Institute of Justice Studies.

Tomison, AM & Wise, S (1999) *Community Based Approaches to Preventing Child Maltreatment* Issues Paper No 11 National Child Protection Clearing House AIFS.

Torrey, EF (1999) "How did so many mentally ill persons get into Americas jails and prisons?", *American Jails*, November.

Travis, J & Waul, M (2003) in J Travis & M Waul (eds) *Prisoners Once Removed: The Impact of Incarceration and Reentry on Children, Families and Communities*, The Urban Institute Press.

Travis, J (2000) *But they all come back: rethinking prisoner re-entry*, National Institute of Justice.

Turnbull, P, Stimson, G & Stillwell, G (1994) *Drug Use in Prison*, Avert.

UNAFEI (2003) "Reports of the course", 121st International Training Course "Enhancement of community-based alternatives to incarceration at all stages of the criminal justice process", Annual Report for 2002 and Resource Material Series No 61.

United Nations Economic and Social Council (2003) "Use and application of United Nations standards and norms in crime prevention and criminal justice", Report of the Secretary-General, Commission on Crime Prevention and Criminal Justice, 12th session, Item 7 of the provisional agenda, Vienna, 13-22 May.

United States of America Bureau of Justice (2004) Statistics, United States Department of Justice office of justice programs, 12 May 2004, <http://www.ojp.usdoj/gov/bjs/correct.htm>.

United States Department of Justice (2003) Reentry, <http://www.ojp.gov/reentry/learn.html>.

United States General Accounting Office (2001) Prisoner Releases, Available: <http://www.gao.gov/new.items/d01483.pdf>.

Vitelli, R (1993), "The homeless inmate in a maximum security prison setting", *Canadian Journal of Criminology* 35(3).

Van Heeringen, K, Hawton, K, & Williams, JMG (2000) "Pathways to suicide: An integrative approach", in K Hawton & K Van Heeringen (eds) *The international handbook of suicide and attempted suicide*, Wiley.

Vennard, J, Hedderman, C, & Sugg, D, (1997) *Changing offenders attitudes and behaviour: What Works?* Research Findings No 61, Home Office Research and Statistics Directorate.

Verdeyen, R (1995) "Correctional Industries: Making Inmate work productive", *Corrections Today* August.

Victorian Department of Justice, (2000) *Annual Report 1999-2000*, Victorian Government.

Vinson, A (1982) *Wilful Obstruction*, Methuen.

Vinson, A (2004) "Implementing the key principles of the Nagle Commission" in The Nagle Report – 25 Years On Symposium, *Current Issues in Criminal Justice* 93.

Vito, GF & Allen, HE (1981) "Shock Probation in Ohio: A Comparison of Outcomes", *International Journal of Offender Therapy and Comparative Criminology* 25.

Von Hirsch, A (1976) *Doing Justice: The Choice of Punishments*, Hall & Wang.

Wagner, P (2003) *The Prison Index: Taking the Pulse of the crime Control Industry*, The Western Prison Project and The Prison Policy Initiative.

Wahler, C & Gendreau, P (1985) "Assessing correctional officers", *Federal Probation*, 49.

Walker, J (2004) *Projections of Prison Populations*, John Walker Consulting.

Walker, J (2000) *Tasmanian Prisoner Projections 2000-2019*, Tasmanian Government.

Walker, J (1987) "Prison Cells with Revolving Doors: A Judicial or Societal Problem", in KM Hazlehurst (ed) *Ivory Scales: Black Australia and the Law*, University of New South Wales Press.

Walker, N (1985) *Sentencing: Theory, Law and Practice*, Butterworths.

Walmsley, R (2003) *World prison population list*, 5th edn, Findings 234, Home Office. available: <www.csdp.org/research/r234.pdf>.

Walmsley, R (2001) *An overview of world imprisonment: global prison populations, trends and solutions*, Paper presented at the United Nations Programme Network Institutes Technical Assistance Workshop Vienna, Austria, 10 May.

Walmsley, R (1998) *Prison population growth in Europe: Its extent and causes*, Paper presented at the "Beyond Prisons" Symposium, Kingston, Ontario, March.

Walrath, C (2001) "Evaluation of an inmate-run alternatives to violence project: The impact of inmate-to-inmate intervention", *Journal of Interpersonal Violence* 16(7).

Walters, GD (1998) "Time series and correlational analyses of inmate-initiated assaultive incidents in a large correctional system", *International Journal of Offender Therapy and Comparative Criminology* 42(2).

Watt, BD & Howells, K (1999) "Skills training for aggression control: Evaluation of an anger management programme for violent offenders", *Legal and Criminological Psychology* 4(2).

Weatherburn, D & Lind, B (2001) *Delinquent-Prone Communities*, Cambridge University Press.

Weatherburn D, Fitzgerald, J and Hua, J (2003) "Reducing Aboriginal Over-representation in Prison", *Australian Journal of Public Administration*, September.

Webster, R, Hedderman, C, Turnbull, P & May, T (2001) *Prison based employment schemes*, Home Office Research, Development and Statistics Directorate.

Welsh, BC & Farrington DP (2000) "X intervention programs and cost-benefit analysis, *Criminal Justice and Behaviour*, 27(1), February.

Weissbrodt, D (1988) "Human Rights: An Historical Perspective", in P Davies (ed) *Human Rights*, Routledge.

Western Australia Ministry of Justice, (2000) *Annual Report 1999-2000*, Western Australian Government.

Wexler, D (1990) *Therapeutic Jurisprudence The Law as a Therapeutic Agent*, Carolina Academic Press.

White, R & Perrone, S (1997) *Crime and Social Control: An Introduction*, Oxford University Press.

Wicks, RJ (1980) *Guard! Society's Professional Prisoner*, Gulf Publications.

Wiles, P (2004) "Policy and Sociology", *The British Journal of Sociology* 55(1)

Williams, M (1997) *Cry of pain: Understanding suicide and self-harm*, Penguin.

Williams, JMG & Pollock, LR (2000) "Psychological aspects of the suicidal process", in K van Heeringen (ed) *Understanding Suicidal Behaviour*, John Wiley.

Williams, P (2001) "Deaths in Custody: 10 years on from the Royal Commission", *Trends and Issues in Crime and Criminal Justice No 203*, Australian Institute of Criminology.

Willmott, Y (1997) "Prison Nursing: the Tension between Custody and Care", *British Journal of Nursing* 6(6).

Wilson, JQ (1980) "What Works Revisited: New Findings on Criminal Rehabilitation", *The Public Interest* 61.

Wines, F (1910) *Punishment and reformation: a study of the penitentiary system*, Thomas A Crowell.

Winter, N, Holland, AJ & Collins, S (1997), "Factors predisposing to suspected offending by adults with self-reported learning disabilities", *Psychological Medicine* 27(3).

Wirth, W, (1993) *Offender Training and Employment in Germany: Models and problems of good practice in European offender employment group, Models of good practice in Europe: What works*, European Offender Employment Group, Surrey.

Woods, R (1990) "Solitary confinement: the criminal in popular literature", Unpublished doctoral dissertation, University of California.

Wolfus, B & Bierman, R (1996) "An evaluation of a group treatment program for incarcerated male batterers", *International Journal of Offender Therapy & Comparative Criminology* 40(4).

Wortley, R (2002) *Situational Prison Control: Crime Prevention in Correctional Institutions*, Cambridge University Press

World Health Organisation (1998) *Population Aging – A Health Challenge, WHO Fact Sheet No 135*, revised September 1998, (accessed online 11 November 2003). <http://www.who.int/inf-fs/en/fact135.html>.

Zamble, E (1998) *Community supervision: current practices and future directions*, Paper presented at the "Beyond Prisons" Symposium, Kingston, Ontario, March.

Zapf, PA, Roesch, R & Hart, SD (1996) "An examination of the relationship of homelessness to mental disorder, criminal behaviour, and health care in a pre-trial jail population", *Canadian Journal of Psychiatry* 41(7).

Zdenkowski, G & Brown, D (1982) *The Prison Struggle*, Penguin Books.

Zdenkowski, G (2000) "Sentencing Trends: Past Present and Prospective", in D Chappell & P Wilson (eds) *Crime and the Criminal Justice System in Australia: 2000 and Beyond*, Butterworths.

Zupan, LL & Menke, BA (1991) "The new generation jail: An overview", in JA Thompson & GL Mays (eds) *American Jails: Public Policy Issues*, Nelson Hall.

Index

Women (*cont*)
prisons
overcrowding, 118
risk and responsibilities, 117-123
proportion of overall prison population, 4, 19, 110
psychological damage, 117
quality of life, 119-120
reduction in numbers required, 120

return to prison, likelihood, 189
self-harm, 147, 153
social science research, 36-37
staff, 107
Woolf Report 1991, 88
Workshops, 56
World prison population
features, 10-11, 226
pre-trial detainees, 10

Also available from The Federation Press:

Islam

Its law and society

Jamila Hussain

Recent events have brought Islam and Muslims to the centre of the West's attention, leading many to ask what it means to be Muslim, keen to know what is fact and what is misconception.

Jamila Hussain explains the basic principles of the religion of Islam and its law, the Shariah, and how the Shariah is lived in the context of many different cultures throughout the World. The discussion includes:

- A brief survey of Islamic history and civilisation
- The development of Islamic law and how it is applied in modern conditions
- The position of women in Islam and the growth of Islamic feminism
- Family law and inheritance
- Modern reproductive technology
- Criminal law and evidence
- Banking and commercial law
- The Australian Muslim community

A new chapter examines Islamic laws of war and peace, and contemporary rulings on the conduct of Muslims in times of war.

Now in its second edition, this book is ideal for those who wish to acquire an introductory knowledge of Islamic culture and law in general and within Australian society in particular.

Praise for the first edition:

> *This book makes a timely and significant contribution to Australians' knowledge of Islamic civilisation*
>
> Law Institute of Victoria Journal

> *Addresses a number of commonly held misconceptions of Islam*
>
> Alternative Law Journal

> *An interesting and thorough introduction to a way of life*
>
> Tasmanian Law Society Newsletter

2003 • **ISBN 1 86287 499 9** • **paperback** • **260 pp** • **$39.95**

Seddon's Domestic Violence in Australia

The legal response – 3rd edition

Renata Alexander

This practical book analyses the law in each Australian State and Territory and provides a summary of the available legal remedies.

It covers criminal law and family law issues in detail, and has a lengthy chapter on protection orders. It has a solid section on social security and related benefits; relates domestic violence to other legal issues such as the evidentiary value or otherwise of the Battered Woman Syndrome; and includes lists of specialist domestic violence agencies in each jurisdiction and of legal centres specialising in social security law.

The book is written in the firm belief that those assisting victims of domestic violence should take a holistic approach, best achieved by one helper having knowledge of a network of helpers and agencies who can deal with the various problems the victims face. The law is one possible remedy; it will be helpful in many cases but not in all. All helpers need to be aware of the law and of its strengths and limitations.

> *An invaluable text for anyone whose work brings him/her into contact with this issue. From the outset, the author … stresses that a holistic, interagency approach is required. … This book is an excellent resource for providing the clients of family therapists and other counsellors with accurate and essential information about the legal avenues for addressing domestic violence.*
>
> ANZ Journal of Family Therapy, Vol 24 No 3 (Sept 200), 170

> *This exceptionally useful book explains the wide range of available legal responses to domestic violence in each Australian jurisdiction.*
>
> Educational Book Review (India), Nov-Dec 2002

> *This practical guide … will make useful reading for anyone involved in providing services/assistance to victims of domestic violence.*
>
> Family Matters No 62 (Winter 2002) 56

> *A fantastic reference for lawyers, Domestic Violence in Australia: the Legal Response serves also as a functional summary for social workers and anyone involved in the support of families disrupted by violence. … Ms Alexander explains practically every option the law provides to victims of domestic violence. She also analyses their relative merits.*
>
> Law Institute Journal (Vic) December 2000

2002 • ISBN 1 86287 425 5 • paperback • 192 pp • $33

Court in the Act

Humorous Moments from Australian Courts

Beverley Tait

Here is a bonanza of inadvertent moments of levity in our Australian courtrooms –
the flashes of humour and humanity that break up otherwise serious proceedings.

Beverley Tait was a court reporter for 16 years, a front row spectator of those moments
really worth waiting for.

> *Beverley's great sense of humour and acute appreciation of the faux pas, malapropisms
> and human foibles ... This collection of wit is sure to entertain*
>
> Justice Marcus Einfeld

> *There are many laughs*
>
> The Examiner

> *It plucks some hilarious little asides from the most pompous of cases*
>
> Weekend Courier Mail

> *A delightful book of amusing anecdotes*
>
> Maryborough Chronicle

1992 • ISBN 1 86287 100 0 • paperback • 128 pp • $21.95

Everyday Law

2nd edition

Stella Tarakson

The law is often seen as something intimidating and remote – but it shouldn't be. It exists to serve the people.

Everyday Law de-mystifies the law by explaining in simple, plain language how the Australian legal system works and all the most common legal issues that affect lives on a daily basis.

This edition thoroughly revises and updates all the material in its predecessor. It also covers many new issues which have become serious concerns for Australians, such as personal privacy and the increasing complexities of the financial world.

This 2nd edition of *Everyday Law* is divided into four Parts:

- The workings of the legal system and how to access it;
- Personal matters, such as family law, children, employment law and health and safety;
- Property issues, including buying, renting and building a home, neighbourhood disputes, car ownership; and
- Money matters, providing an overview of investments, insurance, consumers' rights, debt, wills and estate administration.

This book is the essential first step in recognising and tackling legal problems.

Stella Tarakson, the author, studied Economics and Law at the University of Sydney since when she has worked as a researcher, writer and editor. She has been writing regular articles on law and finance in popular Australian magazines for over ten years. She is also the author of several books, including *What to do When Someone Dies* and *Raising Kids ... Without Breaking the Bank.*

2004 • ISBN 1 86287 494 8 • paperback • 283 pp • $29.95

Sweet and Sour

Stories from the Working World of Police, Social Workers, Lawyers, Judges, Gaolers and Occasional Villains

Professionals working in the criminal justice industry share a life of sordid boredom punctuated by moments of exposure to human farce and tragedy in a stark, face-to-face manner.

To maintain their sanity they sometimes recount to colleagues the occasional moments of humanity which light up an otherwise dark world.

Sweet and Sour is a collection of short stories representing such a sharing of experiences. It is served as a 'sweet and sour' dish, alternating episodes of hilarious farce with those of chilling tragedy.

Rod Settle worked in the criminal justice systems of Australia and Papua New Guinea for over 35 years. He performed a wide variety of roles from probation officer and social worker to judge's associate and police education officer.

> *A shrewd and sceptical observer of the human condition, Rod's work is informed by an uncommon humanity and a considerable compassion. ... You'll find moral indignation leavened with humour and may be affronted, from time to time, by his readiness to be politically incorrect. Nonetheless you'll be impressed ... a lot of the best characteristics of the Australian can be found in this unpretentious book.*
>
> Phillip Adams

1995 • ISBN 1 86287 182 5 • paperback • 181 pp • $21.95

Prisoners as Citizens

Human rights in Australian prisons

Editors: David Brown & Meredith Wilkie

Should prisoners be deprived of rights to such things as voting, personal safety, health, family connection, information, and education? In a series of 17 essays, many of them research-based, writers look at aspects of the surprisingly varied Australian prison situation. Topics include the nature of prison systems and populations, and historical and international perspectives. Also considered are the situations of particular prisoners, such as women and Indigenous Australians, as well as those from non-English speaking backgrounds, and those with intellectual disabilities. The collection is a timely and thought-provoking source of information.

SCAN

One of the most poignant aspects of this collection is the contribution that prisoners themselves make ... Collectively, [their] testimonies depict a deep-seated sense of feeling 'forgotten', anonymous and utterly disenfranchised ...
Practical measures that will immediately improve the recognition of human rights for prisoners are usefully discussed ...The book possesses a certain clarity and common-sense tone ... With a wide variety of contributors, the book represents a rich sourcebook of opinions on prisoners' rights. ... it is an important publication

Howard Journal of Criminal Justice

a landmark collection on prisoners' citizenship rights in Australia ... disturbing reading for citizens concerned about the decency and social justice of our democracy ...

Professor John Braithwaite

Australia's leading academics, activists and prison experts ... highlight why it is critical that these rights [of prisoners] be recognized by the Australian community. This is a timely, well-researched and important book.

Educational Book Review

A valuable and well-informed contribution to the debate about prisons and prisoners.

UNSW Law Journal

This outstanding and comprehensive collection of essays ... This is thoughtful but disturbing reading.

Reform

[A] very valuable analysis into many, if not most, of the changes [of the past two decades]. ... a scholarly contribution to the history and contemporary views of punishment and corrections [which] is full of surprises.

Civil Liberty

2002 • ISBN 1 86287B424 7 • paperback • 396 pp • $49.50